= The Complete Wok = Cookbook

500 Delicious Stir-fry Recipes for Your Wok or Skillet

Lucy Lynn

Table of Contents

Chapter 5: Fish and Seafood

Chapter 6: Poultry

Chapter 7: Beef, Pork, and Lamb

Chapter 8: Soups, Rice, and Noodles

Chapter 9: Appetizers and Dessert

Chapter 10: Sauces

Appendix 1 Measurement Conversion Chart

Appendix 2 Index

Introduction

Wok, thin-walled cooking pan, shaped like a shallow bowl with handles, widely used in Chinese-style cooking. The wok has a round bottom that concentrates heat, cooking food quickly with relatively little oil. Food when cooked may be moved up the sloping side of the wok to stay warm without cooking further, while other food is cooked at the bottom. The wok was developed as an implement to conserve scarce fuel. It is generally made of iron, carbon steel, copper, or aluminum. Although woks come in sizes ranging from 25 to 80 cm (10 to 32 inches) in diameter, household woks average from 30 to 36 cm.

Woks have been used for some many years in China for a variety of cooking methods, including stir-frying, boiling, and stewing. The addition of a rack and cover converts the wok into a steamer. Originally designed for use on wood- or charcoal-burning Chinese stoves, woks have been adapted for Western use by the addition of a metal ring, which is set on top of a gas or electric stove to hold the wok and prevent it from tipping. Electrically heated woks, with a removable heating element and thermostat, may be used for cooking meals at the dining table.

The secret to cooking delicious Chinese food at home is the wok; with just this one pan, you can make thousands of tasty dishes quickly and cheaply. And although it is the perfect pan to use for great-tasting stir-fries, the wok has so much more potential. There's a reason that the Chinese have used the wok for more than two thousand years with very few changes to the pan itself. In addition to stir-frying, you can also steam, boil, stew, braise, deep-fry, poach, smoke, sear, and sauté in a wok. The recipes in this book were designed to highlight the versatility of this time-tested piece of kitchen equipment—the wok will make it easy for you to cook your way through these pages.

The recipes in this cookbook are designed with the take-out lover in mind. You won't miss anything by cooking with a wok. In fact, you may even come to prefer it.

[1]

Chapter 1: Wok History and Basics

A wok is defined as a round bottomed cooking utensil with high sides, commonly designed with two side handles or one larger handle. The round bottom of a wok allows for heat to be distributed more evenly than a saucepan, meaning food is able to cook in less amount of time. The high walls allow for food to be tossed easier, such as when cooking a stir fry, meaning the ingredients can be mixed and cooked evenly throughout.

Woks are traditionally made by hammering a disk of carbon steel into a bowl shape and attaching one or two handles. Wok-like pans are used throughout Asia, and different cultures have customized the versatile pan to fit their needs. For example, the Cantonese wok, also known as a "two-eared wok," has two small, curved handles on each side. A Northern-style wok usually has one long removable wooden handle, sometimes with a handle on the opposite side for lifting when the wok is full. The Japanese refer to their wok-shaped pans as chukanabe, while in Southern India, their wok-shaped pans are referred to as cheena chatti. Both translate roughly to "Chinese pot."

Nowadays, woks come in many different shapes, sizes, and materials. When it comes to shape, woks are typically either round-bottomed or flat-bottomed. Round-bottomed woks were designed to be used over an open flame, so they are best suited for a gas stovetop.

A Brief History of Wok

The wok is believed to have first been invented in China, over 2000 years ago during the Han dynasty. Derived from the Cantonese word meaning 'Cooking pot', the early models of the wok were made of cast iron metals, allowing them to be more durable and long lasting.

Historians and food experts have a number of theories as to why the wok was invented. Some say that due to the shortage of food back in the Han dynasty, the wok allowed for a wide variety of meals to be cooked using the same ingredients due to its versatility.

There is also a theory that due to tribes travelling across the country many years ago and having to carry all their belongings with them, they needed a utensil that was not only portable but also able to quickly cook large amounts of food to feed the tribe.

A third theory is that due to a shortage of fuel and oil in the Han dynasty, the wok allowed for people to cook meals using very little oil. You may have already noticed that you only need a small amount of vegetable oil when using a wok at home to cook your ingredients!

The Modern Wok

These days, the wok is used all over the world for a whole range of meals. The majority of woks are made from carbon steel, which allows for them to still be durable and non-stick while also being light to pick up.

Of course, cooking Asian food relies heavily on the wok, but there are so many other uses for the wok. The wok is one of the most versatile cooking tools in the world, and can be used for cooking techniques such as:

- Stir frying
- Steaming
- Pan frying
- Deep frying
- Boiling
- Braising
- Searing
- Smoking
- Stewing

The design of the modern wok allows for heat to be evenly distributed around the whole wok, meaning all your ingredients will cook and be ready at the same time. On top of this, the fact that you can use very little cooking oil with a wok and still have great tasting, non-sticking foods is a massive benefit. Sometimes you may need accessories to go with your wok, such as a wok lid for steaming/boiling or even a wok ring which ensures your wok won't slide around when cooking.

The Wok Basics

The wok is an integral part of Chinese cooking because its unique shape and surface area make it good not just for stir-frying, but also as mentioned earlier, for braising, stewing, poaching, steaming, deep-frying, and even smoking. The traditional wok, used for almost 2,000 years, has a rounded bottom, which easily allows a spatula or other utensil to move the food around the pan.

Wok hay, or wok hei, is a Cantonese phrase used to describe a well-made stir-fry dish. It translates as "breath of a wok," and it refers to the concentrated, rich flavor that can come only from making a stir-fry in a well-seasoned wok over very high heat.

Choosing A Wok and Essential Tools

There are so many different types of woks on the market that it can be dizzying to choose the right one for your needs. When buying a wok, don't be fooled into thinking that the most expensive one is the best choice. A $10 carbon steel wok purchased in Chinatown can be perfect for home cooking needs. Different types of wok include the following:

- **12- or 14-inch Flat-Bottomed Carbon Steel Wok**

  This pan is really your best choice. Light and easy to handle, a carbon steel wok develops a nonstick surface after you season it, so you don't have to use much oil when cooking. It also heats up quickly, conducts heat well, and cools down quickly, which is essential for good stir-fry technique.

  Most home stoves cannot get as hot as professional stoves or traditional Chinese stoves (on which the wok sits in the flames). The flat-bottomed wok makes up for this lack because it covers more of the heat than its round- bottomed cousin. If you don't cook large meals and are cooking for one or two, then a 12-inch wok will be good for you. For families, a 14-inch wok will be perfect.

- **Round-Bottomed Carbon Steel Wok**

  This traditional Cantonese wok has a round bottom and two handles. Because the rounded-bottom wok isn't stable on the stove, you need to use a wok ring underneath it so it doesn't tip over. For this safety reason, cooks new to a wok may not want to start off with a round-bottomed wok.

- **Cast Iron Wok**

  An American cast iron wok is quite heavy and takes longer to heat up, which makes stir-frying a challenge. If that's all you have, don't fret. You can still follow the recipes in this book to make a tasty stir-fry and excellent poached, steamed, braised, and fried dishes. When you get the chance, invest in a lighter, easier-to-use carbon steel wok.

- **Nonstick Wok or Skillet**

  Most stir-fry experts don't recommend using this type of wok or skillet because the food won't taste the same. A nonstick wok or skillet cannot reach the high heat level conducted by a carbon steel or cast iron wok, which is necessary to create the best-tasting stir-fries. But if that's what you have at home, you absolutely can go ahead and make these recipes with your nonstick pan. They will still taste great! Once you're ready, get a carbon steel wok and be impressed with the flavor difference.

- **Electric Wok**

  This isn't ideal for stir-frying because it doesn't retain heat well, making it difficult to achieve wok hay. However, you can use an electric wok happily for poaching, steaming, braising, and stewing.

Other Tools

The essential list of kitchen tools you will need to successfully stir-fry is very short. Here's are some:

- **Skillets**

  No wok? No worries! If you have a heavy skillet, you can still make stir-fry. Cast iron, carbon steel, and stainless steel are the best materials to use. Cast-iron skillets heat very evenly at high temperatures and are easily seasoned, making them good at searing ingredients in a stir-fry. Carbon steel skillets heat faster, are lighter, and will season well, but they will develop hot spots unless the bottom is thick and heavy. Good-quality stainless steel will heat evenly and can, over time, be seasoned to a degree. Note that a skillet, with its shallower sides, will not hold as much stir-fry as a wok of the same diameter; for that reason, you might consider using a 12-inch or larger skillet.

  Also note that a skillet will not heat as evenly as a wok, so you won't be able to get it as hot without some burning and sticking. In order to compensate, you will need to use a little more oil than you would in a wok. Stir-frying with avocado oil is highly recommended, as it can handle temperatures over 500°F before breaking down and burning.

  - **Chinese all-purpose cleaver.** Since stir-frying depends on quickly cooking bite-size pieces of food, you will need a sharp knife. An all-purpose Chinese cleaver is recommended. Its wide blade surface is easy to guide and

[3]

control, and it can also be used to flatten and smash ingredients, such as garlic and ginger. The back of the blade and the handle's butt can even be used to tenderize meat and grind spices.

- **Cutting boards.** Two or three boards large enough to keep all your ingredients on the board while prepping will be fine. Use one board for vegetables and the other for meat and fish. Wood and plastic are preferred; ceramic and glass will dull the edge of your knife.

- **Prep bowls.** With all the slicing and chopping, you'll want a variety of bowls for organizing the prepared ingredients that are going into the hot wok. Three to four different-size bowls should be sufficient for a typical stir-fry.

- **Large stirring spoon or curved spatula. I** use a long-handled metal stirring spoon for stir-frying. Its curved shape works well with the rounded wok surface. The spoon can also mix and serve glazes and gravies to accompany your stir-fry dishes. The traditional curved wok spatula also works well. A well-seasoned wok can withstand the brisk stirring of metal utensils, but if you have a wok or skillet with a nonstick surface, you will need to use high-temperature silicon or wooden utensils.

- **Soup ladle.** Though not strictly used for stir-frying, a ladle is useful for serving tasty soups that begin with stir-fried ingredients.

Caring for Your Wok

You have to employ some simple and basic tips to keep your wok in good condition and ready for use. New woks need oil to continue developing their seasoning layer. So don't do a lot of poaching with a newly seasoned wok—do a lot of stir- frying! It is recommended to make a few batches of popcorn in your wok with peanut oil to speed up the seasoning process. And when cooking, always heat the wok until it's hot before adding oil.

Never wash your seasoned wok with soap. Rinse it with warm water, and wipe it with a gentle sponge or brush. Don't abrasively scrub your wok, as that will affect the seasoning layer. Don't use steel pads or scouring sponges on the inside, though you can use them on the outside of your wok if it gets very dirty.

For a new wok, you might want to dry it over high heat after you rinse it. For a well-seasoned wok, just wipe until dry. Don't let it sit around wet. It could develop rust if that happens. Over time, your wok will become deeper in color and the seasoning layer will develop. Once this happens, you can just wipe out your wok with a paper towel, like you would a nonstick pan.

The more you cook with your wok, the better seasoned it will be. If you don't use your wok often, rub a small amount of peanut oil onto the inside surface of the wok before storing it. If you forget about your wok for a while and it gets rusty or if it gets very burned once you use it again, then do a full re-seasoning of it. Do a "wok facials" from time to time. To do a wok facial, fold three layers of paper towels into a wad, and set the wad aside. Heat the wok over high heat. Once hot, remove it from the heat, and add a couple of teaspoons of peanut or vegetable oil and some kosher salt (use a 2 to 1 ratio of oil and salt). Using the paper towels, gently rub and scrub the oil and salt all over the inside of your wok until it's clean and shiny. Rinse out the wok with warm water, using a textured sponge to remove any lingering salt crystals. Voilà! Your wok is rejuvenated.

Now that you know your tools and how to care for them, and you also have a little history under your belt, you're almost ready for stir-fry mastery. Now, it's time to learn the intricacies of cooking on a wok

Chapter 2: Cooking in a Wok

Wok cooking can be intimidating, but a wok can also be the most versatile and handy tool in your kitchen. A wok's large surface area and its ability to quickly flash cook food at high temperatures, does make it the perfect utensil for stir-fries.

The thing is, though, wok recipes can be so much more than this! We'll even go as far as to say that you can cook everything in a wok (almost!). But recipes for a wok can involve so many different cooking techniques. You can boil, fry, steam, smoke, or even just use a wok for tossing salads! Wok food can be wonderfully versatile, and we really do encourage you to get creative!

The Best Ways to Cook in a Wok

To get the creative juices flowing (and those tasty wok juices too when you start cooking up a feast!), let's take a look at some of the best ways that you can employ a wok when you're cooking at home.

Here are a few ways to cook in a wok:

1. Deep-frying

Deep-drying is a cooking technique that works fantastically well in a wok, because not only is the wok itself a very deep pan, but it can take a huge amount of heat.

Fill your wok with the required quantity of oil and let it heat up, before deep-frying your potatoes, your shrimp, your squid, or anything else!

2. Steaming

Given their large size, woks are perfect for steaming too, and you can keep the Asian-theme going by steaming up a feast of dumplings to go with your stir-fry.

Simply take a suitable container, keep it covered, and place it in the bottom of the wok, semi-submerged in boiling water. When it's hot enough, add your dumplings to the steamer and let them cook.

3. Smoking

You can get really elaborate with your cooking too, and turn your wok into a home-made smoker for cooking up your favorite smoky-flavored meats.

Line the bottom of your wok with a layer of tin foil, and start heating up a few ingredients to give your food the smoky taste you're looking for (you can use anything from burnt rice to coffee beans!). Place a rack or grill over the foil and get cooking.

4. Flash-frying

Flash-frying is the classic way to use a wok. Heat your wok up to a high temperature, add a drizzle of oil to the pan, and cook your stir-fry ingredients quicky, at a high temperature.

Flash-frying s a great way to keep in the taste and the goodness of the food, and it's a super-quick way to cook up a delicious meal!

5. Braising

You can cook up a delicious braised-beef stew using just a wok! Use the pan itself to heat the meat, before making use of the high sides to stew the braised meat at a low temperature to produce the perfect dish.

6. Tossing salad

You don't even need to apply heat to your wok if you're looking for a tasty and healthy salad for dinner.

Woks are the perfect size for tossing salads, especially given their high sides, which will ensure that you don't toss your greens out of the pan and onto the floor!

7. Making popcorn

You can even use a wok to cook popcorn at home! Add a little oil to the bottom of your wok, throw in some corn kernels, and cover the top to stop them popping all over your kitchen!

8. Warming tortillas

We absolutely adore our Mexican food, and woks can come in handy on Taco Tuesday!

They are not only great for cooking up taco fillings quickly, but you can use woks for cooking or warming up the tortillas too. Keep the bottom of the wok dry, heat the pan up to medium heat, and slap down the tortillas for a minute on either side!

9. Making pasta

You can even use woks for making pasta. It's not very orthodox, but the large size of the pan allows you to boil a large quantity of pasta in a wok.

Once the pasta is boiled, you can also use the wok's great surface area for cooking up dishes such as linguine or even a Bolognese sauce to go with your spaghetti!

Now that you know the different ways you can use your wok, you should also know that the best wok recipes will always require a well-seasoned wok, especially if you are flash-frying or searing, because you don't want your food to stick and burn to the bottom of the pan.

How To Prepare A Wok For Cooking

If you've bought a new wok and you want to get it ready for its inaugural recipe. You'll want to prepare your wok for cooking by cleaning, drying, and seasoning it. Here's how:

- Wash the wok with hot water and dish soap.

Scrub it with a textured sponge or steel wool to remove the factory coating. (Note: Unseasoned woks are coated in a particular type of oil to protect them until they are sold. You want to completely remove this coating.)

- Dry the wok well.

- Use a paper towel or dish towel to rub cooking oil over the entire inside surface of the wok.

- Place the wok over a burner turned to high heat. Heat the wok, slowly rotating and tipping it to expose the entire outer surface to the heat. (The oil may smoke slightly.)

- Remove wok from heat and allow it to cool completely.

- Wipe the inside of the wok clean to remove any residue.

- Drizzle about a teaspoon of fresh oil into the wok and rub it all over the inside before storing the wok. It's ready to use!

Seasoning Your Wok

Many woks come pre-seasoned these days, making them much more versatile and making it much easier to prepare those diverse recipes for wok without worrying too much.

Regularly seasoning your wok, though, won't harm the cooking process. When you buy a new carbon steel or cast iron wok, you need to season it before you start cooking with it. Do not season a nonstick wok or an electric wok. Seasoning will take at least 30 minutes, but once done, you'll have created a natural-nonstick surface without the chemicals found in a Teflon coating.

As always when dealing with high heat and oil, be careful and focused during the seasoning process so that you don't burn yourself.

How to Season Your Wok: A Step-by-Step Guide

Your carbon steel or cast iron wok will come home from the store smelling like oil. This oil is a preservative applied by the manufacturer. It will need to be cleaned off the wok. Wash the wok in soapy water, and scrub it clean on the inside and the outside.

Now you need to "burn" the wok. Place it on the stove, and dry it over very high heat.

3. Remove the wok from the heat, and put a few tablespoons of peanut oil in the bottom of the wok. Using a dry cloth, spread a thin layer of the oil completely over the inside surface of the wok. Be careful not to burn yourself.

4. This next part will get smoky, so turn on your oven fan and open your windows. Over very high heat, heat the oil in the wok for a few minutes. Turn off the heat, take the wok off the heat, and let it cool to room temperature.

5. Once the wok is at room temperature, put it on high heat again, making sure the first layer of oil gets "burned" into the wok. Once it is, turn off the heat, take the pan off the stove, and return the pan to room temperature again.

6. Once at room temperature, add another thin layer of oil, and spread it over the inside surface of the wok, as you did in step 3. Heat the wok again for a few minutes, and then turn off the heat, take the pan off the heat, and return it to room temperature once more.

7. Repeat steps 5 and 6 a few more times. Wipe off any excess oil that collects in the bottom center of the wok. Once the wok starts to darken and look shiny, it's ready to use.

8. If you can, do a first stir-fry of sliced onions to remove any unwanted smells from the wok.

9. The more you cook with your wok, the better its seasoning will be and the less oil you'll have to use when cooking with it.

10. Re-season your wok if it becomes necessary.

Types Of Oil to Use in Wok Cooking

Woks are designed to cook foods hot and fast, so you need to use a type of oil that is approved for cooking over high heat. The best oils to use in wok cooking are:

Peanut Oil – Peanut oil has a nutty, subtle peanut flavor which is a great flavor for many wok dishes (especially dishes that are Chinese in origin). It can be used up to 450° F. It spoils and turns rancid faster than the other oils listed below, so only buy it if you're going to be doing a lot of Thai or Chinese cooking within a few months.

Vegetable or Canola Oil – Inexpensive and with a neutral flavor, these are good all-around oils that will work for almost all wok cooking. Both vegetable and canola oil can be used up to 400° F, last a long time in the pantry, and are used in a lot of baking as well as high heat cooking.

Avocado Oil – It has lots of good monounsaturated fats (like avocados) and be used at temperatures up to 500° F, so it's great for stir-fry or frying and has a fresh, mild flavor.

Grapeseed Oil – This is an all-purpose cooking oil. It can be used at temperatures up to 400° F and the flavor is clean and fresh, which makes it work for most anything you're cooking.

The Order to Cook Ingredients in A Wok

If you've watched someone cook with a wok in a professional kitchen, you may have seen them throw all of the ingredients into a wok together, toss it a few times, and transfer it to a plate. These professional cooks are often using stoves and woks that are very hot – likely much hotter than you will ever get at home.

Fortunately, there's an easy way to get everything to cook properly in your home kitchen. Simply cook them in the following order:

- Protein (4 to 7 minutes)
- Aromatics (1 minute)
- Vegetables (1 to 7 minutes, depending on size and sturdiness)
- Sauce (2 minutes)

Step 1: Heat Oil

To get started, place your wok over medium-high heat. When the wok is hot, add about 1 Tablespoon of cooking oil (see above for some good options) and rotate / swirl the wok to distribute the hot oil over the bottom and sides.

Step 2: Sear Protein and Set Aside

Tip: Before adding protein to the wok, pat it dry with paper towels. Dry protein will sear more easily. (Proteins that are not dry will steam instead of sear.)

To heated oil, add protein of choice (chicken, beef, pork, shrimp, tofu, etc) in a single layer. Leave the protein, without stirring, for a couple minutes, until it sears on the bottom. Use a spatula (a wok spatula works great for this) to flip the protein and sear the other side.

Once the protein is seared on both sides, give it a stir and continue cooking until it is nearly cooked through. (Stop just short of cooking it all the way because it will finish cooking in the sauce.) Season the protein with some salt and transfer it to a plate.

Step 3: Cook Aromatics

Return the wok to medium-high heat and add another 1 Tablespoon of cooking oil. Add aromatics (like garlic, onions, ginger, shallots, chilis). Cook these, stirring constantly, for a minute so they start to flavor the oil.

Step 4: Cook Vegetables

To aromatics, add vegetables in order from longest cooking time to shortest cooking time. Here are a few examples:

- 6 to 7 minutes (hard vegetables): broccoli, cauliflower, carrots, potatoes, brussels sprouts
- 4 to 5 minutes (medium-hard vegetables) like zucchini, mushrooms
- 3 to 4 minutes (medium-soft vegetables): bell peppers, snow peas, baby carrots
- 1 to 2 minutes (soft vegetables): leafy greens, tomatoes, peas, corn kernels

With all vegetables, stir them frequently as they cook. You can also shake the wok back and forth or use it to toss the vegetables a few inches into the air if you're feeling brave!

Tip: As you're cooking the vegetables, if the wok starts to look dry or the vegetables start to burn before they are cooked through, add about 1 Tablespoon of water. If you do this with the longer cooking vegetables, you can cover the wok with a lid after adding the water. This will steam the vegetables and help them to soften without burning.

Step 5: Add Protein, Sauce, Rice

When the vegetables are all cooked to tender, add the protein back to the wok and pour the sauce / liquids down the sides of the wok. Pouring the liquids down the sides will help them to heat up before reaching the other ingredients. If cooking fried rice or another grain, add them now too (note: any grain / rice should be pre-cooked and tender before adding them to the wok).

Toss everything together until protein is cooked through and everything is coated in sauce.

The above can generally be followed when cooking with a wok, nevertheless, each recipe in this book will come with specific instructions on how to cook it.

The 10 Commandments to Cooking with a Wok

Wok cooking is all drama—high flames that curve around the underside of the dome-shaped pan as fragrant clouds of smoke cloak the stove, while vegetables and meat soar through the air above the pan, propelled by the chef's practiced toss. Barely a minute or two passes before the finished dish is scooped out into an awaiting bowl.

To start your wok cooking experience, you need some wide-ranging wok expertise, so you'll know all about the crucial components of wok cookery when you shop for and cook with your pan.

. Season every time you cook.

The most annoying thing that can happen when you're stir-frying is that your chicken sticks, and then you scrape it off and you have this stuff sticking to the wok that will burn before the dish is ready. It changes the flavor and makes it hard to move food around. The way to avoid that is to put in some oil and swirl it around the cooking surface of the wok and let it get smoking hot. Then pour that off into a heatproof container and put in fresh oil for cooking. That's how to make a wok into a nonstick pan."

. Pour the right oil.

You want something with a high smoke point, so groundnut oil is very good. Rapeseed [canola] oil is also very good."

. Look beyond stir-frying.

The wok is not only for stir-frying—it's used for pretty much everything. It's very economical. Deep-frying in a wok, you need much less oil than in a regular saucepan. You can put a bamboo steamer in the wok, fill the base of the wok with water and steam like that, or get little metal trivets in the bottom, lay a dish on the trivet, and cover with a wok lid. You can also use it for boiling and making stews, or even as a smoker—you cover the base of the wok with several layers of foil, and then you put some sugar and tea leaves and some flour. Heat it up until the sugar is burning and everything is smoldering, and you can put food on a rack, put the lid on, and do hot-smoking like that.

4. Figure out the right wok for you.

When you're choosing a wok, you need to think about what kind of cooker [stove] you have. If you have a gas flame, you can have a traditional round-bottomed wok. But if you have an electric cooker, then you do need the kind of wok that has a flat bit at the base. You can get woks made of different materials—I favor the Chinese carbon steel ones, which heat up and cool down quickly.

They have different sorts of handles. Some have one long handle—that is the easiest thing if you want to toss your food around. Other woks will have two ear handles. The good thing about those woks is they're very stable, so for boiling or deep-frying, you do want it to be safer. A wok with about a 13-inch diameter wok is very nice for a home cook."

5. Crank up the heat.

Classic stir-fry is often done at very high heat. The Cantonese talk about the wok-hai, the fragrance of the wok from that kind of searing. You can have a bit of drama, a bit of hissing, a bit of smoke when you're stir-frying. But you don't want to heat the oil up too hot before you put in your aromatics. Season the surface and get the wok really hot before you begin. Then put in your cooking oil and pretty quickly put in garlic or chiles or sensitive things so the oil isn't burning hot when you begin. You can extract the flavor without discarding or burning them. For the smoke, you do want a really good extractor fan."

6. Get a brush, scoop, slotted spoon, and ladle.

Dunlop says: "A wok spatula with a long handle is very good tool for scooping off the base of the wok when stir-frying. That's what Chinese home cooks use. The other thing that's useful is a Chinese ladle, whose bowl is at a different angle than the Western soup angle. You can use it for scooping up oil, stock, or water, or for mixing up sauces before adding to the wok. A scoop with holes in it is good for scooping food out of oil or sauce. A bamboo brush whose bristles won't melt is essential for cleaning the pan in between dishes while it's still hot."

7. Learn the toss.

You just push the wok away from you and raise it and flip the food towards you. When you want to cook food very rapidly, it's a way of moving it around. It's always a good idea to practice without too much food and oil first. You could even practice with just some salad in it off the heat."

8. Don't double the recipe.

If you want to make more food, it's better to not just double the quantities for a stir-fry. If you try to stir-fry too much food, you won't get that searing heat. There will be too much liquid and too much stuff. It's better to do two different dishes, or to do the same thing twice. When you plan a meal for friends, don't make every dish a stir-fry or you'll be very tired: do some cold dishes and a stew and have the rice cooking separately."

9. Tweak the timing.

If you have ingredients that cook at different rates, do them separately and incorporate them at the end and they'll both be perfect. For example, say you've got some crunchy vegetable and some slices of pork or chicken. You want the chicken to be really succulent, not dry. Begin by stir-frying your slivers of pork or chicken until they're just right. Take them out and put them in a dish. Then cook the vegetables, and when they're just right, you put the pork or chicken back in the pan. That way, you don't get the situation where something is raw and something else is overcooked."

10. Relax about wok care.

Woks are practically indestructible. If the wok needs a good scrub, give it a good scrub. You just clean it and then you re-season it: After cleaning, heat the wok very hot, then rub it with a thick wad of paper towels and some oil. Let it get very hot and then let it cool again. It may even get a bit rusty. But it doesn't matter! Just rub away the rust with wire wool and then re-season it with a bit of fresh oil."

Some Wok Cooking Tips

- A 14-inch carbon-steel flat-bottomed wok with a long wooden handle and a short helper handle is ideal. It's roomy enough for tossing ingredients; the carbon steel heats quickly and evenly and acquires a natural nonstick surface the more you cook with it; and the flat bottom sits right on the burner so it gets hot enough for stir-frying.

- Use an oil with a high smoke point, such as peanut, grapeseed, safflower, or canola. Cut ingredients into uniform pieces so that everything cooks in the same amount of time.

- Dry vegetables with a salad spinner or kitchen towel before adding to the wok. Line up ingredients next to the stove in the order that you'll use them. Once cooking starts, there's no time for last-minute prep.

- Heat the wok on high to prevent ingredients like meat, poultry, fish, rice, and noodles from sticking. The wok is hot enough when a bead of water vaporizes in 1 to 2 seconds.

- When stir-frying, you should hear constant sizzling. If there's no sizzle, the wok isn't hot enough, it's overcrowded, or the ingredients are wet.

- Stir-fry with a flexible metal pancake or fish spatula (or if you have one, a wok spatula); a wood spatula is too thick to get under ingredients.

- Don't crowd your wok. Too many ingredients will lower the wok's temperature, turning your stir-fry into a braise.

- High-heat cooking requires your full attention.

- If your wok is newly seasoned, don't braise, steam, boil, or poach in it because the liquid will dissolve the new patina.

- Traditional Chinese kitchens have two woks: one for stir-frying, panfrying, and deep-frying, and one for steaming, boiling, poaching, braising, and smoking. If you have just one well-used wok with a heavy patina, you can do all types of cooking in it. A little of the patina will disappear when boiling, poaching, and braising, but it will return with more frying.

- To preserve its patina, wash your wok as you would a cast-iron skillet. Soak in hot water for 5 minutes. Wash with a sponge. Rinse in hot water. Dry over low heat on the stovetop until all the water has evaporated.

- Your spatula will cause scratches, but scratches give your wok character. As you continue to cook with your wok, the scratches will fade as the patina deepens. A new wok is thirsty for fat, so use it to cook bacon or for deep-frying. The fat will help your wok to develop a patina faster.

The recipes in this book will reflect a traditional

alance of ingredients. Since stir-frying originated
n China, most of the recipes are based on Chinese
ngredients. But stir-frying and wok cooking have
pread beyond China, so some recipes with ingredi-
nts and flavors from other countries have also been
ncluded, as well. Now that you have a decent under-
tanding about wok cooking, it's time to heat up your
ok and start some stir-frying. Let's get started!

Chapter 3: Egg and Tofu

Chili Pork with Mapo Tofu

rep time: 10 minutes | Cook time: 6 minutes |
erves 4

- 2 tablespoons peanut oil
- ½ sweet onion, finely chopped
- ½ teaspoon Chinese chili paste
- 1 garlic clove, minced
- ¼ pound (113 g)

- ground pork
- ½ block firm tofu, cut into cubes
- 2 tablespoons black bean sauce
- 1 teaspoon Sichuan peppercorns

Heat your wok over medium-high heat. Add the oil
and swirl to coat the wok.

Add the onion, chili paste, and garlic, and stir-fry
for about 1 minute, making sure the ingredients
do not burn.

Add the pork and stir-fry until it is almost
cooked through, 2 to 3 minutes. Lower the heat to
medium, and add the tofu and black bean sauce.
Stir-fry for 4 to 5 minutes. It doesn't matter if some
of the tofu doesn't stay in perfect cubes.

Remove the wok from the heat, and sprinkle the
pork and tofu with the Sichuan peppercorns.
Serve over rice.

picy Cauliflower with Orange Tofu

rep time: 10 minutes | Cook time: 18 minutes |
erves 4

- 1 (400 g) pack of baked
- 2 tablespoons olive oil, or as needed
- 340 g grated cauliflower
- 2 onions, chopped
- 3 chopped spring onions
- 2 garlic cloves,

- firm tofu, cut into cubes
- chopped
- 2 green peppers, chopped
- 2 tablespoons water
- 1 tablespoon orange liqueur
- 1 tablespoon soy sauce
- 2 red chilies, grated
- 1 pinch salt

1. Wrap tofu in a paper towel and cover with a plate;
   Let it rest for about 10 minutes until the moisture
   is removed. Heat 1 tablespoon olive oil in a pan
   over medium heat. Add cauliflower; Cook and
   stir until soft, about 5 minutes. Preheat the oven
   to 425ºF (220ºC). (When using a convection oven,
   preheat the worktop to 395ºF/202ºC.)

2. Put in the baking sheet to warm up; Remove the
   paper towel from the tofu; discard. Place the tofu
   on the heated baking sheet with heat-resistant
   gloves. Bake in the preheated oven, turn over once
   until the tofu is heated through, about 3 minutes
   per side in the conventional oven and 2 minutes
   per side in the induction oven on the worktop.

3. Heat 1 tablespoon olive oil in a wok over medium
   heat. Add onions and spring onions; cook and
   stir until the onions are slightly softened, about 5
   minutes. Stir in garlic.

4. Mix water and orange liqueur in a bowl and stir
   in. Put 1 tablespoon liqueur mixture in the wok;
   toss with 2 wooden spoons until mixed. Repeat
   with the rest of the liqueur mixture; Cook for 3 to
   5 minutes and stir until evaporated; Scatter soy
   sauce into the wok.

5. Fold in tofu until covered; Place the cauliflower
   in serving bowls and cover with the tofu mixture.
   Garnish with red chilies; season with salt.

Mushroom with Tofu Stir-Fry

Prep time: 15 minutes | Cook time: 8 minutes |
Serves 4

- 2 tablespoons soy sauce and 2 tablespoons tamari
- 3 tablespoons hoisin or oyster sauce
- ¼ cup broth or water

- 1 tablespoon rice wine or sherry
- 2 teaspoons sugar and a little salt
- ¼ cup coarsely chopped coriander plus long, sprigs for garnish
- 280 g package of Chinese egg noodles, cut wide
- 1 package of firm tofu, drained and cut into large cubes
- 2½ tablespoons roasted peanut oil
- 1 heaping tablespoon chopped ginger and garlic
- 1 jalapeño chili, pitted
- and cut into cubes
- 2 pieces of baked tofu, thinly sliced
- 1 onion and 6 shiitake mushrooms, thinly sliced
- 1 large broccoli, the head, cut into florets and sliced
- 1 red or yellow bell pepper, cut into narrow strips then halved
- 2 carrots, peeled and thinly sliced
- 110 g kefen, cut and 1 bunch of spring onions, cut into lengths

1. Mix the sauce ingredients together and set aside. Bring a saucepan of water to a boil for the pasta and tofu. Reduce it to a boil, add the diced tofu and simmer on a low heat for 4 minutes. Lift out the tofu with a sieve and set aside.

2. Bring the water to the boil again, add the pasta and cook according to the instructions on the package. Drain and rinse under cold water. Mix with 1 tablespoon oil and set aside and set up a wok or pan over high heat. Add the remaining oil and swirl around. When it's hot, add the ginger, garlic, chili, and baked tofu. Fry while stirring. When it's hot, add the ginger, garlic, chili, and baked tofu. Fry for 1 minute, stirring constantly, then add onion, mushrooms, broccoli, paprika and carrots.

3. Season to taste with a few pinches of salt and stir-fry the vegetables for 3 minutes in the pan, then add the snow peas, spring onions and cooked tofu. Fry for another minute, stirring, then add the pasta and sauce. Reduce the heat, toggle it so that everything mixes evenly, cover and cook until the noodles are heated through – a matter of minutes. Turn out onto a large platter and garnish with sprigs of coriander.

Cabbage with Shanghai Buns

Prep time: 10 minutes | Cook time: 15 minutes | Serves 4

- 2 cups all-purpose flour
- 2 teaspoons yeast
- 2 teaspoons baking powder
- 2 teaspoons sugar
- ½ cup chopped napa cabbage
- 1½ pounds (680 g) lean ground beef
- 2 tablespoons soy sauce
- 1 teaspoon toasted sesame oil
- Black vinegar, for dipping

1. To make the dough, mix together the flour, yeast, baking powder, and sugar in a medium mixing bowl. Let the dough rest for 30 minutes.

2. In a large bowl, mix the cabbage, ground beef, soy sauce, and sesame oil together.

3. Once the dough has rested, divide it into 15 equal pieces. Roll a dough piece into a circle, about 4 inches in diameter. Put about 1 tablespoon filling in the center of the dough circle. Bring the edges of the dough together at the top, and twist and pinch them together to seal. Repeat this for the remaining dough pieces and the filling.

4. Add about 2 inches of water to your wok. Place a piece of parchment paper in the bottom of a bamboo steamer, and put the steamer in the wok Bring the water to a boil.

5. Place the buns in the bamboo steamer, making sure they do not touch. Cover the steamer and steam the buns until they are cooked, about 15 minutes.

6. Serve with black vinegar or your favorite dumpling dipping sauce on the side.

Sesame with Steamed Eggs

Prep time: 5 minutes | Cook time: 15 minutes | Serves 4

- 3 medium eggs
- 2 teaspoons sea salt
- 1 cup water
- Soy sauce
- Sesame oil
- 1 scallion, finely chopped

In a large bowl, beat the eggs. Pour the eggs through a sieve into a steam-proof dish. Add the sea salt to the dish, and whisk it into the eggs.

In your wok over high heat, bring the water to a boil. Place a steamer rack or colander with legs in the wok. Carefully place the dish with the eggs in the wok, and cover the dish with a heat-proof plate. Turn the heat to low, and steam the eggs for 15 minutes.

Carefully remove the dish. Serve the eggs with soy sauce and sesame oil and garnished with a chopped scallion.

Garlicky Fried Wontons

Prep time: 10 minutes | Cook time: 0 minutes | Serves 4

- 1 pound (454 g) ground pork
- 2 garlic cloves, minced
- 1 teaspoon minced fresh ginger
- 1 teaspoon toasted sesame oil
- 1 tablespoon soy sauce
- 5 scallions, finely chopped
- 2 carrots, finely chopped
- 40 to 50 wonton wrappers
- Peanut oil, for deep-frying

1. In a large bowl, mix together the pork, garlic, ginger, sesame oil, soy sauce, scallions, and carrots.

2. In the center of a wonton wrapper, place about a teaspoon of the pork filling. Dampen the edges of the wonton wrapper with a little water, and fold the edges over to make a triangle. Using your fingers, press the edges together to seal the wonton.

3. To a wok, add enough of the peanut oil so that it is about 1½ inches deep. Heat the oil to 350°F (180ºC). Fry 5 or 6 wontons at a time until they're golden brown. Continue until all are fried.

4. Drain the finished wontons on a rack or a plate covered with paper towels. Serve with chili sauce or sweet and sour sauce.

Spicy Venison Stir Fry

Prep time: 5 minutes | Cook time: 5 minutes | Serves 2

- 2 cups sliced red peppers

- ½ pound (227 g) venison meat
- ½ cup sliced leeks
- 1 tablespoon oil

1. Marinade venison in Superfoods marinade.

2. In a wok, stir fry drained venison in coconut oil for few minutes, add all vegetables and stir fry for 2 more minutes. Add the rest of the marinade and stir fry for 1 minute.

3. Serve with brown rice or quinoa.

Brothy Foo Yong

Prep time: 15 minutes | Cook time: 3 minutes | Serves 4

- 5 large eggs, at room temperature
- Kosher salt
- Ground white pepper
- ½ cup thinly sliced shiitake mushroom caps
- ½ cup frozen peas, thawed
- 2 scallions, chopped
- 2 teaspoons sesame oil
- ½ cup low-sodium chicken broth
- 1½ tablespoons oyster sauce
- 1 tablespoon Shaoxing rice wine
- ½ teaspoon sugar
- 2 tablespoons light soy sauce
- 1 tablespoon cornstarch
- 3 tablespoons vegetable oil
- Cooked rice, for serving

1. In a large bowl, whisk the eggs with a pinch each of salt and white pepper. Stir in the mushrooms, peas, scallions, and sesame oil. Set aside.

2. Make the sauce by simmering the chicken broth, oyster sauce, rice wine, and sugar in a small saucepan over medium heat. In a small glass measuring cup, whisk the light soy and cornstarch until the cornstarch is completely dissolved. Pour the cornstarch mixture into the sauce while whisking constantly and cook for 3 to 4 minutes, until the sauce becomes thick enough to coat the back of the spoon. Cover and set aside.

3. Heat a wok over medium-high heat until a drop of water sizzles and evaporates on contact. Pour in the vegetable oil and swirl to coat the base of the wok. Add the egg mixture and cook, swirling and shaking the wok until the bottom side is golden. Slide the omelet out of the pan onto a plate and invert over the wok or turn over with a spatula to

cook the other side until golden. Slide the omelet out onto a serving platter and serve over cooked rice with a spoonful of sauce.

Eggy Lettuce Wraps

Prep time: 10 minutes | Cook time: 0 minutes | Serves 4 to 6

- 1 head lettuce
- 4 eggs, lightly beaten
- Pinch salt
- Pinch ground white pepper
- ½ teaspoon soy sauce
- 2 scallions, chopped
- 3 tablespoons peanut
- oil
- ½ cup diced water chestnuts
- 1 small onion, thinly sliced
- ¾ cup crabmeat
- ¼ cup Basic Sambal (optional)

1. Wash and separate the lettuce leaves. Chill the lettuce leaves in the refrigerator until just before serving.

2. Put the beaten eggs into a medium bowl. Add the salt, pepper, soy sauce, and scallions to the eggs. Stir gently just to combine.

3. In a wok over medium-high heat, heat the peanut oil.

4. Stir-fry the water chestnuts and onion until the onion is slightly translucent.

5. Add the crabmeat to the wok, then the egg mixture, and let it sit for a moment. When the bottom of the egg is cooked through, flip, and cook on the other side.

6. Using a wok spatula, break up and scramble the egg.

7. Serve with the chilled lettuce leaves and sambal (if using).

Eggy Shrimp with Sesame

Prep time: 10 minutes | Cook time: 3 minutes | Serve 4

- 2 tablespoons kosher salt, plus more for seasoning
- 2 tablespoons sugar
- 2 cups cold water
- 6 ounces (170 g)
- medium shrimp (U41–50), peeled and deveined
- 4 large eggs, at room temperature
- ½ teaspoon sesame oil
- Freshly ground black pepper
- 2 tablespoons vegetable oil, divided
- 2 peeled fresh ginger slices, each about the
- size of a quarter
- 2 garlic cloves, thinly sliced
- 1 bunch chives, cut into ½-inch pieces

1. In a large bowl, whisk the salt and sugar into the water until they dissolve. Add the shrimp to the brine. Cover and refrigerate for 10 minutes.

2. Drain the shrimp in a colander and rinse. Discard the brine. Spread the shrimp out on a paper towel–lined baking sheet and pat dry.

3. In another large bowl, whisk the eggs with the sesame oil and a pinch each of salt and pepper until combined. Set aside.

4. Heat a wok over medium-high heat until a drop of water sizzles and evaporates on contact. Pour in 1 tablespoon of vegetable oil and swirl to coat the base of the wok. Season the oil by adding the ginger and a pinch of salt. Allow the ginger to sizzle in the oil for about 30 seconds, swirling gently.

5. Add the garlic and stir-fry briefly to flavor the oil, about 10 seconds. Do not let the garlic brown or burn. Add the shrimp and stir-fry for about 2 minutes, until they turn pink. Transfer to a plate and discard the ginger.

6. Return the wok to the heat and add the remaining 1 tablespoon of vegetable oil. When the oil is hot, swirl the egg mixture into the wok. Swirl and shake the eggs to cook. Add the chives to the pan and continue cooking until eggs are cooked but not dry. Return the shrimp to the pan and toss to combine. Transfer to a serving plate.

Cinnamon with Tea-Soaked Eggs

Prep time: 10 minutes | Cook time: 39 minutes | Serve 4

- 2 cups water
- ¾ cup dark soy sauce
- 6 peeled fresh ginger slices, each about the size of a quarter
- 2 whole star anise
- 2 cinnamon sticks
- 6 whole cloves
- 1 teaspoon fennel seeds
- 1 teaspoon Sichuan peppercorns or black

peppercorns

1 teaspoon sugar

5 decaf black tea bags

8 large eggs, at room temperature

In a saucepan, bring the water to a boil. Add the dark soy, ginger, anise, cinnamon sticks, cloves, fennel seeds, peppercorns, and sugar. Cover the pot and reduce the heat to a simmer; cook for 20 minutes. Turn off the heat and add the tea bags. Steep the tea for 10 minutes. Strain the tea through a fine-mesh sieve into a large heatproof measuring cup and allow to cool while you cook the eggs.

Fill a large bowl with ice and water to create an ice bath for the eggs and set aside. In a wok, bring enough water to cover the eggs by about an inch to a boil. Gently lower the eggs into the water, reduce the heat to a simmer, and cook for 9 minutes. Remove the eggs with a slotted spoon and transfer to the ice bath until cool.

Remove the eggs from the ice bath. Tap the eggs with the back of a spoon to crack the shells so the marinade can seep in between the cracks, but gently enough to leave the shells on. The shells should end up looking like a mosaic. Place the eggs in a large jar (at least 32-ounce / 907-g) and cover them with the marinade. Store them in the refrigerator for at least 24 hours or up to a week. Remove the eggs from the marinade when ready to serve.

Chapter 4: Vegetables

Garlicky Scallion with Eggplant

Prep time: 10 minutes | Cook time: 5 minutes | Serves 4

- ¼ cup chicken broth
- 1 tablespoon soy sauce
- 1 tablespoon Chinese black vinegar or good balsamic vinegar
- 1 tablespoon brown sugar
- 1 tablespoon chili oil
- ¼ teaspoon red pepper flakes
- 2 tablespoons peanut or vegetable oil
- 2 to 3 Asian eggplants, cut into thin, 1-inch-long strips
- 2 scallions, minced

- 1 tablespoon fresh minced ginger
- 2 garlic cloves, minced

1. In a small bowl, mix together the chicken broth, soy sauce, vinegar, brown sugar, chili oil, and red pepper flakes. Set aside.

2. Place a wok over high heat until a drop of water sizzles on contact. Add the peanut oil and swirl to coat the wok.

3. Add the eggplants to the wok, and stir-fry for 2 to 3 minutes, until the outsides become golden brown. Turn down the heat to medium-high, and add the scallions, ginger, and garlic. Stir-fry for about 30 seconds, and then add in the chicken broth mixture; toss the vegetables until they are coated with the sauce. Simmer the vegetables for 2 to 3 minutes, allowing the eggplant to absorb the sauce.

Brothy Bok Choy with Ginger

Prep time: 10 minutes | Cook time: 2 minutes | Serves 4

- 1½ pounds baby bok choy
- 1½ tablespoons peanut or vegetable oil
- 1 or 2 garlic cloves, minced
- ¼ teaspoon ground ginger
- 3 tablespoons vegetable broth
- Sea salt
- ½ teaspoon toasted sesame oil

1. Trim the root ends of the baby bok choy. Wash and thoroughly drain the leaves.

2. Heat your wok to medium-high; add the peanut oil and swirl to coat the wok. Add the garlic and ginger, and cook them for 30 seconds to 1 minute. Do not let them burn. When the spices become fragrant, add the bok choy leaves. Stir-fry everything together until well combined.

3. Add the vegetable broth to the wok. Cover the wok and cook for about 1 minute. Remove the cover from the wok, and turn off the heat. Season the bok choy with the sea salt, drizzle it with the sesame oil, and toss to coat. Serve immediately.

Carrots with Garlicky Steamed Pancakes

Prep time: 15 minutes | Cook time: 6 minutes | Serves 4

- 2 tablespoons peanut or vegetable oil, divided
- 2 large eggs, beaten
- Sea salt
- 3 tablespoons minced garlic
- 2 tablespoons minced fresh ginger
- 8 ounces (227 g) shiitake or cremini mushrooms, or a combination of both, thinly sliced.
- 4 scallions, green part only, cut into 1-inch sections
- 1 (10-ounce/283 g) package coleslaw mix
- 1 cup shredded carrots
- ¼ cup Shaoxing rice wine
- 3 tablespoons soy sauce
- 1 teaspoon cornstarch
- Freshly ground black pepper
- 12 to 14 Mandarin pancakes or flour tortillas, steamed for 5 minutes
- Hoisin sauce, slightly thinned with warm water

1. Heat a wok over medium-high heat until it is hot. Add 1 tablespoon of peanut oil. When the oil is hot, add the eggs. Season with the sea salt, and stir-fry to scramble the eggs. Remove the eggs to a clean bowl and set aside.

2. Add the remaining 1 tablespoon of peanut oil to the hot wok. When the oil is hot, add the garlic and ginger and stir-fry for 10 seconds. Before they begin to burn, quickly add the shiitake mushrooms and scallions and stir-fry for 1 to 2 minutes.

3. Add the coleslaw mix, carrots, and rice wine to the wok. Cover the wok, reduce the heat to medium, and cook the vegetables for 3 to 4 minutes. Uncover the wok and cook the vegetables until they are crisp-tender.

4. Return the eggs to the wok, and add the soy sauce and cornstarch. Stir-fry to mix everything. Season with additional sea salt and with the pepper.

5. Serve with the steamed Mandarin pancakes and hoisin sauce.

Scallion with Stir-Fried Vegetable

Prep time: 10 minutes | Cook time: 6 minutes | Serves 4 to 6

- 3 tablespoons vegetable oil
- 1 peeled fresh ginger slice, about the size of a quarter
- Kosher salt
- ½ white onion, cut into 1-inch pieces
- 1 large carrot, peeled and cut diagonally into ¼-inch-thick slices
- 2 celery ribs, cut diagonally into ¼-inch-thick slices
- 6 fresh shiitake mushrooms, stems removed and caps thinly sliced
- 1 red bell pepper, cut into 1-inch pieces
- 1 small handful green beans, trimmed
- 2 garlic cloves, finely minced
- 2 scallions, thinly sliced

1. Heat a wok over medium-high heat until a drop of water sizzles and evaporates on contact. Pour in the oil and swirl to coat the base of the wok. Season the oil by adding the ginger slice and a pinch of salt. Let sizzle in the oil for about 30 seconds, swirling gently.

2. Add the onion, carrot, and celery to the wok and stir-fry, moving the vegetables around in the wok quickly using a spatula. When the vegetables begin to look tender, about 4 minutes, add the mushrooms and continue tossing them in the hot wok.

3. When the mushrooms look soft, add the bell pepper and continue to toss, about 4 more minutes. When the bell peppers begin to soften, add the green beans and toss until tender, about 3 more minutes. Add the garlic and toss until fragrant.

4. Transfer to a platter, discard the ginger, and garnish with the scallions. Serve hot.

Carrot with Vegetable Fried Rice

Prep time: 10 minutes | Cook time: 5 minutes | Serves 4

- 2 tablespoons cooking oil
- 1 tablespoon crushed, chopped ginger
- 2 garlic cloves, crushed and chopped
- ½ teaspoon kosher salt
- 4 large eggs, beaten
- 1 medium carrot, julienned
- 1 medium onion, diced
- 1 red bell pepper, diced
- 1 cup frozen peas, thawed
- 2 cups cold, cooked rice
- 1 teaspoon sesame oil
- 1 tablespoon soy sauce
- 4 scallions, cut into ½-inch pieces

1. In a wok over high heat, heat the cooking oil until it shimmers.
2. Add the ginger, garlic, salt, and eggs and stir-fry for 1 minute, or until the eggs are firm.
3. Add the carrot and stir-fry for 1 minute.
4. Add the onion and stir-fry for 1 minute.
5. Add the bell pepper and stir-fry for 1 minute.
6. Add the peas, rice, sesame oil, and soy sauce and stir-fry for 1 minute.
7. Garnish with the scallions and serve immediately.

Scallion Pancakes Dough

Prep time: 5 minutes | Cook time: 14 minutes | Serve 4

- 2 cups all-purpose flour, plus additional for dusting
- ¾ cup warm water
- ½ cup cold water
- 2 to 4 tablespoons
- vegetable or peanut oil, plus additional as needed
- 3 or 4 scallions, thinly sliced

1. In a large bowl, mix the flour and warm water together to form a dough. Work the cold water into the dough, a little bit at a time, until a smooth and not too sticky dough forms.
2. On a clean work surface, knead the dough for 10 minutes. If the dough seems too sticky at first, dust the work surface with a little flour. The dough will become smoother the more it is kneaded, and extra flour should not be necessary. Place the dough back in the bowl, and cover it with a damp cloth or paper towel. Let the dough rest for 30 minutes.

3. Roll out the dough onto a floured cutting board. Divide it into four equal pieces.
4. Roll each piece of dough into a level circle, 7 to 8 inches in diameter. Brush the top of each circle lightly with some of the oil. Top each circle with one quarter of the scallions.
5. Fold the edges of the dough over the top of the scallions to create a ball. Then flatten the dough and roll out each again to incorporate the scallions into the dough.
6. Heat your wok over medium-low heat. Using about ½ to 1 tablespoon oil, lightly fry each dough circle until golden brown, 2 to 3 minutes per side.
7. Serve warm with Sesame Dipping Sauce (here) or regular soy sauce.

Garlicky Spinach

Prep time: 5 minutes | Cook time: 0 minutes | Serve 4

- 4 teaspoons peanut or vegetable oil
- 5 garlic cloves, thinly sliced or crushed
- 1 (10-ounce) bag raw spinach, washed and drained well
- Sea salt

1. Heat your wok and add the peanut oil until it begins to smoke.
2. Add the garlic and stir-fry it very briefly, about 10 seconds.
3. Before the garlic begins to burn, quickly add the spinach and stir-fry. The spinach will reduce in size quickly. After 1 minute or two, once the spinach looks wilted but still bright green, remove it from the wok. Drain off any excess liquid.
4. Season the spinach with the sea salt and serve.

Seared Broccoli with Broth

Prep time: 10 minutes | Cook time: 4 minutes | Serve 4

- 1½ teaspoons peanut or vegetable oil
- 6 cups broccoli florets (about 2 medium bunches), washed and dried well
- ½ sweet onion, thinly
- sliced
- 1 cup chicken or vegetable broth
- 2 tablespoons soy sauce
- 2 teaspoons orange juice

- Sea salt
- Freshly ground black pepper

1. Heat your wok over high heat until a drop of water sizzles on contact. Add the peanut oil and quickly swirl it to coat the wok.

2. Add the broccoli and onion, and toss them in the wok. Reduce the heat to medium-high, and stir-fry the vegetables for a few minutes, allowing parts of the broccoli to brown.

3. Add the chicken broth to the wok and cover it. Cook the broccoli for 2 to 3 minutes longer, until it is crisp-tender.

4. Remove the cover from the wok, and add the soy sauce and orange juice. Season with the sea salt and pepper. Stir-fry the vegetables for 2 to 3 minutes, or until all the liquid has evaporated.

Gingered Broccoli Stir-Fry

Prep time: 10 minutes | Cook time: 9 minutes | Serves 4

- 4 tablespoons soy sauce
- 2 tablespoons sugar
- 1 tablespoon peanut or vegetable oil
- 1½ teaspoons grated fresh ginger
- 1 cup halved cremini or button mushrooms
- 1 red bell pepper, cut

- into strips
- 1 green bell pepper, cut into strips
- 2 scallions, chopped
- 1 cup bite-size pieces of broccoli florets
- ½ cup (trimmed and cut into thirds) green beans

1. In a small bowl, mix the soy sauce and sugar. Set aside.

2. To a wok over medium-high heat, add the peanut oil. Add the ginger and stir-fry it for about 1 minute. Add the mushrooms, red bell pepper, green bell pepper, scallions, broccoli, and green beans. Put a lid on the wok, and cook the vegetables for about 4 minutes. Remove the lid and stir-fry the vegetables for 1 to 2 minutes. Add the sugar and soy sauce mixture, and toss to coat the vegetables. Cook them for about 3 minutes, or until the liquid has cooked off and the vegetables are crisp-tender.

3. Remove the wok from the heat and serve.

Garlicky Fried Green Beans

Prep time: 5 minutes | Cook time: 6½ minutes | Serves 4

- ¼ cup peanut or vegetable oil
- 1 pound string beans, trimmed and completely dry
- 1 garlic clove, crushed
- 2 tablespoons oyster sauce
- 1 teaspoon Shaoxing rice wine
- 3 scallions, thinly sliced

1. Place your wok over high heat. When it is hot, add the peanut oil. Add the string beans to the wok, and cook them until they are crinkly and blistered, tossing them continuously for about 5 minutes. Remove the beans from the wok.

2. Keeping the wok over high heat, add the crushed garlic, oyster sauce, rice wine, and scallions to the wok and stir-fry until fragrant, about 30 seconds. Return the green beans to the wok, and toss them in the sauce until they are coated. Stir-fry the beans for 1 minute. Serve hot.

Spicy Fish Sauce with Vietnamese Vegetables

Prep time: 15 minutes | Cook time: 3 minutes | Serve 4

- 1 tablespoon cooking oil
- 3 scallions, minced
- 1 medium red onion, diced
- 2 garlic cloves, crushed and chopped
- 1 cup sliced mushrooms
- 1 chile, cut crosswise, into ⅛- to ¼-inch rings
- 2 cups sugar snap or
- snow pea pods
- 1 cup sliced Napa cabbage
- 2 tablespoons fish sauce
- 2 tablespoons rice wine
- ¼ teaspoon ground white pepper
- ½ cup coarsely chopped cilantro, parsley, dill, or mint

1. In a wok over high heat, heat the cooking oil until it shimmers.

2. Add the scallions, onion, and garlic and stir-fry for 30 seconds.

- Add the mushrooms and stir-fry for 30 seconds.
- Add the chile and stir-fry for 30 seconds.
- Add the pea pods and stir-fry for 30 seconds.
- Add the cabbage and stir-fry for 30 seconds.
- Toss the fish sauce, rice wine, and white pepper with the vegetables for 30 seconds.
- Serve over steamed rice or noodles, topped with the fresh herbs of your choice.

Vinegary Vegetable Soup

Prep time: 15 minutes | Cook time: 13 minutes | Serve 4

- 4 cups chicken or vegetable broth
- 3 tablespoons soy sauce
- ¼ cup cooked shredded chicken, or pork
- ½ cup shiitake or cremini mushrooms, diced
- 1 tablespoon garlic chili sauce
- ¼ cup white vinegar
- ¼ teaspoon ground pepper
- ⅓ cup canned bamboo shoots, julienned
- 3 ounces (85 g) block of firm tofu, cut into ½-inch-thin strips
- 1 tablespoon cornstarch mixed with 1 tablespoon cold water
- 1 egg, beaten
- 2 scallions, diced
- ½ teaspoon toasted sesame oil

Bring the chicken broth to a simmer in your wok. Add the soy sauce, shredded chicken, shiitake mushrooms, and garlic chili sauce to the broth. Simmer for 3 to 5 minutes. Add the vinegar, pepper, bamboo shoots, and tofu to the wok. Simmer for 5 to 7 minutes more.

Add the cornstarch mixture to the soup, and stir the soup to combine. Simmer for about 5 minutes, until the soup has thickened.

Slowly pour the egg into the wok in a fine stream. Gently stir the soup a few times. Add the scallions and sesame oil to the soup. Give it a gentle stir and serve.

Cornstarch with Garlicky Cabbage

Prep time: 10 minutes | Cook time: 3 minutes |

Serve 4

- 1 tablespoon cornstarch
- 2 tablespoons cold water
- 4 tablespoons peanut oil
- 3 garlic cloves, very thinly sliced
- 1 small napa cabbage, washed and shredded
- 3 tablespoons black vinegar
- Sea salt

1. In a small bowl, mix the cornstarch and cold water to make a smooth paste. Set aside.
2. To a hot wok, add the peanut oil, and then add the garlic and stir-fry it for about 10 seconds. Before the garlic begins to burn, add the cabbage and stir-fry it for about 2 minutes, or until it has softened completely. Add the vinegar to the wok. Season the cabbage mixture with sea salt, and stir-fry until the vinegar and sea salt have combined with the mixture, about 15 seconds.
3. Add the cornstarch mixture to the wok, and stir-fry for 30 seconds or less, until the sauce has thickened. Remove the wok from the heat and serve.

Carrot with Steamed Pancakes

Prep time: 15 minutes | Cook time: 4 minutes | Serve 4

- 2 tablespoons peanut or vegetable oil, divided
- 2 large eggs, beaten
- Sea salt
- 3 tablespoons minced garlic
- 2 tablespoons minced fresh ginger
- 8 ounces (227 g) shiitake or cremini mushrooms, thinly sliced
- 4 scallions, green part only, cut into 1-inch sections
- 1 (10-ounce / 283-g) package coleslaw mix
- 1 cup shredded carrots
- ¼ cup Shaoxing rice wine
- 3 tablespoons soy sauce
- 1 teaspoon cornstarch
- Freshly ground black pepper
- 12 to 14 Mandarin pancakes or flour tortillas, steamed for 5 minutes
- Hoisin sauce, slightly thinned with warm

water

1. Heat a wok over medium-high heat until it is hot. Add 1 tablespoon peanut oil. When the oil is hot, add the eggs. Season with the sea salt, and stir-fry to scramble the eggs. Remove the eggs to a clean bowl and set aside.

2. Add the remaining 1 tablespoon peanut oil to the hot wok. When the oil is hot, add the garlic and ginger and stir-fry for 10 seconds. Before they begin to burn, quickly add the shiitake mushrooms and scallions and stir-fry for 1 to 2 minutes.

3. Add the coleslaw mix, carrots, and rice wine to the wok. Cover the wok, reduce the heat to medium, and cook the vegetables for 3 to 4 minutes. Uncover the wok and cook the vegetables until they are crisp-tender.

4. Return the eggs to the wok, and add the soy sauce and cornstarch. Stir-fry to mix everything. Season with additional sea salt and with the pepper.

5. Serve with the steamed Mandarin pancakes and hoisin sauce.

Sesame with Seasoned Broccoli

Prep time: 5 minutes | Cook time: 6 minutes | Serves 4

- 2 tablespoons peanut oil
- 2 garlic cloves, thinly sliced
- 1 pound (454 g) Chinese broccoli (gai lan), washed and trimmed
- 2 tablespoons soy sauce
- 1 tablespoon oyster sauce
- 1 teaspoon sesame oil

1. Boil 1 cup water in a kettle or small saucepot.

2. Heat your wok over high heat until a drop of water sizzles on contact.

3. Add the oil and then the garlic to the wok and cook for about 15 seconds.

4. Quickly add the Chinese broccoli and stir-fry in the garlic oil.

5. Pour ½ cup boiling water into the wok and cook for 5 to 6 minutes, or until the broccoli is tender-crisp.

6. Add the soy and oyster sauces to the wok, stir-fry to combine with the broccoli, and heat for about 1 minute.

7. Remove the wok from the heat and add the sesame oil.

8. Mix to combine and serve hot.

Celery with Vegetable Egg Rolls

Prep time: 10 minutes | Cook time: 9½ minutes | Serve 4

- 2 tablespoons plus 1 teaspoon peanut oil, divided
- 2 garlic cloves, minced
- 1 tablespoon minced fresh ginger or ⅓ teaspoon ground ginger
- ½ sweet onion, thinly sliced
- 1 celery stalk, thinly sliced
- 2 carrots, cut into matchsticks
- ½ small cabbage, shredded
- 2 tablespoons rice vinegar
- 2 teaspoons soy sauce
- 1 teaspoon sugar
- 40 to 50 egg roll wrappers

1. To a hot wok over medium-high heat, add 1 teaspoon peanut oil, the garlic, and the ginger, and stir-fry for about 30 seconds. Add the onion, celery, and carrots to the wok, and stir-fry for about 2 minutes. Add the cabbage, rice vinegar, soy sauce, and sugar. Stir-fry the mixture for another 2 minutes. Remove the vegetables from the wok, and let them cool until they can be handled.

2. Place the egg roll wrappers on a clean surface with a point facing you. Spread 1 tablespoon the filling in a horizontal line, slightly closer to you. Roll the point of the wrapper closest to you over the filling. Fold in the two side corners. Dampen the remaining open point with water, and finish rolling the egg roll away from you.

3. The egg rolls will be fried in two batches. To a wok over medium-high heat, add 1 tablespoon the peanut oil. Place the egg rolls in the wok, seam-side down. Fry them for about 5 to 8 minutes, turning often so they cook evenly. Repeat this step with the rest of the egg rolls.

. Serve with plum sauce, sweet and sour sauce, chili sauce, or duck sauce.

Mushroom with Cantonese Vegetables

Prep time: 15 minutes | Cook time: 3 minutes | Serve 4

- ¼ cup soy sauce
- 1 tablespoon cornstarch
- 1 tablespoon brown sugar
- 2 tablespoons cooking oil
- 1 medium carrot, roll-cut into ½-inch pieces
- 1 tablespoon crushed, chopped ginger
- 2 garlic cloves, crushed and chopped
- 1 medium onion, quartered and cut into 1-inch pieces
- 1 cup sliced mushrooms
- 1 medium red bell pepper, cut into 1-inch pieces
- 1 cup 1-inch cut bok choy or Chinese cabbage
- 4 scallions, cut diagonally into 1-inch slices

. In a small bowl, whisk together the soy sauce, cornstarch, and brown sugar to form a roux. Set aside.

. In a wok over high heat, heat the cooking oil until it shimmers.

. Add the carrot, ginger, and garlic and stir-fry for 1 minute.

. Add the onion and mushrooms and stir-fry for 1 minute.

. Add the bell pepper and stir-fry for 1 minute.

. Add the bok choy and toss with the other ingredients.

. Add the roux and mix until a light glaze forms.

. Toss in the scallions. Serve immediately over steamed rice.

Limey Fish Sauce with Thai Vegetables

Prep time: 15 minutes | Cook time: 4½ minutes | Serves 4

- 2 tablespoons red Thai curry paste
- 2 tablespoons fish sauce
- 1 teaspoon hot sesame oil
- Juice of 1 lime
- 3 tablespoons brown sugar
- 1 tablespoon cornstarch
- 2 tablespoons cooking oil
- 2 garlic cloves, crushed and chopped
- 1 medium carrot, roll-cut into ½-inch pieces
- 1 medium onion, cut into 1-inch pieces
- 2 cups sugar snap or snow pea pods
- 1 red bell pepper, cut into 1-inch pieces
- 2 cups basil leaves
- 1 cup fresh bean sprouts
- ½ cup chopped cilantro

1. In a small bowl, whisk together the curry paste, fish sauce, sesame oil, lime juice, brown sugar, and cornstarch. Set aside.

2. In a wok over high heat, heat the cooking oil until it shimmers.

3. Add the garlic and carrot and stir-fry for 1 minute.

4. Add the onion and stir-fry for 1 minute.

5. Add the pea pods and stir-fry for 1 minute.

6. Add the bell pepper and stir-fry for 1 minute.

7. Add the curry paste mixture and stir until it forms a glaze.

8. Add the basil and toss for 30 seconds until it wilts.

9. Serve over rice or noodles, topped with the bean sprouts and cilantro.

Sesame with Japanese Stir-Fried Vegetables

Prep time: 10 minutes | Cook time: 3½ minutes | Serves 4

- 2 tablespoons yellow miso
- 2 tablespoons mirin
- 2 tablespoons tamari
- 1 tablespoon toasted sesame oil
- 2 tablespoons cooking oil
- 1 tablespoon crushed, chopped ginger
- 2 garlic cloves, crushed and chopped
- 1 medium carrot, roll-cut into ½-inch pieces
- 1 medium onion, cut into 1-inch pieces
- 4 ounces shiitake mushrooms, cut into slices
- 1 red bell pepper, cut into 1-inch pieces
- 4 scallions, cut into

1-inch pieces • 2 cups bean sprouts

1. In a small bowl, whisk together the miso, mirin, tamari, and sesame oil. Set aside.

2. In a wok over high heat, heat the cooking oil until it shimmers.

3. Add the ginger, garlic, and carrot and stir-fry for 1 minute.

4. Add the onion and mushrooms and stir-fry for 1 minute.

5. Add the bell pepper and scallions and stir-fry for 1 minute.

6. Add the miso mixture and toss for 30 seconds.

7. Serve with steamed Japanese rice and garnish with bean sprouts.

Soy Sauce with Filipino Vegetables

Prep time: 10 minutes | Cook time: 4 minutes | Serves 4

- 2 tablespoons cooking oil
- 2 garlic cloves, crushed and chopped
- 1 tablespoon crushed, chopped ginger
- 1 medium carrot, roll-cut into ½-inch pieces
- 1 medium onion, diced
- 12 cherry tomatoes, cut in half
- 2 cups sugar snap or snow pea pods
- 1 red bell pepper, cut into 1-inch pieces
- ¼ cup oyster sauce
- 2 tablespoons soy sauce

1. In a wok over high heat, heat the cooking oil until it shimmers.

2. Add the garlic, ginger, and carrot and stir-fry for 1 minute.

3. Add the onion and stir-fry for 1 minute.

4. Add the cherry tomatoes and stir-fry for 1 minute.

5. Add the pea pods and bell pepper and stir-fry for 1 minute.

6. Add the oyster sauce and soy sauce and stir until a light glaze forms.

7. Serve over steamed rice.

Spicy Kimchi with Korean Vegetables

Prep time: 10 minutes | Cook time: 5 minutes | Serve 4

- 2 tablespoons cooking oil
- 1 tablespoon crushed, chopped ginger
- 2 garlic cloves, crushed and chopped
- 1 medium onion, cut into 1-inch pieces
- 4 ounces shiitake mushrooms, sliced
- 2 cups sugar snap or
- snow pea pods
- 1 red bell pepper, cut into 1-inch pieces
- 2 heads baby bok choy, leaves separated
- 2 tablespoons gochujang
- ½ cup kimchi
- 2 tablespoons soy sauce

1. In a wok over high heat, heat the cooking oil until it shimmers.

2. Add the ginger, garlic, and onion and stir-fry for 1 minute.

3. Add the mushrooms and stir-fry for 1 minute.

4. Add the pea pods and stir-fry for 1 minute.

5. Add the bell pepper and bok choy and stir-fry for 1 minute.

6. Add the gochujang, kimchi, and soy sauce and stir-fry for 1 minute.

7. Serve over steamed jasmine rice.

Spicy Malaysian Vegetable Curry

Prep time: 10 minutes | Cook time: 5 minutes | Serve 4

- 2 tablespoons soy sauce
- 1 tablespoon hot sesame oil
- 1 teaspoon Chinese five-spice powder
- ¼ teaspoon ground cumin
- ¼ teaspoon ground fennel
- ½ teaspoon ground chili powder
- 2 tablespoons coconut oil
- 1 tablespoon crushed, chopped ginger

1 medium carrot, roll-cut into ½-inch pieces

1 medium red onion, diced

2 cups sugar snap or snow pea pods

• ¼ cup unsweetened and shredded dried coconut

In a small bowl, whisk together the soy sauce, sesame oil, five-spice powder, cumin, fennel, and chili powder. Set aside.

In a wok over high heat, heat the coconut oil until it shimmers.

Add the ginger and carrot and stir-fry for 1 minute.

Add the onion and stir-fry for 1 minute.

Add the pea pods and the soy sauce mixture and stir-fry for 1 minute.

Add the coconut and stir-fry for 1 minute.

Serve over steamed rice made with coconut water or coconut milk.

Limey Carrot with Spiced Vegetable

Prep time: 10 minutes | Cook time: 4½ minutes | Serve 4

1 teaspoon hot sesame oil

Juice of 1 lime

1 tablespoon fish sauce

1 tablespoon Chinese five-spice powder

2 tablespoons cooking oil

2 garlic cloves, crushed and chopped

1 medium carrot, roll-

• cut into ½-inch pieces

• 2 to 3 red chiles, cut into ¼-inch pieces

• 2 cups sugar snap or snow pea pods

• 1 red bell pepper, cut into 1-inch pieces

• 1 small mango, peeled and cut into ½-inch pieces

• 2 baby bok choy, leaves separated

In a small bowl, whisk together the sesame oil, lime juice, fish sauce, and five-spice powder. Set aside.

In a wok over high heat, heat the cooking oil until it shimmers.

Add the garlic and carrot and stir-fry for 1 minute.

Add the chiles and stir-fry for 30 seconds.

5. Add the pea pods and bell pepper and stir-fry for 1 minute.

6. Add the mango and stir-fry for 1 minute, then add the sesame oil mixture.

7. Add the bok choy and stir-fry for 1 minute.

8. Serve over steamed jasmine rice.

Egg with Garlicky Vegetables

Prep time: 10 minutes | Cook time: 1⅔ minutes | Serve 4

• 2 tablespoons cooking oil

• 3 garlic cloves, crushed and chopped

• 6 eggs, beaten

• 2 tablespoons rice wine

• 3 scallions, cut into ½-inch pieces

• 1 cup chopped bok choy

• 2 tablespoons soy sauce

• ¼ cup hoisin sauce

1. In a wok over high heat, heat the cooking oil until it shimmers.

2. Add the garlic and stir-fry for 10 to 15 seconds or until lightly browned.

3. Add the eggs and rice wine and stir-fry until the eggs are firm but still moist.

4. Add the scallions and stir-fry for 30 seconds.

5. Add the bok choy and stir-fry for 1 minute.

6. In a small bowl, combine the soy sauce and hoisin sauce. Drizzle over the scrambled eggs. Serve alone or over steamed rice.

Brothy Cornstarch with Curried Tofu

Prep time: 15 minutes | Cook time: 6 minutes | Serves 4

• 2 tablespoons curry of choice

• 2 tablespoons rice vinegar

• 2 tablespoons soy sauce

• ½ cup vegetable or meat broth

• 2 tablespoons

cornstarch

• 2 tablespoons cooking oil

• 2 garlic cloves, crushed and chopped

• 1 tablespoon crushed, chopped ginger

• 1 pound extra-firm tofu, well drained,

patted dry, and cut into 1-inch pieces

- 1 medium carrot, roll-cut into ½-inch pieces
- 1 medium onion, cut into 1-inch pieces
- 4 ounces mushrooms, cut into slices
- 1 red bell pepper, cut into 1-inch pieces

1. In a small bowl, whisk together the curry, rice vinegar, soy sauce, broth, and cornstarch. Set aside.

2. In a wok over high heat, heat the cooking oil until it shimmers.

3. Add the garlic, ginger, and tofu and stir-fry for 2 minutes, or until the tofu begins to brown.

4. Add the carrot and stir-fry for 1 minute.

5. Add the onion and stir-fry for 1 minute.

6. Add the mushrooms and stir-fry for 1 minute.

7. Add the bell pepper and stir-fry for 1 minute.

8. Add the curry mixture to the wok and stir-fry until a glaze forms.

9. Serve over basmati (Indian), coconut jasmine (Thai), or long-grain white rice (Chinese), depending on the type of curry you used.

Spicy Cilantro with Garbanzo Stir Fry

Prep time: 10 minutes | Cook time: 25 minutes | Serves 2

- 2 tablespoon oil
- 1 tablespoon oregano
- 1 tablespoon basil, chopped
- 1 garlic clove, crushed
- Ground black pepper, to taste
- 2 cups cooked
- garbanzo beans
- 1 large zucchini, halved and sliced
- ½ cup sliced mushrooms
- 1 tablespoon chopped cilantro
- 1 tomato, chopped

1. Heat oil in a wok over medium heat. Stir in oregano, basil, garlic and pepper.

2. Add the garbanzo beans and zucchini, stirring well to coat with oil and herbs.

3. Cook for 10 minutes, stirring occasionally. Stir in mushrooms and cilantro; cook 10 minutes, stirring occasionally.

4. Place the chopped tomato on top of the mixture to

steam. Cover and cook 5 minutes more.

Spicy Carrot and Sprouts Stir Fry

Prep time: 5 minutes | Cook time: 5 minutes | Serves 2

- 1 cup sliced shiitake
- 1 cup sprouts
- ½ cup sliced snow peas
- ½ cup sliced carrots
- ½ cup sliced yellow peppers
- 1 tablespoon oil

1. Marinade shiitake in Superfoods marinade.

2. In a wok, stir fry drained shiitake in coconut oil for few minutes, add all vegetables and stir fry for 2 more minutes. Add the rest of the marinade and stir fry for 1 minute.

3. Serve with brown rice or quinoa.

Onion with Kale Stir Fry

Prep time: 5 minutes | Cook time: 6 minutes | Serves 2

- ½ pound (227 g) pumpkin
- 2 cups kale
- ½ cup onions
- 1 tablespoon coconut oil

1. Marinade pumpkin in a Superfoods marinade.

2. In a wok, stir fry drained pumpkin in coconut oil for 4 to 5 more minutes. Add the rest of the marinade, onions and kale and stir fry for 2 minutes more.

3. Serve with brown rice or quinoa.

Sprouts with Choy Stir Fry

Prep time: 5 minutes | Cook time: 5 minutes | Serves 2

- 1½ pound (680 g) sliced okra
- 1 cup sprouts
- ½ cup sliced onions
- 1 tablespoon coconut oil

1. Marinade okra in a Superfoods marinade.

2. In a wok, stir fry drained okra in coconut oil for few minutes, add onions and stir fry for 2 more minutes. Add the rest of the marinade and sprou and stir fry for 1 minute.

3. Serve with brown rice or quinoa.

Eggy Chives Stir-Fry

Prep time: 10 minutes | Cook time: 5 minutes | Serves 6

- 5 large eggs
- ⅛ teaspoon sugar
- ½ teaspoon salt
- 1 teaspoon Shaoxing wine
- ¼ teaspoon ground white pepper
- ¼ teaspoon sesame oil
- 4 teaspoons water
- 2 cups Chinese chives, chopped
- 4 tablespoons vegetable oil

1. Beat eggs with sugar, salt, wine, white pepper, water, chives, and sesame oil in a bowl.
2. Set up a wok on medium heat and add vegetable oil to heat.
3. Pour the egg-wine mixture and stir-fry for 5 to 7 minutes until eggs are set.
4. Serve warm.

Spicy Avocado Salad

Prep time: 10 minutes | Cook time: 5 minutes | Serves 4

- 7 ounces (198 g) silken tofu, sliced
- 1 ripe avocado, peeled and sliced
- 2 garlic cloves, grated
- 1 teaspoon ginger, grated
- 2 tablespoons light soy sauce
- 1 teaspoon sesame oil
- ½ teaspoon sugar
- ½ teaspoon Chinese black vinegar
- ¼ teaspoon white pepper
- 2 teaspoons water
- Salt, to taste
- 1 scallion, finely chopped

1. Sauté tofu with sesame oil in a Mandarin wok for 5 minutes.
2. Toss tofu with rest of the salad in a salad bowl.
3. Mix well and serve.
4. Enjoy.

Vinegar with Ginger and Tofu

Prep time: 5 minutes | Cook time: 25½ minutes |

Serves 6

- 21 ounces (595 g) firm tofu, cut into cubes
- 2 tablespoons oil
- 4 ginger slices
- 1 tablespoon Shaoxing wine
- 2 tablespoons Chinese black vinegar
- 3 tablespoons light soy sauce
- 4 tablespoons sugar
- 5 tablespoons water

1. Sauté ginger with oil in a Cantonese wok for 30 seconds.
2. Stir in tofu, and sauté for 10 minutes until it turns golden.
3. Add wine, black vinegar, soy sauce, water, and sugar.
4. Cover and cook for 15 minutes over medium low heat.
5. Serve warm.

Bean Sauce with Garlicky Mushroom

Prep time: 10 minutes | Cook time: 10 minutes | Serves 6

- 1 pound (454 g) king oyster mushrooms
- 5 tablespoons vegetable oil
- 6 ginger slices
- 8 garlic cloves, sliced
- 1 tablespoon spicy
- bean sauce
- 1 tablespoon light soy sauce
- ½ teaspoon sugar
- 5 long hot peppers, sliced diagonally

1. Sauté mushrooms, ginger, and garlic with oil in a Cantonese wok for 5 minutes.
2. Stir in bean sauce, soy sauce, sugar, and hot peppers.
3. Mix well and cover to cook for 5 minutes on low heat.
4. Serve warm.

Vinegary Roasted Beets

Prep time: 10 minutes | Cook time: 25 minutes | Serves 6

- 1½ pounds (680 g) beets, peeled and cut
- into ¼-inch circles
- Olive oil, for cooking

- 1 to 3 garlic cloves, minced
- 1 teaspoon honey
- 1 tablespoon Chinese black vinegar
- Salt and black pepper, to taste
- Fresh herbs, for garnish

1. Toss beets with olive oil in a baking tray.
2. Roast the beets for 20 minutes in the oven at 400ºF (205ºC).
3. Mix honey with garlic, 2 tablespoons olive oil, black vinegar, black pepper, salt, and herbs in a Mandarin wok.
4. Toss in roasted beets and sauté for 5 minutes.
5. Serve warm.

Eggy Tomato Stir-Fry

Prep time: 10 minutes | Cook time: 7 minutes | Serves 4

- 4 tomatoes, diced
- 1 scallion, chopped
- 4 eggs
- ¾ teaspoons salt
- ¼ teaspoon white pepper
- ½ teaspoon sesame oil
- 1 teaspoon Shaoxing wine
- 3 tablespoons vegetable oil
- 2 teaspoons sugar
- ¼ to ½ cup water

1. Sauté tomatoes and scallions with oil in a Cantonese wok for 2 minutes.
2. Beat eggs with salt, white pepper, sesame oil, wine, sugar, and water in a bowl.
3. Pour the eggs mixture into the wok and stir cook for 5 minutes.
4. Serve warm.

Spiced Tofu with Cornstarch

Prep time: 15 minutes | Cook time: 6 minutes | Serves 6

- 14 ounces (397 g) firm tofu
- ⅓ cup cornstarch
- ¼ teaspoon garlic powder
- ¼ teaspoon onion powder
- ⅛ teaspoon five-spice powder
- ½ teaspoon salt
- ¼ cup water
- 1 tablespoon soy sauce
- ½ teaspoon dark soy

- sauce
- 2 teaspoons sugar
- 1½ teaspoons rice vinegar
- ½ teaspoon sesame oil
- 2 teaspoons cornstarch
- ⅔ cup warm water
- ¼ cup peanut oil
- 1 cup blanched peanuts
- 2 medium carrots chopped
- 1 tablespoon ginger, minced
- 3 to 5 dried chili peppers, chopped
- 3 garlic cloves, chopped
- 3 scallions, diced
- 1 teaspoon Sichuan peppercorn powder

1. For tofu, mix cornstarch with water, salt, five-spice powder, onion powder, and garlic powder in a bowl.
2. Mix soy sauces, sugar, salt, rice vinegar, cornstarch, sesame oil, and warm water in a bowl.
3. Sauté peanut with ¼ cup peanut oil in a Cantonese wok for 5 minutes, then transfer to a plate.
4. Sear the tofu in the same oil until golden-brown, then transfer to a plate.
5. Now sauté ginger and chili peppers with 1½ tablespoons peanut oil in a Cantonese wok for 1 minute.
6. Add tofu, peanuts, and prepared sauce.
7. Mix well and garnish with peppercorn.
8. Enjoy.

Mushroom with Garlicky Braised Tofu

Prep time: 15 minutes | Cook time: 1¾ minutes | Serves 6

- 1 pound (454 g) silken tofu
- 2 cups oil, for frying
- 1 cup chicken stock
- 1 tablespoon oyster sauce
- 1½ tablespoons soy sauce
- 1 teaspoon dark soy sauce
- ½ teaspoon sesame oil
- ¼ teaspoon sugar
- ¼ teaspoon salt
- 3 small ginger slices, ½ inch thick
- 3 garlic cloves, finely minced
- 2 scallions, chopped
- 4 fresh shiitake mushrooms
- 1 medium carrot, thinly sliced

⅔ cup fresh winter bamboo shoots

• ½ cup snap peas
• 1½ tablespoons cornstarch

1 tablespoon Shaoxing wine

In a deep pan, heat 2 cups oil and deep fry the tofu until golden-brown.

Transfer the tofu to a plate and set it aside.

Sauté ginger with oil in a Cantonese wok for 15 seconds.

Stir in mushrooms, carrots, scallions, and bamboo shoots, and cook for 30 seconds.

Add snap peas, wine, all the sauces, sesame oil, sugar, and salt, then cook for 4 minutes

Mix cornstarch with water in a bowl and pour into the wok.

Stir and cook for 1 to 2 minutes until the mixture thickens.

Toss in deep fried tofu and mix well to coat.

Serve warm.

picy Tofu with Black Bean auce

rep time: 10 minutes | Cook time: 10½ minutes | erves 4

• 1 pound (454 g) firm tofu, diced
• 3 tablespoons oil
• 2 garlic cloves, minced
• 2 tablespoons fermented black beans, rinsed
• 2 scallions, whites and greens separated
• 3 dried red chilies, deseeded and chopped

• 1 tablespoon Shaoxing wine
• ½ tablespoon light soy sauce
• ½ teaspoon sesame oil
• ¼ teaspoon ground white pepper
• ¼ teaspoon sugar
• 1 teaspoon cornstarch, mixed with 2 tablespoons water

Sauté garlic with oil in a large wok for 30 seconds.

Stir in tofu and cook it for 5 minutes until golden-brown.

Add black beans, wine, soy sauce, red chillies, white pepper, sugar, and cover to a cook for 3 minutes.

4. Stir in cornstarch, mix well, and cook for 2 minutes.

5. Garnish with scallions.

6. Serve warm.

Cucumber with Vinegary Tofu Salad

Prep time: 10 minutes | Cook time: 15 minutes | Serves 4

• 1 cup red bell pepper, julienned
• 1 cup red onion, sliced
• 1 cup carrot, julienned
• 1 cup cucumber, julienned
• 1 cup celery, julienned
• 8 ounces (227 g) spiced tofu, shredded
• 1 tablespoon light olive oil
• 1 teaspoon garlic, minced

• 1½ teaspoons sugar
• ¼ teaspoon ground white pepper
• 2 tablespoons light soy sauce
• 1 tablespoon Chinese black vinegar
• 1 teaspoon sesame oil
• 1 tablespoon toasted sesame seeds
• ¼ cup cilantro, chopped

1. Sauté garlic, celery, carrot, onion, and bell pepper with oil in a Cantonese wok for 5 minutes.

2. Stir in tofu and sauté for 5 minutes.

3. Add soy sauce, white pepper, sugar, black vinegar, and cook for 5 minutes.

4. Remove it with from the heat and toss in cucumber.

5. Garnish with sesame seeds and cilantro.

6. Serve warm.

Cardamom with Besan Ladoo

Prep time: 10 minutes | Cook time: 10 minutes | Serve 10

• ¾ cup ghee (clarified butter)
• 2 cups chickpea flour (besan)

• 3 tablespoons ground almonds
• ½ cup superfine sugar
• ½ teaspoon ground

cardamom

- ½ cup grated,

sweetened coconut (optional)

1. Heat ghee in a pan over low heat, then mix in the chickpea flour. Cook over low heat for 10 minutes until mixture is flavorful and the chickpea flour is toasted. You should have a pasty and not powdery mixture.

2. Take the heat off and let the mixture cool down a bit until it's just warm. Finely powder the coconut (if used) in a coffee grinder. Add the ground coconut, ground cardamom, superfine sugar and ground almonds to the wok and mix thoroughly.

3. Shape the warm mixture into a round ball 1 to 1¼ cm in diameter. Put the ladoos in an airtight container and set aside for 2 to 3 hours to cool completely. Although the ladoos can be consumed immediately, they taste better after a few hours.

Mushroom with Vegetable Dumplings

Prep time: 10 minutes | Cook time: 29 minutes | Serves 12

- 12 Dumpling wrappers

For the Filling:

- 3 tablespoons oil
- 1 tablespoon ginger, minced
- 1 large onion, chopped
- 2 cups shiitake mushrooms, chopped
- 1½ cups cabbage, shredded
- 1½ cups carrot,

shredded

- 1 cup garlic chives, chopped
- ½ teaspoon white pepper
- 2 teaspoons sesame oil
- 3 tablespoons Shaoxing wine
- 2 tablespoon soy sauce
- 1 teaspoon sugar
- Salt, to taste

1. Sauté onion with oil in a Mandarin wok until soft.

2. Stir in ginger, mushrooms, cabbage, garlic, and rest of the ingredients.

3. Sauté for about 7 to 10 minutes until veggies are cooked and soft.

4. Allow the filling to cool and spread the dumpling wrappers on the working surface.

5. Divide the mushroom filling at the center of each dumpling wrapper.

6. Wet the edges of the dumplings and bring all the

edges of each dumpling together.

7. Pinch and seal the edges of the dumplings to seal the filling inside.

8. Boil water in a suitable pot with a steamer basket placed inside.

9. Add the dumplings to the steamer, cover and steam for 20 minutes.

10. Meanwhile, heat about 2 tablespoons oil in a Mandarin wok.

11. Sear the dumpling for 2 minutes until golden.

12. Serve warm.

Turmeric with Okra Stir-Fr

Prep time: 10 minutes | Cook time: 14 minutes | Serves 4

- 2 tablespoons vegetable oil
- 450 g small okra
- ½ teaspoon of ground turmeric
- 1 garlic clove, chopped
- ½ teaspoon fresh

ginger, chopped

- 2 quartered onions
- 2 quartered romaine tomatoes
- 1 tablespoon chopped fresh coriander

1. Heat a large pan or wok with vegetable oil on medium to high heat, add the okra, and stir-fry fo 3 minutes until soft and golden brown.

2. Place the stir-fried okra on a plate.

3. Add turmeric to the hot oil and heat it for 1 to 2 minutes or until it smells fragrant.

4. Mix in the ginger, tomatoes, onions and garlic an stir-fry for about 10 minutes until the onions are soft.

5. Add the stir-fried okra to the onion mixture.

6. Garnish with coriander.

Gingered Wat Wah Did

Prep time: 10 minutes | Cook time: 16½ minutes Serves 6

- 3 tablespoons vegetable oil
- 2 spring onions, thinly sliced
- 2 garlic cloves,

chopped

- ½ pound (227 g) extra firm tofu, cut into cubes
- ¼ cup fermented bla

beans

¼ cup mushroom and oyster sauce

1 cup water

1 tablespoon rice vinegar

- 1 tablespoon tamari sauce
- ¼ teaspoon ground ginger
- 2 cups dried shiitake mushrooms

. Heat the vegetable oil in a wok or large pan over medium to high heat. Stir in the green onions, garlic and garlic cloves; cook and stir until the vegetables are soft, about 30 seconds.

. Stir in the toru, black beans, mushroom oyster sauce and half of the water. Cover and bring to the boil. Cook for 3 minutes.

. Boil for 3 minutes and stir in the remaining water, rice vinegar, tamaris sauce and ginger. Add the mushrooms (the mushrooms will reconstitute in the sauce during cooking) and top with the spinach.

. Turn the heat down to low. Simmer for about 10 minutes, until the spinach has wilted and the mushrooms are soft.

Fish Sauce with Garlicky Stir-Fry

Prep time: 10 minutes | Cook time: 5¼ minutes | Serves 4 to 6

4 cups halved brussels sprouts

Kosher salt

¼ cup vegetable oil

2 tablespoons garlic, thinly sliced

¼ cup oyster sauce

4 teaspoons Thai fish sauce (nam pla)

- 2 teaspoons soy sauce, preferably thin Thai soy sauce
- 2 teaspoons sugar
- ½ teaspoon sliced red Thai chili pods
- Pinch of ground white pepper
- ½ cup low-salt chicken stock

. Blanch the Brussels sprouts in a large saucepan with salted boiling water until they turn light green, about 15 seconds. Heat the oil in a wok or large pan over medium heat.

. Add garlic and stir until light golden brown, about 30 seconds. Transfer to a small bowl with a slotted spoon. Increase heat to high level. Add Brussels sprouts.

3. Fry, stirring until they start to soften, 2 to 3 minutes. Add the oyster sauce and the next 5 ingredients. Fry for 30 seconds while stirring; Add chicken broth.

4. Bring to a boil; cook until the liquid is slightly reduced, about 2 minutes and add more chilies if desired. Stir in garlic.

Couscous with Vegetable Stir-Fry

Prep time: 15 minutes | Cook time: 6 minutes | Serves 4

- 2 cups diced peeled eggplant
- 1½ teaspoons salt
- 1½ cups water
- 1 cup couscous
- 2½ tablespoons rapeseed oil
- 2½ tablespoons red wine vinegar
- 1 cup diced peeled carrots
- 1 cup diced zucchini
- 1 cup diced yellow

tortoiseshell squash

- 1 cup small broccoli florets
- 1 cup diced red pepper
- ½ cup diced red onion
- 2 garlic cloves, chopped
- 4 tablespoons fresh basil, chopped
- 2 tablespoons fresh mint, chopped
- 2 tablespoons toasted pine nuts

1. Put eggplant and 1 teaspoon salt in a medium bowl; Let stand for 30 minutes. Rinse and drain eggplant. Pat dry. Bring 1½ cups water and ½ teaspoon of salt to a boil in a large saucepan; Stir in the couscous.

2. Take off the stove. Cover and let stand for 10 minutes. Discover; Shake up with a fork. Whisk 1½ tablespoons oil and vinegar in a small bowl.

3. Heat 1 tablespoon oil in a wok or in a large non-stick pan over medium to high heat. Add eggplants and carrots; Fry for 3 minutes while stirring.

4. Add zucchini and the next 5 ingredients; Fry while stirring until the vegetables are crispy and tender, about 2 minutes. Add the couscous and vinegar mixture; Fry for 1 minute while stirring.

5. Stir in basil and mint.

6. Season with salt and pepper.

Mustardy Indian Delicacy

Prep time: 10 minutes | Cook time: 46 minutes | Serve 4

- 2 tablespoons rapeseed oil
- 1 teaspoon cumin seeds
- 1 teaspoon mustard seeds
- 1 tablespoon ground coriander
- ½ teaspoon ground turmeric
- ½ teaspoon red chili
- powder
- ½ sliced head cabbage
- 2 potatoes, chopped
- 1 tablespoon ginger and garlic paste
- 1 teaspoon salt
- ½ cup water, or as needed
- ¼ cup chopped fresh coriander, or to taste

1. Heat the rapeseed oil in a wok over medium heat. Cook the cumin and mustard seeds in the hot oil and stir until they begin to dance, 1 to 2 minutes.

2. Add coriander, turmeric and cayenne pepper; cook for about 1 minute; Stir cabbage, potatoes, ginger-garlic paste and salt into the spice mixture; stir.

3. Pour enough water into the wok to steam vegetables; Cook covered, stirring occasionally, adding more water as needed, until potatoes and cabbage are very tender, about 45 minutes. Take from the fire; Sprinkle the vegetables with coriander.

Brothy Vegetarian Congee Xifan

Prep time: 15 minutes | Cook time: 25 minutes | Serves 4

- 2 tablespoons vegetable oil
- 2 garlic cloves, crushed and finely chopped
- 1 tablespoon freshly grated ginger
- 6 dried Chinese mushrooms, soaked in hot water for 20 minutes, stems
- discarded, finely chopped
- 1 small carrot, diced
- 1 cup brown basmati rice
- 1 cup equal parts green split peas, whole green lentils, whole grains, barley flakes and pearl barley

- 12 cups boiling water
- 1 red pepper, finely diced
- 4 cups vegetable broth
- Handful of canned and chopped bamboo shoots
- 2 tablespoons light soy
- sauce
- 1 tablespoon toasted sesame oil
- Freshly ground black pepper
- Small handfuls of chopped coriander leaves and stalks

1. Fry the garlic and ginger and the Chinese mushrooms for less than 1 minute while stirring. Add the carrot, brown rice, and whole grain mixture.

2. Fry for less than 1 minute while stirring and add 4 cups boiling water. Cook for 25 to 30 minutes, stirring, and adding another 8 cups water to make sure the rice and grains are well cooked.

3. Add the red pepper, stir well then pour in the vegetable stock. Finally, add the bamboo shoots and season with the light soy sauce, sesame oil and ground black pepper.

4. Sprinkle with the chopped coriander and serve immediately.

Garlic with Mixed Vegetable Stir-Fry

Prep time: 10 minutes | Cook time: 1 minutes | Serves 4 to 6

- 1 tablespoon peanut oil
- 1 zucchini, cut into bite-size pieces
- 1 carrot, thinly sliced
- ½ pound (227 g) fresh snow peas, trimmed and strings removed
- 2 garlic cloves, minced
- 4 to 6 large mushrooms, quartered
- 3 tablespoons all-purpose stir-fry Sauce
- ½ teaspoon toasted sesame seeds

1. In a wok over medium-high heat, heat the peanut oil.

2. Add the zucchini and carrot, and stir-fry for about 1 minute.

3. When the zucchini and carrot are almost soft, add the snow peas.

4. When the snow peas turn bright green, add the garlic and mushrooms. Stir-fry until the

mushrooms start to soften a little.

Drizzle in the stir-fry sauce, give it a quick stir to combine, and remove from the heat. Place in a serving dish and serve.

Simple Steamed Quinoa

Prep time: 5 minutes | Cook time: 20 minutes | Serves 4 to 6

- 2 cups quinoa
- 2½ cups water

Put the quinoa in a fine mesh strainer and rinse well under running tap water.

Pour the rinsed quinoa into a medium pot, and add the water.

Over medium-high heat, bring the water to a boil, uncovered.

When the water starts to boil, reduce the heat to low, cover the pot, and cook for 15 minutes.

Turn off the heat and uncover the pot. Fluff the quinoa with a fork then let it sit for about 5 minutes before serving.

Eggy Onion Stir-Fry

Prep time: 5 minutes | Cook time: 3½ minutes | Serves 3

- 2 tablespoons avocado oil, or as needed
- 6 eggs, beaten, 4 ripe tomatoes, cut into
- wedges
- 2 thinly sliced green onions

Heat 1 tablespoon avocado oil in a wok or pan over medium heat. Boil eggs in the hot oil and stir until mostly cooked through, about 1 minute.

Transfer the eggs to a plate. Add 1 tablespoon avocado oil to the wok and cook the tomatoes and stir until most of the liquid has evaporated, about 2 minutes.

Return the eggs to the wok and add the green onions; cook and stir until eggs are fully cooked, about 30 more seconds.

Brothy Ginger with Glazed Carrots

Prep time: 10 minutes | Cook time: 8 minutes | Serves 4

- 2 tablespoons olive oil
- 1 tablespoon minced garlic
- 2 teaspoons minced ginger
- 4 small carrots, peeled and thinly sliced on
- the diagonal into ½ slice
- ¼ teaspoon cayenne pepper
- ½ cup chicken broth
- 2 tablespoons brown sugar

1. Heat a wok or skillet over medium-high heat until it is nearly smoking. Add the oil. When the oil is hot, add the garlic and ginger and stir-fry for 10 seconds.

2. Add the carrots. Stir-fry for 1 to 2 minutes. Stir in the cayenne pepper. Add the chicken broth and the brown sugar. Bring to a boil. Cover and cook for 4 minutes.

3. Uncover and cook, stirring, until the carrots are tender but still crisp and nicely glazed with the broth and sugar mixture, which has been reduced (total cooking time is about 8 minutes). Serve hot.

Vinegary Vegetable Medley

Prep time: 10 minutes | Cook time: 7 minutes | Serves 2

- ¼ cup chicken broth
- 1½ tablespoons red wine vinegar
- 2 teaspoons granulated sugar
- ½ cup cauliflower florets
- 2 tablespoons vegetable or peanut oil
- ½ teaspoon minced garlic
- ½ teaspoon minced ginger
- 1 cup shredded red cabbage
- 1 teaspoon salt
- 1 small carrot, julienned

1. In a small bowl, combine the chicken broth, red wine vinegar, and sugar. Set aside.

2. Fill a large saucepan with enough water to cover the cauliflower and bring to a boil. Blanch the cauliflower in the boiling water for 2 minutes. Remove the cauliflower, rinse under cold running water, and drain thoroughly.

3. Heat a wok or skillet over medium-high heat until it is nearly smoking. Add the oil. When the oil is hot, add the garlic and ginger. Stir-fry for 10 seconds.

4. Add the shredded cabbage. Stir-fry for 2 minutes, sprinkling with the salt to taste. Add the carrot and stir-fry for 1 minute. Add the cauliflower and stir-fry for 1 minute.

5. Add the chicken broth mixture. Bring to a boil and continue cooking for 1 to 2 minutes or until the vegetables are tender but still crisp.

Spicey Gingered Vegetables

Prep time: 10 minutes | Cook time: 4 minutes | Serves 2

- 1½ tablespoons vegetable or peanut oil
- 1 teaspoon minced ginger
- 1 large red bell pepper
- 4 Napa cabbage leaves
- ½ teaspoon salt
- 1 cup canned straw mushrooms
- 2 tablespoons chicken broth or water

1. Cut the bell pepper in half, remove the seeds, and cut into thin strips. Cut the cabbage leaves crosswise into thin strips. Cut the straw mushrooms in half.

2. Heat a wok or skillet on medium-high heat until it is nearly smoking. Add the oil. When the oil is hot, add the ginger. Stir-fry for 10 seconds, until aromatic.

3. Add the pepper and cabbage. Sprinkle with salt to taste. Stir-fry for 1 minute, then add the mushrooms. Stir in the chicken broth or water. Stir-fry for 1 more minute, then remove from the pan. Serve hot.

Buttered Basil with Mushrooms

Prep time: 10 minutes | Cook time: 10 minutes | Serves 2

- ¼ cup burgundy wine
- ½ cup beef broth
- 1½ tablespoons vegetable or peanut oil
- 1 teaspoon minced ginger
- 1 teaspoon minced garlic
- 2 shallots, chopped
- ½ teaspoon dried parsley
- ½ teaspoon dried basil
- 1 pound (454 g) button mushrooms
- ¼ teaspoon black pepper

- 2 tablespoons unsalted butter

1. In a small bowl, combine the burgundy and beef broth. Set aside.

2. Heat a wok or skillet over medium-high heat until it is nearly smoking. Add the oil. When the oil is hot, add the minced ginger and garlic and stir-fry for 10 seconds.

3. Add the chopped shallots. Sprinkle the dried parsley and basil over the shallots and stir-fry for 1 minute, until the shallots begin to soften.

4. Add the mushrooms. Stir-fry for about 2 minutes until they have browned. Stir in the black pepper. Add the burgundy mixture and lower the heat.

5. Simmer the mushrooms for 6 to 8 minutes. Remove from heat and stir in the butter. Serve immediately.

Ginger with Brothy Bamboo Shoots

Prep time: 10 minutes | Cook time: 5 minutes | Serves 4

- 1 (8 ounces / 227 g) can bamboo shoots, rinsed and drained
- 1½ tablespoons dark soy sauce
- 1½ tablespoons chicken broth
- 1 teaspoon granulated
- sugar
- 1½ tablespoons vegetable or peanut oil
- 2 slices ginger
- ½ teaspoon sesame o

1. Slice the bamboo shoots and pat dry with paper towels.

2. In a small bowl, combine the dark soy sauce, chicken broth, and sugar. Set aside.

3. Heat a wok or skillet on medium-high heat. Add the oil, swirling it around the wok or skillet so tha it covers the sides. When the oil is hot, add the ginger and stir-fry for 15 seconds.

4. Add the bamboo shoots. Stir-fry for 1 minute, then add the sauce. Stir for a few more seconds to mix the vegetables with the sauce; turn down the heat. Cover and simmer for 3 minutes or until the vegetables are tender.

5. Remove the wok or skillet from the heat. Stir in t sesame oil. Remove the ginger slices or leave in a

desired. Serve immediately.

Spicy Sage with Brussels Sprouts

Prep time: 15 minutes | Cook time: 4 minutes | Serves 4

- 2 tablespoons olive oil
- 1 tablespoon unsalted butter
- ½ teaspoon red pepper flakes
- 4 fresh sage leaves
- 1 tablespoon minced shallots
- 1 tablespoon minced garlic
- 1 pound (454 g) blanched Brussels sprouts, trimmed and quartered
- ¼ teaspoon kosher salt
- ¼ teaspoon black pepper
- ½ tablespoon lemon zest
- ¼ cup freshly grated Parmesan cheese

1. Heat oil in a wok over medium heat. Add the butter and swirl the wok around until it melts. Add in the red pepper flakes, sage, shallots, and garlic. Stir the ingredients around for 30 seconds.

2. Add in the Brussels sprouts and continue stir-frying for 3 to 4 minutes until the sprouts are browned and edges have begun to caramelize. Season with salt and pepper to taste.

3. Pour the contents of the wok on a platter. Sprinkle with lemon zest and Parmesan cheese over the top. Serve hot.

Shallot with Indian-Spiced Okra

Prep time: 10 minutes | Cook time: 6 minutes | Serves 4

- 2 tablespoons peanut or vegetable oil
- 3 cloves garlic, minced
- ¼ teaspoon cumin
- 1 teaspoon red pepper flakes
- 1 shallot, chopped
- 1 pound (454 g) okra, cut on the diagonal into slices ¼-½ thick
- 1 large tomato, cut into 6 wedges, each wedge halved
- 1 teaspoon curry powder
- 1 teaspoon brown sugar

1. Heat a wok or skillet over medium-high heat until it is nearly smoking. Add the oil. When the oil is hot, add the garlic, cumin, red pepper flakes, and the shallot. Stir-fry for 30 seconds or until the shallot begins to soften.

2. Add the okra. Stir-fry for about 4 minutes or until is the okra just starts to turn golden brown.

3. Add the tomato, curry powder, and the brown sugar, and stir-fry for 1 minute. Serve hot or cold.

Vinegar with Stir-Fried Cauliflower

Prep time: 10 minutes | Cook time: 6 minutes | Serves 4

- 1 pound (454 g) cauliflower
- 1½ tablespoons white wine vinegar
- 2½ tablespoons water
- 1½ teaspoons granulated sugar
- 2 tablespoons olive oil
- 2 teaspoons minced ginger

1. Remove the outer leaves and the stalk from the cauliflower. Cut off the florets, leaving part of the stem attached. Soak the florets in cold water for 15 minutes. Drain thoroughly.

2. Fill a large saucepan with enough water to cover the cauliflower, and bring to a boil. Blanch the cauliflower in the boiling water for 2 minutes. Remove the cauliflower, rinse under cold running water, and drain thoroughly.

3. In a small bowl, combine the white wine vinegar, water, and sugar in a bowl. Set aside.

4. Heat a wok or skillet over medium-high heat until it is nearly smoking. Add the oil. When the oil is hot, add the ginger. Stir-fry for 10 seconds.

5. Add the cauliflower florets. Stir-fry for 1 minute, then pour the white wine and vinegar mixture over the top. Stir-fry for another 2 minutes or until the cauliflower is tender but still crisp, stirring vigorously to keep the cauliflower from browning. Serve immediately.

Lettuce with Goji Berries

Prep time: 10 minutes | Cook time: 5 minutes | Serves 4 to 6

- 2 heads baby romaine lettuce

- 1 tablespoon olive oil
- 2 garlic cloves, minced
- ¼ cup dried goji berries
- 1 teaspoon chicken
- stock granules
- Pinch salt to taste
- 2 teaspoons Shaoxing wine

1. Separate the romaine leaves, rinse them, and drain well.
2. In a wok over high heat, heat the olive oil.
3. Add the garlic, followed by the lettuce leaves, goji berries, chicken stock granules, salt, and Shaoxing wine, stirring occasionally.
4. Give all the ingredients a quick stir. Transfer to a serving plate and serve immediately.

Eggy Tomato Stir-fry

Prep time: 10 minutes | Cook time: 5 minutes | Serves 4 to 6

- 4 eggs
- Pinch salt to taste
- Pinch pepper to taste
- 1 teaspoon Shaoxing wine
- 2 tablespoons peanut
- oil
- 2 medium tomatoes, cut into wedges
- ½ teaspoon sugar
- 1 scallion, cut into 1-inch pieces

1. In a medium bowl, add the eggs and the Shaoxing wine. Season them with the salt and pepper to taste and beat together until well combined.
2. In a wok over medium-high heat, heat the peanut oil.
3. Pour the egg mixture into the wok and allow the bottom to cook before gently scrambling.
4. Just before the egg starts to cook all the way through, remove it from the wok.
5. Toss the tomato wedges into the wok and stir-fry until they become a little soft.
6. Return the scrambled eggs to the wok with the tomato, then sprinkle the sugar over the stir-fry.
7. Turn off the heat, add the scallion, and give one last stir before transferring to a serving plate.

Garlic Spiced Indian Vegetables

Prep time: 15 minutes | Cook time: 6 minutes |

Serves 4

- 2 tablespoons cooking oil
- 2 garlic cloves, crushed and chopped
- 1 medium carrot, roll-cut into ½-inch pieces
- 1 medium onion, cut into 1-inch pieces
- 2 cups sugar snap pea pods
- 1 medium poblano pepper, cut into 1-inch pieces
- 1 red bell pepper, cut into 1-inch pieces
- 4 scallions, cut into 1-inch slices
- ¼ teaspoon ground cumin
- ¼ teaspoon ground coriander
- ¼ teaspoon ground cloves
- ¼ teaspoon ground turmeric
- ¼ teaspoon ground fennel
- 1 teaspoon hot sesame oil

1. In a wok over high heat, heat the cooking oil until it shimmers.
2. Add the garlic and carrot and stir-fry for 1 minute.
3. Add the onion and stir-fry for 1 minute.
4. Add the pea pods and stir-fry for 1 minute.
5. Add the poblano and bell peppers and stir-fry for 1 minute.
6. Add the scallions and stir-fry for 30 seconds.
7. Add the cumin, coriander, cloves, turmeric, fennel, and sesame oil and stir-fry for 30 seconds.
8. Serve over steamed basmati rice.

Eggy Vietnamese Melon

Prep time: 10 minutes | Cook time: 5 minutes | Serves 4

- 2 tablespoons cooking oil
- 1 bitter melon, halved and seeded, pulp removed, cut into ¼-inch pieces
- 2 garlic cloves, crushed and chopped
- 1 tablespoon crushed
- and chopped peeled ginger
- 1 teaspoon spicy sesame oil
- 1 teaspoon fish sauce
- 4 large eggs, beaten
- Cooked rice, for serving

1. In a wok, heat the cooking oil over high heat until it begins to smoke.

[33]

Add the bitter melon, garlic, and ginger. Stir-fry for 1 minute, or until the garlic and ginger are fragrant.

Add the sesame oil and fish sauce. Stir for about 30 seconds, or until the melon is coated.

Add the eggs and stir-fry until the eggs have set. Serve over rice.

TIP: Winter melon, which has a milder flavor, can be used in place of bitter melon.

Garlicky Buddha's Delight

Prep time: 15 minutes | Cook time: 5 minutes | Serves 4

- ¼ cup cooking oil
- 4 garlic cloves, crushed and chopped
- 1 tablespoon crushed and chopped peeled ginger
- 4 ounces (113 g) extra-firm tofu, drained and diced into ½-inch pieces
- 1 small carrot, julienned (½ cup)
- 8 sugar snap pea pods
- 1 small onion, cut into ½-inch dice
- 1 (4-ounce / 113-g)) can baby corn, drained and rinsed
- 1 cup chopped (½-inch) napa cabbage
- 1 (8-ounce / 227-g) can straw mushrooms, drained and rinsed
- 1 (8-ounce / 227-g) can bamboo shoots, drained and rinsed
- 1 (8-ounce / 227-g) can sliced water chestnuts, drained and rinsed
- 2 tablespoons cornstarch
- 2 tablespoons Shaoxing rice wine
- 2 tablespoons soy sauce
- 1 tablespoon toasted sesame oil
- 2 scallions, green and white parts, cut diagonally into ¼-inch pieces
- Cooked rice or noodles, for serving

In a wok, heat the cooking oil over high heat until it begins to smoke.

Add the garlic, ginger, tofu, and carrot. Stir-fry for 2 minutes, or until the tofu begins to brown.

Add the pea pods and onion. Stir-fry for 1 minute, or until they are lightly coated with oil.

Add the corn, cabbage, mushrooms, bamboo shoots, and water chestnuts. Stir-fry for 1 minute, or until the ingredients are well combined.

5. Add the cornstarch, wine, soy sauce, and sesame oil. Stir for about 1 minute, or until the liquid is well distributed.

6. Add the scallions and toss. Serve over rice or noodles.

Oyster Sauce with Chinese Broccoli

Prep time: 10 minutes | Cook time: 5 minutes | Serves 6 to 8

- 2 tablespoons peanut oil
- 4 garlic cloves, peeled and halved
- ½ (2-inch) piece ginger, peeled and julienned
- 1 pound (454 g)
- Chinese broccoli (kai lan), rinsed and cut into bite-size pieces
- 2 tablespoons oyster sauce
- 1 teaspoon sugar
- Pinch ground white pepper

1. In a wok over medium heat, heat the peanut oil.

2. Add the garlic. As soon as it starts to turn golden brown, add the ginger and give it all a quick stir.

3. Increase the heat to high and immediately add the kai lan, oyster sauce, sugar, and pepper.

4. Stir the kai lan well. Add a tablespoon or two of water to help steam it, if desired.

5. When the kai lan turns bright green and softens a little, remove it from the heat and serve immediately.

Spicy Seitan with Mushrooms

Prep time: 15 minutes | Cook time: 16 minutes | Serves 6

- ⅓ cup dried wood ear mushrooms, soaked
- ½ cup dried lily flowers, soaked
- 4 large dried shiitake mushrooms, soaked
- 1 ½ cups seitan, cut into bite-sized pieces
- ½ cup mushroom
- soaking liquid
- 1 tablespoon vegetable oil
- ½ teaspoon sesame oil
- 1 tablespoon Shaoxing wine
- 1 tablespoon oyster sauce
- ½ teaspoon sugar

- ¾ teaspoon salt
- ¼ teaspoon white pepper
- 1 teaspoon ginger, grated
- 1 scallion, chopped
- 1 ½ tablespoons cornstarch

1. Drain the mushrooms, lily flowers, and wood ears, and transfer to a wok.
2. Add ginger, oil, soaking liquid, oyster sauce, sugar, salt, white pepper, and white part of scallions.
3. Cook until the liquid is absorbed then add green parts of scallions.
4. Stir and cook for 30 seconds then add cornstarch, seitan, and rest of the ingredients.
5. Mix well, cover, and cook for 15 minutes on medium-low heat.
6. Serve warm.

Gingered Teriyaki Tofu

Prep time: 15 minutes | Cook time: 8 minutes | Serves 4

- ¼ cup plus 2 tablespoons tamari, divided
- 2 tablespoons mirin wine
- 2 tablespoons rice vinegar
- 2 tablespoons toasted sesame oil
- 2 tablespoons brown sugar
- 1 tablespoon white miso
- 1 tablespoon cornstarch
- 2 tablespoons cooking oil
- 1 pound extra-firm tofu, drained and cut into 1-inch cubes
- 2 garlic cloves, crushed and chopped
- 1 tablespoon crushed, chopped ginger
- 1 medium onion, cut into 1-inch pieces
- 4 red bell pepper, cut into 1-inch pieces
- 4 ounces shiitake mushrooms, cut into slices
- 2 tablespoons toasted sesame seeds

1. In a small bowl, whisk together ¼ cup of the tamari, the mirin, rice vinegar, sesame oil, brown sugar, miso, and cornstarch. Set aside.
2. In a wok over high heat, heat the cooking oil until it shimmers.
3. Add the tofu, garlic, ginger, and remaining 2 tablespoons of tamari and stir-fry for 2 minutes, or

until the tofu starts to brown.
4. Add the onion and stir-fry for 1 minute.
5. Add the bell pepper and stir-fry for 1 minute.
6. Add the mushrooms and stir-fry for 1 minute.
7. Add the tamari mixture to the wok and stir-fry until a light glaze forms.
8. Sprinkle with the sesame seeds and serve over Japanese medium-grain white rice.

Gingered Scallions with Carrots

Prep time: 10 minutes | Cook time: 4 minutes | Serves 4

- 2 tablespoons cooking oil
- 2 garlic cloves, crushed and chopped
- 1 tablespoon crushed and chopped peeled ginger
- 1 cup julienned carrots
- 1 (15-ounce / 425-g) can straw mushrooms, drained and rinsed
- 2 cups sliced (½-inch napa cabbage
- ¼ cup hoisin sauce
- 1 teaspoon spicy sesame oil
- 4 scallions, green and white parts, cut diagonally into ¼-inc pieces
- Cooked rice or noodles, for serving

1. In a wok, heat the cooking oil over high heat unti it begins to smoke.
2. Add the garlic, ginger, and carrots. Stir-fry for 1 minute, or until the garlic and ginger are fragran
3. Add the mushrooms and stir-fry for 1 minute, or until they are lightly coated with oil.
4. Add the cabbage and stir-fry for 1 minute, or unti it is lightly coated with oil.
5. Add the hoisin sauce and sesame oil. Stir-fry for 30 seconds, or until all of the ingredients are coated with the sauce.
6. Add the scallions and toss. Serve over rice or noodles.

Sauce with Fried String Beans

Prep time: 10 minutes | Cook time: 5 minutes |

Vegetab

Serves 4 to 6

For the Sauce:

1 tablespoon Shaoxing wine

1 teaspoon chili bean sauce

1 teaspoon sesame oil

1 teaspoon sugar

½ teaspoon salt

For the String Beans:

- 1 tablespoon peanut oil

- 1 pound (454 g) fresh string beans, trimmed

- 8 dried red chile peppers

- ½-inch piece ginger, peeled and julienned

- 3 garlic cloves, minced

. In a small bowl, prepare the sauce by mixing together the Shaoxing wine, chili bean sauce, sesame oil, sugar, and salt to taste. Set it aside.

. In a wok over medium-high heat, heat the peanut oil.

. As soon as the wok starts to smoke, toss in the green beans. Stir-fry until they are blistered and bright green, for about 5 minutes. If they start to burn, reduce the heat to medium.

. Add the dried red chiles, ginger, and garlic to the wok. Fry until aromatic, then add the sauce. Stir to combine all the ingredients.

. Remove from the heat, and transfer to a serving plate.

Sauce with Vegan Tso's Dish

Prep time: 15 minutes | Cook time: 15 minutes | Serves 8

For the Sauce:

1/3 cup Asian vegetable stock

1 teaspoon dark soy sauce

1 tablespoon soy sauce

2 teaspoons rice vinegar

1 teaspoon Shaoxing wine

3 ½ tablespoons brown sugar

¼ teaspoon white pepper

For the Dish:

- 1 pound cauliflower floret

- 2 cups broccoli florets

- 1 tablespoon vegetable oil

- 4 to 5 dried red chili peppers

- 3 garlic cloves, minced

- 1 tablespoon cornstarch, whisked with 2 tablespoons water

1. Mix all the sauce ingredients in a bowl and set it aside.

2. Saute cauliflower, broccoli, and garlic with oil in a Cantonese wok for 5 minutes.

3. Pour in sauce and add cornstarch then mix well.

4. Cover and cook for 10 minutes on medium-low heat.

5. Serve warm.

Vinegar with Shredded Potatoes

Prep time: 10 minutes | Cook time: 15 minutes | Serves 4

- 2 medium low-starch potatoes (such as red-skinned potatoes), scrubbed

- 3 tablespoons peanut or vegetable oil

- 2 or 3 garlic cloves, crushed

- 2 whole dried chiles (optional)

- 2 scallions, thinly sliced

- 1 tablespoon black vinegar

- 1 tablespoon soy sauce

1. Cut the potatoes into matchsticks, taking care to make them uniform in size. Soak the potato shreds in cold water for 10 minutes to remove some of their starch. Then drain, rinse, and thoroughly pat them dry.

2. In a hot wok over high heat, heat the peanut oil until it starts to smoke. Add the garlic and chiles (if using), and stir-fry for 15 seconds. Before they begin to burn, add the scallions and stir-fry for about 30 seconds.

3. Add the potatoes to the wok, and stir-fry for 2 to 3 minutes. Then add the black vinegar and toss to combine. Add the soy sauce and stir-fry for another 2 to 3 minutes, or until the potatoes are cooked through.

Chili Eggplant with Broth

Prep time: 10 minutes | Cook time: 10 minutes | Serves 4

- ¼ cup chicken broth

- 1 tablespoon soy sauce

- 1 tablespoon Chinese black vinegar or good

- balsamic vinegar

- 1 tablespoon brown sugar

- 1 tablespoon chili oil

- ¼ teaspoon red pepper flakes
- 2 tablespoons peanut or vegetable oil
- 2 to 3 Asian eggplants, cut into thin, 1-inch-long strips
- 2 scallions, minced
- 1 tablespoon fresh minced ginger
- 2 garlic cloves, minced

1. In a small bowl, mix together the chicken broth, soy sauce, vinegar, brown sugar, chili oil, and red pepper flakes. Set aside.
2. Place a wok over high heat until a drop of water sizzles on contact. Add the peanut oil and swirl to coat the wok.
3. Add the eggplants to the wok, and stir-fry for 2 to 3 minutes, until the outsides become golden brown. Turn down the heat to medium-high, and add the scallions, ginger, and garlic. Stir-fry for about 30 seconds, and then add in the chicken broth mixture; toss the vegetables until they are coated with the sauce. Simmer the vegetables for 2 to 3 minutes, allowing the eggplant to absorb the sauce.

Garlicky Bok Choy with Ginger

Prep time: 10 minutes | Cook time: 5 minutes | Serves 4

- 1½ pounds baby bok choy
- 1½ tablespoons peanut or vegetable oil
- 1 or 2 garlic cloves, minced
- ¼ teaspoon ground ginger
- 3 tablespoons vegetable broth
- Sea salt to taste
- ½ teaspoon toasted sesame oil

1. Trim the root ends of the baby bok choy. Wash and thoroughly drain the leaves.
2. Heat your wok to medium-high; add the peanut oil and swirl to coat the wok. Add the garlic and ginger, and cook them for 30 seconds to 1 minute. Do not let them burn. When the spices become fragrant, add the bok choy leaves. Stir-fry everything together until well combined.
3. Add the vegetable broth to the wok. Cover the wok and cook for about 1 minute. Remove the cover from the wok, and turn off the heat. Season the bok choy with the sea salt to taste, drizzle

it with the sesame oil, and toss to coat. Serve immediately.

Garlicky Stir-Fry with Spinach

Prep time: 10 minutes | Cook time: 5 minutes | Serves 4

- 1 tablespoon light soy sauce
- 1 teaspoon sugar
- 2 tablespoons vegetable oil
- 4 garlic cloves, thinly sliced
- Kosher salt to taste
- 8 ounces / 227 g prewashed baby spinach

1. In a small bowl, stir together the light soy and sugar until the sugar is dissolved and set aside.
2. Heat a wok over medium-high heat until a drop of water sizzles and evaporates on contact. Pour in the oil and swirl to coat the base of the wok. Add the garlic and a pinch of salt to taste and stir-fry, tossing until the garlic is fragrant, about 10 seconds. Using a slotted spoon, remove the garlic from the pan and set aside.
3. Add the spinach to the seasoned oil and stir-fry until the greens are just wilted and bright green. Add the sugar and soy mixture and toss to coat. Return the garlic to the wok and toss to incorporate. Transfer to a dish and serve.

Spicy Zucchini Stir-Fry

Prep time: 5 minutes | Cook time: 5 minutes | Serves 2

- 1 tablespoon vegetable oil
- 1 large zucchini, cut on the diagonal into 1" slices
- ¼ teaspoon salt
- ¼ teaspoon black pepper
- 1 tablespoon soy sauc

1. Heat a wok or skillet over medium-high heat unti it is nearly smoking. Add the oil.
2. When the oil is hot, add the zucchini. Sprinkle the salt and pepper to taste over the zucchini. Stir-fry for 1 minute, then stir in the soy sauce.
3. Stir-fry the zucchini until it turns dark green and

is tender but still crisp (about 3 minutes). Serve hot.

Garlicky Sausage and Sauce Stir-Fry

Prep time: 5 minutes | Cook time: 5 minutes | Serves 4

1 tablespoon vegetable oil	cabbage
2 cloves of garlic, chopped	• 1 tablespoon soy sauce
450 g chopped	• 1 tablespoon Chinese cooking wine (Shaoxing wine)

Heat the vegetable oil in a wok or large pan over medium heat. Stir in the garlic and cook for a few seconds until it begins to brown.

Stir in the cabbage until it is covered in oil; cover the wok and cook for 1 minute.

Add the soy sauce and cook for another minute and stir. Turn the heat on high and stir in the Chinese cooking wine.

Cook and stir until the cabbage is tender, about 2 more minutes.

Spicy Sauce with Ma Po Tofu

Prep time: 15 minutes | Cook time: 15 minutes | Serves 4

For the Sauce:

1 teaspoon black bean paste	• ½ teaspoon sugar
1 teaspoon spicy bean paste	• For the Stir-fry:
1 teaspoon soy sauce	• 1 tablespoon peanut oil
1 teaspoon oyster sauce	• 2 garlic cloves, minced
Pinch ground black pepper	• ½ pound (227g) ground pork
2 teaspoons cornstarch	• 1 package firm tofu, cut into 1-to 1½-inch cubes
¼ cup water	• 1 scallion, chopped

In a small bowl, prepare the sauce by mixing together the black bean paste, spicy bean paste, soy sauce, oyster sauce, black pepper, cornstarch,

water, and sugar. Set it aside.

2. In a wok over medium-high heat, heat the peanut oil.

3. Stir-fry the garlic and ground pork until the pork is fully cooked.

4. Add the sauce and stir well.

5. When the sauce starts to thicken, add the tofu. Give it a gentle quick stir, taking care not to break the tofu.

6. Remove from the heat and transfer to a serving plate.

7. Garnish with the chopped scallion.

Garlicky Sesame with Asparagus

Prep time: 10 minutes | Cook time: 8 minutes | Serves 4

• 2 tablespoons light soy sauce	trimmed and cut diagonally into 2-inch-long pieces
• 1 teaspoon sugar	
• 1 tablespoon vegetable oil	• Kosher salt to taste
	• 2 tablespoons sesame oil
• 2 large garlic cloves, coarsely chopped	• 1 tablespoon toasted sesame seeds
• 2 pounds asparagus,	

1. In a small bowl, stir the light soy and sugar together until the sugar dissolves. Set aside.

2. Heat a wok over medium-high heat until a drop of water sizzles and evaporates on contact. Pour in the vegetable oil and swirl to coat the base of the wok. Add the garlic and stir-fry until fragrant, about 10 seconds.

3. Add the asparagus and stir-fry until crisp-tender, about 4 minutes, seasoning with a small pinch of salt to taste while stir-frying. Add the soy sauce mixture and toss to coat the asparagus, cooking for about 1 minute more.

4. Drizzle the sesame oil over the asparagus and transfer to a serving bowl. Garnish with the sesame seeds and serve hot.

Gingered Snow Peas Stir-Fry

Prep time: 5 minutes | Cook time: 5 minutes | Serves 4

- 2 tablespoons vegetable oil
- 2 peeled fresh ginger slices, each about the size of a quarter
- Kosher salt to taste
- ¾ pound (340g) snow peas or sugar snap peas, strings removed

1. Heat a wok over medium-high heat until a drop of water sizzles and evaporates on contact. Pour in the oil and swirl to coat the base of the wok. Season the oil by adding the ginger slices and a pinch of salt to taste. Allow the ginger to sizzle in the oil for about 30 seconds, swirling gently.

2. Add the snow peas and, using a wok spatula, toss to coat with oil. Stir-fry for 2 to 3 minutes, until bright green and crisp tender.

3. Transfer to a platter and discard the ginger. Serve hot.

Limey Thai Tofu with Basil

Prep time: 10 minutes | Cook time: 15 minutes | Serves 6

- ⅓ cup olive oil
- 2 large red peppers, pitted, thinly sliced 3 tablespoons of chopped, peeled fresh ginger
- 3 large cloves of garlic, (finely chopped)
- 1 (400 to 450 g) package of extra firm tofu, drained well, cut into cubes
- 3 green onions, thinly sliced on a diagonal
- 3 tablespoons of soy sauce
- 2 tablespoons of fresh lime juice
- ½ to ¾ teaspoon dried, crushed red pepper
- 1 (170 g) sachet of baby spinach leaves
- ⅓ cup chopped fresh basil
- ⅓ cup lightly salted, roasted peanuts

1. Heating oil in a wok over high heat. Add peppers, ginger and garlic; Fry until the peppers just soften, about 2 minutes. Add tofu and spring onions; Swirl for 2 minutes.

2. Add the next 3 ingredients. Fold in to puree,

about 1 minute. Add the spinach in 3 servings and toss until it begins to wither, about 1 minute per serving.

3. Mix in the basil. Season with salt and pepper to taste. Sprinkle with peanuts per serving.

Spicy Chives Stir-Fry

Prep time: 5 minutes | Cook time: 10 minutes | Serves 4

- 1 tablespoon of peanut oil
- 300 g green garlic chives (also called Chinese chives; flat parts only), cut into pieces (4 cups)
- 1 teaspoon dried hot red pepper flakes
- ¼ teaspoon salt, or to taste
- To serve: steamed white rice

1. Heat wok over high heat until a drop of water evaporates immediately on contact. Add oil to coat the wok evenly and heat until hot and only smoking.

2. Add chives and red pepper flakes and sauté while stirring, allowing the chives to rest on the bottom and sides of the wok for a few seconds between stirring operations, until soft and lightly browned 2 to 4 minutes.

3. Stir in salt. Serve over rice.

Gingered Tempeh with Miso Vegetables

Prep time: 15 minutes | Cook time: 5 minutes | Serves 4

- 8 ounces / 227 g tempeh, diced into ½-inch pieces
- 1 tablespoon cornstarch
- 2 tablespoons Shaoxing rice wine
- 2 tablespoons honey
- 1 tablespoon soy sauce
- 2 tablespoons cooking oil
- 2 garlic cloves, crushed and chopped
- 2 tablespoons crushed and chopped peeled ginger
- 2 tablespoons white miso
- 1 medium carrot, roll cut into ½-inch pieces
- 1 medium eggplant, diced into ½-inch pieces
- 1 medium onion, cut into ½-inch pieces
- 1 tablespoon sesame

seeds

4 scallions, green and white parts, cut diagonally into ¼-inch

pieces

• Cooked rice or noodles, for serving

. In a medium bowl, combine the tempeh, cornstarch, wine, honey, and soy sauce. Mix well.

. In a wok, heat the cooking oil over high heat until it begins to smoke.

. Add the garlic, ginger, and tempeh. Stir-fry for 1 minute, or until the garlic and ginger are fragrant.

. Add the miso and carrot. Stir-fry for 1 minute, or until they are lightly coated with oil.

. Add the eggplant and stir-fry for 1 minute, or until it is lightly browned.

. Add the onion and stir-fry for 1 minute, or until it is tender crisp.

. Add the sesame seeds and scallions. Toss. Serve over rice or noodles.

Spicy Thai-Style Milky Corn

Prep time: 10 minutes | Cook time: 15 minutes | Serves 4

4 ears corn

1 teaspoon cornstarch

4 teaspoons water

2 tablespoons palm oil

3 cloves garlic, crushed

2 tablespoons fish

sauce

• ½ cup coconut milk

• 2 Kaffir lime leaves

• 1 tablespoon palm sugar

• 1 teaspoon white pepper

. Remove the outer husk and the silky threads covering the corn kernels. Use a sharp knife to cut off the kernels. Rinse the corn kernels under warm running water. Drain thoroughly.

. In a small bowl, dissolve the cornstarch into the water. Set aside.

. Heat a wok or skillet over medium-high heat until it is almost smoking. Add the palm oil. When the oil is hot, add the crushed garlic and stir-fry for 10 seconds.

. Add the corn. Stir-fry the corn for 1 minute, then add in the fish sauce and stir-fry for 1 minute. Add the coconut milk and Kaffir leaves. Stir in the palm sugar.

5. Bring the coconut milk mixture to a boil. Stir in the cornstarch and water mixture and keep stirring for 1–2 minutes or until thickened. Stir in the white pepper. Remove the crushed garlic before serving.

Garlicky Fiddlehead Greens

Prep time: 10 minutes | Cook time: 5 minutes | Serves 4

• 1 pound (454 g) fiddlehead greens, fresh or frozen

• 2 tablespoons olive oil

• 2 teaspoons minced ginger

• 1 teaspoon garlic salt

• 2 teaspoons sesame oil

• 2 tablespoons toasted sesame seeds

1. If using freshly picked fiddleheads, wash to remove any dirt and drain thoroughly.

2. Heat a wok or skillet over medium-high heat until it is nearly smoking. Add the olive oil. When the oil is hot, add the ginger and stir-fry for 10 seconds. Add the greens. Stir-fry for 1 minute, then stir in the salt.

3. Stir-fry for 1 to 2 more minutes, until the greens are tender but still firm. Remove from the heat and stir in the sesame oil. Garnish with sesame seeds.

Spicy Sichuan Potatoes with Vinegar

Prep time: 10 minutes | Cook time: 5 minutes | Serves 4

• 3 tablespoons cooking oil

• 3 garlic cloves, crushed and chopped

• 1 large potato, julienned or shredded (2 cups)

• 1 teaspoon red pepper flakes

• 1 teaspoon five-spice powder

• 2 tablespoons Chinese black vinegar

• 1 tablespoon soy sauce

• 2 tablespoons Shaoxing rice wine

• 1 teaspoon spicy sesame oil

• 4 scallions, green and white parts, cut diagonally into ¼-inch pieces

1. In a wok, heat the cooking oil over high heat until it begins to smoke.

2. Add the garlic and potato. Stir-fry for 2 minutes, or until the potato begins to brown.

3. Add the red pepper flakes, five-spice powder, vinegar, soy sauce, wine, and sesame oil. Stir-fry for 1 minute, or until all of the ingredients are well combined.

4. Toss in the scallions. Serve immediately.

Chapter 5: Fish and Seafood

Gingered Sea Bass with Scallions

Prep time: 10 minutes | Cook time: 3½ minutes | Serves 6

- 6 (4- or 5-ounce / 113- to 142-g) sea bass fillets, with skin on
- Sea salt and pepper to taste
- 3 tablespoons vegetable oil, divided
- ½ inch fresh peeled ginger, thinly sliced
- 2 garlic cloves, thinly sliced
- 2 red chile peppers, de-seeded and slivered
- 1 bunch scallions, thinly sliced
- 1 tablespoon soy sauce

1. Season the sea bass with salt and pepper and make a couple of small diagonal cuts in the skin of each fillet.

2. Heat a wok over high heat until a drop of water sizzles on contact and add 1 tablespoon oil.

3. In two different batches, fry the fillets, skin-side down, for 3 minutes or until the skin is crisp.

4. Turn the fillets over and cook for a further 30 seconds to 1 minute.

5. Transfer the fillets to a serving plate and cover with foil to keep warm.

6. Heat the remaining tablespoon oil and fry the ginger, garlic, and chile peppers for 1 minute or until fragrant.

7. Remove the wok from the heat, add the scallions, and toss to combine.

8. Add the soy sauce to the wok and stir.

9. Spoon the sauce from the wok over the sea bass fillets and serve.

Peppered Shrimp with Cornstarch

Prep time: 10 minutes | Cook time: 2 minutes | Serves 4

- 1 tablespoon kosher salt
- 1½ teaspoons Sichuan peppercorns
- 1½ pounds (680 g) large shrimp (U31–35), peeled and deveined, tails left on
- ½ cup vegetable oil
- 1 cup cornstarch
- 4 scallions, sliced diagonally
- 1 jalapeño pepper, halved and seeded, thinly sliced
- 6 garlic cloves, thinly sliced

1. In a small sauté pan or skillet over medium heat, toast the salt and peppercorns until aromatic, shaking and stirring frequently to avoid burning. Transfer to a bowl to cool completely. Grind the salt and peppercorns together in a spice grinder or with a mortar and pestle. Transfer to a bowl and set aside.

2. Blot the shrimp dry with a paper towel.

3. In a wok, heat the oil over medium-high heat to 375°F (190°C), or until it bubbles and sizzles around the end of a wooden spoon.

4. Put the cornstarch in a large bowl. Just before you are ready to fry the shrimp, toss half the shrimp to coat in the cornstarch and shake off any excess cornstarch.

5. Fry the shrimp for 1 to 2 minutes, until they turn pink. Using a wok skimmer, transfer the fried shrimp to a rack set over a baking sheet to drain. Repeat the process with the remaining shrimp of tossing in cornstarch, frying, and transferring to the rack to drain.

6. Once all of the shrimp have been cooked, carefull remove all but 2 tablespoons of the oil and return the wok to medium heat. Add the scallions, jalapeño, and garlic and stir-fry until the scallion and jalapeño turn bright green and the garlic is aromatic. Return the shrimp to the wok, season to taste with the salt and pepper mixture (you may not use it all), and toss to coat. Transfer the shrim

to a platter and serve hot.

Eggy Scallops with Soy Sauce

Prep time: 15 minutes | Cook time: 31 minutes | Serves 4

- 1 large egg white
- 2 tablespoons cornstarch
- 2 tablespoons Shaoxing rice wine, divided
- 1 teaspoon kosher salt, divided
- 1 pound (454 g) fresh sea scallops, rinsed, muscle removed, and patted dry
- 3 tablespoons vegetable oil, divided
- 1 tablespoon light soy sauce
- ¼ cup freshly squeezed orange juice
- Grated zest of 1 orange
- Red pepper flakes (optional)
- 2 scallions, green part only, thinly sliced, for garnish

In a large bowl, combine the egg white, cornstarch, 1 tablespoon of rice wine, and ½ teaspoon of salt and stir with a small whisk until the cornstarch completely dissolves and is no longer lumpy. Toss in the scallops and refrigerate for 30 minutes.

Remove the scallops from the fridge. Bring a medium-size pot of water to boil. Add 1 tablespoon of vegetable oil and reduce to a simmer. Add the scallops to the simmering water and cook for 15 to 20 seconds, stirring continuously until the scallops just turn opaque (the scallops will not be completely cooked through). Using a wok skimmer, transfer the scallops to a paper towel–lined baking sheet and pat dry with paper towels.

In a glass measuring cup, combine the remaining 1 tablespoon of rice wine, light soy, orange juice, orange zest, and a pinch of red pepper flakes (if using) and set aside.

Heat a wok over medium-high heat until a drop of water sizzles and evaporates on contact. Pour in the remaining 2 tablespoons of oil and swirl to coat the base of the wok. Season the oil by adding the remaining ½ teaspoon salt.

Add the velveted scallops to the wok and swirl in the sauce. Stir-fry the scallops until they are just cooked through, about 1 minute. Transfer to a serving dish and garnish with the scallions.

Gingered Shrimp with Rice Wine

Prep time: 10 minutes | Cook time: 38 minutes | Serves 4

- 2 cups Shaoxing rice wine
- 4 peeled fresh ginger slices, each about the size of a quarter
- 2 tablespoons dried goji berries (optional)
- 2 teaspoons sugar
- 1 pound (454 g) jumbo
- shrimp (U21–25), peeled and deveined, tails left on
- 2 tablespoons vegetable oil
- Kosher salt
- 2 teaspoons cornstarch

1. In a wide mixing bowl, stir together the rice wine, ginger, goji berries (if using), and sugar until the sugar is dissolved. Add the shrimp and cover. Marinate in the refrigerator for 20 to 30 minutes.

2. Pour the shrimp and marinade into a colander set over a bowl. Reserve ½ cup of the marinade and discard the rest.

3. Heat a wok over medium-high heat until a drop of water sizzles and evaporates on contact. Pour in the oil and swirl to coat the base of the wok. Season the oil by adding a small pinch of salt, and swirl gently.

4. Add the shrimp and vigorously stir-fry, adding a pinch of salt as you flip and toss the shrimp around in the wok. Keep moving the shrimp around for about 3 minutes, until they just turn pink.

5. Stir the cornstarch into the reserved marinade and pour it over the shrimp. Toss the shrimp and coat with the marinade. It will thicken into a glossy sauce as it begins to boil, about another 5 minutes more.

6. Transfer the shrimp and goji berries to a platter, discard the ginger, and serve hot.

Ginger Steamed Fish with Scallion

Prep time: 10 minutes | Cook time: 8 minutes | Serves 4

- 4 (4-ounce/113 g)
- white fish fillets, such

as flounder, sea bass, or red snapper

- 2 tablespoons soy sauce
- 1 tablespoon Shaoxing rice wine or dry sherry
- 1 tablespoon very finely sliced, peeled fresh ginger
- 1 tablespoon very finely sliced scallion, both green and white parts
- 1 teaspoon toasted sesame oil

1. Pat the fish dry with paper towels.

2. In a small bowl, mix together the soy sauce, rice wine, ginger, sliced scallion, and sesame oil. Drizzle the sauce over the fish fillets. Gently place the fish in a bamboo steamer.

3. Add 2 inches of water to your wok, and bring the water to a boil. Place the steamer in the wok, and cover the steamer with its lid. Steam the fish for 7 to 8 minutes, or until the fish is opaque and starts to flake.

Honey with Smoked Salmon

Prep time: 10 minutes | Cook time: 5 minutes | Serve 4

- ½ cup soy sauce
- ¼ cup Shaoxing rice wine
- 1 tablespoon minced fresh ginger
- 1 teaspoon honey
- 1 pound (454 g) fresh salmon fillet, cleaned and patted dry
- 4 tablespoons brown
- sugar
- ⅓ cup uncooked long-grain rice
- ¼ cup black tea leaves, such as oolong
- 2 star anise pods
- 1 teaspoon cornstarch, mixed with 4 teaspoons cold water

1. In a large bowl, make a marinade by mixing together the soy sauce, rice wine, ginger, and honey. Cut the salmon fillet into 2-inch pieces, and add the pieces to the bowl; toss to coat with the marinade. Let the salmon marinate for 15 minutes.

2. Line your wok with a large piece of aluminum foil, letting the excess foil hang over the edges of the wok. Prepare the smoking layer by mixing together the brown sugar, rice, black tea leaves, and star anise pods in a small bowl. Spread this on the foil in the bottom of your wok.

3. Set a wire rack or a metal steamer basket with

little legs on top of the smoking layer. Heat the wok over high heat until the smoking layer begin to smoke, about 5 to 6 minutes. Gently place the marinated salmon on the rack in a single layer, skin-side down. Reserve the marinade to make th sauce for the fish. Reduce the heat to medium-lo cover the wok, and smoke the salmon for about 10 minutes. Turn off the heat and remove the wo from the heat. Do not remove the lid from the wo

4. Pour the marinade into a small saucepan and bring it to a boil. Remove it from the heat, and slowly add the cornstarch mixture to the marinade, stirring constantly until the sauce thickens.

5. Remove the smoked salmon from the wok, and place on a serving dish. Drizzle it with the sauce and serve with rice.

Spicy Wok-Seared Scallops

Prep time: 10 minutes | Cook time: 5 minutes | Serve 4

- ½ stick butter (4 tablespoons), divided
- Splash chili oil
- 24 large scallops, patted dry
- Sea salt
- Freshly ground black pepper
- 2 teaspoons peanut o
- ½ sweet onion, diced
- 2 red bell peppers, diced
- 2 teaspoons hoisin sauce, thinned with 1 teaspoon water

1. Heat your wok over high heat until a drop of wat sizzles on contact. Melt 1 to 2 tablespoons of butt with a splash of chili oil in the wok. Working in batches, add the scallops to the wok. The scallop should not crowd each other. Sear the bottoms of the scallops until browned, about 1 minute. Turn the scallops and sear the other sides, about minute. Season the scallops with the sea salt and pepper after you have turned them to sear on the second side. Transfer the finished scallops to a plate, and cover them with foil. Repeat this step until all the scallops are cooked.

2. Over high heat, add the peanut oil to the wok. When the oil is hot, add the onion and peppers, and stir-fry for 2 to 3 minutes. Add the hoisin sauce and toss to coat the vegetables.

3. When the vegetables are done, return the scallop

to the wok. Toss them to combine with the vegetables, and remove the wok from the heat. Serve.

Vinegary Chili Shrimp

Prep time: 15 minutes | Cook time: 12 minutes | Serve 4

- 8 ounces (227 g) cellophane noodles
- 1 pound (454 g) shrimp, peeled, cleaned, and deveined
- 2 teaspoons cornstarch
- ½ teaspoon sea salt
- ¼ teaspoon freshly ground black pepper
- 1 tablespoon soy sauce
- 1 tablespoon honey
- 1 tablespoon rice vinegar
- 2 teaspoons chili sauce
- 1 tablespoon Shaoxing rice wine or dry sherry
- 1 tablespoon peanut or vegetable oil
- 2 teaspoons minced garlic
- 1 teaspoon minced fresh ginger

1. Soak the cellophane noodles in hot water for 10 minutes, or until soft. Drain and set aside.

2. In a large bowl, toss the shrimp with the cornstarch, sea salt, and pepper. Let it sit for 5 minutes.

3. In a small bowl, make the sauce by mixing together the soy sauce, honey, rice vinegar, chili sauce, and rice wine. Set the bowl aside.

4. Heat your wok over high heat until a drop of water sizzles on contact. Add the peanut oil and swirl to coat the wok. Add the garlic and ginger, and stir-fry them for about 20 seconds. Add the shrimp and stir-fry them for 2 to 3 minutes, or until they become bright pink.

5. Remove the wok from the heat. Pour the sauce over the shrimp, add the cellophane noodles, and toss to combine everything. Transfer to a plate and serve immediately.

Brothy Shrimp with Lobster Sauce

Prep time: 15 minutes | Cook time: 12 minutes | Serve 4

- 2 tablespoons peanut or vegetable oil
- 2 garlic cloves, minced
- 12 ounces (340 g) shrimp, peeled, cleaned, and deveined
- 1 tablespoon Shaoxing rice wine or dry sherry
- 1½ cups low-sodium chicken broth
- ½ teaspoon sesame oil
- ½ teaspoon sugar
- ½ teaspoon sea salt
- Freshly ground white pepper
- ½ cup peas, fresh or frozen
- 1 tablespoon cornstarch mixed with 2 tablespoons cold water
- 1 egg, beaten
- 1 scallion, chopped

1. Heat your wok over medium-high heat. Add the peanut oil, garlic, and shrimp, and stir-fry for about 20 seconds. Add the rice wine and toss for another 20 seconds. Add the chicken broth, sesame oil, sugar, and sea salt to the wok. Season the mixture with white pepper. Stir in the peas.

2. Bring the mixture to a simmer, and then slowly stir the cornstarch mixture into the sauce. The sauce will thicken as the cornstarch is stirred into it. If the sauce gets too thick, thin it with a little water or broth, and stop adding the cornstarch mixture if there is any left.

3. Slowly add the egg to the wok, creating threads of egg throughout the sauce. Add the chopped scallion to the wok and stir to combine. Cook for about 15 minutes, stirring occasionally. If the sauce becomes too thick, thin it with a little water.

4. Take the wok off the heat, and serve the shrimp and sauce immediately with rice.

Chili Poached Fish

Prep time: 10 minutes | Cook time: 12 minutes | Serve 4

- 2 tablespoons cornstarch
- 2 teaspoons sea salt
- 1 teaspoon freshly ground black pepper
- 1 pound (454 g) meaty fish fillet, such as tuna or mahi mahi, cleaned and cut into even pieces
- 1 tablespoon soy sauce
- 1 tablespoon honey
- 1 tablespoon apple cider vinegar
- 1 teaspoon toasted sesame oil
- 2 teaspoons chili sauce
- 1 scallion, julienned, both green and white parts

1. Mix the cornstarch with the sea salt and pepper.

Dip the fish fillet into the cornstarch mixture, and coat the fish evenly on both sides. Gently place the fish in your wok.

2. Bring water to a boil in another pot or kettle. It needs to be enough water to fully cover the fish in the wok. Once the water comes to a boil, pour it over the fish so that it's completely covered. Tightly cover the wok with a lid or aluminum foil. Poach the fish for 12 to 14 minutes.

3. While the fish is poaching, create the sauce by mixing together the soy sauce, honey, apple cider vinegar, sesame oil, and chili sauce in a small bowl.

4. When the fish is ready, drain it and transfer it to a serving dish, pour the sauce over the fish, and garnish it with the julienned scallion.

Spicy Shrimp and Beef Pot Stickers

Prep time: 10 minutes | Cook time: 9 minutes | Serves 4

- ½ pound (227 g) raw shrimp, peeled and deveined
- 2 pounds (907 g) ground beef
- 1½ teaspoons minced fresh ginger
- 1 shallot, minced
- 2 leaves napa cabbage, chopped
- 1½ tablespoons soy sauce
- ¾ teaspoon toasted

- sesame oil
- Salt, to taste
- Freshly ground black pepper
- 30 to 40 round pot sticker, dumpling, or gyoza
- 1½ tablespoons vegetable or peanut oil
- ½ cup water, at room temperature or warm

1. Finely chop the shrimp or process it in a food processor. Set it aside.

2. Finely chop the ground beef by running a knife through it so it is in small chunks.

3. In a large bowl, mix the shrimp and beef with the ginger, shallot, cabbage, soy sauce, and sesame oil. Season with the salt and pepper. Continue mixing until well combined.

4. To make each dumpling, place a packed tablespoon filling in the center of a wrapper.

Wet your finger and trace the entire edge of the wrapper to dampen it. Fold the wrapper in half, and press the wet edges together. Pinch the edges to create small pleats. Repeat this for all the wrappers.

5. Heat your wok over medium heat, add the vegetable oil to it, and then add the dumplings, seam-side up, for about 2 minutes, or until they are golden brown on the bottom. Pour the water over the dumplings. Cover the wok with a lid, and let the dumplings steam for 5 to 6 minutes.

6. Uncover the wok and let the dumplings cook for another 2 minutes, or until the water has boiled off.

Spicy Squid Stir-Fry

Prep time: 15 minutes | Cook time: 3½ minutes | Serves 4

- 2 tablespoons brown sugar
- 1 tablespoon soy sauce
- 1 teaspoon rice vinegar
- 2 teaspoons fish sauce
- 2 tablespoons water
- 1 pound (454 g) squid, cleaned and cut into rings or 2-inch tentacles
- 1½ tablespoons

- peanut or vegetable oil, divided
- 2 Chinese dried red chiles
- 2 garlic cloves, minced
- 1 teaspoon minced ginger
- ½ sweet onion, thinly sliced
- 1 red or green bell pepper, cut into strips

1. In a small bowl, mix together a sauce of the brown sugar, soy sauce, rice vinegar, fish sauce, and water. Set aside.

2. Bring a large pot of water to a boil. Parboil the squid for 10 seconds. Drain it and set aside.

3. Heat a wok on medium-high until it is hot. Add 1 tablespoon peanut oil to the wok, and then add the chiles, garlic, and ginger. Stir-fry for about 30 seconds until it is fragrant, and then add the sauce. Stir everything for about 30 seconds to prevent it from burning.

4. Add the squid to the wok, and stir-fry for 30 to 40 seconds. Quickly remove the wok from the heat. Don't overcook the squid, which becomes rubbery when overcooked. Transfer the squid and sauce

to a plate, reserving 1 tablespoon the sauce for the vegetables.

Heat the wok over medium-high heat. Add the remaining 1½ teaspoons peanut oil to the wok, and swirl to coat the bottom of the wok. Add the onion, red bell pepper, and reserved sauce to the wok, and stir-fry until the vegetables are crisp-tender, 2 to 3 minutes.

Place the vegetables on a plate, and top with the squid. Serve immediately with steamed rice.

Quick Chili Squid

Prep time: 10 minutes | Cook time: ½ minute | Serve 4

- ½ teaspoon sea salt
- ½ teaspoon freshly ground black pepper
- ¼ teaspoon Sichuan peppercorns
- 1 tablespoon peanut or vegetable oil

- 1 pound (454 g) squid, cleaned and cut into rings or 2-inch tentacles
- Lemon wedges, for garnish
- Chili soy sauce, for garnish

In a small bowl, mix the sea salt, pepper, and Sichuan peppercorns.

Heat your wok over high heat until a drop of water sizzles on contact, and then add the peanut oil. Swirl the oil to coat the bottom of the wok. Add the squid and toss it for about 30 seconds. Then sprinkle it with the salt-and-pepper mix. Stir-fry the squid for another minute but no more, as it cooks almost instantly. Overcooked squid has a rubbery texture.

Serve immediately with the lemon wedges and chili soy sauce.

Spicy Shrimp Wontons

Prep time: 5 minutes | Cook time: 6 minutes | Serves 4

- ⅓ pound (136 g) raw, peeled shrimp, washed and deveined, tails removed
- ½ teaspoon sesame oil
- Salt

- Freshly ground white pepper
- 14 to 20 wonton wrappers
- 1 egg, beaten

1. Chop the shrimp into a fine mince, and mix it with the sesame oil. Season with the salt and white pepper.

2. Place a teaspoon of the filling in the center of each wonton wrapper. Brush the edges of the wonton wrappers with the beaten egg.

3. Fold the wontons to make triangles. Press the edges together. Let the wontons dry for about 10 minutes. Place the wontons in a steamer basket in a single layer.

4. Fill the wok with 2 inches of water, and bring it to a boil. Turn the heat down to a simmer, and place the steamer basket in the wok. Cover the wok and let the wontons steam for 6 to 8 minutes.

5. Serve with a spicy dipping sauce or chili-garlic sauce.

Chili Clams with Bean Sauce

Prep time: 20 minutes | Cook time: 20 minutes | Serves 4

- 1½ pounds littleneck or Manila clams, scrubbed and rinsed well
- 1 tablespoon peanut or vegetable oil
- 3 garlic cloves, minced
- ¼ small sweet onion, chopped
- 1 teaspoon fresh

- chopped ginger
- 2 dried red chiles
- 1 teaspoon black bean sauce
- ¼ cup room temperature water
- 1 teaspoon Shaoxing rice wine
- 1 teaspoon sugar

1. Discard any of the littleneck clams that have broken shells or that have already opened. If the clams seem extra gritty, soak them in salted water for 1 to 2 hours. Rinse them again before cooking.

2. Heat your wok over high heat until a drop of water sizzles on contact, and then add the peanut oil. Quickly add the garlic, onion, ginger, and chiles, and toss for about 30 seconds.

3. Add the black bean sauce and water to the wok. Stir to combine. Then add the clams, rice wine, and sugar. Bring the liquid up to a boil, place a lid on the wok, and cook until the clams open.

4. Serve with rice or over noodles.

Rice Wine with Salmon and Vegetables

Prep time: 10 minutes | Cook time: 4 minutes | Serve 4

- ½ cup oyster sauce
- 2 tablespoons rice wine
- 1 pound (454 g) thick, center-cut salmon fillet, cut into 1-inch pieces
- 2 tablespoons cooking oil
- 2 garlic cloves, crushed and chopped
- 1 tablespoon crushed and chopped ginger
- 1 red onion, cut into 1-inch pieces
- 1 red bell pepper, cut into 1-inch pieces
- 2 baby bok choy, leaves separated
- 4 scallions, cut into ½-inch pieces

1. In a large bowl, whisk together the oyster sauce and rice wine. Add the salmon and let marinate while you stir-fry.
2. In a wok over high heat, heat the cooking oil until it shimmers.
3. Add the garlic, ginger, and onion and stir-fry for 1 minute.
4. Add the salmon, reserving the marinade, and gently stir-fry for 1 minute.
5. Add the bell pepper and stir-fry for 1 minute.
6. Add the bok choy and stir-fry for 1 minute.
7. Add the reserved marinade and scallions to the wok and gently stir-fry for 1 minute. Serve over steamed rice.

Seafood with Root Vegetables

Prep time: 10 minutes | Cook time: 4½ minutes | Serve 4

- 2 tablespoons cooking oil
- 2 garlic cloves, crushed and chopped
- 1 tablespoon crushed, chopped ginger
- ½ cup julienned
- carrots
- ½ cup julienned parsnips
- ¼ pound (113 g) medium shrimp, shelled and deveined
- ½ cup julienned

zucchini
- ¼ pound (113 g) sea scallops, cut in half widthwise
- ¼ pound (113 g) squid

tentacles, rinsed in cold water
- ¼ cup hoisin sauce
- 4 scallions, cut into ½-inch pieces

1. In a wok over high heat, heat the cooking oil until it shimmers.
2. Add the garlic and ginger and stir-fry for 30 seconds.
3. Add the carrots and parsnips and stir-fry for 1 minute.
4. Add the shrimp and stir-fry for 1 minute.
5. Add the zucchini and stir-fry for 30 seconds.
6. Add the scallops and stir-fry for 30 seconds, or until the edges are just cracked.
7. Add the squid and stir-fry for 30 seconds, or until the tentacles are just curled.
8. Add the hoisin sauce and stir-fry for 30 seconds.
9. Garnish with the scallions and serve over steamed rice.

Brothy Seafood Salpicao

Prep time: 15 minutes | Cook time: 7 minutes | Serve 4

- 1 teaspoon hot sesame oil
- 1 tablespoon brown sugar
- ¼ cup oyster sauce
- ¼ cup vegetable or meat broth
- 1 tablespoon cornstarch
- 2 tablespoons cooking oil
- 4 garlic cloves, crushed and chopped
- 1 medium onion, cut into 1-inch pieces
- 4 ounces (113 g)

shiitake mushrooms sliced
- ¼ pound (113 g) medium shrimp, shelled and deveined
- 1 cup broccoli florets
- ¼ pound (113 g) scallops, cut in half widthwise
- 2 cups sugar snap or snow pea pods
- 1 red bell pepper, cut into 1-inch pieces
- ¼ pound (113 g) squid tentacles, rinsed in cold water

1. In a small bowl, whisk together the sesame oil, brown sugar, oyster sauce, broth, and cornstarch

Set aside.

2. In a wok over high heat, heat the cooking oil until it shimmers.

3. Add the garlic and onion and stir-fry for 1 minute.

4. Add the mushrooms and stir-fry for 1 minute.

5. Add the shrimp and stir-fry for 1 minute.

6. Add the broccoli and stir-fry for 1 minute.

7. Add the scallops and stir-fry for 30 seconds.

8. Add the pea pods and stir-fry for 1 minute.

9. Add the bell pepper and stir-fry for 1 minute.

10. Add the squid and stir-fry for 30 seconds.

11. Add the sesame oil mixture to the wok and stir-fry until a glaze forms. Serve over steamed rice.

Spicy Sichuan Shrimp

Prep time: 10 minutes | Cook time: 4 minutes | Serves 4

- 2 tablespoons cooking oil
- 4 garlic cloves, crushed and chopped
- 2 tablespoons ginger, crushed, chopped
- ½ pound (227 g) large shrimp, with or without shells
- ¼ cup rice wine
- 1 tablespoon red pepper flakes
- 2 tablespoons Chinese five-spice powder
- ¼ cup vegetable or meat broth
- 1 pound (454 g) mussels, cleaned and rinsed
- ¼ cup oyster sauce

1. In a wok over high heat, heat the cooking oil until it shimmers.

2. Add the garlic and ginger and stir-fry until lightly browned.

3. Add the shrimp and stir-fry for 1 minute.

4. Add the rice wine, red pepper, five-spice powder, and broth and bring to a boil.

5. Add the mussels, cover the wok, and cook for 2 minutes, or until the mussels open.

6. Uncover the wok and stir the ingredients for 1 minute, mixing well.

7. Drizzle the oyster sauce over the mussels and shrimp. Serve alone or over a bed of rice on a platter or in a shallow bowl.

Vinegary Thai Fish with Vegetables

Prep time: 15 minutes | Cook time: 3 minutes | Serves 4

- 1 tablespoon fish sauce
- 1 tablespoon mirin
- 2 tablespoons rice vinegar
- 2 tablespoons brown sugar
- Juice of 1 lime
- 1 tablespoon cornstarch
- 1 pound fresh, firm white fish fillet, cut into 1-inch pieces
- 2 tablespoons cooking oil
- 2 garlic cloves, crushed and chopped
- 1 tablespoon crushed, chopped ginger
- 1 bruised lower stalk of lemongrass, outer leaves removed and stalk cut into 1-inch pieces
- 1 onion, cut into 1-inch pieces
- 3 Thai bird's eye chiles, cut into ¼-inch pieces
- 2 cups chopped bok choy
- 4 scallions, cut into 1-inch pieces
- 1 cup bean sprouts

1. In a large bowl, whisk together the fish sauce, mirin, rice vinegar, brown sugar, lime juice, and cornstarch.

2. Add the fish to the bowl and set aside to marinate while preparing the wok.

3. In a wok over high heat, heat the cooking oil until it shimmers.

4. Add the garlic, ginger, lemongrass, and onion and stir-fry for 1 minute.

5. Remove the lemongrass and discard.

6. Add the bird's eye chiles and stir-fry for 30 seconds.

7. Add the marinated fish to the wok, reserving the marinade, and gently stir-fry for 1 minute.

8. Add the bok choy and remaining marinade and gently stir-fry for 30 seconds.

9. Squeeze the scallions to bruise them, then sprinkle over the fish.

10. Garnish with the fresh bean sprouts and serve over steamed jasmine rice.

Limey Vietnamese Scallops

Prep time: 10 minutes | Cook time: 1½ minutes | Serve 4

- ¼ cup rice wine
- ¼ cup fish sauce
- ¼ cup brown sugar
- Juice of 1 lime
- 1 pound (454 g) large sea scallops, cut in half widthwise
- 2 tablespoons cooking oil
- 2 garlic cloves, crushed and chopped
- 4 scallions, cut into 1-inch pieces
- 1 European cucumber, raked and cut into ¼-inch disks
- 1 teaspoon hot sesame oil
- ¼ cup rice vinegar

1. In a large bowl, combine the rice wine, fish sauce, brown sugar, and lime juice. Add the scallops to marinate and set aside.
2. In a wok over high heat, heat the cooking oil until it shimmers.
3. Add the garlic and scallions and stir-fry for 30 seconds.
4. Add the marinated scallops, reserving the marinade, and stir-fry for 30 seconds.
5. Add the cucumber and marinade to the wok and stir-fry for 30 seconds.
6. Turn off the heat and toss the cucumbers and scallops with the sesame oil and rice vinegar. Serve alone or over jasmine rice.

Spicy Korean Squid Stir-Fry

Prep time: 15 minutes | Cook time: 5 minutes | Serve 4

- 2 tablespoons cooking oil
- 2 garlic cloves, crushed and chopped
- 1 tablespoon crushed, chopped ginger
- 1 medium red onion, cut into 1-inch pieces
- 4 ounces (113 g) shiitake mushrooms, cut into slices
- 2 baby bok choy, leaves separated
- ½ pound (227 g) small to medium squid tentacles and rings, rinsed in cold water
- 2 Thai bird's eye chiles, cut into ¼-inch circles
- 2 tablespoons soy sauce
- 2 tablespoons rice wine
- 2 tablespoons gochujang
- 2 tablespoons brown sugar
- 1 teaspoon hot sesame oil
- 1 tablespoon sesame seeds
- 4 scallions, cut into 1-inch pieces

1. In a wok over high heat, heat the cooking oil until it shimmers.
2. Add the garlic, ginger, and onion and stir-fry for 1 minute.
3. Add the mushrooms and stir-fry for 1 minute.
4. Add the bok choy and stir-fry for 1 minute.
5. Add the squid and stir-fry for 30 seconds.
6. Add the bird's eye chiles and stir-fry for 30 seconds.
7. Add the soy sauce, rice wine, gochujang, and brown sugar and stir-fry 30 seconds.
8. Add the sesame oil, sesame seeds, and scallions and stir-fry for 30 seconds.
9. Serve over jasmine rice.

Brothy Clams with Black Bean Sauce

Prep time: 10 minutes | Cook time: 3 minutes | Serves 4

- 1 cup uncooked white rice
- 1 tablespoon cooking oil
- 4 garlic cloves, crushed and chopped
- 2 tablespoons crushed, chopped ginger
- ½ cup vegetable or meat broth
- 2 cups littleneck or mahogany clams, rinsed clean
- ¼ cup rice wine
- 2 tablespoons cornstarch
- 3 tablespoons black bean sauce

1. Prepare the rice as outlined here.
2. In a wok over high heat, heat the cooking oil until it shimmers.
3. Add the garlic and ginger and stir-fry for 1 minute.
4. Add the broth and bring to a boil. While waiting for the broth to boil, line a serving platter with the cooked rice.
5. Add the clams to the broth, cover the pan, and let

steam for 2 minutes, or until the clams open.

Remove the clams and place on top of the rice, leaving the broth in the wok.

In a small bowl, whisk together the rice wine and cornstarch. Add to the broth along with the black bean sauce. Stir until a glaze forms.

Drizzle the sauce over the opened clams and rice and serve.

Garlicky Malaysian Squid

Prep time: 10 minutes | Cook time: 3 minutes | Serves 4

- 2 tablespoons cooking oil
- 2 garlic cloves, crushed and chopped
- 3 stalks celery, cut diagonally into ¼-inch pieces
- ½ pound (227 g) small to medium squid tentacles and rings,
- rinsed in cold water
- 2 tablespoons rice wine
- 2 chiles, cut into ¼-inch pieces
- ½ cup oyster sauce
- 1 teaspoon hot sesame oil

In a wok over high heat, heat the cooking oil until it shimmers.

Add the garlic and celery and stir-fry for 1 minute.

Add the squid and rice wine and stir-fry for 1 minute.

Add the chiles and stir-fry for 30 seconds.

Add the oyster sauce and sesame oil and stir-fry for 30 seconds.

Serve over steamed basmati coconut rice.

Gingered Scallion King Crab

Prep time: 10 minutes | Cook time: 3 minutes | Serves 4

- 1 cup fish or lobster broth
- 2 tablespoons rice wine
- 2 tablespoons cornstarch
- 3 tablespoons cooking oil
- 2 tablespoons crushed, chopped ginger
- 3 garlic cloves, crushed and chopped
- 2 pounds (907 g) king crab legs, cut into 2-inch sections and left in the shell

- ¼ cup hoisin sauce
- 4 scallions, cut into ½-inch pieces

1. In a small bowl, whisk together the broth, rice wine, and cornstarch. Set aside.

2. In a wok over high heat, heat the cooking oil until it shimmers.

3. Add the ginger and garlic and stir-fry for 1 minute.

4. Add the crab legs and stir-fry for 1 minute.

5. Add the broth mixture and stir-fry for 1 minute.

6. Add the hoisin sauce and stir-fry until a glaze forms.

7. Bruise the scallions by squeezing them, then sprinkle them into the wok to garnish the crab legs.

8. Serve alone or over steamed rice.

Garlicky Cod with Tamari

Prep time: 10 minutes | Cook time: 2½ minutes | Serves 4

- 1 cup uncooked rice
- 2 cups genmaicha green tea
- 2 tablespoons white miso
- 2 tablespoons tamari
- 2 tablespoons mirin
- 2 tablespoons honey
- 1 tablespoon toasted sesame oil
- 1 pound (454 g) thick cod, cut into 4 pieces
- 2 tablespoons cooking oil
- 3 garlic cloves, crushed and chopped
- 1 tablespoon sesame seeds
- 2 scallions, cut into ½-inch pieces, for garnish

1. Prepare the rice as directed here, using genmaicha green tea instead of water.

2. In a large bowl, whisk together the miso, tamari, mirin, honey, and sesame oil. Add the cod and coat evenly with the marinade, then set aside.

3. In a wok over high heat, heat the cooking oil until it shimmers.

4. Add the garlic and stir-fry for 30 seconds until browned.

5. Place the marinated cod in the wok, reserving the marinade, and fry for 30 seconds per side, flipping gently.

6. Add the marinade and fry the fish for 30 more

seconds on each side.

7. Garnish with the sesame seeds and scallions and serve on top of the rice.

Spicy Korean Squid Stir Fry

Prep time: 5 minutes | Cook time: 5 minutes | Serve 2

- 1 pound (454 g) squid stripes
- 1 cup sliced carrots
- ½ cup Korean spicy marinade
- ½ cup sliced onions
- 1 tablespoon. coconut oil

1. Marinade squid stripes in a Korean spicy marinade.

2. In a wok, stir fry drained squid in coconut oil for few minutes, add carrots and onions and stir fry for 2 more minutes. Add the rest of the marinade and stir fry for 1 minute.

3. Serve with brown rice or quinoa.

Sprout with Mixed Seafood Stir Fry

Prep time: 5 minutes | Cook time: 6 minutes | Serves 2

- ½ pound (227 g) mixed seafood
- 1 cup green beans
- 1 cup sprouts
- 1 half of the carrot, sliced
- 1 tablespoon coconut oil

1. Marinade seafood in a Superfoods marinade.

2. Stir fry drained seafood and green beans in coconut oil for few minutes, add carrot and stir fry for 4 to 5 more minutes. Add the rest of the marinade and sprouts and stir fry for 1 minute.

3. Serve with brown rice or quinoa.

Calamari and Shrimp Stir Fry

Prep time: 5 minutes | Cook time: 5 minutes | Serves 2

- 1 cup shrimp
- 1 cup calamari
- 1 cup sliced bok choy
- 1 teaspoon oil

1. Marinade calamari and shrimp in a Superfoods

marinade.

2. In a wok, stir fry drained calamari & shrimp in coconut oil for few minutes, add bok choy and stir fry for 2 more minutes.

3. Add the rest of the marinade and stir fry for 1 minute. Serve with brown rice or quinoa.

Celery with Fish Stir Fry

Prep time: 5 minutes | Cook time: 5 minutes | Serves 2

- ½ pound (227 g) fish fillets
- 1 cup Chinese celery
- 1 cup mushrooms,
- sliced in half
- ½ cup peppers, sliced diagonally
- 1 teaspoon oil

1. Marinade fish in a Superfoods marinade.

2. In a wok, stir fry drained fish in coconut oil for few minutes, add all vegetables and stir fry for 2 more minutes.

3. Add the rest of the marinade and stir fry for 1 minute. Serve with brown rice or quinoa.

Bok Choy with Bass Stir Fry

Prep time: 5 minutes | Cook time: 3 minutes | Serves 2

- ½ pound (227 g) bass fillets
- 1 cup celery
- ½ cup sliced tomatoes
- ½ cup sliced bok choy
- ½ cup sliced carrots and cucumbers
- 1 teaspoon oil

1. Marinade bass in a Superfoods marinade.

2. Stir fry drained bass in coconut oil for few minutes, add all vegetables and stir fry for 2 more minutes.

3. Add the rest of the marinade and stir fry for 1 minute. Serve with brown rice or quinoa.

Gingered Shrimp with Chicken Broth

Prep time: 10 minutes | Cook time: 1½ minutes | Serve 4

- 1 pound (454 g) shrimp, peeled and deveined
- 2 tablespoons oil
- 1 tablespoon minced ginger

3 garlic cloves, sliced thinly

½ pound (227 g) snow peas, strings removed

2 teaspoons fish sauce

¼ cup chicken broth

4 green onions, white and light green parts, sliced diagonally

- 2 teaspoons dark roasted sesame oil

For the Marinade:

- 2 teaspoons arrowroot flour
- 1 tablespoon red wine
- ½ teaspoon salt

- Mix all the ingredients for the marinade in a bowl and then add the shrimp. Mix to coat. Let it marinade 15 minutes while you prepare the peas, ginger, and garlic.

- Add the coconut oil in the wok and let it get hot. Add the garlic and ginger and combine. Stir-fry for about 30 seconds.

- Add the marinade to the wok, add the snow peas, fish sauce and chicken broth. Stir-fry until the shrimp turns pink.

- Add the green onions and stir-fry for 1 more minute. Turn off the heat and add the sesame oil. Toss once more and serve with steamed brown rice or soba gluten free noodles.

Spicy Octopus with Carrot Stir Fry

Prep time: 5 minutes | Cook time: 5 minutes | Serves 2

½ pound (227 g) baby octopus

1 cup sliced green peppers

½ cup sliced carrots

- 2 sliced green onions
- ½ cup cashews
- 1 teaspoon oil

- Marinade octopus in a Superfoods marinade.

- In a wok, stir fry drained octopus in coconut oil for few minutes, add all vegetables and stir fry for 2 more minutes. Add the rest of the marinade and stir fry for 1 minute.

- Serve with brown rice or quinoa.

Spicy Sweet and Sour Fish

Prep time: 15 minutes | Cook time: 3 minutes | Serve 4

For the Fish:

- 12 ounces (340 g) cod fillet, cut into cubes
- 3 cups canola oil, for frying
- ¾ cup all-purpose flour
- ¼ teaspoon baking powder
- 1 tablespoon cornstarch
- ½ teaspoon salt
- ⅛ teaspoon turmeric powder
- ⅛ teaspoon white pepper
- ¼ teaspoon sesame oil
- ⅔ cup cold seltzer or club soda

Sauce:

- ¼ cup red onion, diced
- ¼ cup red bell peppers, diced
- ¼ cup green bell peppers, diced
- 1 tablespoon ketchup
- ¾ cup canned pineapple chunks
- ¾ cup pineapple juice
- 2½ tablespoons red wine vinegar
- ⅓ cup water
- ¼ teaspoon salt
- 2 tablespoons sugar
- 1½ tablespoons cornstarch

For the Sweet and Sour

1. Mix cornstarch, flour, salt, turmeric, white pepper, sesame oil, club soda, and baking powder in a bowl.

2. Dip the fillets in the soda-flour mixture to coat well.

3. Add 3 cups oil to a deep wok and heat to 350ºF (180ºC). Deep fry the fish fillets until golden-brown.

4. Transfer the fillets to a plate lined with paper towel then cover with a foil sheet.

5. Sauté onion and peppers with oil in a cooking pan for 30 seconds.

6. Stir in ketchup and sauté for 20 seconds.

7. Stir in sugar, salt, vinegar, pineapple, and pineapple juices.

8. Cook this sauce for 2 minutes on a low simmer.

9. Stir in cornstarch then mix gently and cook until it makes a thick sauce.

10. Pour this sauce over the fillets.

11. Serve warm.

Peppered Scallions and Shrimp Stir-Fry

Prep time: 10 minutes | Cook time: 5 minutes |

- 12 ounces (340 g) large, shell-on headless shrimp
- 2 tablespoons vegetable oil
- 7 fresh ginger slices, cut ⅛-inch thick
- 1 garlic clove, sliced
- 2 scallions, chopped
- ¼ cup ketchup
- 1 teaspoon Worcestershire sauce
- ⅛ teaspoon white pepper
- ½ teaspoon sugar
- 2 tablespoons Shaoxing wine
- 1 tablespoon soy sauce

1. Mix ketchup, Worcestershire sauce, white pepper, sugar, wine, soy sauce, scallions, garlic, and ginger in a cooking pan.

2. Cook the sauce for 5 minutes on medium heat, then remove it from the heat.

3. Sauté shrimp with 1 tablespoon canola oil in a Cantonese wok until they turn golden brown in color.

4. Pour in the sauce and toss gently to coat the shrimp.

5. Serve warm.

Broth with Steamed Mussels

Prep time: 10 minutes | Cook time: 6 minutes | Serves 6

- 3 pounds (1.4 kg) mussels, debearded
- Sliced rustic bread
- 2 tablespoons olive oil
- 4 garlic cloves, chopped
- 2 sprigs fresh thyme
- ½ cup onion, chopped
- ¼ teaspoon salt
- ½ cup broth
- ¼ teaspoon sugar
- ⅓ cup dry white wine
- ¼ cup fresh parsley, chopped
- Black pepper

1. Sauté onion, with olive oil, garlic, and thyme in a Mandarin wok until soft.

2. Stir in white wine, broth, black pepper, and mussels.

3. Reduce its heat to low, cover, and cook the mussels for 6 to 7 minutes.

4. Serve warm.

Spicy Hunan-Style Fish

Prep time: 10 minutes | Cook time: 10 minutes | Serves 2

- 1½ pounds (680 g) fresh tilapia
- 16 ounces (454 g) silken tofu
- ⅛ teaspoon salt
- 3 tablespoons canola oil
- 1 ½ tablespoons ginger, minced
- 6 tablespoons duo jiao
- 3 garlic cloves, minced
- 1 scallion, diced
- ⅔ cup hot water
- 2 tablespoons soy sauce
- 1 teaspoon sugar
- ¼ teaspoon white pepper

1. Mix hot water, soy sauce, sugar, white pepper, garlic, ginger, salt, scallions, and Duo Jiao in a Mandarin wok.

2. Cook this sauce until the sauce is reduced to half, then allow it to cool.

3. Soak the tofu and fillets in the prepared sauce, rub well, and cover to marinate for 30 minutes.

4. Add oil to a cooking pan and place it over medium heat.

5. Sear the tofu and fish in the skillet for 5 minutes per side until golden-brown.

6. Serve warm.

Spiced Shrimp with Garlic

Prep time: 10 minutes | Cook time: 7 minutes | Serves 6

- 1 pound (454 g) large, head-on shrimp
- ¼ teaspoon white pepper powder
- 2 teaspoons Shaoxing wine
- 3 to 4 ginger slices, minced
- 7 garlic cloves, minced
- 2 scallions, chopped
- 3 red chilies, chopped
- 1 cup panko breadcrumbs
- 1 cup vegetable oil
- ½ teaspoon salt
- ¼ teaspoon sugar
- ⅛ teaspoon five-spice powder

1. Sauté ginger and garlic with vegetable oil in a Mandarin wok until golden-brown.

Stir in white pepper, wine, red chilies, scallions, salt, sugar, and spice powder.

Mix and toss in shrimp, then cook for 5 to 6 minutes.

Spread the shrimp in a baking dish and drizzle the panko crumbs on top.

Bake the shrimp for 2 minutes in the oven at 350ºF (180ºC).

Serve warm.

Sauce with Shrimp and Broccoli

Prep time: 10 minutes | Cook time: 5 minutes | Serves 8

- 16 shrimps, peeled, deveined, and butterflied
- 10 ounces (283 g) broccoli florets
- ½ cup chicken stock
- ¼ teaspoon granulated sugar
- 1½ tablespoons soy sauce
- ½ teaspoon dark soy sauce
- 1 tablespoon oyster sauce
- ½ teaspoon sesame oil
- ⅛ teaspoon white pepper
- 2 tablespoons canola oil
- 2 garlic cloves, chopped
- 1 tablespoon Shaoxing wine
- 1½ tablespoons cornstarch, whisked with 2 tablespoons water

Add sesame oil to a large wok and stir in garlic.

Sauté until the garlic turns golden, then add broccoli.

Stir and cook for 5 minutes until soft.

Add shrimp, sugar, soy sauce, chicken stock, oyster sauce, white pepper, and wine to the saucepan.

Cook the mixture until the shrimp are tender.

Stir in cornstarch, mix and cook until the mixture thickens.

Serve warm.

Milky Fish Masala

Prep time: 15 minutes | Cook time: 8⅓ minutes | Serves 4 to 6

- 1 can unsweetened coconut milk, not shaken
- 2 tablespoons coconut oil or rapeseed oil
- 2 teaspoons black mustard seeds
- 5 slices of peeled crushed fresh ginger
- 2 large cloves of crushed garlic
- 1 to 4 fresh hot green chilies such as Thai or Serrano, halved lengthways
- 2 tablespoons ground coriander
- 1 teaspoon
- ½ teaspoon ground turmeric
- ½ teaspoon curry powder
- 3 medium-sized tomatoes, roughly chopped
- ¾ cup water
- 900 g black sea bass fillet including skin, cut into cubes
- ¾ teaspoon salt
- ⅓ cup diced mango
- Boiled rice

1. Take a scoop of ¼ cup heavy cream from the top of the coconut milk from the can. Set aside the milk and remaining cream for another use.

2. Heat a wok with oil over medium heat until the pan is hot but not smoking. Add the mustard seeds and cook for 15 seconds or until the seeds make a popping sound. Stir in the chilies, ginger and garlic and stir for 1 minute.

3. Stir in the chili powder, curry powder, coriander and turmeric for 5 to 10 seconds until it is fragrant. Stir in the tomatoes and cook for 1 minute. Stir in water and bring to a boil.

4. Reduce the heat setting, cover the pan and let it simmer for 5 minutes. Add the coconut cream and stir until well mixed. Then add the fish and the salt and simmer without the lid for 3 to 5 minutes or until the fish is just cooked through, stirring occasionally.

5. Carefully add the mango and stir in.

6. Serve it with rice.

Eggy Shrimp Tempura

Prep time: 10 minutes | Cook time: 1½ minutes | Serves 4

- 1 cup all-purpose flour
- 2 tablespoons cornstarch
- 1 pinch salt
- 1 cup water
- 1 egg yolk

- 2 egg whites, lightly beaten
- 450 g Medium-sized shrimp, peeled and
- peeled
- 2 cups vegetable oil for frying

1. Heat the oil in a deep fryer to 190ºF (88ºC) and whisk the flour, cornstarch and salt in a large bowl. Make a well in the middle of the flour.

2. Mix in the water and egg yolk. Mix only until it is damp; the dough becomes lumpy. Stir in the egg whites and dip the prawns one after the other in the batter.

3. Carefully place a few prawns one after the other in the hot oil. Fry for 1½ minutes until golden brown. Drain on paper towels.

Avocado with Crab and Corn Salad

Prep time: 10 minutes | Cook time: 4 minutes | Serve 6

- 4 ears of corn, kernels cut from the cob
- 2 leeks, only the white parts, thinly sliced
- 2 garlic cloves, chopped
- 2 avocados, peeled, pitted and diced into pieces
- ½ lemon, squeezed
- 5 tablespoons vegetable oil
- 1 tablespoon rice vinegar vegetable oil
- 1 tablespoon rice vinegar
- 1 tablespoon fresh basil, chopped
- 1 teaspoon salt
- ½ teaspoon chopped fresh tarragon
- 2 cans lumpy crab meat, drained and flaked

1. Put the corn kernels in a sieve to separate the small pieces; put in a bowl. In a separate bowl, stir together the lemon juice and diced avocado so they don't turn brown.

2. Heat vegetable oil in a pan over high heat; Add corn mixture. Cook for 4 to 8 minutes, stirring, until the corn is evenly brown.

3. Mix the tarragon, corn mixture, salt, avocado, basil and rice vinegar in a serving bowl.

4. Put the crab meat on top.

Milky Prawn Thai Curry

Prep time: 10 minutes | Cook time: 17 minutes | Serves 4

- 2 tablespoons sesame oil
- 1½ tablespoons red curry paste, or more to taste
- 1 red onion, cut into cubes
- 2 large peppers, cut into pieces
- 2 (400 ml) cans coconut milk
- ½ cup chicken broth
- 3½ tablespoons maple syrup
- 3 tablespoons fish sauce
- 3 lemongrass stalks, crushed and chopped
- 4 kaffir lime leaves, torn into quarters
- 450 g medium-sized shrimp, peeled and boned
- ¼ cup wrapped chopped fresh basil
- 2 tablespoons chopped fresh coriander

1. Heat the oil in a wok over medium to high heat; Stir in curry paste and cook for about 1 minute until fragrant. Stir the onion into the curry paste; Cook for about 3 minutes, until just tender. Stir coconut milk, chicken broth, maple syrup, fish sauce, lemongrass and lime leaves into the vegetable mixture.

2. Bring the curry to a boil; Reduce heat to low and simmer until vegetables are tender, about 8 minutes. Stir in prawns; cook until the prawns are pink in the middle, about 5 minutes; Take the wok off the stove; Stir basil and coriander into curry.

3. Serve spicy.

Mustardy Cancer Curry

Prep time: 15 minutes | Cook time: 16 minutes | Serves 4

- 2 fresh crabs, cleaned and cracked with their shells
- 2 teaspoons ground turmeric and ½ teaspoon salt
- 1 tablespoon mustard seeds
- 1 tablespoon hot water
- 1 tablespoon mustard oil
- 3 cups sliced red onion
- 1¾ cups boiling potatoes, peeled, halved lengthways, cut into slices
- 2 whole cloves

1 piece of cinnamon stick

2 pods of green cardamom pods and 2 large tomatoes, roughly chopped

5 whole black peppercorns

4 Thai green chilies

1½ teaspoons garlic paste

- ½ teaspoon ginger paste
- 1 teaspoon cayenne pepper and salt to taste
- 1 teaspoon white sugar
- 1 piece of fresh lemon
- ½ cup chopped fresh coriander

Rub the crabs with 1 teaspoon turmeric and ½ teaspoon salt and leave to marinate for 1 hour. Put mustard seeds and 1 tablespoon hot water in a small bowl and let steep for 10 minutes. Use a mortar and pestle to grind the seeds into a coarse paste and heat the oil in a wok or kadhai over medium heat. Add the crabs and stir-fry until they change color, about 4 minutes.

Put the sliced onions in the wok and cook over medium heat and stir until the onions are translucent (about 5 minutes). Turn the heat on high, add the potatoes and cook for about 2 minutes, stirring constantly. Add the cloves, cinnamon stick, cardamom pods, and peppercorns and stir for thirty seconds. Stir in tomatoes, ginger and garlic paste.

Halve three of the chilies and put them in the wok. Boil and stir over high heat for another minute or two. Reduce the heat to medium heat; add the remaining 1 teaspoon of turmeric, cayenne pepper and mustard paste and stir everything together. Put the shrimps in the wok and pour in enough water to cover the vegetables. Bring the water to a boil and stir in sugar and salt to taste. Cover and cook the wok on a low heat until the potatoes are tender and the water is reduced by half, about 10 minutes.

Remove the lid, stir and simmer until the sauce has thickened, about another 5 minutes. Squeeze the lemon wedge over the finished dish. Garnish with chopped coriander and sliced green chili and serve hot with rice.

Garlicky Prawn with Fish Sauce

Prep time: 10 minutes | Cook time: 1 minutes |

Serves 4

- 8 garlic cloves, minced or more to taste
- 2 tablespoons tapioca flour
- 2 tablespoons fish sauce
- 2 tablespoons light soy sauce

- 1 tablespoon white sugar
- ½ teaspoon of ground white pepper
- ¼ cup vegetable oil, split or as needed
- 450 g unpeeled prawns, divided

1. Mix white pepper, garlic, sugar, tapioca flour, soy sauce and fish sauce in a bowl; turn the prawns in it to coat them.

2. Put half of the prawns in a single layer; Fry 1 to 2 minutes per side until crispy and golden brown.

3. Repeat the process with the remaining prawns and the oil.

Eggy Shrimp with Green Peas

Prep time: 5 minutes | Cook time: 2 minutes | Serves 4

- 450 g uncooked medium-sized shrimp, peeled and boned
- 2¼ teaspoons salt
- 1 large egg white
- 2 teaspoons cornstarch
- ¼ cup low-salt chicken stock
- 2 tablespoons Shaoxing wine or dry sherry

- 1 teaspoon Asian sesame oil
- ¼ teaspoon of ground white pepper
- 4 cups peanut oil or vegetable oil
- ½ cup (1½ cm long pieces) green onions
- 4 quarter-size slices of peeled fresh ginger
- ¾ cup frozen green peas, thawed

1. Place the prawns in a colander; Rinse under cold running water. Drain. Sprinkle the prawns with 1 teaspoon salt; stir for 1 minute. Rinse again under cold running water; drain. Repeat with the prawns and 1 teaspoon salt. Rinse well and drain. Place the shrimp on several layers of paper towels and pat dry.

2. Whisk egg white, 1 tablespoon cornstarch and remaining ¼ teaspoon salt in a medium-sized bowl; stir until the shrimp are covered with batter. Whisk the stock, rice wine, sesame oil, white

pepper, and the remaining 1 teaspoon cornstarch in a small bowl and set aside. Pour 4 cups oil into the wok or saucepan and heat over medium to high heat until the thermometer reads 180ºF (82ºC). Using a slotted spoon, add shrimp (with the batter sticking to the surface) in batches of 5 or 6 pieces; just cook until the prawns turn pink, stirring, and separating whatever holds together for about 30 seconds.

3. Place the prawns on the plate with a slotted spoon. Put 1 tablespoon oil from the wok in a small bowl and save. Carefully pour the remaining oil from the wok into a metal bowl. Heat the same wok or a heavy, large pan over high heat until the drop of water evaporates on contact. Add 1 tablespoon reserved oil and toss. Add green onions and ginger; stir for 10 seconds. Add the prawns and peas. Stir in the stock mixture; Fry while stirring until the prawns are just opaque in the middle and the sauce envelops the prawns, about 30 seconds. Transfer to a bowl and serve.

Turmeric and Garlic Prawns

Prep time: 10 minutes | Cook time: 2½ minutes | Serve 4

- ¾ cup mayonnaise
- 2 tablespoons soy sauce
- 2 tablespoons mirin
- 2 garlic cloves, chopped
- 2 tablespoons dried chopped onion
- ¼ teaspoon onion powder
- 1 teaspoon curry powder
- 1 teaspoon ground

- turmeric
- 1 teaspoon dried basil
- 1 tablespoon cayenne pepper
- ¼ teaspoon salt
- ½ cup flavored dry breadcrumbs
- 16 peeled and chopped jumbo prawns, tails still attached
- 2 tablespoons sesame oil
- ¼ cup water

1. In a bowl, stir together mayonnaise, soy sauce, mirin, chopped garlic, dried chopped onion, onion powder, curry powder, turmeric, basil, cayenne pepper and salt. Fold in the breadcrumbs until they are evenly moistened.

2. Cut open the back of each shrimp and open the halves like a book. Place a strong teaspoon of the mayonnaise mixture on each shrimp and cover the

top completely. In a large pan, heat the sesame oil over high heat until it begins to smoke.

3. Place the prawns in the pan with the mayonnaise side up and add the water. Cover and steam until the prawns are no longer transparent (2½ to 3 minutes).

Garlicky Fried Prawns

Prep time: 10 minutes | Cook time: 1 minutes | Serves 4

- 8 garlic cloves, minced, or more to taste
- 2 tablespoons tapioca flour
- 2 tablespoons fish sauce
- 2 tablespoons light soy sauce

- 1 tablespoon white sugar
- ½ teaspoon of ground white pepper
- ¼ cup vegetable oil, divided or as needed
- 450 g Whole unpeeled prawns, divided

1. Mix the garlic, tapioca flour, fish sauce, soy sauce, sugar and white pepper in a bowl, add the prawns and place in the coat.

2. Heat 2 tablespoons oil in a heavy pan over high heat. Add ½ of the prawns in a single layer; Fry until golden brown and crispy, 1 to 2 minutes per side.

3. Repeat with the remaining oil and the remaining shrimp.

Brothy Mushrooms with Bok Choy

Prep time: 10 minutes | Cook time: 1¼ minutes | Serves 4

- 1½ cups chicken broth
- 5 tablespoons fish sauce and 1 tablespoon granulated sugar
- 12 plantation or tiger prawns
- 110 g shiitake mushrooms
- 400 to 450 g baby-bok choy

- 3 tablespoons rapeseed oil
- ½ teaspoon minced garlic
- 2 tablespoons mirin (rice wine)
- ⅓ cup stir-fry sauce
- Steamed rice for serving

Fish and Seafood

For the Stir-Fry Sauce:

Mix the fish sauce, sugar, and chicken broth in a medium bowl. Mix well until the sugar has completely dissolved.

For the Prawns:

Peel the shells of the shrimp and cut the shrimp in half lengthways. Core the shrimp. Rinse the shrimp under cold water, pat dry with paper towels, and set aside. Clean the shiitake mushrooms with a brush or a dry, clean towel.

Cut the mushrooms into pieces. Rinse the baby bok choi and cut it into pieces. Set aside and let dry. Heat a skillet or wok over high heat until the pan smokes. Add 1 tablespoon oil to the pan. Add the shrimp and cook for 20 to 30 seconds until the shrimp change color.

Remove the prawns from the pan and set aside. Without cleaning the pan, add the remaining 2 tablespoons oil. Add the garlic and sauté for about 10 seconds until fragrant. Add the bok choy and mushrooms. Fry for 30 seconds to 1 minute, stirring, until vegetables are soft. Add the prawns to the vegetable mixture and stir-fry for 10 seconds.

Pour in the rice wine and keep stirring. Stir in the stir fry sauce and cook for about 15 seconds, until the prawns are cooked through and well coated with the sauce. Remove the pan from the heat and serve immediately with steamed rice. The remaining sauce can be stored in the refrigerator or frozen for up to 4 days.

Eggy Prawn Tempura

Prep time: 10 minutes | Cook time: 1½ minutes | Serves 6

- 1 cup all-purpose flour
- 2 tablespoons cornstarch
- 1 pinch salt
- 1 cup water
- 1 egg yolk
- 2 egg whites, lightly beaten
- 450 g medium-sized prawns, peeled and deveined, tails left on
- 2 cups vegetable oil, for deep frying

Heat the oil in a deep fryer to 190°F (88°C).

In a large bowl, mix the salt, flour and cornstarch. Make a well in the center of the flour mixture. Add the egg yolks and water. Mix until the batter is almost moist and lumpy.

3. Dip the prawns one at a time in the batter and brush with it. Leave the tails uncoated with batter.

4. Carefully put the prawns piece by piece into the hot oil.

5. Fry for about 1½ minutes until the topping is golden brown. Put the cooked shrimp. Tempuras on paper towels to drain off excess oil.

Vinegary Shrimp with Ketchup

Prep time: 15 minutes | Cook time: 1¼ minutes | Serves 4

- 2 cups peanut oil, for frying
- 450 g peeled and chopped large shrimp
- ¼ cup cornstarch
- 2 large garlic cloves, chopped
- ½ teaspoon chopped fresh ginger
- ½ teaspoon cayenne pepper
- 1 tablespoon white wine
- 1 tablespoon white vinegar
- 1 tablespoon ketchup
- 5 teaspoons white sugar
- ½ teaspoon salt
- ¼ cup water
- 2 teaspoons cornstarch
- 2 teaspoons water
- 5 green onions, sliced

1. Heat the peanut oil in a wok to 375°F (190°C), brush the shrimp with ¼ cup cornstarch, then dip in the hot oil and fry quickly until golden brown, about 45 seconds.

2. Pour everything but a tablespoon oil out of the wok and then stir in the garlic, ginger and cayenne pepper. Cook and stir until the garlic is fragrant and begins to brown, about 30 seconds.

3. Pour in the wine, vinegar, ketchup, sugar, salt and ¼ cup water and bring to a boil over high heat. Dissolve the cornstarch in 2 teaspoons water, stir into the boiling sauce and cook for about 1 minute until it has thickened.

4. Stir the prawns and green onions into the sauce until covered.

Cornstarch with Spicy Prawns

Prep time: 15 minutes | Cook time: 4½ minutes | Serves 4

- 2 tablespoons rapeseed oil
- 10 garlic cloves, chopped
- 1 teaspoon chopped fresh ginger root
- 1 can chopped water chestnuts, drained
- 1 cup sugar peas
- 1 cup small white mushrooms
- 1 teaspoon crushed red pepper flakes
- ½ teaspoon ground
- black pepper and salt
- 450 g peeled and deveined jumbo prawns
- ½ cup chicken broth
- 1 tablespoon rice vinegar
- 2 tablespoons fish sauce
- 2 tablespoons dry sherry
- 1 tablespoon cornstarch
- 1 tablespoon water

1. Heat a large pan or wok with oil until the oil is very hot. Add the ginger and garlic and fry in the hot oil for 30 seconds or until fragrant.

2. Mix in the mushrooms, shrimp, red pepper flakes, water chestnuts, sugar snap peas, pepper and salt. Boil and stir the mixture for 2 to 3 minutes until the shrimp are pink in color.

3. In a small bowl, mix rice vinegar, dry sherry, chicken broth and fish sauce together.

4. Add the sauce mixture to the shrimp mixture and cook and stir for a few seconds to mix well.

5. Mix the water and cornstarch together and add it to the wok. Cook and stir the mixture for 2 minutes or until the sauce is thick.

Gingered Cantonese-Style Sea Bass

Prep time: 10 minutes | Cook time: 10 minutes | Serves 4

- 600 g whole sea bass, with head and tail, scaled and without gills
- ¼ cup plus 2
- tablespoons white wine
- 3 garlic cloves, roughly chopped
- 4 tablespoons chopped green onions, including greens
- 2 tablespoons fresh
- ginger, finely choppe
- 2 teaspoons sugar
- ¼ cup olive oil 3 tablespoons soy sauc

1. Choose a round or oval plate that is big enough to hold the fish but fits in the top of a steamer. This can be a traditional Chinese bamboo or metal steamer, or a western steamer for clams.

2. Place the fish on the plate and place the plate on top of the steamer. Cover the plate with boiling water and steam covered for 10 to 15 minutes. Mix 2 tablespoons wine, garlic, spring onions, ginger and sugar in a small bowl and prepare the sauce the meantime.

3. When cooked, the meat is white and easy to remove from the bones. Take out the plate and pour off any liquid that has accumulated around the fish.

4. Heat the oil in a wok or saucepan and add the sauce base when it is hot. Pour the soy sauce over the sea bass first then pour the cooked sauce ove the fish.

Orange with Shrimp Stir-Fry

Prep time: 15 minutes | Cook time: 24 minutes | Serves 4

- 450 g peeled and boned prawns
- 2 tablespoons freshly squeezed orange juice
- 1 teaspoon minced garlic
- 1 teaspoon chopped fresh ginger root
- Salt and ground black pepper, to taste
- 1 tablespoon vegetable oil
- 1 tablespoon sesame oil
- 1 tablespoon vegetab oil
- 1 diced green pepper
- 1 sliced yellow summer squash
- 1 cup chopped broccoli
- ½ cup diced onion
- ½ cup chopped oran carrot, with peel
- ¼ teaspoon cayenne pepper
- 1½ cups cooked rice

1. Mix the shrimp, orange juice, garlic and ginger in a bowl; Season with salt and pepper. Put in the fridge for 15 minutes. Heat 1 tablespoon vegetabl

oil and sesame oil in a wok or large pan over medium-high heat.

. Remove the prawns from the marinade; cook and stir in the hot oil until opaque, about 2 minutes per side. Put the prawns on a plate.

. Heat 1 tablespoon vegetable oil with the oil remaining in the wok. Cook the bell pepper, pumpkin, broccoli, onion, carrot, orange peel and cayenne pepper in the hot oil and stir until the vegetables are soft, about 5 minutes.

. Return the prawns to the pan, stir into the vegetable mixture and continue cooking for another minute. Serve over cooked rice.

Gingered Scallions and Bass

Prep time: 10 minutes | Cook time: 30 minutes | Serves 4

1 (1 kg) whole black bass or sea bass, head and tail intact	1 piece of fresh ginger, peeled and cut into very thin matches
½ teaspoon salt	3 tablespoons light soy sauce
1 bunch of spring onions, white and pale green pieces cut into very thin strips and kept separately for green	¼ teaspoon sugar
	1 tablespoon peanut or vegetable oil

Put the oven rack in the middle position and preheat the oven to 200ºF (93ºC). Wash the fish and pat dry, then rub salt inside and out.

Put in a baking pan and sprinkle with spring onion strips (white and light green) and ginger, stir together soy sauce and sugar until the sugar is dissolved, then pour over the fish. Pour boiling hot water into the frying pan until it is halfway through the baking pan.

Oil a large sheet of heavy-duty foil then place the tent foil (with the oiled side down) over the fish and close the frying pan tightly. Carefully slide the frying pan into the oven and bake for 30 to 35 minutes, until the fish is just cooked through.

While the fish is baking, cut enough spring onions diagonally into very thin slices to measure out half a cup (save the rest for another use). Just before serving, remove the foil from the fish and sprinkle with spring onions.

5. Woke over high heat until a bead of water evaporates immediately. Pour oil around the side of the wok, then tilt the wok to swirl oil, coat the side and heat until smoked.

6. Remove from heat and immediately pour oil over shallot greens and fish.

Spicy Coconut Rice with Prawns

Prep time: 10 minutes | Cook time: 25 minutes | Serves 6

1½ cups long grain white rice	2½ tablespoons sriracha sauce
1½ cups water	2 teaspoons cornstarch
1½ teaspoons sugar	½ cup chicken broth with reduced sodium content
1½ cups well-stirred unsweetened coconut milk (not low-fat)	1 tablespoon vegetable oil
1½ teaspoons salt	Lime wedges
450 g broccolini	
900 g peeled and chopped large shrimp	

1. Rinse the rice in a sieve under cold water, then shake well, drain and place in a heavy saucepan. Add 1½ cups water, sugar, 1 cup coconut milk and ¾ teaspoon salt.

2. Bring to a boil, partially covered, then reduce the heat to a low level and cover completely. Cook for 20 minutes then remove from heat and cover and let stand for 5 minutes. While the rice is cooking, cut off the broccolini, then cut into lengths diagonally.

3. Put the prawns with Sriracha sauce and the remaining ¾ teaspoon salt in a bowl; mix the cornstarch, ¼ cup chicken stock, and the remaining ½ cup coconut milk in another bowl until the cornstarch is completely dissolved; heat a well-seasoned flat-bottomed wok or pan over high heat until it just begins to smoke; then add oil and toss covered.

4. Add the broccolini and stir-fry until light green, then add the remaining ¼ cup chicken stock and stir-fry until the liquid has evaporated, about 3 minutes.

5. Add the shrimp mixture and cook for 2 minutes, stirring frequently. Stir the cornstarch mixture, then pour on the wok side and cook while stirring until the sauce has thickened slightly and the prawns have just cooked through, another 3 minutes.

6. Open the rice with a fork and serve immediately with the prawns.

Corn with Veggie Stir-Fry

Prep time: 10 minutes | Cook time: 5 minutes | Serves 2

- ½ pound (227 g) shrimp
- 1 cup sliced broccoli
- ½ cup julienned carrots
- ½ cup sprouts
- 1 cup baby corn
- 1 teaspoon oil

1. Marinade shrimp in a Superfoods marinade. Stir fry drained shrimp in coconut oil for few minutes, add all vegetables and stir fry for 2 more minutes.

2. Add the rest of the marinade and stir fry for 1 minute. Serve with brown rice or quinoa.

Sugared Sauce with Stir-Fried Clams

Prep time: 15 minutes | Cook time: 1⅔ minutes | Serves 4

For the Sauce:
- ¼ cup water
- 1 tablespoon oyster sauce
- 2 teaspoons soy sauce
- ½ teaspoon Shaoxing wine
- ½ teaspoon brown sugar
- ¼ teaspoon chicken stock granules

For the Stir-Fry:
- 1 teaspoon cornstarch
- 2 tablespoons water

- 2 tablespoons peanut oil
- 2 stalks lemongrass, white portion only, halved
- ½-inch piece ginger, peeled and thinly sliced
- 2 garlic cloves, minced
- 1½ pounds (680 g) fresh clams
- 1 fresh red chile, thinly sliced
- 1 scallion, cut into 1-inch pieces

1. In a small bowl, make the sauce by mixing

together the water, oyster sauce, soy sauce, Shaoxing wine, brown sugar, and chicken stock granules. Set it aside.

2. In a separate small bowl, mix together the cornstarch and water. Set it aside.

3. In a wok over medium-high heat, heat the peanut oil.

4. Add the lemongrass and stir-fry for 1 to 2 minutes, or until the edges start to brown a little.

5. Add the ginger and garlic and stir-fry for about 20 seconds until it's aromatic.

6. Add the clams, and give all the ingredients a good stir.

7. Stir in the sauce and let it simmer.

8. When the clams start to open up, stir in the cornstarch mixture. Cover the wok if desired. By the time the sauce thickens, 20 to 30 seconds, most if not all of the clams should be open. Discard any unopened clams.

9. Turn off the heat, and transfer the clams to a serving plate. Garnish with the red chile and scallion.

Spicy Chinese Steamed Fish Fillet

Prep time: 10 minutes | Cook time: 5 minutes | Serves 4

For the Sauce:
- 2 tablespoons soy sauce
- 1 tablespoon water
- 2 teaspoons Shaoxing wine
- 1 teaspoon sesame oil
- ½ teaspoon sugar
- Pinch ground white pepper

For the Steamed Fish Fillet:
- 1 teaspoon sesame oil

- 1½ pounds white fish fillet
- ½ teaspoon salt
- 2 pinches ground white pepper
- 2-inch piece ginger, peeled, half sliced and half julienned
- 1 tablespoon peanut oil
- 2 scallions, julienned
- ¼ cup fresh cilantro leaves

1. In a small bowl, make the sauce by combining the soy sauce, water, Shaoxing wine, sesame oil, sugar, and pepper. Set it aside.

Fish and Seafood

Set up a metal steaming rack in a wok and pour water into the wok halfway up to the bottom of the steaming plate. Turn the heat to medium-high.

Rub the sesame oil over the entire surface of the fish fillet and season both sides with salt and pepper.

Place the fish fillet on a heatproof dish and arrange the sliced ginger on top of the fish.

Cover and steam for 5 minutes or until the fish is cooked (It should flake easily with a fork).

Transfer the fish to a serving plate, discarding the ginger slices.

Discard the water from the wok, return the wok to the burner, and dry over medium heat.

Once the wok has completely dried, add the peanut oil to the wok followed by the julienned ginger. When the ginger starts to turn golden brown, add the sauce. Allow the sauce to boil for just a few seconds, then use a wok spatula or ladle to spoon the sauce over the fish.

Garnish with the scallions and cilantro leaves, and serve immediately.

Walnut with Shrimp Marinade

Prep time: 15 minutes | Cook time: 1 minutes | Serves 4 to 6

For the Shrimp Marinade:

2 teaspoons baking soda

1 pound (454 g) shrimp, peeled and deveined

Pinch salt

Pinch ground white pepper

For the Walnuts:

¼ cup sugar

¼ cup water

½ cup walnuts

For the Sauce:

- 1½ tablespoons mayonnaise
- 1 teaspoon honey
- 1 teaspoon sweetened condensed milk
- ½ teaspoon lemon juice

For the Stir-Fry:

- 2 tablespoons peanut oil
- 3 teaspoons cornstarch

Pour the baking soda over the shrimp and gently massage it into the shrimp. Let the shrimp rest in the refrigerator for 30 minutes, then thoroughly

wash off the baking soda. Use a paper towel to blot any excess water from the shrimp. Sprinkle with the salt and pepper.

2. While the shrimp is marinating in the cornstarch, pour the sugar and water into a wok over medium-high heat. Stir until the syrup turns a light caramel color. Pour in the walnuts, stirring to coat. After about 1 minute, pour the walnuts onto parchment paper or aluminum foil and spread them out with a wok spatula. Let them cool.

3. In a small bowl, prepare the sauce by combining the mayonnaise, honey, condensed milk, and lemon juice. Set it aside.

4. In a wok over medium-high heat, heat the peanut oil.

5. Dredge the shrimp in the cornstarch, shake off the excess, and place them in the wok in a single layer. Cook for about 1 minute on one side, then stir-fry until they are fully cooked and transfer them to a bowl.

6. Add the candied walnuts to the shrimp, followed by the sauce, stirring to coat.

7. Serve immediately.

Egg with Chicken and Sauce

Prep time: 15 minutes | Cook time: 5 minutes | Serves 8

- 4 packs of tofu
- ½ cup shrimp, peeled and chopped
- 1 egg, lightly beaten
- 50 g ground chicken
- 1 chopped green onion
- 2 tablespoons cornstarch
- 1 tablespoon sesame oil
- Salt and ground white pepper, to taste

For the Dough:

- 1 egg
- 6 tablespoons all-purpose flour
- Cold water, or as needed

For the Sauce:

- ⅓ cup water
- ¼ cup dry roasted peanuts, coarsely chopped
- 1 fresh red chili pepper, finely chopped
- 2 garlic cloves, finely chopped
- 2 tablespoons white vinegar
- 1 teaspoon white sugar
- 1 teaspoon salt
- Oil, for frying

1. Cut 4 tofu squares diagonally to make 8 triangles. For the filling, mix the shrimp, ground chicken, egg, hollowed tofu pieces, pepper, salt, cornstarch, green onion and sesame oil in one shot.

2. Carefully place the filling mixture in each triangular tofu pocket (the filling bulges out). Place a steamer insert on a saucepan and fill the saucepan with water just below the bottom of the steamer insert. Let the water boil.

3. Put the filled tofu triangles in the steamer and cover them with the steamer lid. While the tofu triangles are cooking in the steamer, start preparing the batter.

4. Mix the flour and egg in a bowl. In a separate bowl, mix the vinegar, water, sugar, salt, red chili pepper, garlic and peanuts together. In a separate bowl, mix the vinegar, water, sugar, salt, red chili pepper, garlic, and peanuts well until the sugar and salt are completely dissolved then set the sauce aside.

5. Remove the cooked tofu triangles from the steamer.

6. Heat a wok with oil until it is hot. Brush the steamed tofu triangles with the batter and carefully pour them into the hot oil.

7. Fry the coated, steamed tofu triangles in portions for about 5 minutes or until the dough is cooked through and has a golden brown color.

8. Place the fried tofu triangles on paper towels so that the excess oil drains off. Serve hot with the peanut sauce on the side.

Peppered Shrimp with Cilantro

Prep time: 10 minutes | Cook time: 5 minutes | Serves 4 to 6

- 3 tablespoons cornstarch
- 1 teaspoon freshly ground black pepper
- 1 teaspoon sea salt
- 1 pound (454 g) large shrimp, deveined, tail on
- 2 tablespoons peanut oil
- ½ jalapeño or 1 Thai bird's eye chile, thinly sliced (optional)
- 1 sprig fresh cilantro, roughly chopped

1. In a medium bowl, combine the cornstarch, pepper, and sea salt. Mix well and set it aside.

2. Just before frying the shrimp, add the shrimp to the cornstarch mixture and toss to coat.

3. In a wok over medium-high heat, heat the peanut oil.

4. Shake any excess cornstarch off the shrimp and place them in the wok in a single layer.

5. Allow the shrimp to cook on one side for about 30 seconds before flipping.

6. Add the sliced jalapeño or chile to the wok (if using) and gently stir-fry to combine.

7. Transfer to a serving dish and garnish with the cilantro.

Spicy Bacon-Wrapped Shrimp

Prep time: 5 minutes | Cook time: 4 minutes | Serves 6

- 24 extra-large shrimp, deveined and shelled, with tails on
- ½ teaspoon black pepper
- 6 slices bacon, quartered
- 1 tablespoon vegetable oil
- 2 cups Basil Pesto

1. Season shrimp with pepper. One at a time, wrap a piece of bacon around each shrimp. Use a toothpick to secure.

2. Heat oil in a wok over medium heat. Add the wrapped shrimp in a single layer. Cook for 2 minutes on each side or until the bacon is crispy and the shrimp turn pink. Drain the shrimp on plates lined with paper towels. Repeat until all the shrimp have been cooked.

3. Serve warm with pesto as a dipping sauce.

Carrot and Shrimp with Lobster Sauce

Prep time: 15 minutes | Cook time: 5 minutes | Serves 4 to 6

FOR THE SAUCE:

- 1 cup Basic Chinese Chicken Stock, or store bought
- 2 teaspoons soy sauce
- 2 teaspoons cornstarch
- 1 teaspoon Shaoxing wine
- ½ teaspoon sugar

Pinch ground white pepper to taste

FOR THE STIR-FRY:

1 tablespoon peanut oil

2-inch piece ginger, peeled and julienned

- 2 garlic cloves, minced
- ½ cup frozen peas and carrots
- 1 pound (454 g) large shrimp, peeled and deveined
- 1 egg, lightly beaten

. In a small bowl, prepare the sauce by combining the chicken stock, soy sauce, cornstarch, Shaoxing wine, sugar, and pepper. Stir well, breaking up any lumps. Set it aside.

. In a wok over medium-high heat, heat the peanut oil.

. Add the ginger and garlic and stir-fry until aromatic, or for about 20 seconds.

. Add the frozen peas and carrots and stir-fry for 10 seconds.

. Pour in the sauce and the shrimp. Stir with a wok spatula to combine all the ingredients.

. Slowly pour in the beaten egg while using the wok spatula to swirl it into the sauce.

. As soon as the shrimp are cooked (they curl into a "C" shape), transfer the dish to a serving plate and serve immediately.

Scallops with Gingered Snow Peas

Prep time: 15 minutes | Cook time: 10 minutes | Serves 6

FOR THE SAUCE:

2 tablespoons water

1 tablespoon oyster sauce

1 teaspoon soy sauce

½ teaspoon sugar

½ teaspoon sesame oil

FOR THE STIR-FRY:

1 tablespoon water

1 teaspoon cornstarch

1 pound (454 g) fresh bay scallops

In a small bowl, prepare the sauce by combining

- ½ teaspoon salt
- Pinch ground white pepper to tatse
- Pinch sugar to taste
- 2½ tablespoons peanut oil, divided
- 2-inch piece ginger, peeled and minced
- 2 garlic cloves, minced
- ¾ pound (340g) snow peas, trimmed and strings removed.

the water, oyster sauce, soy sauce, sugar, and sesame oil. Set it aside.

2. In a separate small bowl, mix together the water and cornstarch. Set it aside.

3. Rinse the scallops and pat them dry with paper towel. Season them with the salt, pepper, and pinch of sugar to taste.

4. In a wok over medium-high heat, heat 1½ tablespoons of peanut oil.

5. Add the scallops and stir-fry for about 4 minutes. Remove the scallops and set them aside.

6. Add the remaining 1 tablespoon of peanut oil to the wok. Add the ginger and garlic and stir-fry until aromatic, or for about 30 seconds.

7. Add the snow peas and stir-fry until bright green, for about 1 minute. Stir in the sauce.

8. Once the snow peas have softened, add the cornstarch mixture. Stir-fry until the sauce begins to thicken.

9. Return the scallops to the wok and after a very quick stir-fry, transfer the dish to a serving plate.

Vinegary Kung Pao Shrimp

Prep time: 15 minutes | Cook time: 10 minutes | Serves 6

FOR THE SAUCE:

- 2 tablespoons rice vinegar
- 2 tablespoons soy sauce
- 2 teaspoons brown sugar
- 1 teaspoon dark soy sauce
- 1 teaspoon sesame oil
- 1 teaspoon cornstarch

FOR THE STIR-FRY:

- 2 tablespoons peanut oil
- 8 to 10 dried red chiles

- 1 small green bell pepper (or ½ a large one), cut into bite-size pieces
- 2-inch piece ginger, peeled and julienned
- 2 garlic cloves, minced
- 1 pound (454 g) shrimp, peeled and deveined
- ¼ cup unsalted roasted peanuts
- 1 or 2 scallions, cut into 1-inch pieces

1. In a small bowl, prepare the sauce by combining the rice vinegar, soy sauce, brown sugar, dark soy sauce, sesame oil, and cornstarch. Set it aside.

2. In a wok over medium heat, heat the peanut oil.

3. Add the chiles and bell pepper and stir-fry slowly, allowing the skin of the bell pepper to blister.

4. Add the ginger and garlic and stir-fry for about 20 seconds until aromatic.

5. Add the shrimp, spreading them in a single layer. Cook the bottom side of the shrimp, then flip and stir-fry them for about 1 minute or until fully cooked.

6. Add the roasted peanuts and stir in the sauce.

7. When the sauce thickens, turn off the heat and toss in the scallions. Transfer to a serving dish and serve with steamed rice.

Garlicky Crab Rangoon

Prep time: 10 minutes | Cook time: 4 minutes | Serves 6

- 8 ounces (227 g) softened cream cheese
- 4 ounces (113 g) cooked lump crab meat
- 1 tablespoon minced chives
- ¼ teaspoon cayenne powder
- ¼ teaspoon garlic powder
- ¼ teaspoon black pepper
- ½ teaspoon kosher salt
- 24 wonton skins
- 2 cups peanut or vegetable oil
- 1 cup Sweet-and-Sour Sauce

1. In a medium bowl, mix the cream cheese, crab meat, chives, and seasonings together.

2. Take one wonton skin and brush the edge of each side with water. Place about 1 tablespoon of the mixture in the center of the skin. Fold 2 ends of the wrapper together, pinching to seal. Fold the other ends together to make a little parcel. Use your fingers and pinch together all the seams to thoroughly seal. Repeat with the remaining wonton skins.

3. Heat the oil in a wok to 375°F. In batches, fry the wontons for 2 to 3 minutes until golden brown. Remove to a plate lined with paper towels to drain. Repeat until all parcels have been fried.

4. Serve with immediately with Sweet-and-Sour Sauce.

Gingered Crab with Scallion

Prep time: 10 minutes | Cook time: 5 minutes | Serves 4 to 6

- **FOR THE SAUCE:**
- 4 tablespoons water
- 1½ tablespoons oyster sauce
- 1 teaspoon soy sauce
- ½ teaspoon sesame oil
- ½ teaspoon sugar
- ½ teaspoon cornstarch
- Pinch ground white pepper to taste
- **FOR THE STIR-FRY:**
- 1 tablespoon peanut oil
- 2-inch piece ginger, peeled and sliced
- 4 whole Dungeness or blue crabs (about 2 pounds each), cooked, cleaned, and cut (see here)
- 2 scallions, cut into 1-inch pieces

1. In a small bowl, make the sauce by mixing together the water, oyster sauce, soy sauce, sesame oil, sugar, cornstarch, and pepper.

2. Pour the peanut oil into the wok along with the ginger slices. Turn the heat to medium-high. Stir-fry the ginger until it is aromatic.

3. Add the crab and the sauce to the wok. Toss to coat the crab in the sauce.

4. Once the sauce thickens, turn off the heat and add the scallions. Stir-fry for a few seconds.

5. Transfer to a serving dish and serve immediately.

Spicy Cornstarch with Pan-Fried Fish

Prep time: 10 minutes | Cook time: 5 minutes | Serves 4

FOR THE PAN-FRIED FISH

- 1½ pounds (680 g) white fish fillet (cod, tilapia, or red snapper), cut into two or three pieces
- Salt and Pepper to taste
- 1 to 2 tablespoons cornstarch
- 1½ tablespoons peanut oil
- 2 tablespoons chopped scallions (optional)
- **FOR THE SAUCE**
- 1 tablespoon soy sauce
- ½ teaspoon sesame oil
- ½ teaspoon sugar

Pat the fish dry with a paper towel. Season on both sides with salt and pepper to taste, and dust with the cornstarch.

In a wok over medium-high heat, heat the peanut oil.

When the wok is smoking very slightly, place the fillets in the wok and leave untouched for about 3 minutes.

While the fish is cooking, make the sauce by whisking together the soy sauce, sesame oil, and sugar. Set it aside.

Gently flip the fish to cook on the other side for about 1 minute.

Test the fish with a fork. If it flakes easily, it is cooked.

Turn off the heat and pour the sauce into the wok around around the fish. Flip the fish one more time to coat and transfer it to a serving plate.

Garnish with the chopped scallions (if using), and serve immediately.

Honey with Mirin Teriyaki Salmon

Prep time: 15 minutes | Cook time: 8 minutes | Serves 4

- 2 tablespoons tamari
- 2 tablespoons honey
- 2 tablespoons mirin
- 2 tablespoons rice vinegar
- 1 tablespoon white miso
- 1 pound (454 g) thick, center-cut salmon fillet, cut into 1-inch pieces
- 2 tablespoons cooking oil
- 2 garlic cloves, crushed and chopped
- 1 tablespoon crushed, chopped ginger
- 1 medium onion, diced
- 4 ounces shiitake mushrooms, cut into slices
- 2 cups sugar snap or snow pea pods
- 2 scallions, cut into 1-inch pieces
- 1 tablespoon sesame seeds

In a large bowl, whisk together the tamari, honey, mirin, rice vinegar, and miso. Add the salmon, making sure to coat evenly with the marinade, and set aside.

2. In a wok over high heat, heat the cooking oil until it shimmers.

3. Add the garlic, ginger, and onion and stir-fry for 1 minute.

4. Add the mushrooms and stir-fry for 1 minute.

5. Add the pea pods and stir-fry for 1 minute.

6. Add the marinated salmon, reserving the marinade, and gently stir-fry for 1 minute.

7. Add the marinade and scallions and gently stir-fry for 30 seconds.

8. Sprinkle the sesame seeds on top. Serve over steamed medium-grain Japanese rice.

Eggy Scallops with Soy Sauce

Prep time: 10 minutes | Cook time: 4 minutes | Serves 4

- 1 large egg white
- 2 tablespoons cornstarch
- 2 tablespoons Shaoxing rice wine, divided
- 1 teaspoon kosher salt, divided
- 1 pound fresh sea scallops, rinsed, muscle removed, and patted dry
- 3 tablespoons vegetable oil, divided
- 1 tablespoon light soy sauce
- ¼ cup freshly squeezed orange juice
- Grated zest of 1 orange
- Red pepper flakes (optional)
- 2 scallions, green part only, thinly sliced, for garnish

1. In a large bowl, combine the egg white, cornstarch, 1 tablespoon of rice wine, and ½ teaspoon of salt and stir with a small whisk until the cornstarch completely dissolves and is no longer lumpy. Toss in the scallops and refrigerate for 30 minutes.

2. Remove the scallops from the fridge. Bring a medium-size pot of water to boil. Add 1 tablespoon of vegetable oil and reduce to a simmer. Add the scallops to the simmering water and cook for 15 to 20 seconds, stirring continuously until the scallops just turn opaque (the scallops will not be completely cooked through). Using a wok skimmer, transfer the scallops to a paper towel–lined baking sheet and pat dry with paper towels.

3. In a glass measuring cup, combine the remaining

1 tablespoon of rice wine, light soy, orange juice, orange zest, and a pinch of red pepper flakes (if using) and set aside.

4. Heat a wok over medium-high heat until a drop of water sizzles and evaporates on contact. Pour in the remaining 2 tablespoons of oil and swirl to coat the base of the wok. Season the oil by adding the remaining ½ teaspoon salt.

5. Add the velveted scallops to the wok and swirl in the sauce. Stir-fry the scallops until they are just cooked through, about 1 minute. Transfer to a serving dish and garnish with the scallions.

Spicy Fried Flounder

Prep time: 10 minutes | Cook time: 20 minutes | Serves 4

- 1-1¼ pounds (454-567g) whole flounder, sole, or fluke
- 2 teaspoons Shaoxing wine
- ¾ teaspoon salt
- ½ teaspoon white pepper
- 3 tablespoons cornstarch
- ⅔ cup canola oil

- 1 ½ tablespoons hot water
- ¼ teaspoon sugar
- 1 ½ tablespoons soy sauce
- 2 teaspoons Shaoxing wine
- 3 tablespoons oil
- 1 scallion, julienned
- 1 small handful cilantro, chopped

For the Sauce:

1. Mix hot water, sugar, soy sauce, wine, scallion, cilantro, and oil in a saucepan.

2. Cook this mixture for 5 minutes with occasional stirring, then allow the sauce to cool.

3. Mix cornstarch with white pepper, salt, and wine in a bowl.

4. Coat the flounder with the cornstarch mixture.

5. Heat oil in a deep wok for deep frying and deep fry the flounder until golden-brown.

6. Transfer the flounder to a plate lined with a paper towel.

7. Pour the prepared sauce over the fillet.

8. Serve warm.

Mushroom with Seafood and Broth

Prep time: 15 minutes | Cook time: 8 minutes | Serves 4

- 1 teaspoon hot sesame oil
- 1 tablespoon brown sugar
- ¼ cup oyster sauce
- ¼ cup vegetable or meat broth
- 1 tablespoon cornstarch
- 2 tablespoons cooking oil
- 4 garlic cloves, crushed and chopped
- 1 medium onion, cut into 1-inch pieces
- 4 ounces (113 g)

- shiitake mushrooms, sliced
- ¼ pound (114g) medium shrimp, shelled and deveined
- 1 cup broccoli florets
- ¼ pound scallops, cut in half widthwise
- 2 cups sugar snap or snow pea pods
- 1 red bell pepper, cut into 1-inch pieces
- ¼ pound (114g) squid tentacles, rinsed in cold water

1. In a small bowl, whisk together the sesame oil, brown sugar, oyster sauce, broth, and cornstarch. Set aside.

2. In a wok over high heat, heat the cooking oil until it shimmers.

3. Add the garlic and onion and stir-fry for 1 minute.

4. Add the mushrooms and stir-fry for 1 minute.

5. Add the shrimp and stir-fry for 1 minute.

6. Add the broccoli and stir-fry for 1 minute.

7. Add the scallops and stir-fry for 30 seconds.

8. Add the pea pods and stir-fry for 1 minute.

9. Add the bell pepper and stir-fry for 1 minute.

10. Add the squid and stir-fry for 30 seconds.

11. Add the sesame oil mixture to the wok and stir-fry until a glaze forms. Serve over steamed rice.

Soy Sauce with Steamed Fish

Prep time: 10 minutes | Cook time: 15 minutes | Serves 4

4 (4-ounce / 113-g) white fish fillets, such as flounder, sea bass, or red snapper

2 tablespoons soy sauce

1 tablespoon Shaoxing rice wine or dry sherry

1 tablespoon very

finely sliced, peeled fresh ginger

- 1 tablespoon very finely sliced scallion, both green and white parts

- 1 teaspoon toasted sesame oil

. Pat the fish dry with paper towels.

. In a small bowl, mix together the soy sauce, rice wine, ginger, sliced scallion, and sesame oil. Drizzle the sauce over the fish fillets. Gently place the fish in a bamboo steamer.

. Add 2 inches of water to your wok, and bring the water to a boil. Place the steamer in the wok, and cover the steamer with its lid. Steam the fish for 7 to 8 minutes, or until the fish is opaque and starts to flake.

Peppered Smoked Fish with Cinnamon Sauce

Prep time: 15 minutes | Cook time: 15 minutes | Serves 4

For the Fish and Marinade:

2 ½ pounds (1.1kg) small buffalo carp, cut into ¾-inch-thick sections

4 tablespoons Shaoxing wine

½ teaspoon ground white pepper

½ teaspoon salt

3 teaspoons ginger, grated

For the Sauce:

3 cups water

4 ginger slices

- 2-star anise
- 1 cinnamon stick
- 5 bay leaves
- 90 g brown rock sugar
- ½ cup Shaoxing wine
- 1 tablespoon oyster sauce
- 5 tablespoons light soy sauce
- 1 ½ tablespoons dark soy sauce
- ½ teaspoon Chinese black vinegar
- 4 scallions
- ½ cup orange juice

Mix wine with white pepper, salt, and ginger in a shallow large bowl.

Add the fish fillets to the wine mixture and cover

to marinate for 24 hours in the refrigerator.

3. Prepare the sauce, add water, ginger, star anise, cinnamon, bay leaves, brown sugar, wine, soy sauce, black vinegar, scallions, and orange juice in a saucepan.

4. Cook this mixture on medium heat until the sauce is reduced to half.

5. Strain the mixture and allow it to cool.

6. Meanwhile, remove the fish from the marinade, and set it aside.

7. Heat oil in a deep wok for deep frying and fry the fish until golden-brown.

8. Transfer the fish to a plate lined with a paper towel.

9. Pour the prepared sauce on top.

10. Serve warm.

Vinegary Poached Fish

Prep time: 10 minutes | Cook time: 20 minutes | Serves 4

- 2 tablespoons cornstarch
- 2 teaspoons sea salt
- 1 teaspoon freshly ground black pepper
- 1 pound (454 g) meaty fish fillet, such as tuna or mahi mahi, cleaned and cut into even pieces
- 1 tablespoon soy sauce
- 1 tablespoon honey
- 1 tablespoon apple cider vinegar
- 1 teaspoon toasted sesame oil
- 2 teaspoons chili sauce
- 1 scallion, julienned, both green and white parts

1. Mix the cornstarch with the sea salt and pepper. Dip the fish fillet into the cornstarch mixture, and coat the fish evenly on both sides. Gently place the fish in your wok.

2. Bring water to a boil in another pot or kettle. It needs to be enough water to fully cover the fish in the wok. Once the water comes to a boil, pour it over the fish so that it's completely covered. Tightly cover the wok with a lid or aluminum foil. Poach the fish for 12 to 14 minutes.

3. While the fish is poaching, create the sauce by mixing together the soy sauce, honey, apple cider vinegar, sesame oil, and chili sauce in a small

bowl.

4. When the fish is ready, drain it and transfer it to a serving dish, pour the sauce over the fish, and garnish it with the julienned scallion.

Chili Squid with Lemon Wedges

Prep time: 10 minutes | Cook time: 5 minutes | Serves 4

- ½ teaspoon sea salt
- ½ teaspoon freshly ground black pepper
- ¼ teaspoon
- Sichuan peppercorns
- 1 tablespoon peanut or vegetable oil
- 1 pound (454 g) squid, cleaned and cut into rings or 2-inch tentacles
- Lemon wedges, for garnish
- Chili soy sauce, for garnish

1. In a small bowl, mix the sea salt, pepper, and Sichuan peppercorns.

2. Heat your wok over high heat until a drop of water sizzles on contact, and then add the peanut oil. Swirl the oil to coat the bottom of the wok. Add the squid and toss it for about 30 seconds. Then sprinkle it with the salt-and-pepper mix. Stir-fry the squid for another minute but no more, as it cooks almost instantly. Overcooked squid has a rubbery texture.

3. Serve immediately with the lemon wedges and chili soy sauce.

Peppered Squid with Goat Cheese

Prep time: 10 minutes | Cook time: 5 minutes | Serves 4

- ½ teaspoon sea salt
- ½ teaspoon freshly ground black pepper
- ¼ teaspoon
- Sichuan peppercorns
- 1 tablespoon peanut or vegetable oil
- 1 pound (454 g) squid, cleaned and cut into rings or 2-inch tentacles
- Lemon wedges, for garnish
- Chili soy sauce, for garnish

1. In a small bowl, mix the sea salt, pepper, and Sichuan peppercorns.

2. Heat your wok over high heat until a drop of water sizzles on contact, and then add the peanut oil. Swirl the oil to coat the bottom of the wok. Add the squid and toss it for about 30 seconds. Then sprinkle it with the salt-and-pepper mix. Stir-fry the squid for another minute but no more, as it cooks almost instantly. Overcooked squid has a rubbery texture.

3. Serve immediately with the lemon wedges and chili soy sauce.

Garlicky Shrimp with Vinegar

Prep time: 15 minutes | Cook time: 5 minutes | Serves 4

- 8 ounces / 227 g cellophane noodles
- 1 pound (454 g) shrimp, peeled, cleaned, and deveined
- 2 teaspoons cornstarch
- ½ teaspoon sea salt
- ¼ teaspoon freshly ground black pepper
- 1 tablespoon soy sauce
- 1 tablespoon honey
- 1 tablespoon rice vinegar
- 2 teaspoons chili sauce
- 1 tablespoon Shaoxing rice wine or dry sherr
- 1 tablespoon peanut or vegetable oil
- 2 teaspoons minced garlic
- 1 teaspoon minced fresh ginger

1. Soak the cellophane noodles in hot water for 10 minutes, or until soft. Drain and set aside.

2. In a large bowl, toss the shrimp with the cornstarch, sea salt, and pepper . Let it sit for 5 minutes.

3. In a small bowl, make the sauce by mixing together the soy sauce, honey, rice vinegar, chili sauce, and rice wine. Set the bowl aside.

4. Heat your wok over high heat until a drop of wate sizzles on contact. Add the peanut oil and swirl to coat the wok. Add the garlic and ginger, and stir-fry them for about 20 seconds. Add the shrim and stir-fry them for 2 to 3 minutes, or until they become bright pink.

5. Remove the wok from the heat. Pour the sauce over the shrimp, add the cellophane noodles, and toss to combine everything. Transfer to a plate an

serve immediately.

Spicy Chinese Shrimp Cakes

Prep time: 15 minutes | Cook time: 10 minutes | Serves 10

- 1 pound (454 g) shrimp, chopped
- 1 small carrot, blanched and chopped
- 5 water chestnuts, minced
- ¼ cup cilantro, finely chopped
- 1 teaspoon ginger, grated
- 2 teaspoons Shaoxing wine
- ½ teaspoon salt
- ⅛ teaspoon ground white pepper
- 2 teaspoons oyster sauce
- 1 teaspoon sesame oil
- ¼ teaspoon sugar
- 1 teaspoon cornstarch
- 3 tablespoons oil

Mix water chestnuts, shrimp, carrot, ginger, cilantro, wine, white, and rest of the ingredients (except oil) in a bowl.

Add oil to a Cantonese wok and place it over medium-high heat.

Make 10 patties out of this mixture and sear the patties in batches in the skillet.

Cook the patties for 5 minutes per side until golden-brown.

Serve warm.

Scallions with Stir-Fried Shrimp

Prep time: 5 minutes | Cook time: 10 minutes | Serves 4

- 1 pound (454 g) medium-large shrimp (U31–40), peeled and deveined, tails left on
- 2 tablespoons vegetable oil
- Kosher salt to taste
- 2 teaspoons Shaoxing rice wine
- 2 scallions, finely julienned

Using sharp kitchen scissors or a paring knife, slice the shrimp in half lengthwise, keeping the tail section intact. As the shrimp is stir-fried, cutting it this way will give more surface area and create a unique shape and texture!

2. Blot the shrimp dry with paper towels and keep dry. The drier the shrimp, the more flavorful the dish. You can keep the shrimp refrigerated, rolled up in a paper towel, for up to 2 hours before cooking.

3. Heat a wok over medium-high heat until a drop of water sizzles and evaporates on contact. Pour in the oil and swirl to coat the base of the wok. Season the oil by adding a small pinch of salt to taste, and swirl gently.

4. Add the shrimp all at once to the hot wok. Toss and flip quickly for 2 to 3 minutes, until the shrimp just begins to turn pink. Season with another small pinch of salt to taste, and add the rice wine. Let the wine boil off while you continue stir-frying, about another 2 minutes. The shrimp should separate and curl, still attached at the tail.

5. Transfer to a serving platter and garnish with the scallions. Serve hot.

Cilantro with Deep-Fried Squid

Prep time: 10 minutes | Cook time: 10 minutes | Serves 4

- 3 cups vegetable oil
- 1 pound (454 g) squid tubes and tentacles, cleaned and tubes cut into ⅓-inch rings
- ½ cup rice flour
- Kosher salt to taste
- ¼ teaspoon freshly ground black pepper
- ¾ cup sparkling water, kept ice cold
- 2 tablespoons coarsely chopped fresh cilantro

1. Pour the oil into the wok; the oil should be about 1 to 1½ inches deep. Bring the oil to 370ºF (188ºC) over medium-high heat. You can tell the oil is at the right temperature when the oil bubbles and sizzles around the end of a wooden spoon when it is dipped in. Blot the squid dry with paper towels.

2. Meanwhile, in a shallow bowl, stir the rice flour with a pinch of salt and the pepper to taste. Whisk in just enough sparkling water to form a thin batter. Fold in the squid and, working in batches, lift up the squid from the batter using a wok skimmer or slotted spoon, shaking off any excess. Carefully lower into the hot oil.

3. Cook the squid for about 3 minutes, until golden

brown and crisp. Using a wok skimmer, remove the calamari from the oil and transfer to a paper towel–lined plate and season lightly with salt to taste. Repeat with the remaining squid.

4. Transfer the squid to a platter and garnish with the cilantro. Serve hot.

Gingered Bean Sauce with Mussels

Prep time: 10 minutes | Cook time: 10 minutes | Serves 4

- 3 tablespoons vegetable oil
- 2 peeled fresh ginger slices, each about the size of a quarter
- Kosher salt to taste
- 2 scallions, cut into 2-inch-long pieces
- 4 large garlic cloves, thinly sliced
- 2 pounds (907 g) live PEI mussels, scrubbed

and debearded
- 2 tablespoons Shaoxing rice wine
- 2 tablespoons Black Bean Sauce or store-bought black bean sauce
- 2 teaspoons sesame oil
- ½ bunch fresh cilantro, coarsely chopped

1. Heat a wok over medium-high heat until a drop of water sizzles and evaporates on contact. Pour in the vegetable oil and swirl to coat the base of the wok. Season the oil by adding the ginger slices and a small pinch of salt to taste. Allow the ginger to sizzle in the oil for about 30 seconds, swirling gently.

2. Toss in the scallions and garlic and stir-fry for 10 seconds, or until the scallions are wilted.

3. Add the mussels and toss to coat with the oil. Pour the rice wine down the sides of the wok and toss briefly. Cover and steam for 6 to 8 minutes, until the mussels are opened.

4. Uncover and add the black bean sauce, tossing to coat the mussels. Cover and let steam for another 2 minutes. Uncover and pick through, removing any mussels that have not opened.

5. Drizzle the mussels with the sesame oil. Toss briefly until the sesame oil is fragrant. Discard the ginger, transfer the mussels to a platter, and garnish with the cilantro.

Milky Curry Crab

Prep time: 15 minutes | Cook time: 15 minutes | Serves 4

- 2 tablespoons vegetable oil
- 2 peeled slices fresh ginger, about the size of a quarter
- Kosher salt to taste
- 1 shallot, thinly sliced
- 1 tablespoon curry powder
- 1 (13.5-ounce / 382-g) can coconut milk
- ¼ teaspoon sugar
- 1 tablespoon Shaoxin rice wine
- 1 pound canned crabmeat, drained and picked through t remove shell pieces
- Freshly ground black pepper to taste
- ¼ cup chopped fresh cilantro or flat-leaf parsley, for garnish
- Cooked rice, for serving

1. Heat a wok over medium-high heat until a drop of water sizzles and evaporates on contact. Pour in the oil and swirl to coat the base of the wok. Season the oil by adding the ginger slices and a pinch of salt to taste. Allow the ginger to sizzle in the oil for about 30 seconds, swirling gently.

2. Add the shallot and stir-fry for about 10 seconds. Add the curry powder and stir until fragrant for another 10 seconds.

3. Stir in the coconut milk, sugar, and rice wine, cover the wok, and cook for 5 minutes.

4. Stir in the crab, cover with the lid, and cook until heated through, about 5 minutes. Remove the lid adjust the seasoning with salt and pepper to tast and discard the ginger. Ladle over the top of a bowl of rice and garnish with chopped cilantro.

Panko Crab Cakes with Tartar Sauce

Prep time: 15 minutes | Cook time: 20 minutes | Serves 4

For the Crab Cakes:

- ¼ cup mayonnaise
- 2 scallions, chopped
- 2 eggs
- 1 tablespoon Dijon

mustard
- 2 teaspoons Old Bay seasoning
- 2 teaspoons lime jui
- 1 pound (454 g) lum crabmeat

Fish and Seafo

1 ½ cups panko breadcrumbs

2 tablespoons toasted sesame seeds

Salt and black pepper, to taste

Oil, for cooking

or the Tartar Sauce:

½ cup mayonnaise

- 2 tablespoons pickles, chopped

- 2 tablespoons red onion, chopped

- ¼ cup cilantro, chopped

- 1 tablespoon lime juice

- Mix crabmeat with breadcrumbs, sesame seeds, salt, black pepper, lime juice, Old Bay seasoning, mayonnaise, scallions, eggs, and mustard in a bowl.

- Make 8 equal-sized patties out of this mixture and refrigerate the patties for 10 minutes.

- Meanwhile, blend all ingredients for tartar sauce in a blender.

- Sear the crab cakes in hot oil in a Mandarin wok over medium heat until golden-brown.

- Serve warm with tartar sauce.

Basic Fried Oysters

rep time: 10 minutes | Cook time: 10 minutes | erves 4

1 ½ cups all-purpose bleached flour with a high gluten content

280 ml of cold water

¾ teaspoon salt

2 tablespoons of baking powder

2 tablespoons of

- peanut oil

- 5 cups of peanut oil

- 20 medium-sized fresh oysters, opened, removed from the shells, patted dry and dusted with flour

Mix all ingredients for the dough in a bowl and set aside. Heat the wok over high heat for 1 minute. Add the peanut oil and heat it to a temperature of 375ºF (190ºC).

Spread the batter evenly on each oyster. When a little smoke picks up in the air, add the coated oysters to the hot oil. Fry 5 coated oysters in batches for 3 minutes or until the oysters are light brown in color.

Place the fried oysters in a colander that you place on a bowl to drain off excess oil.

4. Fry the last batch of oysters for about 4 minutes or until golden brown. Return the other fried oysters to the hot oil and fry for another 2 minutes until golden brown.

5. Always pay attention to the heating level of the oven during deep-frying. Reduce the heat if the oysters are getting too brown or increase the heat if the oysters cook slowly.

Mushrooms with Garlicky Prawns

Prep time: 15 minutes | Cook time: 10 minutes | Serves 4

- 2 tablespoons of rapeseed oil

- 10 cloves of garlic (chopped)

- 1 teaspoon of chopped fresh ginger root

- 225 g can of chopped water chestnuts (drained)

- 1 cup of snow peas

- 1 cup of small white mushrooms

- 1 teaspoon of crushed red pepper flakes

- ½ teaspoon salt

- 1 teaspoon ground

- black pepper

- 450 g peeled and chopped jumbo prawns

- ½ cup of chicken broth

- 1 tablespoon rice vinegar

- 2 tablespoons of fish sauce

- 2 tablespoons of dry sherry

- 1 tablespoon of cornstarch

- 1 tablespoon of water

1. Heat the oil in a wok or in a large pan until it is very hot. Cook the garlic and ginger in the hot oil and stir until they are fragrant, about 30 seconds. Add the water chestnuts, sugar snap peas, mushrooms, red pepper flakes, salt, pepper and prawns to the pan.

2. Cook, stirring, until the prawns turn pink (2 to 3 minutes). Mix the chicken broth, rice vinegar, fish sauce, and dry sherry in a small bowl for 2 to 3 minutes. Pour into the shrimp mixture; boil and stir briefly to combine.

3. Mix the corn starch with water and add to the wok. Stir until the sauce thickens, about 2 minutes.

Eggy Shrimp Tempura with Cornstarch

Prep time: 10 minutes | Cook time: 10 minutes | Serves 4

- 1 cup all-purpose flour
- 2 tablespoons of cornstarch
- 1 pinch of salt
- 1 cup of water
- 1 egg yolk
- 2 egg whites, lightly beaten
- 450 gr. Medium-sized shrimp (peeled and peeled)
- 2 cups of vegetable oil for frying

1. Heat the oil in a deep fryer to 375ºF (190ºC) and whisk the flour, cornstarch and salt in a large bowl. Make a well in the middle of the flour.

2. Mix in the water and egg yolk. Mix only until it is damp; the dough becomes lumpy. Stir in the egg whites and dip the prawns one after the other in the batter.

3. Carefully place a few prawns one after the other in the hot oil. Approx. Fry for 1 ½ minutes until golden brown. Drain on paper towels.

Spicy Buttered Scallops

Prep time: 10 minutes | Cook time: 10 minutes | Serves 4

- ½ stick butter (4 tablespoons), divided
- Splash chili oil
- 24 large scallops, patted dry
- Sea salt to taste
- Freshly ground black pepper to taste
- 2 teaspoons peanut oil
- ½ sweet onion, diced
- 2 red bell peppers, diced
- 2 teaspoons hoisin sauce, thinned with 1 teaspoon water

1. Heat your wok over high heat until a drop of water sizzles on contact. Melt 1 to 2 tablespoons of butter with a splash of chili oil in the wok. Working in batches, add the scallops to the wok. The scallops should not crowd each other. Sear the bottoms of the scallops until browned, about 1 minute. Turn the scallops and sear the other sides, about 1 minute. Season the scallops with the sea salt and pepper to taste after you have turned them to sear on the second side. Transfer the finished scallops to a plate, and cover them with foil. Repeat this step until all the scallops are cooked.

2. Over high heat, add the peanut oil to the wok. When the oil is hot, add the onion and peppers, and stir-fry for 2 to 3 minutes. Add the hoisin sauce and toss to coat the vegetables.

3. When the vegetables are done, return the scallops to the wok. Toss them to combine with the vegetables, and remove the wok from the heat. Serve.

Syrupy Teriyaki Salmon

Prep time: 15 minutes | Cook time: 5 minutes | Serves 4

- 8 ounces / 227 g fresh salmon fillet, skin removed, diced into 1-inch pieces
- 1 tablespoon cornstarch
- 2 tablespoons Shaoxing rice wine
- 2 tablespoons soy sauce
- 2 tablespoons maple syrup
- 2 tablespoons cooking oil
- 2 garlic cloves, crushed and chopped
- 1 tablespoon crushed
- and chopped peeled ginger
- 1 medium carrot, roll-cut into ½-inch pieces
- 1 medium onion, dice into 1-inch pieces
- 1 cup sugar snap pea pods
- 1 red bell pepper, diced into 1-inch pieces
- 4 scallions, green and white parts, cut diagonally into ¼-inch pieces
- Cooked rice or noodles, for serving

1. In a medium bowl, combine the salmon, cornstarch, wine, soy sauce, and maple syrup. Mix well.

2. In a wok, heat the cooking oil over high heat until it begins to smoke.

3. Add the garlic, ginger, and carrot. Stir-fry for 1 minute, or until the garlic and ginger are fragrant.

4. Add the onion and stir-fry for 1 minute, or until it is lightly coated with oil.

5. Add the salmon and stir-fry for 1 minute, or until it begins to turn opaque.

6. Add the pea pods and bell pepper. Stir-fry for 1 minute, or until the peas are bright green but still.

crisp.

Add the scallions and toss. Serve over rice or noodles.

Brothy Stir-Fried Cod

Prep time: 15 minutes | Cook time: 7 minutes | Serves 4

- 1 pound (454 g) cod fillets
- 2 tablespoons light soy sauce
- 1 tablespoon Chinese rice wine or dry sherry
- ½ teaspoon sesame oil
- 3 teaspoons cornstarch, divided
- ⅓ cup chicken broth
- 1 tablespoon oyster sauce
- 1 teaspoon granulated sugar
- 4 teaspoons water
- 3 tablespoons vegetable or peanut oil, divided
- 2 teaspoons minced ginger, divided
- 2 ribs celery, cut on the diagonal into ½" pieces
- ¼ teaspoon salt
- 1 small red bell pepper, seeded and cut into bite-sized cubes
- 1-2 tablespoons additional water, optional

Cut the fish into cubes. Place the cubes in a large bowl, and add the light soy sauce, rice wine or sherry, Asian sesame oil, and 2 teaspoons cornstarch. Marinate the fish for 15 minutes.

In a small bowl, combine the chicken broth, oyster sauce, and sugar. Set aside.

In a separate small bowl, dissolve 1 teaspoon cornstarch into the water. Set aside.

Heat a wok or skillet over medium-high heat until it is nearly smoking and add 2 tablespoons oil. When the oil is hot, add half the ginger. Stir-fry for 10 seconds.

Add the fish cubes. Stir-fry the fish cubes for about 2 minutes or until they begin to brown. Remove the fish and drain in a colander or on paper towels.

Heat 1 tablespoon oil in the wok or skillet. When the oil is hot, add the remainder of the ginger. Stir-fry for 10 seconds, then add the celery. Stir-fry the celery for 1 minute, sprinkling with the salt to taste. Add the red bell pepper, and stir-fry for 1 minute. Splash the vegetables with 1–2

tablespoons of water if they begin to dry out.

7. Push the vegetables to the sides of the pan. Add the chicken broth mixture and bring to a boil. Stir the cornstarch and water and add into the sauce, stirring quickly to thicken.

8. Once the sauce has thickened, add the fish back into the pan. Stir-fry for 1 minute to mix the ingredients. Serve hot.

Limey Mussels with Mixed Greens

Prep time: 15 minutes | Cook time: 5 minutes | Serves 4

- 2 tablespoons coconut oil
- 4 garlic cloves, crushed and chopped
- 2 tablespoons crushed and chopped peeled ginger
- 1 medium carrot, roll-cut into 1-inch pieces
- 1 large onion, diced into 1-inch pieces
- Grated zest and juice of 1 lime
- ¼ cup green or red curry paste
- ½ cup coconut milk
- 1 tablespoon fish
- sauce
- 2 pounds mussels, cleaned and debearded
- 1 cup sliced (1-inch) napa cabbage
- 1 cup sliced (1-inch) bok choy
- 4 scallions, green and white parts, cut diagonally into 1-inch pieces
- Fresh cilantro, coarsely chopped, for garnish
- Cooked rice, for serving

1. In a wok, heat the coconut oil over high heat until it begins to smoke.

2. Add the garlic, ginger, and carrot. Stir-fry for 1 minute, or until the garlic and ginger are fragrant.

3. Add the onion and stir-fry for 1 minute, or until it is lightly coated with oil.

4. Add the lime zest, lime juice, curry paste, coconut milk, and fish sauce. Bring to a boil.

5. Add the mussels, cover, and cook for 1 minute. Stir, cover, and cook for 1 more minute, or until they begin to open.

6. Stir in the cabbage, bok choy, and scallions. Cover and cook for 1 minute, or until the bok choy leaves

7. Discard any unopened mussels. Remove from the heat.

8. Garnish with the cilantro and serve over rice.

Chapter 6: Poultry

Brothy Cornstarch with Mushrooms

Prep time: 15 minutes | Cook time: 25 minutes | Serves 4

- 1 tablespoon light soy sauce
- 1 tablespoon Shaoxing rice wine
- 2 teaspoons sesame oil
- ¾ pound (340 g) boneless, skinless chicken breasts, sliced into thin strips
- ½ cup low-sodium chicken broth
- 2 tablespoons oyster sauce
- 1 teaspoon sugar
- 1 tablespoon cornstarch

- 3 tablespoons vegetable oil, divided
- 4 peeled fresh ginger slices, each about the size of a quarter
- Kosher salt
- 4 ounces fresh button mushrooms, thinly sliced
- 1 (4-ounce/113 g) can sliced bamboo shoots, drained
- 1 (4-ounce/113 g) can sliced water chestnuts, drained
- 1 garlic clove, finely minced

1. In a large bowl, whisk together the light soy, rice wine, and sesame oil until smooth. Add the chicken and toss to coat. Marinate for 15 minutes.

2. In a small bowl, whisk together chicken broth, oyster sauce, sugar, and cornstarch until smooth and set aside.

3. Heat a wok over medium-high heat until a drop of water sizzles and evaporates on contact. Pour in 2 tablespoons of vegetable oil and swirl to coat the base of the wok. Season the oil by adding the ginger and a small pinch of salt. Allow the ginger to sizzle in the oil for about 30 seconds, swirling gently.

4. Add the chicken and discard the marinade. Stir-fry for 2 to 3 minutes, until the chicken is no

longer pink. Transfer to a clean bowl and set asid[e]

5. Add the remaining 1 tablespoon of vegetable oil. Stir-fry the mushrooms for 3 to 4 minutes, tossing and flipping quickly. As soon as the mushrooms become dry, stop stir-frying and let the mushrooms sit against the hot wok for about [a] minute. Toss again and then rest again for anoth[er] minute.

6. Add the bamboo shoots, water chestnuts, and garlic. Stir-fry for 1 minute, or until the garlic is fragrant. Return the chicken to the wok and toss [to] combine.

7. Stir the sauce together and add to the wok. Stir-f[ry] and cook until the sauce begins to boil, about 45 seconds. Keep tossing and flipping until the sauc[e] thickens and becomes glossy. Remove the ginger and discard. Transfer to a platter and serve while hot.

Eggy Chicken with Snow Peas

Prep time: 10 minutes | Cook time: 16 minutes | Serves 4

- 2 large egg whites
- 2 tablespoons cornstarch, plus 1 teaspoon
- ¾ pound(340 g) boneless, skinless chicken breasts, cut into bite-size slices
- 3½ tablespoons vegetable oil, divided
- ⅓ cup low-sodium chicken broth
- 1 tablespoon Shaoxing rice wine

- Kosher salt
- Ground white peppe[r]
- 4 peeled fresh ginger slices, each about the size of a quarter
- 1 (4-ounce/113 g) ca[n] sliced bamboo shoot[s] rinsed and drained
- 3 garlic cloves, minc[ed]
- ¾ pound (340 g) sno[w] peas or sugar snap peas, strings remove[d]

1. In a mixing bowl, using a fork or whisk, beat the egg whites until frothy and the tighter clumps of egg white are foamy. Stir in the 2 tablespoons of cornstarch until well blended and no longer clumpy. Fold in the chicken and 1 tablespoon of vegetable oil and marinate for 10 minutes or up [to] 30 minutes.

2. In a small bowl, stir together the chicken broth,

rice wine, and remaining 1 teaspoon of cornstarch, and season with a pinch each of salt and white pepper. Set aside.

Bring a medium saucepan filled with water to a boil over high heat. Add ½ tablespoon of oil and reduce the heat to a simmer. Using a wok skimmer or slotted spoon to allow the marinade to drain off, transfer the chicken to the boiling water. Give the chicken a stir so that the pieces do not clump together. Cook for 40 to 50 seconds, until the chicken is white on the outside but not cooked through. Drain the chicken in a colander and shake off the excess water. Discard the simmering water.

Heat a wok over medium-high heat until a drop of water sizzles and evaporates on contact. Pour in the remaining 2 tablespoons of oil and swirl to coat the base of the wok. Season the oil by adding the ginger slices and salt. Allow the ginger to sizzle in the oil for about 30 seconds, swirling gently.

Add the bamboo shoots and garlic and, using a wok spatula, toss to coat with oil and cook until fragrant, about 30 seconds. Add the snow peas and stir-fry for about 2 minutes until bright green and crisp tender. Add the chicken to the wok and swirl in the sauce mixture. Toss to coat and continue cooking for 1 to 2 minutes, until the chicken is completely cooked.

Transfer to a platter and discard the ginger. Serve hot.

Green Bean Chicken

Prep time: 10 minutes | Cook time: 21 minutes | Serves 4

- ¾ pound (340 g) boneless, skinless chicken thighs, sliced across the grain into bite-size strips
- 3 tablespoons Shaoxing rice wine, divided
- 2 teaspoons cornstarch
- Kosher salt
- Red pepper flakes
- 3 tablespoons vegetable oil, divided
- 4 peeled fresh ginger slices, each about the size of a quarter
- ¾ pound (340 g) green beans, trimmed and halved crosswise diagonally
- 2 tablespoons light soy sauce
- 1 tablespoon seasoned

rice vinegar
- ¼ cup slivered almonds, toasted
- 2 teaspoons sesame oil

1. In a mixing bowl, combine the chicken with 1 tablespoon of rice wine, cornstarch, a small pinch of salt, and a pinch of red pepper flakes. Stir to evenly coat the chicken. Marinate for 10 minutes.

2. Heat a wok over medium-high heat until a drop of water sizzles and evaporates on contact. Pour in 2 tablespoons of vegetable oil and swirl to coat the base of the wok. Season the oil by adding the ginger and a small pinch of salt. Allow the ginger to sizzle in the oil for about 30 seconds, swirling gently.

3. Add the chicken and marinade to the wok and stir-fry for 3 to 4 minutes, or until the chicken is slightly seared and no longer pink. Transfer to a clean bowl and set aside.

4. Add the remaining 1 tablespoon of vegetable oil and stir-fry the green beans for 2 to 3 minutes, or until they turn bright green. Return the chicken to the wok and toss together. Add the remaining 2 tablespoons of rice wine, light soy, and vinegar. Toss to combine and coat and allow the green beans to simmer for 3 more minutes, or until the green beans are tender. Remove the ginger and discard.

5. Toss the almonds in and transfer to a platter. Drizzle with the sesame oil and serve hot.

Vinegar with Spiced Chicken

Prep time: 10 minutes | Cook time: 10 minutes | Serves 4

- 2 teaspoons cornstarch
- 2 tablespoons water
- 3 tablespoons vegetable oil, divided
- 4 peeled fresh ginger slices, each about the size of a quarter
- Kosher salt
- ¾ pound (340 g) boneless, skinless chicken thighs, cut into bite-size chunks
- ½ red bell pepper, cut into ½-inch pieces
- ½ green bell pepper, cut into ½-inch pieces
- ½ yellow onion, cut into ½-inch pieces
- 1 (8-ounce/227 g) can pineapple chunks, drained, juices reserved
- 1 (4-ounce/113 g) can sliced water chestnuts, drained

- ¼ cup low-sodium chicken broth
- 2 tablespoons light brown sugar
- 2 tablespoons apple cider vinegar
- 2 tablespoons ketchup
- 1 teaspoon Worcestershire sauce
- 3 scallions, thinly sliced, for garnish

1. In a small bowl, stir together the cornstarch and water and set aside.

2. Heat a wok over medium-high heat until a drop of water sizzles and evaporates on contact. Pour in 2 tablespoons of oil and swirl to coat the base of the wok. Season the oil by adding the ginger and a pinch of salt. Allow the ginger to sizzle in the oil for about 30 seconds, swirling gently.

3. Add the chicken and sear against the wok for 2 to 3 minutes. Flip and toss the chicken, stir-frying for about 1 minute more, or until no longer pink. Transfer to a bowl and set aside.

4. Add the remaining 1 tablespoon of oil and swirl to coat. Stir-fry the red and green bell peppers and onion for 3 to 4 minutes, until soft and translucent. Add the pineapple and water chestnuts and continue to stir-fry for another minute. Add the vegetables to the chicken and set aside.

Soy Sauce with Chicken and Honey

Prep time: 10 minutes | Cook time: 10 minutes | Serves 4

- ¾ pound (340 g) fresh green beans, trimmed
- 2 tablespoons soy sauce
- 1 garlic clove, minced
- 1 teaspoon chili sauce
- 1 teaspoon honey
- 2 teaspoons peanut or vegetable oil
- 1 pound (454 g) boneless, skinless chicken breasts, cut into thin strips

1. Parboil the green beans in a small pot for 2 to 3 minutes, until vibrant green. Drain the beans and set aside.

2. In a small bowl, mix together the soy sauce, garlic, chili sauce, and honey. Set aside.

3. Heat your wok on high heat until a drop of water sizzles on contact. Add the peanut oil and swirl to coat the wok. Add the chicken to the wok, and stir-fry for 1 to 2 minutes. Add the green beans to the wok, and continue stir-frying for about 2 minutes.

4. Pour in the soy sauce mixture and stir to combine. Continue cooking for another 2 to 3 minutes, or until the sauce has thickened slightly.

Spicy Chicken with Brothy Sauce

Prep time: 15 minutes | Cook time: 10 minutes | Serves 4

- 3 large egg whites
- 3 tablespoons cornstarch, divided
- 1½ tablespoons light soy sauce, divided
- 1 pound (454 g) boneless, skinless chicken thighs, cut into bite-size pieces
- 3 cups vegetable oil
- 3 peeled fresh ginger slices, each about the size of a quarter
- Kosher salt
- Red pepper flakes
- 3 garlic cloves, coarsely chopped
- ¼ cup low-sodium chicken broth
- 2 tablespoons sesame oil
- 2 scallions, thinly sliced, for garnish
- 1 tablespoon sesame seeds, for garnish

1. In a mixing bowl, using a fork or whisk, beat the egg whites until frothy and the tighter clumps of egg white are foamy. Stir together 2 tablespoons of cornstarch and 2 teaspoons of light soy until well blended. Fold in the chicken and marinate for 10 minutes.

2. Pour the oil into the wok; the oil should be about 1 to 1½ inches deep. Bring the oil to 375°F (135°C) over medium-high heat. You can tell the oil is at the right temperature when you dip the end of a wooden spoon into the oil. If the oil bubbles and sizzles around it, the oil is ready.

3. Using a slotted spoon or wok skimmer, lift the chicken from the marinade and shake off the excess. Carefully lower into the hot oil. Fry the chicken in batches for 3 to 4 minutes, or until the chicken is golden brown and crispy on the surface. Transfer to a paper towel–lined plate.

4. Pour out all but 1 tablespoon of oil from the wok and set it over medium-high heat. Swirl the oil to coat the base of the wok. Season the oil by adding

the ginger and a pinch of salt and red pepper flakes. Allow the ginger and pepper flakes to sizzle in the oil for about 30 seconds, swirling gently.

Add the garlic and stir-fry, tossing and flipping with a wok spatula for 30 seconds. Stir in the chicken broth, remaining 2½ teaspoons of light soy, and remaining 1 tablespoon of cornstarch. Simmer for 4 to 5 minutes, until the sauce thickens and becomes glossy. Add the sesame oil and stir to combine.

Turn off the heat and add the fried chicken, tossing to coat with the sauce. Remove the ginger and discard. Transfer to a platter and garnish with the sliced scallions and sesame seeds.

Gingered Chicken with Spiced Vegetables

Prep time: 10 minutes | Cook time: 9 minutes | Serves 4

- 1 tablespoon light soy sauce
- 1 teaspoon sesame oil
- 1 teaspoon cornstarch
- ¾ pound (340 g) boneless, skinless chicken thighs, cut into bite-size pieces
- 3 tablespoons vegetable oil, divided
- 1 peeled fresh ginger slice, about the size of a quarter
- Kosher salt

- 1 small yellow onion, cut into bite-size pieces
- ½ red bell pepper, cut into bite-size pieces
- ½ yellow or green bell pepper, cut into bite-size pieces
- 3 garlic cloves, chopped
- ⅓ cup Black Bean Sauce or store-bought black bean sauce

In a large bowl, stir the light soy, sesame oil, and cornstarch together until the cornstarch dissolves. Add the chicken and toss to coat in the marinade. Set the chicken aside to marinate for 10 minutes.

Heat a wok over medium-high heat until a drop of water sizzles and evaporates on contact. Pour in 2 tablespoons of vegetable oil and swirl to coat the base of the wok. Season the oil by adding the ginger and a pinch of salt. Allow the ginger to sizzle in the oil for about 30 seconds, swirling gently.

Transfer the chicken to the wok and discard the

marinade. Let the pieces sear in the wok for 2 to 3 minutes. Flip to sear on the other side for another 1 to 2 minutes more. Stir-fry by tossing and flipping around in the wok quickly for 1 more minute. Transfer to a clean bowl.

4. Add the remaining 1 tablespoon of oil and toss in the onion and bell peppers. Quickly stir-fry for 2 to 3 minutes, tossing and flipping the vegetables with a wok spatula until the onion looks translucent but is still firm in texture. Add the garlic and stir-fry for another 30 seconds.

5. Return the chicken to the wok and add the black bean sauce. Toss and flip until the chicken and vegetables are coated.

6. Transfer to a platter, discard the ginger, and serve hot.

Ginger with Sugared Smoked Chicken

Prep time: 10 minutes | Cook time: 30 minutes | Serves 4

- ¼ cup low-sodium soy sauce
- 5 tablespoons Shaoxing wine
- 1 tablespoon cornstarch
- 2 pounds (907 g) skinless, boneless chicken thighs, trimmed of fat, and cut

- into 2-inch pieces
- 1 tablespoon brown sugar
- ¼ cup uncooked rice
- ¼ cup black tea leaves, preferably oolong
- 2 tablespoons Chinese five-spice powder
- 4 slices ginger

1. In a large bowl, mix the soy sauce, rice wine, and cornstarch. Add the chicken, toss to coat the pieces, and let them marinate for at least 30 minutes.

2. In a small bowl, mix together the brown sugar, rice, tea leaves, Chinese five-spice powder, and ginger. These are the ingredients used for smoking the chicken.

3. Prepare the wok to smoke the chicken. Line the bottom of your wok with a piece of aluminum foil large enough that it hangs over the edges of the wok. Place the smoking ingredients on the foil, and spread them around evenly. Place a wire rack or metal steamer basket on top of the smoking

ingredients. Cover the rack with foil.

4. Place the chicken on top of the foil-covered rack, and cover it with the wok lid. Fold the overhanging foil over the wok lid. Turn the heat to medium-high. Once you start to see smoke, turn the heat down to medium.

5. Smoke the chicken for 10 minutes without removing the lid. After 10 minutes, turn off the heat. Do not remove the lid from the wok. Let the chicken smoke in the wok for another 20 minutes.

Garlicky Chicken with Bean Sauce

Prep time: 10 minutes | Cook time: 6 minutes | Serves 4

- 2 tablespoons peanut oil
- 1 pound (454 g) boneless, skinless chicken thighs, trimmed of fat and cut into bite-size pieces
- 1 tablespoon grated fresh ginger
- 2 garlic cloves, minced
- 1 sweet onion, thinly sliced
- 1 green and 1 red bell pepper, cut into bite-size pieces
- 4 tablespoons Shaoxing wine
- 5 tablespoons black bean sauce

1. Heat your wok over high heat until a drop of water sizzles on contact.

2. Add the peanut oil and then the chicken, stir-frying it for 4 to 6 minutes, or until the chicken becomes golden.

3. Add the ginger, garlic, onion, green bell pepper, and red bell pepper, and stir-fry for another 2 minutes, or until the vegetables are crisp-tender.

4. Add the rice wine and black bean sauce. Stir to combine.

5. Serve with rice or noodles.

Scallion with Crispy Chicken Wings

Prep time: 10 minutes | Cook time: 30 minutes | Serves 3

- 24 chicken wingettes
- 3 garlic cloves, minced
- 1 teaspoon ginger powder
- 1 tablespoon peanut oil, more if needed
- ½ tablespoon fish sauce
- 2 tablespoons soy sauce
- 6 tablespoons honey
- 3 tablespoons chili-garlic sauce
- 1 scallion, chopped (optional)

1. Preheat the oven to 350°F (180°C).

2. Bake the chicken wings on a parchment-lined pa for 30 minutes, turning once.

3. In a large bowl, mix the cooked chicken with the minced garlic and ginger powder.

4. Heat your wok over high heat until a drop of wate sizzles on contact. Add the oil and then fry the chicken in batches, adding more oil if needed.

5. Remove the chicken when the skin is crispy and brown.

6. Turn the heat under the wok down to low and then add the fish sauce, soy sauce, honey, and chili-garlic sauce.

7. Cook until the sauce starts to bubble.

8. Add the chicken back to the wok and toss to coat with the sauce.

9. Garnish with the scallion, if using.

Brothy Chicken with Cashews

Prep time: 10 minutes | Cook time: 6½ minutes Serves 4 to 6

- 2 pounds (907 g) skinless, boneless chicken thighs
- Sea salt
- Freshly ground black pepper
- 3 tablespoons peanut or vegetable oil, divided
- 1 cup unsalted roasted cashews
- 1 teaspoon crushed
- dried chile pepper
- 1 tablespoon honey
- 2 jalapeño peppers, deseeded and thinly sliced
- 1 large sweet onion, cut into large chunk
- 2 tablespoons oyster sauce
- ¼ cup chicken broth
- 1 scallion, chopped, for garnish (optiona

1. Cut the chicken into 1-inch pieces, and season th pieces by sprinkling them on all sides with the s

salt and pepper.

Heat your wok over high heat until a drop of water sizzles on contact. Add 1 tablespoon peanut oil, and swirl to coat the wok. Add the cashews and stir-fry and toss for about 30 seconds. Transfer the nuts to a medium bowl, and toss them with the chile pepper and honey. Set aside.

Add the remaining 2 tablespoons peanut oil to the wok. Add the chicken to the wok, and stir-fry for 4 to 5 minutes. Add the jalapeños and onion to the wok, and stir-fry for about 2 minutes. Add the oyster sauce, chicken broth, and cashew mix to the wok and stir to combine. Season with additional sea salt and pepper, if necessary.

Transfer the chicken and cashews to a platter, and garnish with the chopped scallion (if using).

Lemony Chicken with Cornstarch

Prep time: 10 minutes | Cook time: 3 minutes | Serves 4

- 2 teaspoons Shaoxing rice wine or dry sherry
- 1 tablespoon soy sauce
- ½ teaspoon salt
- 2 pounds (907 g) skinless, boneless chicken breast meat
- 2 eggs, beaten
- 3½ tablespoons cornstarch, divided
- ⅓ teaspoon baking

- powder
- 1½ cups peanut or vegetable oil
- 3 tablespoons sugar
- ⅔ cup chicken broth
- 1 tablespoon lemon juice
- ½ teaspoon salt
- 1 lemon, sliced into thin rounds

In a large bowl, mix the rice wine, soy sauce, and salt. Add the chicken to the bowl, toss it to coat on all sides, and marinate the chicken for at least 15 minutes.

In a small bowl, make a batter by combining the eggs, 3 tablespoons cornstarch, and the baking powder.

In your wok, heat the peanut oil to 350°F (180°C). Dip each chicken breast into the batter, and then gently fry them until lightly browned, 3 to 4 minutes. When the chicken is finished, remove it with a slotted spoon, and place it on a paper

towel–lined plate. Discard the oil left in the wok, and wipe the wok clean with a paper towel.

4. In a medium bowl, make the sauce by mixing the sugar, the remaining ½ tablespoon cornstarch, the chicken broth, lemon juice, and salt.

5. Heat your wok over medium heat. Add the lemon sauce. When the sauce begins to bubble, add the lemon slices, stir, and then turn off the heat.

6. Pour the lemon sauce over the chicken and serve.

Vinegar with Tea-Smoked Duck

Prep time: 10 minutes | Cook time: 14 minutes | Serve 4

- 2 tablespoons Chinese five-spice powder, plus additional, if needed
- 3 duck breasts, skin scored in a diamond pattern through the fat
- Sea salt
- Freshly ground black pepper

- 2 tablespoons rice wine vinegar
- ½ cup jasmine rice
- ½ cup black tea leaves, such as oolong
- ½ cup brown sugar
- Rind of 1 lemon or 1 orange, or a combination of both

1. Rub the Chinese five-spice powder all over the duck. Season with the sea salt and pepper by sprinkling them on all sides of the duck. Place the duck breasts in a zip-top bag, and then coat them with the rice wine. Let the duck marinate for at least 4 hours in the refrigerator.

2. In a small bowl, mix the rice, tea leaves, brown sugar, and lemon rind. Set aside. These are the ingredients used for smoking the duck.

3. Prepare the smoker in your wok. Line the bottom of the wok with a piece of aluminum foil large enough that it hangs over the edges of the wok. Place the smoking ingredients on the foil, and spread them around evenly. Place a wire rack or metal steamer basket on top of the smoking ingredients. Place the duck on the rack, skin-side up, and cover the wok with a lid. Fold the overhanging foil over the top of the lid to better enclose the smoke.

4. Heat the wok on high until smoke begins to

appear. Then turn the heat down to medium, and smoke the duck for 10 minutes. Do not open the wok lid. Remove the wok from the heat, and let the duck sit in the wok for 2 to 3 more minutes.

5. For crisp duck skin, place the duck breasts, skin-side down, in a hot sauté pan for 2 to 3 minutes. Remove the breasts from the pan, and let them rest for about 5 minutes.

6. Slice the duck across the grain, and serve over rice, noodles, or a salad.

Scallion with Ketchup and Chicken

Prep time: 10 minutes | Cook time: 5 minutes | Serves 4

- ¼ cup rice vinegar
- 2 tablespoons ketchup
- 1 (8-ounce / 227-g) can pineapple chunks, drained, juice reserved
- ¼ cup plus 2 tablespoons cornstarch, divided
- 1 pound (454 g) boneless chicken thighs, cut into 1-inch pieces
- ¼ cup cooking oil
- 1 tablespoon crushed, chopped ginger
- 2 garlic cloves, crushed and chopped
- 2 cups sugar snap or snow pea pods
- 1 medium red bell pepper, cut into 1-inch pieces
- 4 scallions, cut into 1-inch pieces

1. In a small bowl, whisk together the rice vinegar, ketchup, pineapple juice, and 2 tablespoons the cornstarch. Set aside.

2. Coat the chicken with the remaining ¼ cup cornstarch by tossing in a resealable plastic bag or covered bowl. Set aside.

3. Heat the cooking oil in a wok over high heat until it shimmers.

4. Add the ginger and garlic and stir-fry for 30 seconds to lightly brown.

5. Add the chicken and shallow-fry for 3 to 4 minutes until lightly browned.

6. Remove the chicken from the wok and set aside.

7. Remove and discard all but 2 tablespoons oil from the wok.

8. Add the pea pods and stir-fry for 30 seconds.

9. Add the bell pepper and stir-fry for 30 seconds.

10. Add the pineapple chunks and stir-fry for 30 seconds.

11. Add the rice vinegar mixture and stir until a glaze forms.

12. Return the chicken to the wok, toss with the other ingredients, and garnish with the scallions. Serve with steamed rice.

Spiced Mushroom with Cashew Chicken

Prep time: 15 minutes | Cook time: 5 minutes | Serve 4

- 2 tablespoons cooking oil
- 1 tablespoon crushed, chopped ginger
- 2 garlic cloves, crushed and chopped
- 1 medium carrot, roll-cut into ½-inch pieces
- 1 pound (454 g) boneless chicken thighs, cut into 1-inch pieces
- 1 medium onion, cut into 1-inch pieces
- 4 ounces sliced mushrooms
- 1 red bell pepper, cut into 1-inch pieces
- 2 cups sugar snap or snow pea pods
- ½ cup whole cashews
- ¼ cup oyster sauce
- 2 tablespoons soy sauce
- 4 scallions, cut into 1-inch pieces

1. In a wok over high heat, heat the cooking oil until it shimmers.

2. Add the ginger, garlic, and carrot and stir-fry for 1 minute.

3. Add the chicken and onion and stir-fry for 1 minute.

4. Add the mushrooms and bell pepper and stir-fry for 1 minute.

5. Add the pea pods and cashews and stir-fry for 1 minute.

6. Add the oyster sauce and soy sauce and stir-fry for 1 minute.

7. Garnish with the scallions and serve over steamed rice.

Gingered Vegetables with Hoisin Sauce

Prep time: 10 minutes | Cook time: 3½ minutes | Serves 4

- 2 tablespoons cooking oil
- 1 tablespoon crushed, chopped ginger
- 2 garlic cloves, crushed and chopped
- 1 medium carrot, roll-cut into ½-inch pieces
- 1 pound (454 g) ground chicken
- 1 medium onion, cut into 1-inch pieces
- 2 cups sugar snap or snow pea pods
- ¼ cup hoisin sauce

In a wok over high heat, heat the cooking oil until it shimmers.

Add the ginger, garlic, carrot, and chicken and stir-fry for 1 minute.

Add the onion and stir-fry for 1 minute.

Add the pea pods and stir-fry for 1 minute.

Add the hoisin sauce and stir-fry for 30 seconds.

Serve over steamed rice.

Spicy Turkey with Broccoli Stir Fry

Prep time: 5 minutes | Cook time: 5 minutes | Serves 2

- 2 cups sliced red peppers
- ½ pound (227 g) turkey meat
- ½ cup sliced broccoli
- ½ cup sliced yellow peppers
- ½ cup sliced red peppers
- ½ cup julienned zucchini
- 1 tablespoon oil

Marinade turkey in Superfoods marinade.

In a wok, stir fry drained turkey in coconut oil for few minutes, add all vegetables and stir fry for 2 more minutes. Add the rest of the marinade and stir fry for 1 minute.

Serve with brown rice or quinoa.

Mushrooms with Asparagus Stir Fry

Prep time: 5 minutes | Cook time: 5 minutes | Serves 2

- ½ pound (227 g) chicken breast meat
- 1 cups sliced asparagus
- ½ cup sliced carrot
- ½ cup sliced mushrooms
- 1 tablespoon coconut oil

1. Marinade chicken in a Superfoods marinade.
2. In a wok, stir fry drained chicken in coconut oil for few minutes, add all vegetables and stir fry for 2 more minutes.
3. Add the rest of the marinade and stir fry for 1 minute.
4. Serve with brown rice or quinoa.

Egg with Thai Basil Chicken

Prep time: 10 minutes | Cook time: ½ minutes | Serves 1

For the Egg:
- 1 egg
- 2 tablespoons coconut oil for frying

For the Basil Chicken:
- 200 g chicken breast
- 5 garlic cloves
- 4 Thai chilies
- 1 tablespoon oil for frying
- Fish sauce
- 1 handful Thai holy basil leaves

1. In a wok, fry the egg.
2. Cut the chicken into small pieces. Peel the garlic and chilies, and chop them fine. Add basil leaves.
3. Add about 1 tablespoon. of oil to the wok.
4. When the oil is hot, add the chilies and garlic. Stir fry for half 1 minute.
5. Toss in your chicken and keep stir frying. Add fish sauce.
6. Add basil into the wok, fold it into the chicken, and turn off the heat.

Brothy Chicken and Lemon Stir Fry

Prep time: 10 minutes | Cook time: 2½ minutes | Serves 3 to 4

- 1 lemon
- ½ cup chicken broth

- 3 tablespoons fish sauce
- 2 teaspoons arrowroot flour
- 1 tablespoon oil
- 1 pound (454 g) boneless, skinless chicken breasts, trimmed and cut into 1-inch pieces
- 10 ounces (283 g)

- mushrooms, halved or quartered
- 2 cups snow peas, stems and strings removed
- 1 bunch scallions, cut into 1-inch pieces, white and green parts divided
- 1 tablespoon. chopped garlic

1. Grate the lemon, have the lemon juice. Mix 3 tablespoons the juice with broth, fish sauce and arrowroot flour in a small bowl.
2. Heat oil in a wok over high heat. Add chicken and cook, stirring occasionally, until just cooked through. Transfer to a plate.
3. Add mushrooms to the wok and cook until the mushrooms are tender.
4. Add snow peas, garlic, scallion whites and the lemon zest. Cook, stirring, around 30 seconds.
5. Add the broth to the wok and cook, stirring, 2 to 3 minutes.
6. Add scallion greens and the chicken and any accumulated juices and stir.
7. Serve.

Carrot with Chicken Chop Suey

Prep time: 20 minutes | Cook time: 5½ minutes | Serve 4

- 12 ounces (340 g) boneless chicken breast, sliced
- 3 tablespoons water
- 1 tablespoon oyster sauce
- 1 teaspoon Shaoxing wine
- 1 teaspoon vegetable oil
- 2 teaspoons cornstarch

- 3 tablespoons vegetable oil
- 2 garlic cloves, chopped
- 4 mushrooms, sliced
- ½ small carrot, sliced
- ⅔ cup celery, sliced
- 6 ounces (170 g) bok choy, cut into 2-inch pieces
- 1 tablespoon Shaoxing wine

- ¾ cup mung bean sprouts
- 1 cup snow peas
- 1½ tablespoons cornstarch

For the Sauce:

- ⅔ cup chicken stock
- ¼ teaspoon granulated sugar

- 1½ tablespoons soy sauce
- 1 teaspoon dark soy sauce
- 1½ tablespoons oyster sauce
- ½ teaspoon toasted sesame oil
- ⅛ teaspoon white pepper

1. Mix water, wine, and oyster sauce in a bowl, and soak the chicken slices in this mixture.
2. Whisk 2 teaspoons cornstarch with 1 teaspoon oil in a bowl.
3. Mix the remaining sauce in a bowl.
4. Add 2 tablespoons vegetable oil in a Mandarin wok and sear the chicken for 5 to 10 minutes until golden-brown.
5. Transfer the chicken slices to a plate and keep it aside.
6. Sauté garlic with oil in a Cantonese wok for several seconds, then add carrots, mushrooms, and celery. Sauté for 30 seconds.
7. Stir in bok choy and Shaoxing wine, then mix well
8. Pour in the prepared sauce and mix well, then cook to a simmer.
9. Stir in snow peas, bean sprouts, and chicken.
10. Mix cornstarch with 2 tablespoons water in a bowl and pour the mixture into the chicken.
11. Cook this mixture until the sauce thickens.
12. Serve warm.

Garlic with Braised Duck Legs

Prep time: 10 minutes | Cook time: 1 minutes | Serves 4

- 4 duck legs
- ¼ cup Shaoxing wine
- 2 cups chicken stock
- 2 tablespoons soy sauce
- 2 tablespoons oyster

- sauce
- ½ teaspoon sesame o
- ¼ teaspoon white pepper
- 3 ginger slices
- 3 garlic cloves, slice

Pou

12 scallions, cut into 2-inch pieces

- Sauté ginger and garlic with sesame oil in a large wok for 1 minute.
- Stir in chicken stock, wine, soy sauce, oyster sauce, and white pepper.
- Mix well and cook this mixture to a simmer.
- Toss in duck legs, cover, and cook until the duck is tender.
- Garnish with scallions.
- Serve warm.

Ginger with Scallion Poached Chicken

Prep time: 10 minutes | Cook time: 45 minutes | Serves 6

3 pounds (1.4 kg) whole chicken, cut into pieces	scallions, minced
2 scallions, chopped	• 2 tablespoons ginger, minced
5 ginger slices, chopped	• 3 tablespoons vegetable oil
3 tablespoons	• Salt, to taste

- Add 18 cups water to a large cooking pot and place the whole chicken in the pot.
- Set this pot over medium heat and add ginger and scallions.
- Cook and boil the chicken for 40 minutes until chicken is tender.
- sauté ginger with vegetable oil in a large wok.
- Add chicken to the oil and cook for 5 minutes per side until golden.
- Serve warm.

Spicy Baked Chicken Wings

Prep time: 5 minutes | Cook time: 35 minutes | Serves 6

3 pounds (1.4 kg) whole chicken wings	• 1 teaspoon Sichuan peppercorn powder
1 to 2 tablespoons white pepper powder	• 2 teaspoons vegetable oil
2 teaspoons salt	• ½ cup all-purpose flour

- ¼ cup cornstarch
1. Mix cornstarch with all-purpose flour, peppercorn powder, salt, and white pepper powder in a bowl.
2. Toss in chicken wings to the flour mixture, then coat well.
3. Grease a wok vegetable oil and sear the chicken for 5 minutes on medium heat.
4. Transfer the wings to the baking pan and bake them for 30 to 35 minutes in the oven at 475ºF (245ºC).
5. Serve warm.

Garlicky Chicken with Brown Sauce

Prep time: 15 minutes | Cook time: 1¼ minutes | Serves 4

12 ounces (340 g) boneless and skinless chicken breast	sauce
3 tablespoons water	• 1 teaspoon sesame oil
1 tablespoon oyster sauce	• ⅛ teaspoon white pepper
1 teaspoon cornstarch	• 4 cups broccoli florets
1½ teaspoon vegetable oil	• 3 tablespoons vegetable oil
⅔ cup chicken stock, warmed	• 2 garlic cloves, minced
1½ teaspoons sugar	• ¼ teaspoon fresh ginger, grated
1½ tablespoons soy sauce	• 1 tablespoon Shaoxing wine
2 teaspoons dark soy sauce	• 2 tablespoons cornstarch, whisked with 2 tablespoons water
1 tablespoon oyster	

1. Mix chicken with water, cornstarch, oyster sauce, and vegetable oil in a bowl.
2. Prepare the sauce by mixing chicken stock with oyster sauce, soy sauce, white pepper, and sesame oil in a bowl.
3. Boil broccoli in water for 1 minute, then drain.
4. Sauté chicken with 2 tablespoons vegetables in a Cantonese wok until golden-brown. Transfer the chicken to a plate.

5. Sauté ginger and garlic with 1 tablespoon oil in a Cantonese wok then add wine.

6. Stir in prepared sauce, chicken, and broccoli.

7. Mix well and cook for 15 seconds. Mix cornstarch with 2 tablespoons water.

8. Pour this slurry into the chicken and cook until mixture thickens.

9. Serve warm.

Pancake with Turmeric Gravy

Prep time: 10 minutes | Cook time: 6 minutes | Serves 6

- **For the Pancakes:**
- 10 ounces (283 g) chicken mince
- 1 tablespoon water
- 1 teaspoon soy sauce
- 2 teaspoons cornstarch
- 1 tablespoon peanut oil
- 1 medium onion, diced
- 2 cups mung bean sprouts, boiled
- 6 large eggs
- ¼ teaspoon sesame oil
- 1 scallion, chopped
- Sesame seeds
- **For the Gravy:**
- 1 tablespoon vegetable
- oil
- 1 tablespoon flour
- ½ teaspoon turmeric
- ½ teaspoon paprika
- ⅛ teaspoon garlic powder
- ⅛ teaspoon onion powder
- 3 cups chicken stock
- 2 teaspoons soy sauce
- 1 tablespoon oyster sauce
- ½ teaspoon sesame oil
- ¼ teaspoon white pepper
- ¼ cup cornstarch
- Salt, to taste
- ¼ cup chicken stock

1. Mix chicken cubes with 1 tablespoon water, 1 teaspoon cornstarch, and 1 teaspoon soy sauce in a bowl. Cover and set it aside.

2. Prepare the sauce, add oil to a Mandarin wok, and stir in 1 tablespoon flour.

3. Stir and cook this mixture for 20 seconds, then stir in paprika, turmeric, onion powder, and garlic powder.

4. Mix and cook for 15 seconds, then add chicken stock.

5. Cook this mixture to a simmer then add sesame oil, oyster sauce, white pepper, and soy sauce.

6. Cook and mix this sauce for 30 seconds, then remove from the heat.

7. Add 1 tablespoon oil and chicken in a skillet until golden-brown.

8. Mix bean sprouts with onion, chicken, eggs, cornstarch, in a bowl.

9. Make medium-sized patties out of this mixture.

10. Set a skillet over medium heat and pour in sesame oil.

11. Sear the patties for 5 minutes per side until golden-brown.

12. Pour the prepared sauce on top of the patties.

13. Serve warm.

Soy Sauce with Braised Duck

Prep time: 10 minutes | Cook time: 30 minutes | Serve 8

- 4 pounds (1.8 kg) duck, cut into pieces
- 1½ pounds (680 g) large taro
- ½ cup oil
- 1 small piece of rock sugar
- 5 ginger slices
- 8 garlic cloves, smashed
- 3 scallions, white and green parts separated
- ¼ cup Shaoxing wine
- 1 tablespoon oyster sauce
- 3 tablespoons light soy sauce
- 2 tablespoons dark soy sauce
- 2 cups water

1. Sauté ginger, garlic, and scallions with oil in a Mandarin wok.

2. Stir in wine, oyster sauce, soy sauce, water, sugar, and duck to the wok.

3. Sear the duck for 3 minutes then pour in water.

4. Cover and cook the duck for 20 minutes on medium-low heat.

5. Stir in taro and cook for 7 minutes.

6. Serve warm.

Spicy Chicken with Zucchini Dumplings

Prep time: 10 minutes | Cook time: 27 minutes | Serves 12

- 1 medium zucchini, shredded
- 2½ tablespoons vegetable oil
- 1 tablespoon ginger, minced
- ½ pound (227 g) ground chicken
- ¼ teaspoon white pepper
- ½ teaspoon sugar
- 1 teaspoon sesame oil
- 1 ½ tablespoons soy sauce
- 1 tablespoon Shaoxing wine
- 1 package dumpling wrappers

Sauté ginger and zucchini with oil in a Cantonese wok until soft.

Stir in chicken, soy sauce, and rest of the ingredients.

Sauté for about 5 minutes until chicken are cooked and golden.

Allow the filling to cool and spread the dumpling wrappers on the working surface.

Divide the chicken filling at the center of each dumpling wrapper.

Wet the edges of the dumplings and bring all the edges of each wrapper together.

Pinch and seal the edges of the dumplings to seal the filling inside.

Boil water in a suitable pot with a steamer basket placed inside.

Add the dumplings to the steamer, cover and steam for 20 minutes.

Meanwhile, heat about 2 tablespoons oil in a skillet.

Sear the dumpling for 2 minutes until golden.

Serve warm.

Limey Fish Sauce with Chicken

Prep time: 10 minutes | Cook time: 4½ minutes | Serves 4

- 450 g boneless skinless chicken breast
- 1 tablespoon vegetable oil
- 3 garlic cloves, finely chopped
- 2 small fresh red or green Thai chilies, pitted and chopped
- ¼ cup chicken broth or water
- 1 tablespoon Asian
- fish sauce
- 2 teaspoons sugar
- 1 teaspoon soy sauce
- ¼ teaspoon freshly ground black pepper
- 1½ cups loosely wrapped fresh holy basil leaves or Asian basil leaves
- 2 tablespoons fresh lime juice, or to taste
- Thai sticky rice or Thai jasmine rice

1. Wrap the chicken in cling film and put it in the fridge for 30 minutes to make it easier to cut. Cut the chicken lengthways into thin slices and then into thin strips lengthways. Finally, cut the chicken strips crosswise into pieces.

2. Heat a heavy pan or wok over high heat until hot. Pour the oil in and let it get hot until it stops smoking. Add the garlic and sauté until golden brown. Add the chicken and cook, stirring, for 3 to 4 minutes, or until all of the chicken is opaque white; keep stirring the chicken so it doesn't stick in the wok.

3. Add the broth or water, soy sauce, chilies, fish sauce, black pepper and sugar and stir until all ingredients are completely combined.

4. Mix in the basil and fry for 30 seconds while stirring. If using holy basil, stir-fry for 1 minute or until the basil has wilted but is still green. Add the lime juice.

5. Serve the fried chicken with rice.

Vinegary Chicken in Lettuce Leaves

Prep time: 10 minutes | Cook time: 2¾ minutes | Serves 4

- 2 tablespoons vegetable oil
- 1 tablespoon finely chopped peeled fresh ginger
- ½ teaspoon salt
- 2 spring onions, chopped
- 2 (225 g) boneless chicken breast halves without skin, cut into pieces

- 1 can chopped water chestnuts, roughly chopped
- ¼ cup hoisin sauce from the bottle
- 1½ teaspoons Worcestershire sauce
- 1 teaspoon rice vinegar, not seasoned
- ½ cup pine nuts
- 12 large red or green lettuce leaves

1. Heat a pan (no non-stick coating) or wok over moderately high heat until the pan is almost smoking then add the oil. Add 2 tablespoons spring onions, ginger and salt.

2. Fry for about 45 seconds, stirring, until the ginger smells fragrant. Add the chicken and stir-fry for about 2 minutes until it is almost cooked through.

3. Add the Worcestershire sauce, water chestnuts, pine nuts, hoisin sauce and vinegar. Boil and stir for 1 minute or until mixture is heated through.

4. Put the mixture in a bowl and garnish with the remaining 2 tablespoons spring onions.

5. Have guests make their own lettuce wrap by taking a spoonful of the chicken mixture and adding it to the lettuce leaves, then wrap the lettuce leaves to enclose the chicken mixture.

Spicy Paprika with Chicken

Prep time: 10 minutes | Cook time: 8⅓ minutes | Serves 4

- 1 teaspoon Chinese cooking wine
- ½ teaspoon salt
- 225 g boneless chicken, cut into cubes
- ¼ cup cornstarch or as needed
- 3 cups peanut oil, for frying
- 4 garlic cloves, chopped
- 1 tablespoon chopped fresh ginger root
- 2 green onions, cut
- 2 long, green chilies, cut into pieces
- 2 cups dried chilies, chopped
- 2 tablespoons Szechuan peppercorns
- 2 teaspoons soy sauce
- 2 teaspoons Chinese cooking wine
- ½ teaspoon white sugar
- ½ teaspoon salt

1. Combine ½ teaspoon salt and 1 teaspoon cooking wine in a bowl and stir them together. Add the chicken and cover by stirring in. Let it marinate

for 2 to 3 minutes. Combine the marinated chicken and cornstarch in a large, sealable plastic bag and shake it to coat the chicken.

2. Heat the peanut oil in a large frying pan or wok over high heat. Fry the chicken in the oil for 7 to 10 minutes until the edges start to get crispy. Take the chicken to a plate lined with paper towels to drain. Discard the oil, leaving 2 tablespoons.

3. Reheat the remaining 2 tablespoons oil in the wok over medium to high heat. Fry the garlic, spring onions and ginger in the oil for 1 minute until they are fragrant. Add the green chilies, Szechuan peppercorns, and crushed dried chilies and cook for another 20 seconds.

4. Put the chicken back in the wok and add 2 teaspoons cooking wine, soy sauce, ½ teaspoon of salt and sugar while stirring until everything is well mixed. Turn off the heat and serve immediately.

Garlicky Fettuccine Bombay

Prep time: 10 minutes | Cook time: 39 minutes | Serves 4

- 1 pack of fettuccine
- 3 tablespoons olive oil
- 1 teaspoon cumin
- 1 large onion, chopped
- 4 garlic cloves, crushed
- 2 skinless and boned chicken breasts, cut
- into cubes
- 2 tablespoons divided curry powder
- 1 (400 g) can diced tomatoes
- 2 tablespoon tomato paste

1. Bring a large saucepan with water and a little salt to a boil over high heat, add the fettuccine and let it boil. Let the noodles cook in the open pot for about 8 minutes or until the noodles are cooked through but are still firm to the bite.

2. Heat a large pan or wok with olive oil over medium to high heat. Fry the cumin seeds in the hot oil for 2 to 3 minutes or until they start to pop.

3. Add the garlic and onion and fry for about 5 minutes until the garlic is lightly brown. Add the chicken and cook for 4 to 5 minutes or until the chicken is well cooked. Add 1 tablespoon curry powder and stir-fry for 3 to 4 minutes.

4. Add the diced tomatoes and turn the heat on low

Add the remaining 1 tablespoon curry powder and the tomato paste. Let simmer for 15 minutes.

Pour in the cooked fettuccine and mix until well covered in sauce. Let it simmer for 2 to 5 minutes or until the noodles are heated.

Spicy Caribbean Jerk Stir-Fry

Prep time: 10 minutes | Cook time: 8 minutes | Serves 2

1 tablespoon vegetable oil	boned chicken breast, cut into strips
1 green pepper, pitted and diced	2½ teaspoons Caribbean jerk seasoning
1 red pepper, pitted and diced	½ cup plum sauce
¼ cup sliced sweet onions	1 tablespoon soy sauce
350 g skinless and	¼ cup chopped roasted peanuts

Heat the oil in a large pan over medium heat, add the onion and paprika and stir-fry in the hot oil for 5 to 7 minutes until they are slightly soft.

Take the onion and peppers out of the pan and save them. Put the chicken in the pan. Then season with the jerk seasoning.

Fry the chicken, stirring, until it's no longer pink in color. Add the plum sauce to the chicken. Add the onions and peppers and stir.

Cook for 3 to 5 minutes until the onions and peppers are fully heated.

Drizzle with chopped peanuts and soy sauce and serve.

Milky Curry Stir-Fry

Prep time: 10 minutes | Cook time: 17 minutes | Serve 4

1½ cups coconut milk	1 tablespoon oyster sauce
1 tablespoon ginger, chopped	2 tablespoons minced garlic
1 tablespoon lime juice	½ tablespoon chili garlic sauce
1 tablespoon fish sauce	2 tablespoons white

sugar or sugar substitute

1 tablespoon avocado oil

450 g chicken breast, cut into bite-sized pieces

½ sliced onion

1½ teaspoons curry powder

2 cups broccoli florets

1. Mix the oyster sauce, fish sauce, chili-garlic sauce, lime juice, coconut milk, sugar, ginger and garlic in a small bowl. Heat a large pan or wok with avocado oil on medium to high heat.

2. Place the chicken in the hot oil and cook for 8 to 10 minutes or until it is no longer pink on the inside. Take the cooked chicken out of the wok and keep it warm. Save the remaining avocado oil in the wok.

3. Fry the curry powder and the onion in the same wok with hot avocado oil for 2 minutes. Add the broccoli and stir-fry for 3 minutes. Add the coconut milk mixture and let it boil.

4. Reduce the heat to medium setting and let the sauce and vegetables simmer for 3 minutes. Return the cooked chicken to the wok, cover the wok, and cook for another 3 minutes until the vegetables are tender and the chicken is cooked through.

Celery with Chicken Stir-Fry

Prep time: 15 minutes | Cook time: 11 minutes | Serves 4

4 skinless and boned chicken breast halves, cut into bite-sized pieces	25 snow peas, chopped
1 tablespoon Cajun spice mix, or to taste	10 small sticks of fresh asparagus, cut into bite-sized pieces
1¼ cups chicken broth	3 stalks celery, chopped
1 tablespoon cornstarch	½ red bell pepper, cut into thin strips
4 teaspoons soy sauce	2 green onions, chopped
2 tablespoons olive oil, divided	1 can cut and drained bamboo shoots
2 cups shredded cabbage	½ cup cashew nuts
	1 pinch paprika, or to

taste (optional)

1. Sprinkle Cajun seasoning over the chicken pieces. In a bowl, stir together 3 tablespoons soy sauce, cornstarch and chicken stock until everything is well mixed.

2. Heat a tablespoon olive oil in a wok or deep pan over high heat. Fry the chicken in the hot oil for 6 to 10 minutes, until completely cooked. Take the chicken out of the pan and pour off the accumulated liquid.

3. Heat the remaining 1 tablespoon olive oil in a wok or pan over high heat. Fry and stir together bamboo shoots, cabbage, green onions, snow peas, red peppers, asparagus and celery for 1 minute; add a teaspoon of soy sauce.

4. Cook for 3 minutes until the vegetables are crispy and tender. Mix the chicken into the cabbage mixture then add the chicken broth to the chicken mixture.

5. Switch to medium heat and let it simmer for 1 minute until the sauce is thick. Turn on low heat then add the cashews; cook another minute until completely heated. Top with paprika.

Cabbage with Quinoa Bowl

Prep time: 15 minutes | Cook time: 27 minutes | Serves 8

- 4 cups low sodium chicken broth
- 2 cups quinoa, rinsed and drained
- 1 tablespoon coconut oil and 3 eggs
- 1 large boneless and skinless chicken breast, cut into thin strips
- ¾ cup grated cabbage
- ½ cup Edam
- ¼ cup diced broccoli stalks
- 2 carrots, cut into matches
- 2 green onions, chopped
- 1 teaspoon sesame oil
- Thai peanut sauce:
- ¼ cup natural peanut butter and ¼ cup reduced sodium soy sauce
- 3 tablespoons rice vinegar
- 2 tablespoons chili garlic sauce and 2 tablespoons chopped fresh ginger
- 3 garlic cloves, chopped
- 1 teaspoon sesame oil and ½ cup chopped salted peanuts
- 3 tablespoons

chopped fresh coriander

1. Bring chicken broth and quinoa to a boil in a saucepan. Reduce the heat to medium/low, cover and simmer for 15 to 20 minutes, until the quinoa is soft. Put aside. Heat 1½ teaspoons coconut oil in a wok or large pan over medium-high heat.

2. Add chicken; stir until cooked; about 5 minutes. Take the chicken out of the wok. Heat the remaining 1½ teaspoons coconut oil. Add the cabbage, Edam cheese, broccoli, carrots and spring onions and fry until the vegetables are slightly soft (2 to 3 minutes).

3. Whisk eggs and sesame oil in a small bowl for 2 to 3 minutes. Push the vegetables along the sides of the wok so that there is a hollow in the middle; Add the eggs and mix into scrambled eggs, about 3 minutes. Mix peanut butter, soy sauce, rice vinegar, chili and garlic sauce, ginger, garlic and sesame oil in a small bowl.

4. Pour the Thai peanut sauce over the vegetable and egg mixture in the wok, return the chicken to the wok and add the quinoa; mix well to combine. Stir in chopped peanuts and coriander and serve.

Spicy Chicken and Cornstarch Stir Fry

Prep time: 10 minutes | Cook time: 15 minutes | Serves 4

- 1 bunch of spring onions
- 450 g skinless and boned chicken thighs
- ½ teaspoon of salt
- ¼ teaspoon black pepper
- 3 tablespoons vegetable oil
- 1 chopped red pepper
- 4 garlic cloves, finely chopped
- 1½ tablespoons fresh ginger, peeled and
- finely chopped
- ¼ teaspoon dried hot red pepper flakes
- ¾ cup chicken broth with reduced sodium content
- 1½ tablespoons soy sauce
- 1½ teaspoons cornstarch
- 1 teaspoon sugar
- ½ cup salted roasted whole cashew nuts

1. Chop the spring onions and separate the white and green parts. Pat the chicken dry then cut into

pieces and season with salt and pepper. Heat a wok or a 30 cm pan (non-stick pan) over moderate heat until a drop of water evaporates immediately.

Add oil and stir-fry the chicken until it is golden brown in places and cooked for 4 to 5 minutes. Transfer to a plate with a slotted spoon. Add paprika, garlic, ginger, red pepper flakes and shallot white to the wok and stir-fry until the peppers are just tender (5 to 6 minutes).

Mix the stock, soy sauce, corn starch and sugar for 5 to 6 minutes, then stir into the vegetables in a wok. Reduce the heat and simmer for 1 to 2 minutes, stirring occasionally, until thickened. Stir in cashew nuts, spring onions and chicken along with the juice that has accumulated on the plate.

eanuts with Pad Thai

Prep time: 15 minutes | Cook time: 17 minutes | Serves 4

- ½ cup rice wine vinegar
- ½ cup white sugar
- ¼ cup oyster sauce
- 2 tablespoons tamarind pulp
- 1 (340 g) pack of dried rice noodles in cold water, as required
- ½ cup peanut oil
- 4 eggs
- 1½ teaspoons minced garlic
- 340 g chicken breast, cut into strips

- 1½ tablespoons white sugar, or more to taste
- 1½ teaspoons salt
- 1½ cups dry roasted, unsalted peanuts
- 1½ teaspoons dried, ground Asian radish
- 1 teaspoon chili powder, or more to taste
- ½ cup chopped fresh chives
- 2 cups fresh bean sprouts
- 1 lime, cut into wedges

Whisk rice wine vinegar, ½ cup sugar, oyster sauce and tamarind pulp in a saucepan over medium heat until the sugar has dissolved, about 5 minutes; remove from heat and set aside.

Put rice noodles in a large bowl and pour enough cold water to cover the noodles. Let it soften for about 10 minutes. Drain and heat peanut oil in a wok or large pan over medium heat.

Boil the eggs and garlic in hot oil and stir until the eggs are tender, 2 to 3 minutes. Stir the chicken

and noodles into the eggs and cook until the chicken is no longer pink in the center and the juice is clear, about 5 minutes. Pour rice wine vinegar sauce, 1½ tablespoons sugar and 1½ teaspoons salt into the pasta mixture. Stir peanuts, ground radish and chili powder into the pasta mixture; cook until the peanuts soften slightly, about 5 minutes.

4. If desired, add more sugar or chili powder. Remove from the heat and stir the chives with the pasta mixture. Sprinkle with bean sprouts and garnish with lime wedges.

Chili Curry with Broccoli Stir-Fry

Prep time: 15 minutes | Cook time: 19 minutes | Serves 4

- 1½ cups coconut milk
- 1 tablespoon ginger, chopped
- 1 tablespoon lime juice
- 1 tablespoon fish sauce
- 1 teaspoon oyster sauce
- 2 teaspoons minced garlic
- ½ teaspoon chili garlic sauce

- 2 tablespoons white sugar
- 1 tablespoon avocado oil
- 450 g chicken breast, cut into bite-sized pieces
- ½ onion, sliced
- 1½ teaspoons curry powder
- 2 cups of broccoli florets

1. Mix coconut milk, ginger, lime juice, fish sauce, oyster sauce, garlic, chili garlic sauce and sugar in a small bowl and heat the avocado oil in a large pan or in a wok over medium heat.

2. Fry the chicken in the hot oil while stirring until it is no longer pink (8 to 10 minutes). Take out of the wok and keep warm. Leave the remaining avocado oil in the pan.

3. Fry the onion and curry powder in hot oil in the pan for 2 minutes. Stir in broccoli; fry for 3 minutes while stirring. Add coconut milk mixture and bring to a boil.

4. Reduce the heat to medium level and simmer the sauce and vegetables for 3 minutes. Return the chicken to the pan; cook covered until the chicken

is heated through and the vegetables are tender, about 3 minutes.

Chicken Broth with Grape Stir-Fry

Prep time: 5 minutes | Cook time: 5 minutes | Serves 4

- 1 tablespoon vegetable oil
- 1 cup red grapes sliced
- 1 cup cooked chicken,
- cut into cubes
- 2 cups cooked rice
- ¼ cup chicken broth

1. Heat the vegetable oil in a wok or large pan over medium heat. Stir in the grapes and chicken; cook and stir until chicken is hot and grapes are tender, about 3 minutes.

2. Add rice and chicken broth; continue to cook until the rice is hot, about 2 minutes more.

Spicy Pineapple Chicken

Prep time: 10 minutes | Cook time: 37 minutes | Serves 4

- 3 tablespoons soy sauce
- 3 tablespoons olive oil, divided
- ½ teaspoon paprika salt, to taste
- 450g boneless, skinless chicken breast, cut into strips
- 1 red pepper, cut into
- cubes
- 1 bunch spring onions, sliced and cut into lengths
- 340 g canned pineapple pieces (drained and juice reserved)
- 1 tablespoon cornstarch

1. Mix the soy sauce, 2 tablespoons olive oil, paprika and salt in a bowl.

2. Add the chicken strips and let them marinate while you prepare the remaining ingredients. Heat 1 tablespoon olive oil in a wok. Add paprika and stir-fry for 3 minutes.

3. Add spring onions and cook for 2 more minutes. Remove the chicken from the marinade and place in the wok; discard the marinade. Cook for 10 to 15 minutes, stirring occasionally, until the chicken is cooked through and is no longer pink in the middle.

4. Mix the pineapple juice and cornstarch in a bowl for 10 to 15 minutes; stir together. Put the pineapple pieces in the pan and cook for 2 to 3 minutes.

5. Put the pineapple pieces in the pan and cook for to 3 minutes. Pour in the pineapple juice mixture and bring to the boil. Simmer for about 3 minute until the sauce has thickened.

Broccoli with Mushroom and Garlicky Chicken

Prep time: 15 minutes | Cook time: 10½ minutes Serves 3

- 1 tablespoon vegetable oil
- 1 cup fresh mushrooms sliced
- 2 cups broccoli florets, chopped
- 1 (8 ounces / 227 g) can sliced and drained bamboo shoots
- 1 (225 g) can water chestnuts sliced, drained
- 1 (425 g) can be whole straw mushrooms, drained
- 1 tablespoon vegetable oil
- 2 garlic cloves, chopped
- 1 pound (454 g) skinless chicken breast, boneless, cut into strips
- 1 tablespoon cornstarch
- 1 tablespoon white sugar
- 1 tablespoon soy sau
- 1 tablespoon oyster sauce
- 1 tablespoon rice win
- ¼ cup chicken broth

1. Heat 1 tablespoon vegetable oil in a wok or large pan over high heat until it starts to smoke. Stir in fresh mushrooms, broccoli, bamboo shoots, wate chestnuts and straw mushrooms. Cook and stir until all the vegetables are hot and the broccoli i tender, about 5 minutes.

2. Remove from the wok and set aside. Heat the remaining tablespoon the vegetables in the wok until they start to smoke. Stir in the garlic and cook for a few seconds until it turns golden brow

3. Add the chicken and cook until the chicken is lightly browned around the edges and no longer pink in the center, about 5 minutes.

4. Stir cornstarch, sugar, soy sauce, oyster sauce, ri wine and chicken broth together in a small bowl

1. Pour over the chicken and bring to the boil, stirring constantly. Cook for about 30 seconds, until the sauce is thick and no longer cloudy.

2. Put the vegetables back in the wok and toss with the sauce.

Spiced Leeks with Chicken Stir-Fry

Prep time: 5 minutes | Cook time: 5 minutes | Serves 2

- 2 cups sliced red peppers
- ½ pound (227 g) chicken meat
- ½ cup sliced leeks
- 1 tablespoon oil

- Marinade chicken in Superfoods marinade. Stir fry drained chicken in coconut oil for few minutes, add all vegetables and stir fry for 2 more minutes.

- Add the rest of the marinade and stir fry for 1 minute. Serve with brown rice or quinoa.

Ginger and Garlic Sun Chicken

Prep time: 10 minutes | Cook time: 7 minutes | Serves 3

- 2 tablespoons vegetable oil
- 450 g skinless and boneless chicken breast halves, cut into pieces
- 2 sliced carrots
- 2 garlic cloves, pressed
- 1 teaspoon ground ginger
- 4 shallots, chopped
- 1 sliced pepper
- ½ cup water
- 2 tablespoons soy sauce
- 1 tablespoon cornstarch
- 1 teaspoon white vinegar
- ½ teaspoon red pepper flakes

Heat the oil in a large pan or wok over medium to high heat. Saute the carrots and chicken for about 5 minutes, until the carrots are tender and the chicken in the center is no longer pink.

Add the ginger and garlic, stir and cook for another 1 minute.

Add shallots and peppers and cook for 1 more minute.

4. Add paprika flakes, 3 tablespoons the reserved liquid from the canned pineapple pieces, water, vinegar, soy sauce, cornstarch and pineapple pieces.

5. Stir into the vegetable-chicken mixture and bring to the boil. Stir until the sauce thickens.

Scallions with Carrot and Chicken Stock

Prep time: 10 minutes | Cook time: 3 hours | Makes 8 to 13 cups

- 1 whole chicken
- 2 large carrots, peeled and quartered
- 1 large yellow onion, peeled and halved
- 3 scallions
- 2-inch piece ginger, peeled
- 10 to 15 cups water

1. Put the chicken, carrots, onion, scallions, and ginger in a very large pot.

2. Fill the pot with just enough water to cover the chicken.

3. Simmer on low heat for 3 to 4 hours, partially uncovered. Use an ultra-fine mesh skimmer to remove any froth from the surface, along with any excess oil.

4. Allow the stock to cool slightly then remove the solid ingredients.

5. Run the stock through a fine mesh strainer as you pour it into storage jars or containers. You can refrigerate the stock overnight then simply scoop off the solidified fat. The stock will keep in the refrigerator for up to 1 week and in the freezer for up to 6 months.

Garlicky Broccoli with Noodles

Prep time: 10 minutes | Cook time: 12 minutes | Serves 3

- 1 tablespoon dark soy sauce
- 2 tablespoons soy sauce
- 1 tablespoon white sugar, or more to taste
- 1 teaspoon chili garlic sauce, or more to taste
- 1 tablespoon olive oil
- 1 tablespoon chopped garlic
- 170 g chicken breast

fillet, cut into bite-sized pieces

- 1 (450 g) pack of frozen broccoli
- 450 g Fresh flat rice

- noodles
- 1 egg, beaten
- ¼ teaspoon sesame seeds

1. Mix the dark soy sauce, soy sauce, sugar and chili garlic sauce in a small saucepan over medium to low heat; Simmer and stir until the sugar has dissolved in the sauce, about 5 minutes.

2. Take off the stove and set aside. Heat the olive oil in a pan over medium heat. Cook the garlic and chicken in the hot oil and stir until the chicken is no longer pink in the middle (7 to 10 minutes).

3. Stir the broccoli into the chicken mixture; cook and stir until the broccoli is completely heated. Add the pasta and stir until all ingredients are evenly mixed. Pour the sauce over the mixture and stir until everything is evenly covered; keep cooking until the sauce begins to thicken.

4. Press the chicken mixture to the side of the pan with a spatula. Put the egg in the pan in the free space. Stir the egg and cook it through.

5. As soon as the egg is cooked, mix in the ingredients again and heat it thoroughly. Garnish with sesame seeds and paprika flakes and serve.

Carrot and Tomato with Filipino Stew

Prep time: 10 minutes | Cook time: 45 minutes | Serves 6

- 1 tablespoon vegetable oil
- 3 garlic cloves, pressed and chopped
- 1 onion, chopped
- 1 cup pitted and chopped tomatoes
- 1 (450 g) whole chicken, cut into pieces
- 3 cups water

- 3 quartered potatoes
- 1 green pepper, deseeded and cut into sticks
- 1 chopped carrot
- Salt and ground black pepper, to taste
- 1 cup tomato sauce (optional)

1. Heat a large wok with oil on medium heat and add the garlic. Saute the garlic for 3 minutes or until fragrant.

2. Add the onion and cook for 5 minutes or until the onions are translucent. Mix in the tomatoes and cook for 5 minutes, mashing with a fork until the skin and pulp separate.

3. Put the chicken in the wok and stir-fry for about 5 minutes or until the chicken is slightly brown in color. Add water. Cover the wok and bring the mixture to a boil. Stir in tomato sauce and simmer for 15 minutes until all the flavors have combined.

4. Stir in the potatoes and simmer for 10 minutes until the potatoes are tender. Add the carrots and peppers and simmer for 5 minutes until the vegetables are soft.

5. Season to taste with pepper and salt.

Soy Sauce with Gingered Chicken

Prep time: 10 minutes | Cook time: 6 minutes | Serves 4 to 6

- 2 tablespoons sesame oil
- 2-inch piece ginger, peeled and julienned
- 4 chicken drumsticks (bone-in), chopped into 2 or 3 pieces each
- 2 tablespoons

- Shaoxing wine
- 2 teaspoons soy sauce
- ¼ teaspoon dark soy sauce
- ½ cup water
- Pinch ground white pepper

1. In a wok over medium-high heat, heat the sesame oil.

2. Add the ginger and stir-fry until it turns a very light golden brown.

3. Add the chicken pieces and stir-fry for about 1 minute to cook the surface.

4. Stir in the Shaoxing wine, soy sauce, dark soy sauce, water, and pepper.

5. Stir the chicken well, reduce the heat to low, and simmer until tender, 5 to 10 minutes.

6. Transfer to a serving plate and serve immediately.

Scallion with Chicken and Cashew Nuts

Prep time: 10 minutes | Cook time: 0 minutes | Serves 4 to 6

- 2 tablespoons peanut oil
- 2 garlic cloves, minced
- ½ onion, thinly sliced
- 2 boneless skinless chicken breast halves, cut into thin strips
- 1½ tablespoons brown sugar
- 1 tablespoon soy sauce
- 1 tablespoon oyster sauce
- 1 teaspoon fish sauce
- ½ cup cashews, lightly roasted
- 1 scallion, chopped

In a wok over medium heat, heat the peanut oil.

Add the garlic and onion and stir-fry until fragrant.

Add the chicken and stir-fry until the chicken is almost fully cooked.

Combine the brown sugar, soy sauce, oyster sauce, and fish sauce, and add to the chicken.

Increase the heat to high, stir well to mix, and continue stirring until the chicken is fully cooked.

Stir in the cashew nuts.

Garnish with the chopped scallion, and serve.

ggy Marinade with Sesame hicken

ep time: 10 minutes | Cook time: 0 minutes | rves 4 to 6

For the Marinade:

3 teaspoons cornstarch

1 egg white

½ teaspoon salt

Pinch ground white pepper

2 (5-ounce / 142-g) boneless chicken breast halves

For the Sauce:

2 tablespoons honey

- 1½ tablespoons apple cider vinegar
- 1 teaspoon soy sauce
- ½ teaspoon sesame oil
- ½ teaspoon salt
- **For the Stir-Fry:**
- 2 tablespoons peanut oil
- 1 teaspoon toasted sesame seeds
- 1 scallion, chopped

Pour the cornstarch, egg white, salt, and pepper over the chicken and toss to combine. Marinate at room temperature for 20 minutes.

In a small bowl, prepare the sauce by mixing together the honey, apple cider vinegar, soy sauce, sesame oil, and salt.

3. In a wok over medium-high heat, heat the peanut oil.

4. Add the chicken and stir-fry until fully cooked.

5. Stir in the sauce, mixing well to coat the chicken.

6. Sprinkle the sesame seeds over the chicken, stirring well.

7. Transfer to a serving dish and top with the scallion.

Buttered Chicken Pad Thai

Prep time: 10 minutes | Cook time: 16 minutes | Serves 5

- 450 g boneless, skinless chicken breast halves, cut into bite-sized pieces
- Ground black pepper, to taste
- ¾ cup white sugar
- 1 teaspoon ground cayenne pepper
- 3 tablespoons white wine vinegar
- 6 tablespoons fish sauce
- 1 tablespoon creamy
- peanut butter
- 1 tablespoon olive oil
- 5 garlic cloves, chopped
- 4 large eggs, lightly beaten
- 450 g Thai rice noodles
- ½ cup fresh bean sprouts
- 2 cups beef soup
- ½ cup green onion, chopped

1. Bring a large saucepan of water to the boil. Season the chicken with salt and black pepper; In a bowl, whisk together the sugar, cayenne pepper, white wine vinegar, fish sauce and peanut butter.

2. Brush the inside of a large pan or wok with olive oil and heat it over a high flame. Boil the chicken and stir in the hot oil until the meat is white on the outside but still pink on the inside, about 3 minutes.

3. Remove the chicken and set aside in a bowl. Reduce the heat under the pan to medium to low. Boil the garlic in the pan and stir until it becomes translucent (1 to 2 minutes); Boil eggs and stir with garlic until they cook loosely (2 to 3 minutes); Pour peanut sauce in garlic and eggs and stir. Bring sauce to a boil.

4. Stir rice noodles into the boiling water. Cook until

the pasta is still slightly tough, about 5 minutes. Drain the pasta. Return the chicken with the eggs and sauce to the pan. Simmer until the chicken is no longer pink in the middle and the juice is clear, stirring frequently, for another 5 to 8 minutes. Add bean sprouts, rice noodles and beef broth to the pan. Bring to a boil and cook until the pasta is tender and most of the broth has been absorbed, about 10 minutes, sprinkle with green onions and serve.

Spicy Chicken Marinade with Asparagus

Prep time: 15 minutes | Cook time: 8 minutes | Serves 4

- **FOR THE MARINADE**
- 3 teaspoons cornstarch
- 2 teaspoons Shaoxing wine
- ½ teaspoon salt
- Pinch freshly ground black pepper to taste
- 2 (5-ounce / 142-g) boneless skinless chicken breast halves, cut into bite-size pieces
- **FOR THE SAUCE**
- 1 tablespoon oyster sauce
- 1 teaspoon rice vinegar
- ½ teaspoon soy sauce
- ½ teaspoon dark soy sauce
- 1 teaspoon freshly ground black pepper
- **FOR THE STIR-FRY**
- 2 tablespoons peanut oil
- ½ pound (227 g) asparagus (about ½ bunch), stems trimmed, cut into 1-inch pieces

1. Pour the cornstarch, Shaoxing wine, salt, and pepper over the chicken and toss to combine. Marinate at room temperature for 20 minutes.

2. In a small bowl, prepare the sauce by combining the oyster sauce, rice vinegar, soy sauce, dark soy sauce, and pepper, and mix it well. Set it aside.

3. In a wok over medium-high heat, heat the peanut oil.

4. Add the chicken and stir-fry until the chicken is half cooked.

5. Add the asparagus and stir-fry until it turns bright green and the chicken is fully cooked, or for about 2 minutes.

6. Add the sauce to the wok, and stir well to combine all the ingredients.

7. Transfer to a serving dish and serve.

Vinegary Mushroom with Scallion

Prep time: 15 minutes | Cook time: 4 minutes | Serves 4

- 2 tablespoons soy sauce
- 2 tablespoons rice wine
- 2 tablespoons rice vinegar
- 2 tablespoons sugar
- 1 tablespoon cornstarch
- 2 tablespoons cooking oil
- 1 tablespoon crushed, chopped ginger
- 2 cloves garlic, crushed and chopped
- 1 pound (454 g) boneless chicken thighs, cut into 1-inch pieces
- 4 ounces (113 g) sliced mushrooms
- 2 cups sugar snap or snow pea pods
- 1 medium red bell pepper, cut into ½-inch pieces
- 4 scallions, cut into 1-inch pieces

1. In a small bowl, whisk together the soy sauce, rice wine, rice vinegar, sugar, and cornstarch. Set aside.

2. In a wok over high heat, heat the cooking oil until it shimmers.

3. Add the ginger, garlic, and chicken and stir-fry for 1 minute.

4. Add the mushrooms and stir-fry for 1 minute.

5. Add the pea pods and stir-fry for 1 minute.

6. Add the bell pepper and stir-fry for 1 minute.

7. Stir the soy sauce mixture into the wok and stir until a light glaze forms.

8. Garnish with the scallions and serve over steamed rice.

Chicken Marinade with Mushroom Stir-Fry

Prep time: 15 minutes | Cook time: 5 minutes | Serves 4

Pour

OR THE MARINADE

- 2 teaspoons soy sauce
- ½ teaspoon salt
- 2 pinches ground white pepper
- 3 teaspoons cornstarch
- 2 boneless skinless chicken breast halves, cut into bite-size pieces

OR THE STIR-FRY

- 2 tablespoons peanut oil
- 1 medium zucchini, cut into bite-size pieces
- 1-inch piece ginger, peeled and minced
- ½ pound (227 g) cremini or button mushrooms, cut into quarters or slices
- ½ cup Brown Sauce
- ½ teaspoon toasted sesame seeds

Pour the soy sauce, salt, pepper, and cornstarch over the chicken breast and toss to combine. Marinate at room temperature for about 20 minutes.

In a wok over medium-high heat, heat the peanut oil.

Add the chicken and stir-fry until it turns lightly golden brown on all sides. Remove it from the wok and set it aside.

Add the zucchini to the wok and stir-fry until slightly tender, then remove it from the wok and set it aside.

Add a little more oil to the wok if needed. Add the ginger and stir-fry for about 20 seconds, then add the mushrooms. Stir-fry the mushrooms until slightly brown.

Return the chicken and zucchini to the wok with the mushrooms and stir in the brown sauce.

When the sauce thickens, transfer the dish to a serving plate. Top with the sesame seeds.

Ioney with Five-Spice Chicken

rep time: 15 minutes | Cook time: 4 minutes | erves 4

- 2 tablespoons soy sauce
- 2 tablespoons rice wine
- ¼ cup honey
- 1 tablespoon Chinese five-spice powder
- 1 pound (454 g) boneless chicken thighs, cut into 1-inch pieces
- 2 tablespoons cooking oil
- 1 medium carrot, roll-cut into ½-inch pieces
- 1 tablespoon crushed, chopped ginger
- 3 garlic cloves, crushed and chopped
- 1 medium onion, cut into 1-inch pieces
- 1 medium red bell pepper, cut into 1-inch pieces
- 1 tablespoon cornstarch
- 1 teaspoon hot sesame oil
- 4 scallions, cut into 1-inch pieces

1. In a large bowl or resealable plastic bag, mix the soy sauce, rice wine, honey, and five-spice powder. Add the chicken and set aside to marinate.
2. In a wok over high heat, heat the cooking oil until it shimmers.
3. Add the carrot, ginger, and garlic and stir-fry for 1 minute.
4. Add the chicken, reserving the marinade, to the wok and stir-fry for 1 minute.
5. Add the onion and stir-fry for 1 minute.
6. Add the bell pepper and stir-fry for 1 minute.
7. Add the reserved marinade and the cornstarch and stir until a light glaze forms.
8. Add the sesame oil and stir-fry for 30 seconds.
9. Garnish with the scallions. Serve immediately over steamed rice.

Zesty Chicken with Cornstarch

Prep time: 20 minutes | Cook time: 6 minutes | Serves 4

- Zest of 1 orange
- 1 teaspoon hot sesame oil
- ¼ cup plus 2 tablespoons cornstarch, divided
- ¼ cup orange juice
- 2 tablespoons rice vinegar
- 2 tablespoons rice wine
- 2 tablespoons brown sugar
- 2 tablespoons soy sauce
- 1 pound (454 g) boneless chicken thighs, cut into 1-inch pieces
- ¼ cup cooking oil
- 1 tablespoon crushed, chopped ginger

- 2 garlic cloves, crushed and chopped
- 1 medium onion, cut into 1-inch pieces
- 2 cups sugar snap or snow pea pods
- 1 medium red bell pepper, cut into 1-inch pieces
- 4 scallions, cut into 1-inch pieces

1. In a small bowl, whisk together the orange zest, sesame oil, 2 tablespoons of the cornstarch, the orange juice, rice vinegar, rice wine, brown sugar, and soy sauce. Set aside.

2. Coat the chicken with the remaining ¼ cup of cornstarch by tossing in a resealable plastic bag or covered bowl, ensuring the pieces are evenly coated.

3. In a wok over high heat, heat the cooking oil until it shimmers.

4. Add the ginger and garlic and stir-fry for 30 seconds.

5. Shallow-fry (see here) the chicken for 3 to 4 minutes until lightly browned.

6. Remove the chicken and set aside. Remove and discard all but 2 tablespoons of oil from the wok.

7. Add the onion to the wok and stir-fry for 1 minute.

8. Add the pea pods and stir-fry for 30 seconds.

9. Add the bell pepper and stir-fry for 30 seconds.

10. Add the orange juice mixture and stir until a glaze forms.

11. Return the chicken to the wok. Toss, garnish with the scallions, and serve over rice.

Cornstarch with Limey Chicken

Prep time: 15 minutes | Cook time: 3 minutes | Serves 4

- ¼ cup canned coconut milk
- 2 tablespoons fish sauce
- 2 tablespoons lime juice
- 1 teaspoon hot sesame oil
- 1 tablespoon cornstarch
- 2 tablespoons coconut oil
- 1 tablespoon crushed, chopped ginger
- 2 garlic cloves, crushed and chopped
- 1 pound (454 g) boneless chicken

thighs, cut into 1-inch pieces
- 1 medium red onion, cut into 1-inch pieces
- 2 cups sugar snap or snow pea pods
- ½ cup chopped cilantro or parsley

1. In a small bowl, whisk together the coconut milk, fish sauce, lime juice, sesame oil, and cornstarch. Set aside.

2. In a wok over high heat, heat the coconut oil until it shimmers.

3. Add the ginger, garlic, and chicken and stir-fry for 1 minute.

4. Add the onion and stir-fry for 1 minute.

5. Add the pea pods and stir-fry for 1 minute.

6. Add the coconut milk mixture to the wok and stir until a glaze forms.

7. Garnish with the chopped cilantro or parsley and serve over coconut steamed jasmine rice.

Tamari with Mirin and Teriyaki Chicken

Prep time: 15 minutes | Cook time: 3 minutes | Serves 4

- 8 ounces / 227 g boneless chicken thighs, cut across the grain into ⅛-inch pieces
- 1 tablespoon cornstarch
- 2 tablespoons mirin
- 1 tablespoon gluten-free tamari
- ¼ cup honey
- 1 teaspoon toasted sesame oil
- 2 tablespoons cooking oil
- 2 garlic cloves, crushed and chopped
- 1 tablespoon crushed
- and chopped peeled ginger
- 1 medium onion, diced into 1-inch pieces
- 1 red bell pepper, diced into 1-inch pieces
- 4 ounces (113 g) shiitake mushrooms, sliced
- 1 cup diagonally sliced (1-inch) napa cabbage
- 4 scallions, green and white parts, cut diagonally into ¼-inch pieces
- Cooked rice or noodles, for serving

1. In a medium bowl, combine the chicken, cornstarch, mirin, tamari, honey, and sesame oil. Mix well.

In a wok, heat the cooking oil over high heat until it begins to smoke.

Add the garlic, ginger, and chicken. Stir-fry for 1 minute, or until the garlic and ginger are fragrant.

Add the onion, bell pepper, and mushrooms. Stir-fry for 1 minute, or until they are lightly coated with oil.

Add the cabbage and stir-fry for 1 minute, or until well it is combined with the other ingredients.

Add the scallions and toss. Serve over rice or noodles.

Paprika with Kadai Chicken

Prep time: 15 minutes | Cook time: 3 minutes | Serves 4

- 2 tablespoons ghee (see Preparation Tip)
- 1 tablespoon crushed, chopped ginger
- 2 garlic cloves, crushed and chopped
- 1 medium carrot, roll-cut into ½-inch pieces
- 1 pound (454 g) boneless chicken thighs, cut into 1-inch pieces

- 1 medium onion, cut into 1-inch pieces
- 1 teaspoon ground coriander
- 1 teaspoon cumin
- 1 teaspoon paprika
- 2 chiles, sliced into ¼-inch circles (no need to core or seed them)
- ½ cup whole-milk Greek yogurt

In a wok over high heat, heat the ghee until it shimmers.

Add the ginger, garlic, carrot, and chicken and stir-fry for 1 minute.

Add the onion, coriander, cumin, and paprika and stir-fry for 1 minute.

Add the sliced chiles and stir-fry for 1 minute.

Turn off the heat and stir the yogurt into the wok. Serve over basmati rice.

Fish Sauce with Kimchi Chicken

Prep time: 10 minutes | Cook time: 2 minutes | Serves 4

- 2 tablespoons cooking oil
- 1 tablespoon crushed, chopped ginger

- 2 garlic cloves, crushed and chopped
- 1 pound (454 g) ground chicken
- 1 cup chopped kimchi
- 2 heads baby bok choy, leaves separated

- 1 tablespoon fish sauce
- 1 tablespoon gochujang
- 1 tablespoon toasted sesame oil
- 2 tablespoons sesame seeds

1. In a wok over high heat, heat the cooking oil until it shimmers.
2. Add the ginger, garlic, and chicken and stir-fry for 1 minute.
3. Add the kimchi, bok choy, fish sauce, and gochujang and stir-fry for 1 minute.
4. Add the sesame oil and sesame seeds and toss.
5. Serve over steamed rice.

Broccoli with Honey and Spiced Chicken

Prep time: 15 minutes | Cook time: 4 minutes | Serves 4

- 2 tablespoons soy sauce
- 2 tablespoons honey
- 1 tablespoon cornstarch
- 2 tablespoons cooking oil
- 1 tablespoon crushed, chopped ginger
- 3 garlic cloves, crushed and chopped
- 1 medium carrot, roll-cut into ½-inch pieces

- 1 pound (454 g) boneless chicken thighs, cut into 1-inch pieces
- 1 medium onion, cut into 1-inch pieces
- 1 cup broccoli florets, cut into bite-size pieces
- 1 red bell pepper, cut into 1-inch pieces
- 4 scallions, cut into 1-inch pieces

1. In a small bowl, whisk together the soy sauce, honey, and cornstarch. Set aside.
2. In a wok over high heat, heat the cooking oil until it shimmers.
3. Add the ginger, garlic, carrot, and chicken and stir-fry for 1 minute.
4. Add the onion and stir-fry for 1 minute.
5. Add the broccoli and stir-fry for 1 minute.

6. Add the bell pepper and stir-fry for 1 minute.

7. Add soy sauce mixture to the wok and stir until a glaze forms.

8. Garnish with the scallions and serve over steamed rice.

Limey Cilantro with Gingered Chicken

Prep time: 15 minutes | Cook time: 5 minutes | Serves 4

- 1 (8-ounce / 227 g) can of pineapple chunks, drained, juice reserved
- Zest and juice of 1 lime
- 2 tablespoons fish sauce
- 1 tablespoon cornstarch
- 2 tablespoons cooking oil
- 1 tablespoon crushed, chopped ginger
- 2 garlic cloves, crushed and chopped
- 1 pound (454 g) boneless chicken thighs, cut into 1-inch pieces
- 1 medium onion, cut into 1-inch pieces
- 2 cups sugar snap or snow pea pods
- 1 medium red bell pepper, cut into 1-inch pieces
- 1 cup chopped cilantro

1. In a small bowl, whisk together the pineapple juice, lime zest and juice, fish sauce, and cornstarch. Set aside.

2. In a wok over high heat, heat the cooking oil until it shimmers.

3. Add the ginger, garlic, and chicken and stir-fry for 1 minute.

4. Add the onion and stir-fry for 1 minute.

5. Add the pea pods and stir-fry for 1 minute.

6. Add the bell pepper and stir-fry for 1 minute.

7. Add the pineapple chunks to the wok and stir-fry for 1 minute.

8. Add the pineapple and lime juice mixture to the wok and stir until a light glaze is formed.

9. Garnish with the cilantro and serve over jasmine rice.

Coriander with Buttered Chicken

Prep time: 15 minutes | Cook time: 6 minutes | Serves 4

- 2 tablespoons ghee
- 1 tablespoon crushed, chopped ginger
- 2 garlic cloves, crushed and chopped
- 1 medium carrot, roll-cut into ½-inch pieces
- 1 pound (454 g) boneless chicken thighs, cut into 1-inch pieces
- 1 medium onion, cut into 1-inch pieces
- 1 red bell pepper, cut into 1-inch pieces
- 1 teaspoon ground cumin
- 1 teaspoon ground coriander
- 1 teaspoon ground paprika
- 1 teaspoon ground cloves
- 2 tablespoons salted butter
- 1 teaspoon hot sesame oil
- ½ cup whole-milk Greek yogurt

1. In a wok over high heat, heat the ghee until it shimmers.

2. Add the ginger, garlic, and carrot and stir-fry for minute.

3. Add the chicken, onion, bell pepper, cumin, coriander, paprika, and cloves and stir-fry for 1 minute.

4. Add the butter and sesame oil and stir-fry for 1 minute.

5. Turn off the heat and stir in the yogurt.

6. Serve over basmati rice.

Scallion with Gingered Malaysian Chicken

Prep time: 10 minutes | Cook time: 4 minutes | Serves 4

- 2 tablespoons cooking oil
- 1 tablespoon crushed, chopped ginger
- 2 garlic cloves, crushed and chopped
- 1 pound (454 g) boneless chicken thighs, cut into 1-inch pieces
- 1 medium red onion, cut into 1-inch pieces

¼ cup sambal oelek

1 tablespoon fish sauce

1 cup chopped bok choy

- 4 scallions, cut into 1-inch pieces

. In a wok over high heat, heat the cooking oil until it shimmers.

. Add the ginger, garlic, and chicken and stir-fry for 1 minute.

. Add the onion and stir-fry for 1 minute.

. Add the sambal oelek and stir-fry for 30 seconds.

. Add the fish sauce and bok choy and stir-fry for 1 minute.

. Garnish with the scallions and serve over jasmine rice.

Sesame Chicken with Limey Curry

Prep time: 15 minutes | Cook time: 3 minutes | Serves 4

- 8 ounces / 227 g boneless chicken thighs, cut across the grain into ⅛-inch pieces

- 1 tablespoon cornstarch

- 2 tablespoons Shaoxing rice wine

- 1 tablespoon curry powder

- 1 tablespoon soy sauce

- 1 teaspoon spicy sesame oil

- 2 tablespoons freshly squeezed lime juice

- ¼ cup ghee

- 1 garlic clove, crushed and chopped

- 1 tablespoon crushed and chopped peeled ginger

- 1 large carrot, roll-cut into ½-inch pieces

- 4 bird's-eye chiles, coarsely chopped

- 1 large onion, diced into 1-inch pieces

- Grated zest of 1 lime (1 teaspoon)

- 4 scallions, green and white parts, cut diagonally into ¼-inch pieces

In a medium bowl, combine the chicken, cornstarch, wine, curry powder, soy sauce, sesame oil, and lime juice. Mix well.

In a wok, heat the ghee over high heat until it begins to smoke.

Add the garlic, ginger, carrot, and chicken. Stir-

fry for 2 minutes, or until the chicken begins to brown.

4. Add the chiles, onion, and lime zest. Stir-fry for 1 minute, or until all of the ingredients are well combined.

5. Add the scallions and toss. Serve over basmati rice.

Brothy Walnut with Garlicky Chicken

Prep time: 15 minutes | Cook time: 8 minutes | Serves 4

- 1 pound (454 g) boneless, skinless chicken breasts

- 2 tablespoons oyster sauce

- 2 teaspoons cornstarch

- 3 tablespoons chicken broth

- 1 tablespoon soy sauce

- 1 tablespoon rice wine or dry sherry

- 3½ tablespoons vegetable or peanut oil, divided

- 1 teaspoon minced ginger

- 1 teaspoon minced garlic

- 2 tablespoons Chinese brown bean sauce

- 1 cup toasted walnut halves

1. Chop the chicken into thin strips 1½-2 long. Place the chicken in a bowl and add the oyster sauce and cornstarch. Marinate the chicken for 20 minutes.

2. In a small bowl, combine the chicken broth, soy sauce, and rice wine or sherry. Set aside.

3. Heat a wok or skillet over medium-high heat until it is nearly smoking. Add 2 tablespoons oil. When the oil is hot, add the ginger. Stir-fry for 10 seconds.

4. Add the chicken. Let sit briefly, then stir-fry the chicken, stirring and moving it around the pan until it turns white and is nearly cooked through—about 3-4 minutes. Remove the chicken and drain in a colander or on paper towels.

5. Heat 1½ tablespoons oil in the wok or skillet. When the oil is hot, add the garlic and the brown bean sauce. Stir-fry for 10 seconds.

6. Add the walnut halves. Stir-fry for 1 minute, mixing them in with the bean sauce.

7. Add the chicken broth mixture and bring to a boil.

8. Add the chicken back into the pan. Stir-fry for 2 more minutes to mix everything together and make sure the chicken is cooked through. Serve hot.

Shallots with Lemongrass Chicken

Prep time: 10 minutes | Cook time: 4 minutes | Serves 4

- 2 tablespoons fish sauce
- ½ tablespoon sugar
- ¼ teaspoon turmeric powder
- 4 tablespoons vegetable oil, divided
- 1 pound (454 g) boneless, skinless chicken thighs, cut into 1 pieces
- 1 tablespoon minced garlic
- ¼ cup minced shallots
- 2 tablespoons minced lemongrass
- 2 chilies, minced, or ½ teaspoon red pepper flakes
- 2 scallions, cut into 1 pieces

1. In a large bowl, mix the fish sauce, sugar, turmeric powder, and 2 tablespoons oil. Add the chicken and stir to coat well. Allow the chicken to marinate for 15 minutes.

2. Heat a wok over medium heat. Add the remaining oil and cook the garlic, shallots, lemongrass, and chilies until fragrant, about 1 minute.

3. Add in the marinated chicken and increase the heat to medium high. Stir-fry the chicken for 3-4 minutes until browned. Toss in the scallions and serve hot.

Chili Sauce with Thai Basil Turkey

Prep time: 10 minutes | Cook time: 5 minutes | Serves 4

- 1 tablespoon peanut oil
- 2 tablespoons minced garlic
- 3 red Thai chilies, minced
- ¼ cup chopped
- scallions
- 1 pound (454 g) lean ground turkey
- ¼ teaspoon black pepper
- 2 tablespoons fish sauce

- 1½ cups chopped Thai basil

1. Heat a wok over medium heat and add the oil.

2. Add the garlic and cook until fragrant, about 30 seconds.

3. Add chilies and cook for 1 minute before adding in scallions. Cook for an additional minute or until the scallions have softened.

4. Add in the ground turkey. Cook the turkey until it is no longer pink, approximately 3-4 minutes.

5. Remove the wok from heat. Stir in pepper, fish sauce, and basil. Serve immediately.

Cilantro with Tequila Lime Chicken

Prep time: 10 minutes | Cook time: 4 minutes | Serves 4

- ½ cup Tequila Lime Marinade
- 1 pound (454 g) boneless, skinless chicken thighs, chopped into quarters
- 2 tablespoons vegetable oil
- 1 small red onion,
- sliced thinly
- ½ jalapeño pepper, seeded and diced
- 2 garlic cloves, minced
- ¼ cup chopped cilantro
- Lime wedges

1. Pour the marinade into a large resealable bag and add the chicken. Massage the marinade into the chicken and seal the bag. Refrigerate for 15-20 minutes.

2. Heat oil in a wok over medium heat and add the onion, jalapeño, and garlic. Add in the marinated chicken and stir-fry until browned and cooked through—about 4-5 minutes. Serve with cilantro on top and lime wedges on the side.

Cheesy Chicken Saltimbocca

Prep time: 15 minutes | Cook time: 6 minutes | Serves 4

- 4 chicken breast cutlets, pounded to ¼–⅛ thickness
- ½ teaspoon kosher salt
- ¼ teaspoon black
- pepper
- ½ cup all-purpose flour
- ¼ teaspoon cayenne powder

2 tablespoons vegetable oil

3 tablespoons unsalted butter, divided

8 fresh sage leaves

- 4 thin slices prosciutto
- 4 slices mozzarella cheese
- ½ cup dry white wine
- ½ teaspoon dry sage

Use paper towels and blot excess moisture from chicken. Season with salt and pepper to taste.

In a shallow dish, whisk together the flour and cayenne.

Heat the oil in a wok over medium heat and add 1 tablespoon butter. Place each cutlet into the flour mixture. Use your fingers to adhere the flour on both sides. Shake off excess flour and add to the wok. Repeat with the remaining chicken. Cook the cutlets for 2 minutes on each side until golden and transfer to a baking sheet.

On top of each cutlet, place 2 fresh sage leaves, 1 slice prosciutto, and 1 slice mozzarella.

Set the oven to broil. Transfer the baking sheet to the oven and allow the cheese to melt and brown. Remove and cover with foil.

Using the same wok, add the white wine and cook for 2-3 minutes to allow the liquids to reduce by half. Use a wooden spoon to scrape up the brown bits. Whisk in the dry sage and remaining 2 tablespoons butter.

Place the chicken on a platter and top with the sauce.

Ginger and Garlic Scallions with Chicken

Prep time: 15 minutes | Cook time: 8 minutes | Serves 4

12 chicken wings

½ teaspoon black pepper

¼ teaspoon cayenne powder

½ tablespoon garlic salt

½ cup rice flour

½ cup vegetable or peanut oil

- 1 clove garlic, minced
- 2 slices ginger, minced
- 4 tablespoons chopped scallions, divided
- 1 red jalapeño pepper, thinly sliced
- ½ cup Sweet-and-Sour Sauce

1. In a large bowl, season the wings with black pepper, cayenne, and garlic salt to taste.

2. Toss the seasoned wings with the rice flour and set aside.

3. Add the oil to a wok over medium-high heat. Once the oil reaches temperature, gently shake off excess flour from the wings and carefully add them to the wok. Fry until golden brown and cooked through—about 7 to 8 minutes. Remove the chicken wings and drain on a platter lined with paper towels.

4. Carefully drain all but 1 tablespoon of the oil from the wok. Over medium heat, add in the garlic, ginger, 2 tablespoons scallions, and jalapeño. Stir-fry for 15 seconds.

5. Add in the Sweet-and-Sour Sauce. Allow the sauce to come to a boil and return the chicken wings to the wok. Toss the wings to coat well. Transfer to a platter and sprinkle the tops with remaining scallions. Serve immediately.

Hoisin Sauce with Braised Duck

Prep time: 10 minutes | Cook time: 8 minutes | Serves 4

- 2 tablespoons hoisin sauce
- 1 tablespoon honey
- 1 teaspoon Chinese five-spice powder
- 1 tablespoon warm water
- 1 tablespoon peanut

or vegetable oil

- ½ small sweet onion, thinly sliced
- 1 clove garlic, minced
- ½ head napa cabbage, with leaves shredded
- 2 skinless duck breasts, thinly sliced

1. In a bowl, mix the hoisin sauce, honey, Chinese five-spice powder, and water. Set aside.

2. Heat your wok over high heat until a drop of water sizzles on contact. Add the peanut oil and swirl to coat the wok. Add the onion and stir-fry it for 2 minutes. Add the garlic and cabbage, and stir-fry for another 2 to 3 minutes. Remove the vegetables from the wok and set aside.

3. Add the duck slices to the hot wok and stir-fry for 2 minutes. Add the sauce mixture to the wok, and cook for another 2 minutes, or until the sauce thickens. Return the vegetables to the wok, and

toss to combine with the duck and sauce.

4. Serve with rice or noodles.

Five-Spice Peking Duck

Prep time: 15 minutes | Cook time: 10 minutes | Serves 4

- **For the Duck:**
- 4 boneless duck breasts
- ¼ teaspoon salt
- 1 teaspoon light soy sauce
- 1 teaspoon Shaoxing wine
- ⅛ teaspoon five spice powder
- 1 tablespoon oil

- **For the Fixings:**
- 1 cucumber, julienned
- ½ cup cantaloupe, julienned
- 2 scallions, julienned
- 3 garlic cloves, finely minced
- 3 tablespoons hoisin sauce

1. Mix wine, five-spice powder, soy sauce, and salt in a bowl.

2. Soak the duck breasts in the marinade for 20 minutes for marination.

3. Sear the marinated duck breast in a Mandarin wok greased with oil over medium heat for 10 minutes per side until golden-brown.

4. Mix cucumber with cantaloupe, scallions, garlic, and hoisin sauce in a bowl.

5. Serve the duck breast with cucumber mixture.

6. Enjoy.

Quick Vinegary Cornstarch with Chicken

Prep time: 15 minutes | Cook time: 7 minutes | Serves 4

- 2 tablespoons soy sauce
- 2 teaspoons toasted sesame oil
- 1 tablespoon sugar
- 1 tablespoon honey
- 2 tablespoons rice vinegar

- 1 tablespoon grated fresh ginger
- 1 clove garlic, minced
- 1 egg, beaten
- 3 tablespoons cornstarch
- Sea salt to taste
- Freshly ground black

pepper to taste
- 1 pound (454 g) boneless and skinless chicken thighs, trimmed of fat and cut into bite-size pieces
- 1½ tablespoons

peanut or vegetable oil
- 2 tablespoons sesame seeds, for garnish
- 1 scallion, sliced into ½-inch pieces, for garnish

1. In a small bowl, make the sauce by combining the soy sauce, sesame oil, sugar, honey, rice vinegar, ginger, and garlic. Set aside.

2. In a large bowl, mix the egg with the cornstarch, and season with the sea salt and pepper to taste. Let it sit for 10 minutes. Add the chicken to the bowl with the egg mixture, and toss to coat the pieces.

3. Heat your wok on high heat until a drop of water sizzles on contact. Add the peanut oil and swirl to coat the wok. Add the chicken and stir-fry for 5 to 6 minutes, until the pieces are golden brown.

4. Add the sauce to the wok. Toss to combine it with the chicken, and continue stir-frying for about 2 minutes. As soon as the sauce thickens, turn off the heat.

5. Place the chicken on a serving platter, and garnish with the sesame seeds and scallions. Serve with rice.

Chili Peanuts with Spicy Chicken

Prep time: 10 minutes | Cook time: 6 minutes | Serves 4

- 3 tablespoons peanut or vegetable oil, divided
- 1 sweet onion, sliced
- 1 red bell pepper, cut into strips
- 1 pound (454 g) boneless, skinless chicken breasts, cut into 1-inch chunks
- Sea salt to taste

- Freshly ground black pepper to taste
- ½ pound (227 g) snow peas, washed and trimmed
- ⅓ cup hoisin sauce
- ⅓ cup roasted peanut
- Chili sauce, for garnish (optional)

1. Heat your wok over high heat until a drop of water sizzles on contact. Add 1½ tablespoons of peanut

oil, and swirl to coat the wok. Stir-fry the onion and red bell pepper for 3 to 5 minutes, until they are slightly browned. Remove the vegetables from the wok and set aside.

Add the remaining 1½ tablespoons of peanut oil to the wok, and stir-fry the chicken for 2 to 3 minutes, until it is browned on all sides. Season the chicken with the sea salt and pepper to taste. Add the snow peas to the wok, and toss to combine with the chicken. Reduce the heat to medium-low and add the hoisin sauce. Cook for 1 to 2 minutes, or until the snow peas are wilted.

Remove the wok from the heat, sprinkle the chicken and peas with the peanuts, and serve with the chili sauce on the side (if using).

Broth with Vinegar Tso's Chicken

Prep time: 20 minutes | Cook time: 10 minutes | Serves 4

- 3 tablespoons soy sauce
- 1 tablespoon rice vinegar
- 1½ tablespoons honey
- 1 tablespoon sugar
- 2 teaspoons chili sauce
- ¾ cup chicken broth
- 5 teaspoons cornstarch, divided
- Sea salt to taste
- Freshly ground black pepper to taste

- 2 pounds (907 g) skinless, boneless chicken meat, cut into 1-inch pieces
- 2 tablespoons peanut or vegetable oil
- 2 garlic cloves, finely minced
- 2 teaspoons fresh ginger, finely minced
- 4 scallions, chopped
- 1 teaspoon roasted sesame seeds, for garnish

In a small bowl, make the sauce by whisking together the soy sauce, rice vinegar, honey, sugar, chili sauce, chicken broth, and 2 teaspoons of cornstarch. Set aside.

To a medium bowl, add the remaining 3 teaspoons of cornstarch. Season with the sea salt and pepper to taste. Add the chicken and coat it on all sides.

Heat your wok over high heat until a drop of water sizzles on contact. Add the peanut oil and swirl to coat the wok. Cook the chicken, making sure to get

a nice brown crust on all sides. Cook it in batches, if necessary, as the chicken should not crowd the bottom of the wok. When the chicken is almost completely cooked, remove it from the wok and set it aside.

4. Turn the heat down to medium. Add the garlic, ginger, and scallions to the wok, and stir-fry for about 20 seconds. Pour the sauce into the wok, and bring it to a simmer. Return the chicken to the wok, and toss to combine with the sauce. Stir-fry the chicken for another 1 to 2 minutes, or until the chicken is cooked through.

5. Garnish the chicken with the sesame seeds and serve with rice.

Gingered Peanuts with Garlicky Chicken

Prep time: 15 minutes | Cook time: 7 minutes | Serves 4 to 6

- 3 teaspoons light soy sauce
- 2½ teaspoons cornstarch
- 2 teaspoons Chinese black vinegar
- 1 teaspoon Shaoxing rice wine
- 1 teaspoon sesame oil
- ¾ pound (340 g) boneless, skinless, chicken thighs, cut into 1-inch cubes

- 2 tablespoons vegetable oil
- 6 to 8 whole dried red chilies, or 1 teaspoon red pepper flakes
- 3 scallions, white and green parts separated, thinly sliced
- 2 garlic cloves, minced
- 1 teaspoon peeled minced fresh ginger
- ¼ cup unsalted dry roasted peanuts

1. In a medium bowl, stir together the light soy, cornstarch, black vinegar, rice wine, and sesame oil until the cornstarch is dissolved. Add the chicken and stir gently to coat. Marinate for 10 to 15 minutes, or enough time to prepare the rest of the ingredients.

2. Heat a wok over medium-high heat until a drop of water sizzles and evaporates on contact. Pour in the vegetable oil and swirl to coat the base of the wok.

3. Add the chilies and stir-fry for about 10 seconds, or until they have just begun to blacken and the oil is slightly fragrant. (Note: Turn on your stove's

exhaust fan, because stir-frying dried chilies on high heat can get a little smoky.) Add the chicken, reserving the marinade, and stir-fry for 3 to 4 minutes, until no longer pink.

4. Toss in the scallion whites, garlic, and ginger and stir-fry for about 30 seconds. Pour in the marinade and mix to coat the chicken. Toss in the peanuts and cook for another 2 to 3 minutes, until the sauce becomes glossy.

5. Transfer to a serving plate, garnish with the scallion greens, and serve hot.

Brothy Chicken with Bamboo Shoots

Prep time: 15 minutes | Cook time: 6 minutes | Serves 4

- 2 large egg whites
- 2 tablespoons cornstarch, plus 1 teaspoon
- ¾ pound (340 g) boneless, skinless chicken breasts, cut into bite-size slices
- 3 ½ tablespoons vegetable oil, divided
- ⅓ cup low-sodium chicken broth
- 1 tablespoon Shaoxing rice wine
- Kosher salt to taste
- Ground white pepper to taste
- 4 peeled fresh ginger slices, each about the size of a quarter
- 1 (4-ounce / 113-g) can sliced bamboo shoots, rinsed and drained
- 3 garlic cloves, minced
- ¾ pound (340 g) snow peas or sugar snap peas, strings removed

1. In a mixing bowl, using a fork or whisk, beat the egg whites until frothy and the tighter clumps of egg white are foamy. Stir in the 2 tablespoons of cornstarch until well blended and no longer clumpy. Fold in the chicken and 1 tablespoon of vegetable oil and marinate for 10 minutes or up to 30 minutes.

2. In a small bowl, stir together the chicken broth, rice wine, and remaining 1 teaspoon of cornstarch, and season with a pinch each of salt and white pepper to taste. Set aside.

3. Bring a medium saucepan filled with water to a boil over high heat. Add ½ tablespoon of oil and reduce the heat to a simmer. Using a wok skimmer or slotted spoon to allow the marinade to drain

off, transfer the chicken to the boiling water. Give the chicken a stir so that the pieces do not clump together. Cook for 40 to 50 seconds, until the chicken is white on the outside but not cooked through. Drain the chicken in a colander and shake off the excess water. Discard the simmering water.

4. Heat a wok over medium-high heat until a drop of water sizzles and evaporates on contact. Pour in the remaining 2 tablespoons of oil and swirl to coat the base of the wok. Season the oil by adding the ginger slices and salt to taste. Allow the ginger to sizzle in the oil for about 30 seconds, swirling gently.

5. Add the bamboo shoots and garlic and, using a wok spatula, toss to coat with oil and cook until fragrant, about 30 seconds. Add the snow peas and stir-fry for about 2 minutes until bright green and crisp tender. Add the chicken to the wok and swirl in the sauce mixture. Toss to coat and continue cooking for 1 to 2 minutes, until the chicken is completely cooked.

6. Transfer to a platter and discard the ginger. Serve hot.

Cashew Chicken

Prep time: 15 minutes | Cook time: 9 minutes | Serves 4 to 6

- 1 tablespoon light soy sauce
- 2 teaspoons Shaoxing rice wine
- 2 teaspoons cornstarch
- 1 teaspoon sesame oil
- ½ teaspoon ground Sichuan peppercorns
- ¾ pound (340 g) boneless, skinless, chicken thighs, cut into 1-inch cubes
- 2 tablespoons vegetable oil
- ½-inch piece peeled finely minced fresh ginger
- Kosher salt to taste
- ½ red bell pepper, cut into ½-inch pieces
- 1 small zucchini, cut into ½-inch pieces
- 2 garlic cloves, minced
- ½ cup unsalted dry roasted cashews
- 2 scallions, white and green parts separated thinly sliced

1. In a medium bowl, stir together the light soy, rice wine, cornstarch, sesame oil, and Sichuan pepper. Add the chicken and stir gently to coat. Let it

marinate for 15 minutes, or for enough time to prepare the rest of the ingredients.

Heat a wok over medium-high heat until a drop of water sizzles and evaporates on contact. Pour in the vegetable oil and swirl to coat the base of the wok. Season the oil by adding the ginger and a pinch of salt to taste. Allow the ginger to sizzle in the oil for about 30 seconds, swirling gently.

Using tongs, lift the chicken from the marinade and transfer to the wok, reserving the marinade. Stir-fry the chicken for 4 to 5 minutes, until no longer pink. Add the red bell pepper, zucchini, and garlic and stir-fry for 2 to 3 minutes, or until the vegetables are tender.

Pour in the marinade and mix to coat the other ingredients. Bring the marinade to a boil and continue to stir-fry for 1 to 2 minutes, until the sauce turns thick and glossy. Stir in the cashews and cook for another minute.

Transfer to a serving plate, garnish with the scallions, and serve hot.

auce with Cornstarch and hicken

ep time: 15 minutes | Cook time: 8 minutes | rves 4

3 scallions, chopped

4 garlic cloves, cut in half

6 ginger slices, ¼-inch thick

1 tablespoon vegetable oil

24-ounce / 680.4-g boneless chicken thighs, cut into chunks

3 shallots, cut into quarters

¼ cup Shaoxing wine

1 ½ cups chicken stock

- 1 teaspoon light brown sugar
- 2 tablespoons soy sauce
- 1 teaspoon dark soy sauce
- ¼ teaspoon white pepper
- 2 teaspoons oyster sauce
- 1 tablespoon cornstarch, mixed with 1 tablespoon water

Sauté garlic and ginger with oil in a Cantonese wok for 1 minute.

Stir in scallion, chicken thighs, and shallots, and cook for 5 minutes.

3. Add wine, chicken stock, brown sugar, soy sauce, white pepper, and oyster sauce.

4. Mix, cover, and cook on medium-low heat until the chicken is tender.

5. Whisk cornstarch with 1 tablespoon water in a small bowl.

6. Pour this slurry into the pan and cook for 2-3 minutes until the sauce thickens.

7. Serve warm.

Spicy Sesame with Five-Spice Chicken

Prep time: 15 minutes | Cook time: 5 minutes | Serves 4

- 8 ounces / 227 g boneless chicken thighs, cut across the grain into ⅛-inch pieces
- 1 tablespoon cornstarch
- 2 tablespoons Shaoxing rice wine
- 2 tablespoons soy sauce
- 1 teaspoon five-spice powder
- 2 tablespoons cooking oil
- 2 garlic cloves, crushed and chopped
- 1 tablespoon crushed

- and chopped peeled ginger
- 1 medium onion, diced into 1-inch pieces
- 4 ounces (113 g) shiitake mushrooms, sliced
- 2 dozen sugar snap pea pods
- 1 teaspoon spicy sesame oil
- ¼ cup oyster sauce
- 4 scallions, green and white parts, cut diagonally into ¼-inch pieces
- Cooked rice or noodles, for serving

1. In a medium bowl, combine the chicken, cornstarch, wine, soy sauce, and five-spice powder. Mix well.

2. In a wok, heat the cooking oil over high heat until it begins to smoke.

3. Add the garlic, ginger, and chicken. Stir-fry for 1 minute, or until the garlic and ginger are fragrant.

4. Add the onion and mushrooms. Stir-fry for 1 minute, or until the vegetables are lightly coated with oil.

5. Add the pea pods, sesame oil, and oyster sauce. Stir-fry for 1 minute, or until all of the ingredients are coated in the sauce.

6. Add the scallions and toss. Serve over rice or noodles.

Chapter 7: Beef, Pork, and Lamb

Gingered Beef with Broccoli

Prep time: 10 minutes | Cook time: 8 minutes | Serves 4

- 3 tablespoons cornstarch
- 6 tablespoons water, divided
- 1 garlic clove, thinly sliced
- 1 pound (454 g) sirloin or chuck steak, cut into strips
- ⅓ cup soy sauce
- 1½ tablespoons brown sugar
- 1 teaspoon ground ginger
- 2 tablespoons peanut or vegetable oil, divided
- 4 cups broccoli florets
- 1 small sweet onion, cut into wedges

1. In a medium bowl, mix the cornstarch, 2 tablespoons water, and garlic until smooth. Add the beef and toss to coat on all sides. Let it sit for 10 minutes.

2. In a medium bowl, mix the soy sauce, the remaining 4 tablespoons water, the brown sugar, and the ginger until smooth. Set aside.

3. Heat your wok over medium-high heat. Add 1 tablespoon peanut oil, and swirl to coat the wok. Add the beef and stir-fry for 2 minutes, or until the steak is slightly browned. Transfer the beef to a bowl and set aside.

4. Add the remaining 1 tablespoon peanut oil to the wok, and then add the broccoli and onion. Stir-fry the vegetables for about 4 minutes, or until crisp-tender. Return the beef to the wok, and toss it with the vegetables. Add the soy sauce mixture to the wok, and stir to mix it with all the ingredients. Cover the wok and cook for 2 to 3 more minutes. Serve over rice.

Spicy Pork with Bok Choy

Prep time: 10 minutes | Cook time: 8 minutes | Serves 4

- 1 tablespoon light soy sauce
- 1 tablespoon Shaoxing rice wine
- 1 teaspoon Chinese five spice powder
- 1 teaspoon cornstarch
- ½ teaspoon light brown sugar
- ¾ pound (340.5 g) ground pork
- 2 tablespoons
- vegetable oil
- 2 garlic cloves, peeled and slightly smashed
- Kosher salt
- 2 to 3 heads bok choy, cut crosswise into bite-size pieces
- 1 carrot, peeled and julienned
- Cooked rice, for serving

1. In a mixing bowl, stir together the light soy, rice wine, five spice powder, cornstarch, and brown sugar. Add the pork and mix gently to combine. Set aside to marinate for 10 minutes.

2. Heat a wok over medium-high heat until a drop of water sizzles and evaporates on contact. Pour in the oil and swirl to coat the base of the wok. Season the oil by adding the garlic and a pinch of salt. Allow the garlic to sizzle in the oil for about seconds, swirling gently.

3. Add pork to the wok and leave it to sear against the wok's walls for 1 to 2 minutes, or until a golden crust develops. Flip and sear on the other side for another minute more. Toss and flip to stir-fry the pork for 1 to 2 more minutes, breaking it up into crumbles and clumps until no longer pink.

4. Add the bok choy and carrot and toss and flip to combine with the pork. Keep stir-frying for 2 to 3 minutes, until the carrot and bok choy are tender. Transfer to a platter and serve hot with steamed rice.

Sauce and Sugar Pork Belly

Prep time: 10 minutes | Cook time: 8½ minutes Serves 4

- 1 pound (454 g) boneless pork belly
- ⅓ cup Black Bean
- Sauce or store-bought black bean sauce
- 1 tablespoon Shaoxi

rice wine

1 teaspoon dark soy sauce

½ teaspoon sugar

2 tablespoons vegetable oil, divided

4 peeled fresh ginger slices, each about the size of a quarter

- Kosher salt
- 1 leek, halved lengthwise and cut on the diagonal into ½-inch slices
- ½ red bell pepper, sliced

In a large saucepan, place the pork and cover with water. Bring the pan to a boil and then reduce to a simmer. Simmer uncovered for 30 minutes, or until the pork is tender and cooked through. Using a slotted spoon, transfer the pork to a bowl (discard the cooking liquid) and allow to cool. Refrigerate for several hours or overnight. Once the pork is cool, thinly slice into ¼-inch-thick slices and set aside. Allowing the pork to cool completely before slicing will make it easier to thinly slice.

In a glass measuring cup, stir together the black bean sauce, rice wine, dark soy, and sugar and set aside.

Heat a wok over medium-high heat until a drop of water sizzles and evaporates on contact. Pour in 1 tablespoon of oil and swirl to coat the base of the wok. Season the oil by adding the ginger and a pinch of salt. Allow the ginger to sizzle in the oil for about 30 seconds, swirling gently.

Working in batches, transfer half the pork to the wok. Let the pieces sear in the wok for 2 to 3 minutes. Flip to sear on the other side for another 1 to 2 minutes more, until the pork begins to curl. Transfer to a clean bowl. Repeat with the remaining pork.

Add the remaining 1 tablespoon of oil. Add the leek and red pepper and stir-fry for 1 minute, until the leek is soft. Swirl in the sauce and stir-fry until fragrant. Return the pork to the pan and continue stir-frying for 2 to 3 more minutes, until everything is just cooked through. Discard the ginger slices and transfer to a serving platter.

Gingered Lamb with Leeks

Prep time: 15 minutes | Cook time: 8 minutes | Serves 4

¾ pound (340.5 g)   boneless leg of lamb,

cut into 3 chunks, then thinly sliced across the grain

- Kosher salt
- 2 tablespoons Shaoxing rice wine
- 1 tablespoon dark soy sauce
- 1 tablespoon light soy sauce
- 1 teaspoon oyster sauce
- 1 teaspoon honey
- 1 to 2 teaspoons

sesame oil

- ½ teaspoon ground Sichuan pepper corns
- 2 teaspoons cornstarch
- 2 tablespoons vegetable oil
- 1 tablespoon peeled and finely minced fresh ginger
- 2 leeks, trimmed and thinly sliced
- 4 garlic cloves, finely minced

1. In a mixing bowl, season the lamb lightly with 1 to 2 pinches of salt. Toss to coat and set aside for 10 minutes. In a small bowl, stir together the rice wine, dark soy, light soy, oyster sauce, honey, sesame oil, Sichuan pepper, and cornstarch. Set aside.

2. Heat a wok over medium-high heat until a drop of water sizzles and evaporates on contact. Pour in the vegetable oil and swirl to coat the base of the wok. Season the oil by adding the ginger and a pinch of salt. Allow the ginger to sizzle in the oil for about 10 seconds, swirling gently.

3. Add the lamb and sear for 1 to 2 minutes, then begin to stir-fry, tossing and flipping for 2 minutes more, or until no longer pink. Transfer to a clean bowl and set aside.

4. Add the leeks and garlic and stir-fry for 1 to 2 minutes, or until the leeks are bright green and soft. Transfer to the lamb bowl.

5. Pour in the sauce mixture and simmer for 3 to 4 minutes, until the sauce reduces by half and turns glossy. Return the lamb and vegetables to the wok and toss to combine with the sauce.

6. Transfer to a platter and serve hot.

Spiced Marinade with Seared Beef Rolls

Prep time: 15 minutes | Cook time: 3 minutes | Serves 4

For the Marinade:

- 1 tablespoon soy sauce

- 1 teaspoon sesame oil
- Freshly ground black pepper
- 1 pound (454 g) top round London broil

For the Filling:

- 1 carrot, cut into 2-inch matchsticks
- ½ red bell pepper, cut into 2-inch matchsticks
- ½ green bell pepper, cut into 2-inch matchsticks
- 1 English cucumber, cut into 2-inch matchsticks
- 1 green apple, cut into 2-inch matchsticks
- 1 cup pea shoots

For the Sauce:

- 1 tablespoon oyster sauce
- 2 teaspoons soy sauce
- 1 tablespoon Shaoxing wine
- 1 garlic clove, minced
- 4 tablespoons canned chicken or beef broth

For the Beef Rolls:

- 1 tablespoon peanut or vegetable oil

1. In a large bowl, mix the soy sauce and sesame oil. Season with the pepper. Add the beef and coat it all around. Marinate the beef for at least 30 minutes.

2. To prepare the filling, in a large bowl, mix the carrot, red bell pepper, green bell pepper, cucumber, apple, and pea shoots. Set aside.

3. To prepare the sauce, in a saucepan, mix the oyster sauce, soy sauce, rice wine, garlic, and chicken broth. Bring to a simmer and turn off the heat when the sauce thickens slightly, 1 to 2 minutes. Set aside.

4. Heat your wok over high heat until a drop of water sizzles on contact. Add the peanut oil and swirl to coat the wok. Add the beef and sear it for 2 minutes on each side, or until medium-rare.

5. Transfer the beef to a cutting board, and let it rest until it's cool enough to handle. Slice the beef against the grain into thin, long pieces. Lay each beef slice on a flat surface, and top each with an equal amount of the filling. Make sure the vegetables lie flat and length-wise. Roll each beef slice and secure it with toothpicks if necessary.

6. Place the beef rolls on a serving platter, and gently drizzle them with the sauce.

Beef with Pineapples Stir-Fry

Prep time: 15 minutes | Cook time: 2 minutes | Serves 4

For the Marinade:

- 2 tablespoons oyster sauce
- 2 tablespoons soy sauce
- 1 teaspoon sesame oil
- 1 tablespoon brown sugar
- 2 tablespoons Chinese rice wine
- 1 pound beef fillet, cut into strips

For the Stir-Fry:

- 2 tablespoons vegetable or canola oil, divided
- 2 garlic cloves, minced
- 1 green pepper, cut into large dice
- 1 sweet onion, cut into large dice
- 1 teaspoon sugar
- 1 cup cubed mango and pineapple

1. In a large bowl, combine the marinade ingredient together.

2. Add the beef to the marinade, toss to combine, and marinate for at least 2 hours.

3. Heat a wok over high heat until a drop of water sizzles on contact. Add 1 tablespoon oil.

4. Stir-fry the beef for about 1 minute or until mostly done.

5. Remove the beef from the wok.

6. Add the remaining 1 tablespoon oil to the wok. Stir-fry the garlic for about 15 seconds and then add the pepper, onion, and sugar. Cook for 1 to 2 minutes, tossing frequently.

7. Add the fruit and toss to combine, just until coated, and serve immediately.

Spicy Bean Sauce with Pork

Prep time: 10 minutes | Cook time: 48 minutes | Serve 4

- 1 pound (454 g) pork belly
- 1 tablespoon soy sauce
- 1 tablespoon Shaoxing wine
- 1 tablespoon spicy bean paste
- 1 teaspoon sesame oil
- 2 teaspoons sugar
- 1 tablespoon peanut or vegetable oil
- 1 tablespoon black bean sauce
- 1 tablespoon minced fresh ginger
- 3 garlic scapes, cut into 1-inch pieces
- 1 scallion, thinly slice

In a pot of enough salted water to cover the pork, boil the pork belly for about 45 minutes, skimming the fat from the top of the water as needed. Drain and allow the pork belly to cool. Slice the pork into ¼-inch-thick pieces.

While the pork is cooking, mix the soy sauce, rice wine, spicy bean paste, sesame oil, and sugar in a small bowl. Set aside.

Heat the wok over high heat until a drop of water sizzles on contact. Add the peanut oil and swirl to coat the wok. Working in two or three batches, add the pork and stir-fry it until the pieces crisp at the edges and brown on both sides. Transfer the pork to a plate lined with paper towels. Drain any excess oil from the wok, leaving just a little in the wok for the remaining stir-fry.

Reduce the heat to medium-high. Add the soy sauce mixture, black bean sauce, ginger, and garlic scapes to the wok, and let them heat for 2 to 3 minutes. Return the pork to the wok, and stir-fry for 1 to 2 minutes. Transfer everything to a plate, and garnish with the sliced scallion.

Garlicky Chives with Pork Stir-Fry

Prep time: 10 minutes | Cook time: 12½ minutes | Serve 4

- 2 tablespoons soy sauce
- 1 teaspoon sugar
- 1 teaspoon cornstarch
- ¾ pound pork tenderloin, cut into thin strips

- 4 tablespoons peanut or vegetable oil
- 4 garlic cloves, minced
- 2 bunches garlic chives, cut into 2-inch pieces

In a medium bowl, mix together the soy sauce, sugar, and cornstarch. Add the pork and toss to coat it on all sides. Let the pork sit for 10 to 15 minutes.

Heat your wok on high until a drop of water sizzles on contact.

Add the peanut oil and swirl to coat the wok.

Add the garlic and stir-fry for about 30 seconds.

Add the pork and stir-fry until it starts to change color.

6. Then add the garlic chives, and continue to stir-fry until the pork is completely cooked, 2 to 3 minutes.

Spicy Pork Chops with Mushroom

Prep time: 10 minutes | Cook time: 20 minutes | Serves 4

- 4 pork chops, about 1 inch thick, trimmed of fat
- Sea salt
- Freshly ground pepper
- 2 teaspoons peanut or vegetable oil
- 1 large sweet onion, cut into strips
- 4 large dried shiitake mushrooms,

- rehydrated and cut into strips
- 4 small red-skinned potatoes, scrubbed and quartered
- ¼ cup soy sauce
- ¼ cup vegetable broth
- 2 teaspoons cornstarch, mixed with 1 tablespoon water

1. Season the pork chops on both sides with the sea salt and pepper.

2. Heat your wok over medium-high heat. Add the peanut oil and swirl to coat the wok. Brown the pork chops for about 1 minute on each side. Transfer the chops to a plate.

3. Add the onion to the wok, and stir-fry until it softens and becomes translucent, 2 to 3 minutes. Add the mushrooms, potatoes, soy sauce, and vegetable broth to the wok, and give everything a stir to combine. Return the pork chops to the wok. Heat the liquid and simmer for 15 to 20 minutes, or until the potatoes are cooked through.

4. Transfer the chops and vegetables to a platter. Leave the remaining liquid in the wok. Stir the cornstarch slurry into the liquid, and allow it to thicken, 1 to 2 minutes. Pour the sauce over the pork chops and vegetables. Serve.

Cinnamon with Pork in Soy Sauce

Prep time: 10 minutes | Cook time: 32½ minutes | Serves 4

- 3 tablespoons sugar
- 1 tablespoon honey

- 4 tablespoons soy sauce
- 1 tablespoon peanut or vegetable oil
- 1-inch piece peeled ginger, smashed and coarsely chopped
- 1 pound (454 g) pork shoulder, cut into 1-inch pieces
- 1 teaspoon ground cinnamon
- ½ cup Shaoxing wine

1. In a small bowl, mix the sugar, honey, and soy sauce. Set aside.
2. Heat your wok on high heat until a drop of water sizzles on contact.
3. Add the peanut oil and swirl to coat the wok.
4. Add the ginger and stir-fry it for about 30 seconds.
5. Add the pork and stir-fry it for 2 to 3 minutes, browning the pieces on all sides.
6. Add the soy sauce mixture, along with the cinnamon and rice wine. Stir everything to combine. Bring the liquid to a gentle simmer, cover the wok, and simmer for 30 minutes.
7. Serve with rice.

Chili Tofu with Spiced Pork

Prep time: 10 minutes | Cook time: 7 minutes | Serves 4

- 1 tablespoon peanut or vegetable oil
- ¾ pound pork tenderloin, sliced
- 3 scallions, chopped
- ⅓ cup black bean sauce
- 1 pound (454 g) firm tofu, cut into cubes
- Sea salt
- Freshly ground black pepper
- Chili sauce, for garnish

1. Heat your wok over high heat until a drop of water sizzles on contact.
2. Add the peanut oil and swirl to coat the wok.
3. Add the pork and scallions, and stir-fry until the pork is cooked, 4 to 5 minutes.
4. Add the black bean sauce and tofu to the wok, and cook for 3 to 4 minutes, stirring to mix with the pork. It's fine if some of the tofu cubes don't retain their shape. As soon as everything is mixed together and the sauce is distributed, remove the wok from the heat. Season with the sea salt and pepper.

5. Garnish with chili sauce. Serve with rice.

Garlicky Zucchini Stir-Fry

Prep time: 15 minutes | Cook time: 10 minutes | Serves 4

- 2 tablespoons peanut or vegetable oil, divided
- ½ block firm tofu, cut into ½-inch cubes
- 1 cup diced carrots
- 1 cup frozen shelled edamame, thawed
- 1 cup pork tenderloin, trimmed of fat, diced into ½-inch cubes
- 3 garlic cloves, minced
- 1 cup roasted unsalted
- peanuts
- 1 cup diced green bel pepper
- 1 cup diced zucchini
- 2 tablespoons Shaoxing wine
- 2 tablespoons spicy bean paste
- 1 teaspoon sugar
- 2 teaspoons sesame (
- 1 teaspoon chili sauc

1. Heat your wok over high heat until a drop of wat sizzles on contact. Add 1 tablespoon peanut oil, and swirl to coat the wok. Add the tofu and stir-f for about 2 minutes. Transfer the tofu to a bowl.
2. Add the remaining 1 tablespoon peanut oil to th wok. Add the carrots, edamame, pork, and garlic, and stir-fry for 2 to 3 minutes. Add the peanuts and stir-fry for another 2 to 3 minutes. Add the bell pepper and zucchini, and toss everything together. Stir-fry for another 2 to 3 minutes, unti everything is combined.
3. Add the rice wine, bean paste, sugar, sesame oil, and chili sauce, and stir-fry until the sauce has reduced and thickened, 2 to 3 minutes.
4. Serve with rice.

Sugared Lamb with Gingered Scallions

Prep time: 10 minutes | Cook time: 11 minutes | Serve 4

- 2 tablespoons soy sauce
- 3 tablespoons Shaoxing wine
- 1 tablespoon
- cornstarch
- 2 teaspoons sugar
- ½ pound (227 g) boneless lamb, cut into thin strips

3 tablespoons peanut or vegetable oil

6 to 8 scallions, cut into 1-inch pieces

· 1 teaspoon ground ginger

In a medium bowl, mix the soy sauce, rice wine, cornstarch, and sugar. Add the lamb to the bowl, and toss to coat it on all sides. Let the lamb sit for 10 minutes.

Heat your wok over high heat until a drop of water sizzles on contact. Add the peanut oil and swirl to coat the wok.

Add the scallions and ginger, and stir-fry for about 10 seconds, making sure the ingredients do not burn.

Add the lamb and stir-fry for about 1 minute, or until completely cooked through. Serve immediately.

Garlicky Lamb in Soy Sauce

Prep time: 10 minutes | Cook time: 31 minutes | Serve 4

2 tablespoons soy sauce

1 teaspoon sesame oil

2 teaspoons Shaoxing wine

1 teaspoon sugar

½ pound lamb, thinly sliced

1 tablespoon peanut or vegetable oil

2 teaspoons minced ginger

· 2 leeks, cut into 1-inch strips

· 3 dried chiles, Chinese red, Mexican, or Spanish

· 1 teaspoon minced garlic

· 2 teaspoons hoisin sauce

· 2 teaspoons cornstarch mixed with 4 tablespoons water

In a medium bowl, mix the soy sauce, sesame oil, rice wine, and sugar. Add the lamb, toss it to coat on all sides, and allow it to marinate for 30 minutes.

Heat your wok over high heat until a drop of water sizzles on contact. Add the peanut oil and swirl to coat the wok. Add the ginger and leeks, and stir-fry for about 1 minute. Add the chiles and garlic, and stir-fry for 1 minute.

Add the lamb and stir to combine it with the other ingredients. Add the hoisin sauce and cornstarch slurry to the wok, and stir until the sauce thickens,

2 to 3 minutes. If the sauce becomes too thick, add a little more water.

4. Remove the wok from the heat and serve.

Gingered Scallions with Pork Pot Stickers

Prep time: 10 minutes | Cook time: 8 minutes | Serve 4

· 12 ounces (340 g) napa cabbage leaves, chopped

· 1 teaspoon kosher salt

· 1 teaspoon grated fresh ginger

· ¼ cup minced scallions

· 1 pound (454 g) ground pork

· ⅛ teaspoon white pepper

· 1½ tablespoons soy

sauce

· 1 tablespoon Shaoxing wine

· 2 teaspoons toasted sesame oil

· 30 to 40 dumpling wrappers (gyoza, pot sticker, or mandu)

· 1½ tablespoons peanut or vegetable oil

· ¼ cup water, room temperature or warm

1. Put the cabbage in a strainer in the sink or over a bowl, and sprinkle it with the kosher salt. Mix the kosher salt with the cabbage to coat the cabbage. Let the cabbage sit for 15 minutes. Using your hands, squeeze any water from the cabbage, getting as much out as possible.

2. In a medium bowl, mix together the cabbage, ginger, scallions, pork, white pepper, soy sauce, rice wine, and sesame oil. Using your hands, mix the ingredients thoroughly until they are sticky.

3. To make each dumpling, place a packed tablespoon filling in the center of a wrapper. Wet your finger and trace the entire edge of the wrapper to dampen it. Fold the wrapper in half, and press the wet edges together. Pinch the edges to create small pleats. Repeat this for all the wrappers.

4. Heat a wok to medium-high, and add the peanut oil. Place the pot stickers into the wok, seam-side up. Cook the dumplings for about 1 minute, until the bottoms are golden brown.

5. Add the warm water to the wok. Cover the wok and cook the pot stickers for 7 to 8 minutes, or until

the water has boiled off.

6. Remove the wok from the heat.

7. Serve warm with your favorite hot chili sauce or dumpling dipping sauce.

Ginger with Korean Pork

Prep time: 10 minutes | Cook time: 1½ minutes | Serves 4

- ½ cup kimchi, cut into ½-inch pieces, drained and juice reserved
- 2 tablespoons rice wine
- ¼ cup gochujang
- 1 tablespoon cornstarch
- 2 tablespoons cooking oil
- 1 tablespoon crushed, chopped ginger
- 2 garlic cloves, crushed and chopped
- 1 pound (454 g) pork tenderloin, cut into 1-inch pieces
- 4 scallions, cut into 1-inch pieces

1. In a small bowl, whisk together the kimchi juice, rice wine, gochujang, and cornstarch. Set aside.

2. In a wok over high heat, heat the cooking oil until it shimmers.

3. Add the ginger, garlic, and pork and stir-fry for 1 minute.

4. Add the kimchi and stir-fry for 30 seconds.

5. Add the gochujang mixture and stir until a glaze forms.

6. Garnish with the scallions and serve over steamed rice.

Oyster Sauce with Five-Spice Pork

Prep time: 10 minutes | Cook time: 2½ minutes | Serves 4

- 2 tablespoons cooking oil
- 1 tablespoon crushed, chopped ginger
- 2 garlic cloves, crushed and chopped
- 1 pound (454 g) ground pork
- 1 tablespoon Chinese five-spice powder
- 1 teaspoon hot sesame oil
- 2 cups chopped bok choy
- ¼ cup oyster sauce
- 4 scallions, cut into 1-inch pieces

1. In a wok over high heat, heat the cooking oil until it shimmers.

2. Add the ginger, garlic, pork, and five-spice powder and stir-fry for 1 minute.

3. Add the sesame oil and bok choy and stir-fry for 1 minute.

4. Add the oyster sauce, toss with the stir-fry, and cook for 30 seconds.

5. Garnish with the scallions and serve over steamed rice.

Ginger and Sesame Pineapple Pork

Prep time: 10 minutes | Cook time: 2½ minutes | Serve 4

- 1 (8-ounce / 227 g) can pineapple chunks, drained, juice reserved
- ¼ cup rice vinegar
- 2 tablespoons brown sugar
- 2 tablespoons cornstarch
- 2 tablespoons cooking oil
- 1 tablespoon crushed, chopped ginger
- 2 garlic cloves, crushed and chopped
- 1 pound (454 g) pork tenderloin, cut into 1-inch pieces
- 2 chiles, cut into ¼-inch circles (no need to remove seeds or core)
- 1 medium onion, cut into 1-inch pieces
- 1 teaspoon hot sesame oil
- 4 scallions, cut into 1-inch pieces

1. In a small bowl, whisk together the pineapple juice, rice vinegar, brown sugar, and cornstarch. Set aside.

2. In a wok over high heat, heat the cooking oil until it shimmers.

3. Add the ginger, garlic, and pork and stir-fry for 1 minute.

4. Add the chiles and onion and stir-fry for 1 minute.

5. Add the pineapple chunks and sesame oil and stir-fry for 30 seconds.

6. Add the pineapple juice mixture and stir until a glaze forms.

Garnish with the scallions and serve over steamed rice.

Oniony Pork with Mushrooms

Prep time: 10 minutes | Cook time: 3½ minutes | Serve 4

- 2 tablespoons cooking oil
- 1 tablespoon crushed, chopped ginger
- 2 garlic cloves, crushed and chopped
- 1 pound (454 g) pork tenderloin, cut into 1-inch pieces
- 1 medium onion, cut into 1-inch pieces
- 4 ounces (113 g) sliced mushrooms
- 2 cups sugar snap or snow pea pods
- ¼ cup hoisin sauce
- 2 tablespoons soy sauce
- 4 scallions, cut into 1-inch pieces

In a wok over high heat, heat the cooking oil until it shimmers.

Add the ginger, garlic, and pork and stir-fry for 1 minute.

Add the onion and mushrooms and stir-fry for 1 minute.

Add the pea pods and stir-fry for 1 minute.

Add the hoisin sauce and soy sauce and stir-fry for 30 seconds.

Garnish with the scallions and serve over steamed rice.

Peppered Sichuan Pork with Peanuts

Prep time: 10 minutes | Cook time: 2 minutes | Serve 4

- 2 tablespoons cooking oil
- 1 tablespoon crushed, chopped ginger
- 2 garlic cloves, crushed and chopped
- 1 pound (454 g) ground pork
- 1 medium onion, cut into 1-inch pieces
- 1 teaspoon red pepper flakes
- 1 teaspoon hot sesame oil
- 1 tablespoon Chinese five-spice powder
- 1 medium red bell pepper, cut into 1-inch pieces
- 2 tablespoons rice wine
- 2 tablespoons rice vinegar
- 1 tablespoon cornstarch
- ½ cup peanuts

1. In a wok over high heat, heat the cooking oil until it shimmers.

2. Add the ginger, garlic, pork, and onion and stir-fry for 1 minute.

3. Add the red pepper flakes, sesame oil, five-spice powder, and bell pepper and stir-fry for 1 minute.

4. Add the rice wine, rice vinegar, and cornstarch and stir until a glaze forms.

5. Add the peanuts, stir, and serve over steamed rice.

Spicy Pork with Garlicky Tofu

Prep time: 15 minutes | Cook time: 4 minutes | Serves 4

- 2 tablespoons soy sauce
- 2 tablespoons rice wine
- 1 tablespoon cornstarch
- 2 tablespoons cooking oil
- ½ pound (227 g) extra-firm tofu, cut into 1-inch cubes
- 1 medium carrot, roll-cut into ½-inch pieces
- 1 tablespoon crushed, chopped ginger
- 4 garlic cloves, crushed and chopped
- ½ pound (227 g) ground pork
- 1 medium onion, cut into 1-inch pieces
- 1 teaspoon Chinese five-spice powder
- 1 medium red bell pepper, cut into 1-inch pieces
- 4 scallions, cut into 1-inch pieces

1. In a small bowl, whisk together the soy sauce, rice wine, and cornstarch. Set aside.

2. In a wok over high heat, heat the cooking oil until it shimmers.

3. Add the tofu, carrot, ginger, and garlic and stir-fry for 2 minutes.

4. Add the pork, onion, and five-spice powder and stir-fry for 1 minute.

5. Add the bell pepper and stir-fry for 1 minute.

6. Add the soy sauce mixture and stir until a glaze forms.

7. Garnish with the scallions and serve over steamed rice.

Garlicky Pork with Eggplant

Prep time: 10 minutes | Cook time: 3 minutes | Serves 4

- 2 tablespoons cooking oil
- 1 tablespoon crushed, chopped ginger
- 2 garlic cloves, crushed and chopped
- 1 small eggplant, diced into ½-inch cubes
- 1 pound (454 g)

ground pork
- 2 chiles, cut into ¼-inch circles (no need to core or seed)
- ¼ cup sriracha
- 2 tablespoons hoisin sauce
- 4 scallions, cut into 1-inch pieces

1. In a wok over high heat, heat the cooking oil until it shimmers.

2. Add the ginger, garlic, and eggplant and stir-fry for 1 minute.

3. Add the pork and stir-fry for 1 minute.

4. Add the chiles, sriracha, and hoisin sauce and stir-fry for 1 minute.

5. Garnish with the scallions and serve over steamed rice.

Honey with Pork and Brussels Sprouts

Prep time: 10 minutes | Cook time: 3½ minutes | Serves 4

- 2 tablespoons cooking oil
- 1 tablespoon crushed, chopped ginger
- 2 garlic cloves, crushed and chopped
- 1 dozen Brussels sprouts, trimmed and

halved
- 1 medium onion, diced
- 1 pound (454 g) ground pork
- ¼ cup honey
- ¼ cup oyster sauce

1. In a wok over high heat, heat the cooking oil until it shimmers.

2. Add the ginger, garlic, and Brussels sprouts and

stir-fry for 1 minute.

3. Add the onion and pork and stir-fry for 1 minute.

4. Add the honey and stir-fry for 1 minute.

5. Add the oyster sauce and toss for 30 seconds.

6. Serve over steamed rice.

Cornstarch with Red Pork Bowl

Prep time: 10 minutes | Cook time: 2½ minutes | Serves 4

- ¼ cup rice wine
- 1 tablespoon cornstarch
- 2 tablespoons brown sugar
- 2 tablespoons cooking oil
- 1 tablespoon crushed, chopped ginger
- 2 garlic cloves, crushed and chopped
- ½ pound (227 g)

Smithfield ham, cut into ½-inch pieces
- 2 chiles, cut into ¼-inch circles (no need to core or seed)
- 1 teaspoon hot sesame oil
- 2 tablespoons soy sauce
- ¼ cup sriracha
- 4 scallions, cut into ½-inch pieces

1. Fresh chopped cilantro, for garnish

2. In a small bowl, whisk together the rice wine, cornstarch, and brown sugar. Set aside.

3. In a wok over high heat, heat the cooking oil until it shimmers.

4. Add the ginger, garlic, and ham and stir-fry for 1 minute.

5. Add the chiles, sesame oil, soy sauce, and sriracha and stir-fry for 1 minute.

6. Add the rice wine mixture and stir until a glaze forms.

7. Add the scallions and stir-fry for 30 seconds.

8. Garnish with the cilantro and serve over jasmine rice.

Rice Wine with Beef and Broccoli

Prep time: 10 minutes | Cook time: 3½ minutes | Serves 4

2 tablespoons cooking oil

1 tablespoon crushed, chopped ginger

2 garlic cloves, crushed and chopped

1 pound (454 g) sirloin tips, cut into ¼-inch

strips

- 2 tablespoons Shaoxing rice wine
- 1 cup broccoli florets
- 2 tablespoons soy sauce
- ¼ cup oyster sauce

. In a wok over high heat, heat the cooking oil until it shimmers.

. Add the ginger and garlic and stir-fry for 30 seconds until lightly browned.

. Add the steak and rice wine and stir-fry for 1 minute.

. Add the broccoli and stir-fry for 1 minute.

. Add the soy sauce and oyster sauce and stir-fry for 1 minute.

. Serve over steamed rice.

Vinegary Sichuan Beef with Vegetables

Prep time: 15 minutes | Cook time: 3 minutes | Serves 4

2 tablespoons rice wine

2 tablespoons rice vinegar

2 tablespoons soy sauce

1 tablespoon cornstarch

2 tablespoons cooking oil

1 tablespoon crushed, chopped ginger

2 garlic cloves, crushed and chopped

- 1 pound (454 g) sirloin steak, cut into ¼-inch strips
- 1 tablespoon Chinese five-spice powder
- 1 medium onion, diced
- 1 teaspoon red pepper flakes
- 2 cups sugar snap or snow pea pods
- 1 teaspoon hot sesame oil
- 4 scallions, cut into 1-inch pieces

In a small bowl, whisk together the rice wine, rice vinegar, soy sauce, and cornstarch. Set aside.

In a wok over high heat, heat the cooking oil until it shimmers.

Add the ginger, garlic, and steak and stir-fry for 1

minute.

4. Add the five-spice powder, onion, and red pepper flakes and stir-fry for 1 minute.

5. Add the pea pods and sesame oil and stir-fry for 1 minute.

6. Add the rice wine mixture and stir-fry until a glaze forms.

7. Garnish with the scallions and serve over rice.

Rice Wine with Gingered Beef

Prep time: 10 minutes | Cook time: 4 minutes | Serve 4

- 2 tablespoons cooking oil
- 1 tablespoon crushed, chopped ginger
- 2 garlic cloves, crushed and chopped
- 1 pound (454 g) sirloin steak, sliced into ¼-inch strips
- 1 medium onion, cut into 1-inch pieces
- 2 tablespoons soy sauce
- 2 tablespoons Chinese rice wine
- ¼ cup sha cha
- 1 chile, cut into ¼-inch circles
- 2 cups sugar snap or snow pea pods
- 4 scallions, cut into 1-inch pieces

1. In a wok over high heat, heat the cooking oil until it shimmers.

2. Add the ginger, garlic, steak, and onion and stir-fry for 1 minute.

3. Add the soy sauce, rice wine, sha cha, and chile and stir-fry for 1 minute.

4. Add the pea pods and stir-fry for 1 minute.

5. Add the scallions and stir-fry for 1 minute.

6. Serve over steamed rice.

Limey Cardamom with Beef Rendang

Prep time: 10 minutes | Cook time: 2 minutes | Serve 4

- 2 tablespoons coconut oil
- 1 tablespoon crushed,

chopped ginger
- 2 garlic cloves, crushed and chopped

- 1 pound (454 g) sirloin steak, sliced into ¼-inch strips
- 1 teaspoon Chinese five-spice powder
- 1 teaspoon cardamom
- 1 chile, cut into ¼-inch rounds
- Juice of 1 lime
- 1 lemongrass heart
- (the bottom 2 inches of the white inner layers), minced
- 1 tablespoon brown sugar
- 2 tablespoons soy sauce
- 4 scallions, cut into ½-inch pieces

1. In a wok over high heat, heat the coconut oil until it shimmers.
2. Add the ginger, garlic, steak, five-spice powder, and cardamom and stir-fry for 1 minute.
3. Add the chile, lime juice, lemongrass, brown sugar, and soy sauce and stir-fry for 1 minute.
4. Garnish with the scallions and serve over steamed rice cooked in coconut water or coconut milk.

Limey Sauce and Sugar Lamb

Prep time: 15 minutes | Cook time: 3 minutes | Serves 4

- Juice of 1 lime
- 1 tablespoon brown sugar
- 1 tablespoon hot sesame oil
- 1 tablespoon cornstarch
- 1 pound (454 g) lamb tenderloin, cut into 1-inch pieces, across the grain
- 1 tablespoon fish sauce
- 1 tablespoon soy sauce
- 2 tablespoons cooking oil
- 1 tablespoon crushed, chopped ginger
- 2 garlic cloves, crushed and chopped
- 1 medium onion, diced
- 2 or 3 Thai bird's eye chiles
- 4 scallions, cut into 1-inch pieces

1. In a small bowl, whisk together the lime juice, brown sugar, sesame oil, and cornstarch. Set aside.
2. In a large bowl, combine the soy sauce and fish sauce. Add the lamb and massage for 1 minute.
3. In a wok over high heat, heat the cooking oil until it shimmers.

4. Add the ginger, garlic, and lamb and stir-fry for 1 minute.
5. Add the onion and bird's eye chiles and stir-fry for 1 minute.
6. Add the lime juice mixture and stir until a glaze forms.
7. Garnish with the scallions and serve over rice.

Gingered Adobo Lamb with Cabbage

Prep time: 10 minutes | Cook time: 1 minutes | Serves 4

- 2 tablespoons soy sauce
- ¼ cup rice vinegar
- 2 tablespoons brown sugar
- 2 tablespoons cornstarch
- 1 cup Napa cabbage, shredded
- 2 tablespoons cooking oil
- 1 tablespoon crushed, chopped ginger
- 2 garlic cloves, crushed and chopped
- 1 pound (454 g) boneless leg of lamb or shoulder, cut into ¼-inch strips
- 1 medium onion, diced
- 1 teaspoon red pepper flakes

1. In a small bowl, whisk together the soy sauce, rice vinegar, brown sugar, and cornstarch. Set aside.
2. In a wok over high heat, heat the cooking oil until it shimmers.
3. Add the ginger, garlic, lamb, onion, and red pepper flakes and stir-fry for 1 minute.
4. Add the soy sauce mixture and cabbage and stir until a glaze forms.
5. Serve over steamed rice.

Gingered Lamb with Green Beans

Prep time: 10 minutes | Cook time: 3 minutes | Serve 4

- 2 tablespoons cooking oil
- 1 tablespoon crushed, chopped ginger
- 2 garlic cloves,
- crushed and chopped
- 1 pound (454 g) ground lamb
- 1 medium onion, dice

[117]

2 cups fresh green beans

- 1 teaspoon hot sesame oil

1 tablespoon Chinese five-spice powder

- ¼ cup oyster sauce

In a wok over high heat, heat the cooking oil until it shimmers.

Add the ginger, garlic, lamb, and onion and stir-fry for 1 minute.

Add the green beans, five-spice powder, and sesame oil and stir-fry for 1 minute.

Add the oyster sauce and stir-fry for 1 minute.

Serve over steamed rice.

Zucchini and Beef Stir-Fry

Prep time: 10 minutes | Cook time: 5 minutes | Serves 2

½ pound (227 g) beef

peppers

1 cup sliced zucchini

- 1 tablespoon coconut oil

1 cup sliced carrots

½ cup sliced onions

- 2 teaspoons ground cumin

½ cup sliced green

Marinade beef, carrots and zucchini in a Superfoods marinade (add ground cumin).

In a wok, stir fry drained beef and veggies in coconut oil for few minutes, add onions and green peppers and stir fry for 2 more minutes. Add the rest of the marinade and stir fry for 1 minute.

Serve with brown rice or quinoa.

Celery with Beef Liver Stir Fry

Prep time: 5 minutes | Cook time: 5 minutes | Serves 2

½ pound (227 g) beef liver

- 1 cup mushrooms
- 1 teaspoon oil

1 cup Chinese celery

Marinade beef liver in a Superfoods marinade.

In a wok, stir fry drained beef liver in coconut oil for few minutes, add all vegetables and stir fry for 2 more minutes.

Add the rest of the marinade and stir fry for 1 minute.

4. Serve with brown rice or quinoa.

Peppered Pork with Fried Brown Rice

Prep time: 5 minutes | Cook time: 5 minutes | Serve 2

- ½ pound (454 g) cubed pork
- 1 cup peppers
- ½ cup sliced carrots
- 1 tablespoon black

sesame seeds

- 1 cup cooked brown rice
- 1 teaspoon oil

1. Marinade pork in a Superfoods marinade.

2. In a wok, stir fry drained pork in coconut oil for few minutes, add all vegetables and stir fry for 2 more minutes.

3. Add the rest of the marinade and stir fry for 1 minute. Stir in brown rice and black sesame seeds.

Spicy Pork with Tomato Stir-Fry

Prep time: 5 minutes | Cook time: 5 minutes | Serves 2

- ½ pound (454 g) cubed pork
- 1 cup green peppers
- ½ cup sliced tomatoes
- 1 teaspoon ground black pepper
- 1 teaspoon oil

1. Marinade pork in a Superfoods marinade.

2. Stir fry drained pork in coconut oil for few minutes, add all vegetables and stir fry for 2 more minutes.

3. Add the rest of the marinade and stir fry for 1 minute. Serve with brown rice or quinoa.

Sesame with Beef Stir Fry

Prep time: 5 minutes | Cook time: 5 minutes | Serves 2

- ½ pound (227 g) beef
- 1 cup broccoli
- ½ cup sliced yellow peppers
- ½ cup chopped onions
- 1 tablespoon sesame seeds
- 1 teaspoon oil

1. Marinade beef in a Superfoods marinade.

2. In a wok, stir fry drained beef in coconut oil for few minutes, add all vegetables and stir fry for 2 more minutes.

3. Add the rest of the marinade and stir fry for 1 minute.

4. Serve with brown rice or quinoa.

Pork with Bok Choy Stir-Fry

Prep time: 5 minutes | Cook time: 3 minutes | Serves 2

- 10 ounces (283 g) lean pork tenderloin
- 2 cups bok choy
- 1 cup celery, chopped
- 1 teaspoon coconut oil

1. Marinade pork in a Superfoods marinade.

2. In a wok, stir fry drained pork in coconut oil and when it's no longer pink add celery and stir fry for 1 more minute.

3. Add bok choy and stir fry for 1 minute longer and then add the rest of the marinade and stir fry for 1 more minute.

Chestnut with Pork Stir-Fry

Prep time: 5 minutes | Cook time: 5 minutes | Serves 2

- ½ pound (227 g) cubed pork
- 1 cup sliced broccoli
- ½ cup sliced celery
- ½ cup sliced onions
- 1 cup sliced water chestnuts
- 1 teaspoon oil

1. Marinade pork in a Superfoods marinade.

2. In a wok, stir fry drained pork in coconut oil for few minutes, add all vegetables and stir fry for 2 more minutes. Add the rest of the marinade and stir fry for 1 minute.

3. Serve with brown rice or quinoa.

Oregano with Tomato Meat Sauce

Prep time: 10 minutes | Cook time: 5 minutes | Serves 4

- 5 pounds (2.3 kg) ripe tomatoes
- 1 tablespoon sea salt
- 8 tablespoons extra virgin olive oil
- 2 tablespoons

balsamic vinegar
- 6 garlic cloves, minced
- 1½ pounds (680 g) ground beef
- ½ pound (227 g) ground pork
- 1 large onion, finely chopped
- 6 ounces (170 g)
- tomato paste
- 1½ cups beef stock
- ½ cup dry red wine
- 2 teaspoons dried oregano
- 1½ teaspoons ground black pepper
- 1 tablespoon sugar

1. Toss the tomatoes with 4 tablespoons olive oil, 1 tablespoon salt, 2 tablespoons balsamic vinegar, and 3 garlic cloves in a baking tray.

2. Roast the tomatoes for 1 hour in the oven at 400º (205ºC).

3. sauté beef and pork with 4 tablespoons oil in a Mandarin wok until brown.

4. Stir in chopped onion, 3 garlic cloves, black pepper, and salt, then sauté for 5 minutes.

5. Transfer the roasted tomatoes to the beef and pork.

6. Stir in red wine, beef stock, tomato paste, sugar, black pepper, and dried oregano.

7. Cover and cook the mixture for 3 hours on a simmer. Serve warm.

Vinegary Pork Knuckles

Prep time: 10 minutes | Cook time: 3 hours | Serves 4

- 1 pound (454 g) ginger
- 5 cups Chinese sweet vinegar
- ½ cup Chinese black vinegar
- 2 pounds (907 g) pork
- knuckle
- 2 tablespoons Shaoxing wine
- 6 hard-boiled eggs
- Salt, to taste

1. Boil ginger with sweet vinegar and black vinegar in a Cantonese wok for 90 minutes on a simmer.

2. Add pork knuckles, wine, and enough water to cover the pork, and cook for 3 minutes.

3. Cover and cook for another 90 minutes over medium heat.

4. Add the hard-boiled eggs to the pork and cook the mixture to a boil.

Serve warm.

Cumin with Raisins Lamb Rice

Prep time: 10 minutes | Cook time: 33 minutes | Serves 6

- 2 cups uncooked white rice
- 2 pounds (907 g) fatty lamb, cut into chunks
- 4 cups water
- 3 ginger slices
- 3 tablespoons oil
- 1 medium onion, diced
- 2 teaspoons salt
- 2 teaspoons soy sauce
- 1 teaspoon cumin powder
- 1 pound (454 g) carrots, cut into thin strips
- ¼ cup raisins

Sauté onion, ginger, and carrots with oil in a Mandarin wok for 5 minutes until soft.

Stir in lamb, salt, soy sauce, cumin powder then sautés for 8 minutes.

Add water to the lamb and bring it to a boil.

Stir in rice, cover, and cook for 15 minutes on medium-high heat.

Add raisins to the rice and mix well.

Cook for 5 minutes then serve warm.

Anise and Mushroom with Lamb Casserole

Prep time: 15 minutes | Cook time: 1¼ hours | Serves 6

- 1 kg lamb breast, cut into 2-inch pieces
- 15 ginger slices
- 2 tablespoons oil
- 6 scallions
- 10 grams rock sugar
- 3 pieces fermented red bean curd
- ¼ cup Zhu Hou sauce
- 1-star anise
- 3 tablespoons Shaoxing wine
- 1 teaspoon dark soy sauce
- 2 tablespoons light soy sauce
- 2 tablespoons oyster sauce
- 1 dried tangerine peel
- 6 dried Shiitake mushrooms, soaked and cut in half
- 4 small carrots, cut into chunks
- 6 bean thread/sticks,

soaked and cut into large chunks

- Salt, to taste

1. Add lamb and 4 slices of ginger to a cooking pan and fill it with water.
2. Boil the lamb then drain and rinse under cold water.
3. Sauté ginger, and scallions with 2 tablespoons oil in a Cantonese wok.
4. Stir in sugar, red bean curd, and Zha Hou sauce, then cook for 5 minutes.
5. Add lamb, star anise, wine, soy sauces, oyster sauce, mushroom water, mushrooms, peel, and enough water to cover all the ingredients.
6. Cover and cook the lamb mixture for 60 minutes.
7. Add bamboo shoots, bean threads, and carrot, then cook for 20 minutes.
8. Serve warm.

Bok Choy with Steak Stir-Fry

Prep time: 15 minutes | Cook time: 10 minutes | Serves 6

For the Steak and Marinade:

- 1 pound (454 g) beef ribeye, cut into cubes
- 1½ tablespoons vegetable oil
- ⅛ teaspoon baking soda
- 1 teaspoon cornstarch
- ¼ teaspoon salt

For the Sauce:

- 5 tablespoons water
- 1 teaspoon ketchup
- 1 teaspoon Worcestershire sauce
- 2 teaspoons soy sauce
- 2 teaspoons oyster sauce
- ⅛ teaspoon ground

white pepper

- ⅛ teaspoon sesame oil
- 1 tablespoon cornstarch, mixed with 1 tablespoon water

For the Bok Choy:

- 12 ounces (340 g) fresh bok choy, cut and washed
- 1 tablespoon vegetable oil
- 3 to 4 fresh ginger slices, smashed
- 3 garlic cloves, chopped
- ½ teaspoon salt
- ⅛ teaspoon sugar
- ⅛ teaspoon MSG

1. Mix ketchup and all the for the sauce in a bowl.

2. Coat the beef cubes with cornstarch, salt, and baking soda.

3. Sear the beef with vegetable oil in a skillet until golden-brown.

4. Sauté ginger, bok choy, salt, sugar, msg, and garlic with oil in a Cantonese wok for 5 minutes.

5. Add beef cubes and sauce into the wok then mix well.

6. Stir and cook the mixture for 5 minutes until beef is done.

7. Serve warm.

Celery with Cinnamon and Meat

Prep time: 25 minutes | Cook time: 46 minutes | Serve 6

- ⅓ cup Chinese celery, chopped, to serve
- ¼ cup roasted peanuts, chopped, to serve
- 2 tablespoons cilantro, chopped, to serve
- **For the Meat:**
- 2 pounds (907 g) beef shank
- 1½ pounds (680 g) honeycomb beef tripe
- 5 ginger slices
- 3 scallions
- 2 teaspoons Sichuan peppercorns
- 1 teaspoon cumin seeds
- 1 teaspoon coriander seeds
- 1 teaspoon black or white peppercorns
- 3 cloves
- 3 bay leaves
- 1 cinnamon stick
- ½ dried tangerine peel

- 2-star anise
- 1 black cardamom pod
- 2 white cardamom pods
- ⅓ cup Shaoxing wine
- ⅓ cup light soy sauce
- 1 tablespoon dark soy sauce
- 2 tablespoons rock sugar
- **For the Sauce:**
- ¼ cup braising liquid
- ¼ cup chili oil
- 2 garlic cloves, finely minced
- 1 teaspoon Sichuan peppercorn powder
- 1 tablespoon toasted sesame seeds
- 2 teaspoons Chinese black vinegar
- 1 tablespoon light soy sauce
- 1½ teaspoon sugar
- ¼ teaspoon salt

1. Add tripe, ginger, and beef shank to a cooking pot and pour in water to cover them.

2. Boil the meat for 1 minute, then drain and rinse the meat.

3. Add the beef and tripe to a wok and pour enough water to cover it.

4. Stir in scallions, sugar, soy sauce, and all the for meat.

5. Cover and cook this meat for 45 minutes on a simmer.

6. Strain and reserve the braising liquid.

7. Mix all the for liquid sauce in a bowl.

8. Slice the tripe and beef then transfer to a serving platter.

9. Pour the sauce and celery on top.

10. Garnish with cilantro and peanuts.

11. Enjoy!

Spicy Japanese Dumplings

Prep time: 10 minutes | Cook time: 29 minutes | Serves 12

- 5 cups Napa cabbage
- 8 ounces (227 g) ground pork
- 1 garlic clove, smashed
- 1½ teaspoons fresh ginger, minced
- 1 scallion, chopped
- 2 tablespoons vegetable oil

- ½ teaspoon sesame oil
- 2 teaspoons soy sauce
- ¾ teaspoon sugar
- ½ teaspoon salt
- ⅛ teaspoons white pepper
- 24 store-bought gyoza wrappers

1. Sauté garlic, ginger, and scallions with oil in a Mandarin wok until soft.

2. Stir in cabbage, pork, and rest of the ingredients.

3. Sauté for about 7 minutes until veggies are cooked and soft.

4. Allow the filling to cool and spread the gyoza wrappers on the working surface.

5. Divide the pork filling at the center of each gyoza wrapper.

6. Wet the edges of the dumplings and bring all the edges of each wrapper together.

7. Pinch and seal the edges of the dumplings to seal

Beef, Pork, and Lar

the filling inside.

Boil water in a suitable pot with a steamer basket placed inside.

Add the dumplings to the steamer, cover and steam for 20 minutes.

Meanwhile, heat about 2 tablespoons oil in a skillet.

Sear the dumpling for 2 minutes until golden.

Serve warm.

Honeyed Beef Stir-Fry

Prep time: 10 minutes | Cook time: 8 minutes | Serves 4

- ⅓ cup soy sauce
- ½ teaspoon sesame oil
- 1 tablespoon honey
- 1 garlic clove, finely chopped or grated
- 1 teaspoon fresh ginger, finely chopped or grated
- 1 teaspoon corn starch

- 1 teaspoon water
- 450 g boneless sirloin, flank or rock steak cut into strips
- 1 package (400 g) frozen or fresh broccoli florets
- 3 teaspoons vegetable oil

Mix honey, soy sauce, sesame oil, ginger and garlic together. In a Ziploc plastic bag (or glass bowl), mix the beef and half of the sauce mixture together until the beef is coated.

Set the marinade aside for 20 minutes or keep covered in the refrigerator overnight. Mix the water and cornstarch and add to the remaining sauce mixture.

Heat a large pan or wok with 2 teaspoons oil over high heat and add the marinated beef. Cook for 4 minutes and then transfer the cooked beef to a clean bowl.

Put the remaining 1 teaspoon oil in the wok, then add the broccoli and cook for 2 minutes. Return the cooked beef to the wok. Return the cooked beef to the wok.

Make a well in the middle and add the sauce. Cook the sauce for about 2 minutes or until the whole mixture is heated through and the sauce has thickened.

Serve with brown rice.

Asparagus with Steak Stir-Fry

Prep time: 15 minutes | Cook time: 13 minutes | Serves 6

- ½ cup soy sauce
- ½ cup white sugar
- ⅓ cup rice wine vinegar
- ⅓ cup chopped garlic
- 1 tablespoon sesame seeds
- 450 g thinly sliced steak
- ¼ cup peanut oil
- 2 cups sliced asparagus
- 1 cup sliced fresh mushrooms, or more to taste

- 1 chopped sweet onion
- 1 sliced red pepper
- 1 bunch of green onions, chopped into pieces
- 1 cup whole cashews
- 1 tablespoon sesame seeds
- 1 tablespoon sesame seeds
- 1 tablespoon corn starch (optional)
- 1 tablespoon water (optional)

1. Mix rice wine vinegar, soy sauce, 1 tablespoon sesame seeds, garlic and sugar in a bowl and place the mixture in a zippered plastic bag. Pour the beef in, seal the bag and squeeze out as much air as you can, then gently massage the beef to evenly cover it with the marinade.

2. Heat a large pan or wok with peanut oil on medium to high heat and fry the marinated beef with the marinade for 5 minutes or until the beef is well browned.

3. Add the mushrooms, peppers, asparagus, spring onions and onions and cook for 3 to 4 minutes, stirring until the vegetables start to soften. Add 1 tablespoon sesame seeds and cashew nuts and cook the mixture for another 2 to 3 minutes until the vegetables are soft.

4. Mix the water and cornstarch in a small bowl until the cornstarch is completely dissolved, then add it to the beef roast and cook the sauce for 3 minutes or until it is thick. Top with the remaining 1 tablespoon sesame seeds.

Garlicky Beef with Soy Sauce

Prep time: 10 minutes | Cook time: 5 minutes |

Serves 4

- ¼ cup soy sauce
- 1 tablespoon hoisin sauce
- 1 tablespoon sesame oil
- 2 teaspoons white sugar
- 1 tablespoon chopped garlic
- 450 g beef flank steak, thinly sliced
- 1 tablespoon peanut oil
- 2 large green onions, thinly sliced
- 1 tablespoon red pepper flakes (optional)

1. Whisk the soy sauce, hoisin sauce, sesame oil, sugar, garlic and red pepper flakes in a bowl.

2. Pour the marinade over the beef, cover and place in the fridge for 1 hour overnight. Heat the peanut oil in a wok or in a large, non-stick pan over high heat.

3. Add the green onions and cook for 5 to 10 seconds before stirring in the beef.

4. Boil and stir until the beef is no longer pink and begins to brown, about 5 minutes.

Vinegary Pork Ribs with Soy Sauce

Prep time: 10 minutes | Cook time: 9 minutes | Serves 4

- Salt and ground black pepper, to taste
- 450 g pork ribs
- 1 tablespoon oil
- ¼ celery, grated
- 1 slice of fresh ginger, grated
- ½ garlic clove, grated
- 2 tablespoons soy sauce
- 1 fresh chili pepper, finely chopped
- 1 tablespoon sake
- 1 tablespoon tomato puree
- 1 tablespoon white sugar
- 1 teaspoon balsamic vinegar
- Salt, to taste

1. Place the oven rack about 15 cm away from the heat source and preheat the griddle of the oven.

2. Line a baking sheet with aluminum foil; put a baking rack on it; Sprinkle the pork ribs with salt and pepper; place on the prepared baking sheet; Cook in the preheated oven, turning once, until the meat loosens easily from the bone, 7 to 10

minutes per side.

3. An instant thermometer inserted into the center should read 145ºF (63ºC) . Heat the oil in a large pan or stir it over medium heat. Add celery, ginger and garlic; cook and stir until fragrant, 2 to 3 minutes.

4. Reduce heat to low. Mix in the soy sauce, chili pepper, sake, tomato puree, sugar, balsamic vinegar and salt; stir until the sauce is thickened. Remove from heat and toss the pork ribs in the sauce until coated.

Sesame with Pork Apple Stir-Fry

Prep time: 10 minutes | Cook time: 2½ minutes | Serves 3

- 2 tablespoons hoisin sauce
- 2 tablespoons brown sugar
- 6 tablespoons soy sauce
- ½ cup applesauce
- 450 g pork loin, sliced and cut into thin strips
- 1½ tablespoons cornstarch
- 2 tablespoons peanut oil
- ½ teaspoon sesame oil
- 1 tablespoon chopped fresh ginger root
- 3 cups broccoli florets

1. Whisk the hoisin sauce, brown sugar, soy sauce and apple sauce in a small bowl; Set aside and combine the pork and cornstarch in a bowl.

2. Heat the peanut oil and sesame oil in a large pan or heat in a wok over medium heat. Cook the pork in the hot oil in three separate batches until it is no longer pink in the middle, 2 to 3 minutes per batch.

3. Place the pork on a plate lined with paper towels to drain and save the oil. Add ginger to the pan, cook and stir for 30 seconds.

4. Stir in the broccoli and cook until tender. Return the pork to the pan and pour in the sauce; swivel to pull over. Cook until all ingredients are hot.

Peppered Pork Meatballs

Prep time: 10 minutes | Cook time: 2 minutes | Makes 20 portions

1 pound (454 g) ground pork

1 tablespoon cornstarch

1 teaspoon minced ginger

3 garlic cloves, minced

2 teaspoons brown

sugar

- 2 teaspoons soy sauce

- 1 teaspoon five-spice powder

- 2 pinches ground white pepper

- 3 tablespoons peanut oil

In a large bowl, combine the pork, cornstarch, ginger, garlic, brown sugar, soy sauce, five-spice powder, and pepper, and mix well.

Roll 1 heaping tablespoon of pork mixture into a ball and continue until all the pork mixture is used.

In a wok over medium heat, heat the peanut oil. Using a wok spatula, spread the oil to coat enough of the wok surface to fry about 10 meatballs at a time.

Lower the meatballs into the wok in batches. Cook without moving for about 2 minutes, or until the bottoms are cooked through. Use the spatula to carefully rotate the meatballs to cook on the other sides.

Keep rotating the meatballs gently until cooked through.

Eggy Pork with Cornstarch

Prep time: 10 minutes | Cook time: 15 minutes | Serves 4 to 6

½ pound (227 g) ground pork

2 teaspoons soy sauce

1 teaspoon cornstarch

½ teaspoon salt

Pinch freshly ground black pepper

3 eggs

- ½ cup water

- 1 teaspoon Shaoxing wine

- 2 teaspoons finely diced Chinese preserved radish (optional)

In a medium bowl, combine the ground pork, preserved radish (if using), soy sauce, cornstarch, salt, and pepper, mixing it well. Marinate at room temperature for about 15 minutes.

Set up a steaming rack in a wok, fill it with water halfway up to the rack, and set the heat to medium.

3. In a separate bowl, whisk the eggs with the water and Shaoxing wine. Set it aside.

4. Transfer the ground pork mixture to a shallow heatproof dish. Spread the ground pork in a single layer to cover the dish.

5. Pour the egg mixture evenly over the ground pork.

6. Cover the dish with aluminum foil. This will prevent water from dripping onto the custard.

7. When the water in the wok starts to boil, place the dish on the steaming rack.

8. Steam for about 15 minutes or until the custard is set, then serve.

Spicy Ketchup with Pork Ribs

Prep time: 15 minutes | Cook time: 6 minutes | Serves 4 to 6

For the Marinade:

- 2 teaspoons Chinese rose wine

- 2 pounds (907 g) pork ribs, cut into about 1½-inch pieces

- ½ teaspoon salt

- Pinch ground white pepper

- ¼ teaspoon five-spice powder

- 3 teaspoons cornstarch

For the Sauce:

- 2 tablespoons ketchup

- 1½ tablespoons apple cider vinegar

- 2 teaspoons brown sugar

- 1 teaspoon soy sauce

- ½ teaspoon dark soy sauce

- Pinch five-spice powder

For the Stir-Fry:

- 2 tablespoons peanut oil

- 2 garlic cloves, minced

1. Pour the Chinese rose wine over the pork. Add the salt, pepper, and five-spice powder. Mix well, then coat the pork with the cornstarch. Marinate at room temperature for 20 minutes.

2. In a small bowl, prepare the sauce by mixing together the ketchup, apple cider vinegar, brown sugar, soy sauce, dark soy sauce, and five-spice powder.

3. In a wok over medium-high heat, heat the peanut oil.

4. Arrange the pork ribs in the wok in a single layer. Cook without stirring for about 30 seconds,

reduce the heat to medium, and stir-fry for about 5 minutes or until the pork is cooked and golden brown.

5. Add the garlic and stir-fry for about 20 seconds until aromatic.

6. Stir in the sauce, coating the ribs.

7. Transfer the ribs and sauce to a serving plate.

Spiced Pork Ribs in Soy Sauce

Prep time: 15 minutes | Cook time: 23 minutes | Serves 4 to 6

For the Marinade:

- 2 teaspoons Shaoxing wine
- 2 teaspoons cornstarch
- ½ teaspoon salt
- Pinch ground white pepper
- 2 pounds (907 g) pork ribs, cut into 1½-inch pieces

For the Sauce:

- 1½ cups water
- 2 tablespoons black bean sauce
- 2 teaspoons sugar
- 2 teaspoons soy sauce
- 1 teaspoon dark soy sauce

For the Stir-Fry:

- 2 tablespoons peanut oil
- 1-inch piece ginger, peeled and minced
- 2 garlic cloves, minced
- 1 scallion, chopped

1. Pour the Shaoxing wine, cornstarch, salt, and pepper over the pork and toss to combine. Marinate at room temperature for about 20 minutes.

2. In a small bowl, prepare the sauce by mixing together the water, black bean sauce, sugar, soy sauce, and dark soy sauce. Set it aside.

3. In a wok over medium-high heat, heat the peanut oil.

4. Arrange the pork ribs in the wok in a single layer. Let them cook without stirring for 30 seconds, add the ginger and garlic, then flip the ribs with a wok spatula.

5. Cook, stirring every 10 seconds or so, for about 2 minutes.

6. Add the sauce, stir, and cover the wok.

7. Reduce the heat to low and simmer for about 20 minutes. Peek every few minutes to make sure the sauce is not evaporating too quickly. If it is, add water when necessary to keep it simmering until the last minute.

8. Transfer the ribs to a serving plate and garnish with the chopped scallion. Serve immediately.

Honeyed Sauce with Five-Spice Pork

Prep time: 15 minutes | Cook time: ⅓ minutes | Serves 4 to 6

For the Marinade:

- 2 teaspoons Shaoxing wine
- 2 teaspoons cornstarch
- ½ teaspoon Chinese five-spice powder
- ½ teaspoon salt
- Pinch ground white pepper
- 1 pound pork tenderloin or shoulder, cut into thin strips

For the Sauce:

- 1 tablespoon soy sauce
- 2 teaspoons honey
- ½ teaspoon brown sugar
- ½ teaspoon dark soy sauce
- ½ teaspoon Chinese five-spice powder

For the Stir-Fry:

- 2 tablespoons peanut oil
- 2 garlic cloves, minced

1. Pour the Shaoxing wine, cornstarch, five-spice powder, salt, and pepper over the pork and toss to combine. Marinate at room temperature for 20 minutes.

2. In a small bowl, prepare the sauce by combining the soy sauce, honey, brown sugar, dark soy sauce, and five-spice powder.

3. In a wok over medium-high heat, heat the peanut oil.

4. Add the pork and stir-fry until slightly golden brown.

5. Add the garlic and stir-fry for about 20 seconds.

6. Stir in the sauce, tossing well to coat the pork, and transfer to a serving dish. Serve immediately.

Chili Bean Paste with Pork

Prep time: 10 minutes | Cook time: 1⅓ minutes |

- 1 pound (454 g) pork shoulder
- Water, for boiling pork shoulder

or the Sauce:

- 1 tablespoon black bean paste
- 1 tablespoon soy sauce
- 1 teaspoon chili bean paste
- ½ teaspoon sugar
- Pinch salt

For the Stir-Fry:

- 1 tablespoon peanut oil
- 2 garlic cloves, minced
- 1 leek, cut into 1-inch pieces
- 1 green bell pepper, cut into bite-size pieces

Fill a medium pot with enough water to cover the pork shoulder. Bring the water to a boil over high heat and lower the pork into the pot.

Reduce the heat to medium, cover, and simmer for 20 minutes.

Remove the pork from the water and let it cool. Keep it in the refrigerator until you are ready to cook the dish.

In a small bowl, prepare the sauce by mixing together the black bean paste, soy sauce, chili bean paste, sugar, and salt.

When the meat has cooled and you are ready to prepare the dish, slice it into the thinnest pieces possible with a very sharp knife.

In a wok over medium-high heat, heat the peanut oil.

Add the pork and stir-fry the slices until they turn slightly brown around the edges. Remove the pork from the wok and set it aside.

Add more oil to the wok if needed, add the garlic, and stir-fry for about 20 seconds, until aromatic.

Add the leek and bell pepper, stir-fry for about 1 minute, and return the pork to the wok.

Add the black bean sauce, stir well, and transfer the dish to a serving plate.

esame and Spicy Beef Stir-
ry

Prep time: 15 minutes | Cook time: 1⅓ minutes |
erves 4 to 6

For the Marinade:

- 2 teaspoons cornstarch
- ½ teaspoon salt
- ½ teaspoon ground black pepper
- 1 pound (454 g) flank steak, thinly sliced

For the Sauce:

- 1 tablespoon soy sauce
- 1 teaspoon black bean sauce
- ½ teaspoon dark soy sauce
- ½ teaspoon sugar
- ½ teaspoon sesame oil

For the Stir-Fry:

- 2 tablespoons peanut oil
- 2 garlic cloves, minced
- 1 red bell pepper, cut into thin strips
- 1 green bell pepper, cut into thin strips
- 1 onion, cut into rings
- 1 fresh red or green chile, cut into strips (optional)

1. Sprinkle the cornstarch, salt, and pepper over the beef, and toss to combine. Marinate at room temperature for about 20 minutes.

2. In a small bowl, prepare the sauce by mixing together the soy sauce, black bean sauce, dark soy sauce, sugar, and sesame oil. Set it aside.

3. In a wok over high heat, heat the peanut oil.

4. Arrange the beef in the wok in a single layer. Cook without stirring for about 20 seconds, flip the beef, and continue to stir-fry until fully cooked, about 1 minute.

5. Remove the beef from the wok.

6. Add a little more oil to the wok if needed, then add the garlic, red and green bell peppers, chile (if using), and onion. Avoid stirring too much, just toss lightly so the high heat can blister the peppers.

7. Return the beef to the wok and add the sauce. Stir to combine all the ingredients and transfer to a serving dish.

Honeyed Sauce with Beef Marinade

Prep time: 15 minutes | Cook time: 0 minutes |
Serves 4 to 6

For the Marinade:

- 3 teaspoons cornstarch
- ½ teaspoon salt
- ¼ teaspoon black pepper
- 1 pound beef tenderloin or steak,

cut into thin slices

For the Sauce:

- 3 tablespoons honey
- 2½ tablespoons low-sodium soy sauce
- 2 tablespoons water
- 2 teaspoons oyster sauce

- 1 teaspoon freshly ground black pepper

For the Stir-Fry:

- 2 tablespoons peanut oil
- ½ onion, thinly sliced
- 2 garlic cloves, minced

1. Sprinkle the cornstarch, salt, and pepper over the beef and toss to combine. Marinate at room temperature for 15 minutes.

2. In a small bowl, prepare the sauce by mixing together the honey, soy sauce, water, oyster sauce, and pepper.

3. In a wok over medium-high heat, heat the peanut oil.

4. Add the beef and stir-fry until just browned, remove from the wok, and set it aside.

5. Toss the onion and garlic into the wok and stir-fry until the onion turns slightly translucent.

6. Return the beef to the wok and add the sauce, stirring to coat the beef.

7. Turn off the heat and transfer to a serving plate.

Vinegary Pork with Cornstarch Marinade

Prep time: 20 minutes | Cook time: 1 minutes | Serves 4 to 6

- 1 head lettuce

For the Marinade:

- 2 teaspoons soy sauce
- 2 teaspoons Shaoxing wine
- 2 teaspoons cornstarch
- ½ teaspoon salt
- Pinch ground white pepper
- 1 pound (454 g) pork tenderloin, cut into thin strips

For the Sauce:

- 2 tablespoons hoisin sauce
- 1 tablespoon rice vinegar
- 1 tablespoon oyster sauce
- 1 teaspoon sugar
- 1 teaspoon soy sauce
- ½ teaspoon sesame oil

For the Stir-Fry:

- 2 tablespoons peanut oil
- 2-inch piece ginger, peeled and julienned

- 2 garlic cloves, minced
- 4 or 5 large shiitake mushrooms, thinly sliced
- 4 cups shredded cabbage
- ½ carrot, julienned
- 1 scallion, chopped
- ½ cup fresh cilantro, chopped

1. Separate and wash the lettuce leaves. Chill the leaves in the refrigerator until ready to serve.

2. Pour the soy sauce, Shaoxing wine, cornstarch, salt, and pepper over the pork and toss to combine and coat the meat. Marinate at room temperature for 20 minutes.

3. Meanwhile, in a small bowl, make the sauce by mixing together the hoisin sauce, rice vinegar, oyster sauce, sugar, soy sauce, and sesame oil. Set it aside.

4. In a wok over medium-high heat, heat the peanut oil.

5. Add the ginger and garlic and stir-fry until aromatic, or for about 20 seconds.

6. Add the pork and stir-fry for about 30 seconds.

7. Toss in the sliced shiitake mushrooms.

8. Once the pork and mushrooms are cooked all the way through, stir in the sauce and mix well.

9. Toss in the shredded cabbage and carrot, stir, and turn off the heat.

10. Transfer to a serving dish, garnish with the chopped scallion and cilantro, and serve with the chilled lettuce.

Spicy Sauce with Garlicky Broccoli

Prep time: 10 minutes | Cook time: 4¼ minutes | Serves 4

- 2 teaspoons dark soy sauce
- 2 teaspoons cornstarch
- 2 teaspoons fish sauce, divided
- ½ teaspoon kosher salt
- Ground white pepper
- ¾ pound (340 g) flank steak, sliced across the grain into ⅛-inch thick slices
- 2 tablespoons oyster sauce
- 1 tablespoon light soy sauce
- ½ teaspoon sugar
- 1½ pounds fresh wide rice noodles or dried

rice noodles

5 tablespoons vegetable oil, divided

4 garlic cloves, thinly sliced

1 bunch Chinese broccoli (gai lan), stems sliced diagonally into ½-inch pieces, leaves cut into bite-size pieces

- 2 large eggs, beaten

In a mixing bowl, stir together the dark soy, cornstarch, 1 teaspoon fish sauce, salt, and a pinch of white pepper. Add the beef slices and toss to coat. Set aside to marinate for 10 minutes.

In another bowl, stir together the oyster sauce, light soy, remaining 1 teaspoon fish sauce, and sugar. Set aside.

If using fresh rice noodles, rinse them under hot water to keep them separated, and set aside. If using dried rice noodles, cook them according to package instructions, drain, and set aside.

Heat a wok over medium-high heat until a drop of water sizzles and evaporates on contact. Pour in 2 tablespoons oil and swirl to coat the base of the wok. Using tongs, transfer the beef to the wok and reserve the marinade. Sear the beef against the wok for 2 to 3 minutes, until it's brown and a seared crust develops. Return the beef to the marinade bowl and stir in the oyster sauce mixture.

Add 2 more tablespoons oil and stir-fry the garlic for 30 seconds. Add the Chinese broccoli stems and stir-fry for 45 seconds, keeping everything moving to prevent the garlic from burning.

Push the broccoli stems to the sides of the wok, leaving the bottom of the wok empty. Add the remaining 1 tablespoon oil and scramble the eggs in the well, then toss them together.

Add the noodles, sauce, and beef, and toss and flip quickly to combine all of the ingredients, stir-frying for 30 more seconds. Add the broccoli leaves and stir-fry for 30 seconds more, or until the leaves begin to wilt. Return to a platter and serve immediately.

Honeyed Sesame Pork

Prep time: 15 minutes | Cook time: 5 minutes | Serves 4

- 2 tablespoons cooking oil
- 1 tablespoon crushed, chopped ginger
- 2 garlic cloves, crushed and chopped
- 1 medium carrot, roll-cut into ½-inch pieces
- 1 pound (454 g) pork tenderloin, cut into 1-inch pieces
- 1 medium onion, cut into 1-inch pieces
- 1 medium red bell pepper, cut into 1-inch pieces
- 1 teaspoon hot sesame oil
- 2 tablespoons soy sauce
- 2 tablespoons honey
- 1 tablespoon cornstarch
- 2 tablespoons sesame seeds
- 4 scallions, cut into 1-inch pieces

1. In a wok over high heat, heat the cooking oil until it shimmers.

2. Add the ginger, garlic, and carrot and stir-fry for 1 minute.

3. Add the pork and stir-fry for 1 minute.

4. Add the onion and bell pepper and stir-fry for 1 minute.

5. Add the sesame oil, soy sauce, honey, and cornstarch and stir until a light glaze forms.

6. Sprinkle with the sesame seeds, garnish with the scallions, and serve over steamed rice.

Oniony Pork with Garlic

Prep time: 15 minutes | Cook time: 5 minutes | Serves 4

- 1 (8-ounce / 227-g) can pineapple chunks, drained, juice reserved
- ¼ cup rice vinegar
- ¼ cup plus 2 tablespoons cornstarch, divided
- 2 tablespoons brown sugar
- 1 pound (454 g) pork tenderloin, cut into 1-inch pieces
- ¼ cup cooking oil
- 1 tablespoon crushed, chopped ginger
- 2 garlic cloves, crushed and chopped
- 1 medium red onion, cut into 1-inch pieces
- 1 red bell pepper, cut into 1-inch pieces
- 4 scallions, cut into 1-inch pieces

1. In a small bowl, whisk together the reserved pineapple juice, rice vinegar, 2 tablespoons of the cornstarch, and brown sugar. Set aside.

2. Add the pork to a resealable plastic bag or covered bowl. Toss with the remaining ¼ cup of cornstarch

to coat completely.

3. In a wok over high heat, heat the cooking oil until it shimmers.

4. Add the ginger and garlic and stir-fry for 1 minute.

5. Add the pork and shallow-fry until lightly browned. Remove the pork and set aside.

6. Remove and discard all but 2 tablespoons of oil from the wok.

7. Add the onion to the wok and stir-fry for 1 minute.

8. Add the bell pepper and pineapple chunks and stir-fry for 1 minute.

9. Add the pineapple juice mixture and stir until a glaze forms. Stir in the cooked pork.

10. Garnish with the scallions and serve over steamed rice.

Kimchi with Vietnamese Pork

Prep time: 10 minutes | Cook time: 5 minutes | Serves 4

- 2 tablespoons coconut oil
- 1 tablespoon crushed, chopped ginger
- 2 garlic cloves, crushed and chopped
- 1 medium onion, diced
- 1 pound (454 g) ground pork
- 1 teaspoon ground black pepper
- 1 tablespoon fish sauce
- ¼ cup brown sugar
- ½ cup chopped kimchi
- 4 scallions, cut into ½-inch pieces

1. In a wok over high heat, heat the coconut oil until it shimmers.

2. Add the ginger, garlic, onion, and pork and stir-fry for 1 minute.

3. Add the black pepper, fish sauce, and brown sugar and stir-fry for 1 minute.

4. Add the kimchi and stir-fry for 30 seconds.

5. Garnish with the scallions and serve over steamed rice cooked in coconut water.

Sake with Japanese Ginger Pork

Prep time: 10 minutes | Cook time: 4 minutes |

Serves 4

- 1 tablespoon white miso
- 2 tablespoons tamari
- 2 tablespoons cooking oil
- 2 tablespoons crushed, chopped ginger
- 2 garlic cloves, crushed and chopped
- 1 pound (454 g) pork tenderloin, cut into 1-inch pieces
- 2 tablespoons sake
- 2 tablespoons mirin
- 2 tablespoons brown sugar

1. In a small bowl, whisk together the miso and tamari. Set aside.

2. In a wok over high heat, heat the cooking oil until it shimmers.

3. Add the ginger, garlic, pork, and sake and stir-fry for 1 minute.

4. Add the mirin and brown sugar and stir-fry for 1 minute.

5. Stir in the miso and tamari mixture and toss.

6. Serve the pork over sushi rice.

Sugar and Pepper with Basil Pork

Prep time: 10 minutes | Cook time: 5 minutes | Serves 4

- 2 tablespoons cooking oil
- 1 tablespoon crushed, chopped ginger
- 2 garlic cloves, crushed and chopped
- 1 pound (454 g) ground pork
- 1 medium red bell pepper, cut into ½-inch pieces
- 1 tablespoon fish sauce
- 2 tablespoons brown sugar
- 1 tablespoon soy sauce
- 1 handful fresh Thai basil leaves

1. In a wok over high heat, heat the cooking oil until it shimmers.

2. Add the ginger, garlic, and pork and stir-fry for 1 minute.

3. Add the bell pepper, fish sauce, brown sugar, and soy sauce and stir-fry for 1 minute.

4. Add the basil and stir-fry until just wilted.

5. Serve over steamed rice.

Lemon and Milk with Tonkatsu Sauce

Prep time: 10 minutes | Cook time: 5 minutes | Serves 4

- 1 cup panko bread crumbs
- ½ cup all-purpose flour
- 2 large eggs
- 2 tablespoons milk
- ¼ teaspoon kosher salt
- ¼ teaspoon black
- pepper
- 4 pork loin pieces, pounded to ½ thickness
- ½ cup vegetable oil
- ½ cup Tonkatsu Sauce
- 4 lemon wedges

Place bread crumbs in a shallow dish, and place the flour in another dish.

In a small bowl, whisk together the eggs and milk.

Season the pork with salt and pepper to taste. Working in batches, dredge a few pieces of the pork in the flour, then the egg mixture, and finally the bread crumbs to coat, shaking off the excess between each step. Repeat with the remaining pork.

Heat the oil in a wok to medium-high heat. In batches, slide in 2 pieces of pork and fry until golden brown, approximately 2-3 minutes on each side. Remove from pan and drain the cutlets on plates lined with paper towels. Repeat with remaining pork.

To serve, drizzle the Tonkatsu Sauce over the pork and serve with lemon wedges and rice.

Chili Beef Tostadas

Prep time: 15 minutes | Cook time: 5 minutes | Serves 4

- 1 pound (454 g) lean ground beef
- 1 teaspoon kosher salt
- ½ teaspoon pepper
- ¼ teaspoon cumin powder
- ½ teaspoon chili powder
- 2 tablespoons
- vegetable oil
- 2 cloves garlic, crushed
- 1 small white onion, diced
- 8 tostada shells, toasted
- 16 ounces (454 g) refried beans, warmed
- 2 cups shredded lettuce
- 1 cup diced tomatoes
- 1 cup shredded Cheddar cheese

1. In a bowl, combine the ground beef with the salt, pepper, cumin, and chili powder. Let the beef stand for 10 minutes.

2. Heat a wok or skillet over medium-high heat and add the oil. When the oil is hot, add the garlic and onions. Cook for 2 minutes or until they are softened.

3. Add the ground beef. Cook the beef, stirring and tossing for 2 minutes in the wok until there is no trace of pink. Using a slotted spoon, remove the beef mixture to a large plate.

4. One at a time, spread 2 ounces (57 g) of refried beans in an even layer on top of a tostada shell. Place several spoonfuls of the beef mixture over the beans and top with the lettuce, tomatoes, and cheese. Repeat with the remaining shells. Serve warm.

Buttered Steak Diane

Prep time: 15 minutes | Cook time: 7 minutes | Serves 4

- 4 (3-ounce / 85-g) filet mignon medallions, pounded to ½ thick
- 1½ teaspoons kosher salt, divided
- 1 teaspoon black pepper, divided
- 2 tablespoons unsalted butter
- 1 tablespoon vegetable oil
- 2 tablespoons minced shallots
- 1 teaspoon minced garlic
- 1 cup sliced crimini mushrooms
- 2 tablespoons cognac
- ¾ cup low-sodium beef stock
- 2 teaspoons Dijon mustard
- ⅓ cup heavy cream
- 1 tablespoon chopped parsley

1. Season both sides of the beef medallions with 1 teaspoon salt and ½ teaspoon black pepper.

2. Bring a wok to medium-high heat. Melt the butter and oil together. Add the beef and cook for 1 minute on each side. Transfer the medallions to a plate and tent with aluminum foil.

3. Lower the heat to medium and add shallot, garlic, and mushrooms. Cook the mushrooms for 3-4

minutes or until softened and then deglaze the pan with cognac.

4. Once the cognac has nearly evaporated, add in the beef stock and Dijon mustard. When the liquid comes to a boil, whisk in the heavy cream. Allow the sauce to reduce for another 2-3 minutes and season with the remaining salt and pepper to taste.

5. Return the beef and any juices to the wok and thoroughly cover the steak with the sauce.

6. Plate the steaks and mushrooms and spoon the sauce over the top. Sprinkle the tops with parsley and serve immediately.

Oniony Beef Stir-Fry with Potato

Prep time: 15 minutes | Cook time: 15 minutes | Serves 6

- 1 pound (454 g) rib eye steak, thinly sliced
- 1 tablespoon minced garlic
- 1½ teaspoons cornstarch
- ½ teaspoon black pepper
- 2 cups plus 3 tablespoons vegetable oil, divided
- 2 large Russet potatoes, peeled and cut into ¼-wide strips
- 1 small yellow onion, quartered
- 1½ cups white mushrooms, sliced
- 2 Roma tomatoes, sliced into wedges
- 1 tablespoon unsalted butter
- 2 tablespoons Maggi Seasoning or low-sodium soy sauce
- ¼ cup cilantro leaves

1. In a bowl, mix together the beef, garlic, cornstarch, black pepper, and 1 tablespoon vegetable oil. Set aside.

2. Heat 2 cups oil in a heavy pot until it reaches 375ºF (190ºC). Carefully add a handful of the potatoes into the pot and cook, stirring occasionally, until they are golden brown—about 7-8 minutes. Drain the potatoes on paper towels and keep warm on a baking sheet in a 200ºF (93ºC) oven while frying remaining batches.

3. Heat 2 tablespoons oil in a large wok over medium heat. Add onion and mushrooms and cook until both have softened but not browned,

approximately 3-4 minutes.

4. Add the tomatoes and cook for an additional 2 minutes.

5. Push the items to the side of your wok (or remove to a plate if your wok is not large enough) and ad the beef. Quickly stir-fry the beef for 2-3 minutes or until lightly browned. Stir in the onion, tomato and mushroom mixture to combine well.

6. Remove from heat and stir in the butter and Mag Seasoning.

7. To serve, place the potatoes in a layer on a rimme plate. Pour beef stir-fry over the top and garnish with cilantro. Serve immediately.

Sugared Sesame with Vinegary Beef

Prep time: 15 minutes | Cook time: 10 minutes | Serves 4

- 1 tablespoon light soy sauce
- 2 tablespoons sesame oil, divided
- 2 teaspoons cornstarch, divided
- 1 pound (454 g) hanger, skirt, or flat iron steak, cut into ¼-inch-thick strips
- ½ cup freshly squeezed orange juice
- ½ teaspoon rice vinegar
- 1 teaspoon sriracha (optional)
- 1 teaspoon light brow sugar
- Kosher salt to taste
- Freshly ground blac pepper to taste
- 3 tablespoons vegetable oil, divide
- 4 peeled fresh ginge slices, each about th size of a quarter
- 1 small yellow onion thinly sliced
- 3 garlic cloves, minc
- ½ tablespoon white sesame seeds, for garnish

1. In a large bowl, stir together the light soy, 1 tablespoon of sesame oil, and 1 teaspoon of cornstarch until the cornstarch dissolves. Add th beef and toss to coat in the marinade. Set aside t marinate for 10 minutes while you prep the sauc

2. In a glass measuring cup, stir together the orang juice, remaining 1 tablespoon of sesame oil, rice vinegar, sriracha (if using), brown sugar, remaining 1 teaspoon of cornstarch, and a pinch each of salt and pepper to taste. Stir until the

cornstarch is dissolved and set aside.

. Heat a wok over medium-high heat until a drop of water sizzles and evaporates on contact. Pour in 2 tablespoons of vegetable oil and swirl to coat the base of the wok. Season the oil by adding the ginger and a pinch of salt to taste. Allow the ginger to sizzle in the oil for about 30 seconds, swirling gently.

. Using tongs, transfer the beef to the wok and discard the marinade. Let the pieces sear in the wok for 2 to 3 minutes. Flip to sear on the other side for another 1 to 2 minutes. Stir-fry by tossing and flipping around in the wok quickly for 1 more minute. Transfer to a clean bowl.

. Add the remaining 1 tablespoon of vegetable oil and toss in the onion. Quickly stir-fry, tossing and flipping the onion with a wok spatula for 2 to 3 minutes, until the onion looks translucent but is still firm in texture. Add the garlic and stir-fry for another 30 seconds.

. Swirl in the sauce and continue to cook until the sauce starts to thicken. Return the beef to the wok, tossing and flipping so the beef and onion are coated with sauce. Season to taste with salt and pepper.

. Transfer to a platter, discard the ginger, sprinkle with the sesame seeds, and serve hot.

Carrot with Beef Lettuce Cups

Prep time: 15 minutes | Cook time: 5 minutes | Serves 4

- ¾ pound (340 g) ground beef
- 2 teaspoons cornstarch
- Kosher salt to taste
- Freshly ground black pepper to taste
- 3 tablespoons vegetable oil, divided
- 1 tablespoon peeled finely minced ginger
- 2 garlic cloves, finely minced

- 1 carrot, peeled and julienned
- 1 (4-ounce / 113-g) can diced water chestnuts, drained and rinsed
- 2 tablespoons hoisin sauce
- 3 scallions, white and green parts separated, thinly sliced
- 8 broad iceberg (or Bibb) lettuce leaves,

trimmed to neat round cups

1. In a bowl, sprinkle the beef with the cornstarch and a pinch each of salt and pepper to taste. Mix well to combine.

2. Heat a wok over medium-high heat until a bead of water sizzles and evaporates on contact. Pour in 2 tablespoons of oil and swirl to coat the base of the wok. Add the beef and brown on both sides, then toss and flip, breaking up the beef into crumbles and clumps for 3 to 4 minutes, until the beef is no longer pink. Transfer the beef to a clean bowl and set aside.

3. Wipe the wok clean and return it to medium heat. Add the remaining 1 tablespoon of oil and quickly stir-fry the ginger and garlic with a pinch of salt to taste. As soon as the garlic is fragrant, toss in the carrot and water chestnuts for 2 to 3 minutes, until the carrot becomes tender. Lower the heat to medium, return the beef to the wok, and toss with the hoisin sauce and the scallion whites. Toss to combine, about another 45 seconds.

4. Spread out the lettuce leaves, 2 per plate, and evenly divide the beef mixture among the lettuce leaves. Garnish with the scallion greens and eat as you would a soft taco.

Mirin with Beef and Teriyaki Sauce

Prep time: 10 minutes | Cook time: 5 minutes | Serves 4

- 1 pound (454 g) flank steak
- 4 ½ teaspoons low-sodium soy sauce
- 3 teaspoons Japanese mirin
- 1 teaspoon granulated sugar
- 1 pound (454 g)

- broccoli florets
- 3 tablespoons vegetable oil, divided
- 1 tablespoon minced garlic
- 2 teaspoons minced ginger
- ¼ cup Teriyaki Sauce

1. Cut the beef into thin strips. In a medium bowl, combine the soy sauce, mirin, and sugar. Add the beef strips. Marinate the beef for 20 minutes.

2. Blanch the broccoli florets in boiling water for 2-3 minutes, until the broccoli turns bright green. Plunge the broccoli into cold water to stop the

cooking process. Drain thoroughly.

3. Heat a wok or skillet until it is nearly smoking. Add 1½ tablespoons oil. When the oil is hot, add the garlic. Stir-fry for 10 seconds.

4. Add the steak, laying it flat in the pan. Let sear (brown) briefly, then stir-fry the meat, stirring and tossing for 2 minutes or until it is no longer pink. Remove and drain in a colander or on paper towels.

5. Heat 1½ tablespoons oil in the wok or skillet. When the oil is hot, add the ginger. As soon as the ginger starts sizzling, add the broccoli florets. Stir-fry for 1 minute.

6. Add the Teriyaki Sauce. Bring to a boil. Add the beef back into the pan. Cook for another minute, stirring to mix everything together, then serve hot.

Cilantro with Buttered Beef

Prep time: 10 minutes | Cook time: 5 minutes | Serves 4

- 1 pound (454 g) filet mignon or rib eye steak, cut into ½ cubes
- 1 tablespoon minced garlic
- 1 small shallot, thinly sliced
- ½ teaspoon black pepper
- 2 tablespoons vegetable oil, divided
- 1 tablespoon unsalted butter
- 1 tablespoon Maggi Seasoning or low-sodium soy sauce
- ¼ cup fresh cilantro

1. In a large bowl, mix the beef, garlic, shallots, black pepper, and 1 tablespoon oil.

2. Heat a large wok over medium-high heat. Add 1 tablespoon oil to the wok and when it begins to slightly smoke, carefully toss in the beef mixture. Quickly stir-fry for 2-3 minutes and remove from heat.

3. Stir in the butter and Maggi Seasoning. Remove to a plate and top with cilantro.

Sugared Flank Steak

Prep time: 10 minutes | Cook time: 10 minutes | Serves 2

- ½ pound (227 g) flank steak
- 2 teaspoons tomato paste

- 1 tablespoon Worcestershire sauce
- 2 teaspoons soy sauce
- 1 tablespoon water
- 1 teaspoon brown sugar
- 2 tablespoons vegetable or peanut oil
- 2 cloves garlic, chopped
- 1 medium yellow onion, chopped

1. Cut the steak across the grain into thin strips 1½- long, ⅛ wide, and ⅛ thick.

2. In a small bowl, combine the tomato paste, Worcestershire sauce, soy sauce, water, and brow sugar. Set aside.

3. Heat a wok or skillet over medium-high heat unti it is nearly smoking. Add the oil. When the oil is hot, add the garlic. Stir-fry for 10 seconds.

4. Add the onion. Stir-fry until it begins to soften (about 2 minutes).

5. Add the steak. Sear briefly, then stir-fry for 2 minutes or until the beef is no longer pink and is nearly cooked.

6. Add the sauce and bring to a boil. Stir-fry for 2-3 more minutes, to blend the flavors. Serve hot.

Peppered Chimichurri Steak

Prep time: 5 minutes | Cook time: 5 minutes | Serves 4

- 1 pound (454 g) skirt steak, thinly sliced crosswise
- ½ tablespoon kosher salt
- ¼ tablespoon black
- pepper
- 2 tablespoons vegetable oil
- 1 cup Chimichurri Sauce

1. Season the beef with salt and pepper to taste.

2. Heat wok over medium-high heat and add the vegetable oil. Once the oil is hot, add in the beef and stir-fry for 3-4 minutes until browned.

3. Transfer the beef to a platter and drizzle the Chimichurri Sauce over the steak. Serve immediately.

Sesame Beef with Peanut Stir-Fry

Prep time: 15 minutes | Cook time: 5 minutes | Serves 4

Beef, Pork, and Lar

- 2 teaspoons cornstarch
- 1 teaspoon sesame oil
- 1 teaspoon soy sauce
- 1 pound (454 g) beef tenderloin or sirloin, cut into ¼-inch strips (like French fries)

FOR THE SAUCE:

- 1 tablespoon soy sauce
- 1 teaspoon brown sugar
- 1 teaspoon sesame oil
- 1 teaspoon chili oil
- ½ tablespoon oyster sauce
- ¼ teaspoon dark soy sauce

FOR THE STIR-FRY:

- 2 tablespoons peanut oil
- 2 garlic cloves, minced
- 5 or 6 dried red chiles
- ½ carrot, julienned
- 1 scallion, chopped

Pour the cornstarch, sesame oil, and soy sauce over the beef and toss to combine. Marinate at room temperature for 15 minutes.

In a small bowl, prepare the sauce by mixing together the soy sauce, brown sugar, sesame oil, chili oil, oyster sauce, and dark soy sauce. Set it aside.

In a wok over medium-high heat, heat the peanut oil.

Add the beef and stir-fry for about 30 seconds.

Add the garlic and stir-fry until the beef is almost cooked.

Add the sauce and dried red chiles, tossing to combine all the ingredients.

Turn off the heat, add the carrot, and give the dish one last stir.

Transfer the beef to a serving plate and garnish with the chopped scallion.

eef Stir-Fry with Shiitake Mushrooms

Prep time: 15 minutes | Cook time: 5 minutes | Serves 4

- 2 cups whole dried shiitake mushrooms
- 5 cups boiling water

FOR THE MARINADE

- 2 teaspoons soy sauce
- 2 teaspoons cornstarch
- Pinch freshly ground black pepper to taste
- 1 pound (454 g) beef tenderloin or sirloin, cut into thin strips

FOR THE SAUCE

- 2 tablespoons oyster sauce
- 1 tablespoon soy sauce
- 2 teaspoons brown sugar
- ½ teaspoon sesame oil

FOR THE STIR-FRY

- 2 tablespoons peanut oil
- 1 scallion, chopped

1. Soak the dried shiitake mushrooms in boiling water for about 20 minutes.

2. Meanwhile, pour the soy sauce, cornstarch, and pepper over the beef, and toss to combine. Marinate at room temperature for about 20 minutes.

3. In a small bowl, make the sauce by mixing together the oyster sauce, soy sauce, brown sugar, and sesame oil. Set it aside.

4. Drain and discard the water from the mushrooms, cut off and discard the mushroom stems, and gently squeeze the caps to remove excess water.

5. Cut the mushrooms into thin slices.

6. In a wok over medium-high heat, heat the peanut oil.

7. Add the beef and stir-fry for about 30 seconds, then remove it from the wok.

8. Add the sliced mushrooms, along with a little more peanut oil if needed. Stir-fry for about 2 minutes, then stir in the sauce.

9. Return the beef to the wok, toss to combine all the ingredients, and transfer to a serving dish.

10. Garnish with the chopped scallion and serve immediately.

Rice Wine with Crispy Sesame Beef

Prep time: 15 minutes | Cook time: 10 minutes | Serves 4

- ¼ cup soy sauce
- 2 tablespoons rice vinegar
- 2 tablespoons brown sugar
- ¼ cup plus 2 tablespoons
- cornstarch, divided
- 1 teaspoon hot sesame oil
- 1 pound (454 g) sirloin steak, thinly sliced
- 1 tablespoon Shaoxing rice wine

- ¼ cup cooking oil
- 1 tablespoon crushed, chopped ginger
- 2 garlic cloves, crushed and chopped
- 1 medium onion, diced
- 1 chile, cut into ¼-inch circles
- 2 tablespoons sesame seeds
- 4 scallions, cut into ½-inch pieces

1. In a small bowl, whisk together the soy sauce, rice vinegar, brown sugar, 2 tablespoons of the cornstarch, and the sesame oil. Set aside.
2. In a large bowl, toss the steak with the rice wine and the remaining ¼ cup of cornstarch, ensuring the steak is coated evenly.
3. In a wok over high heat, heat the cooking oil until it shimmers.
4. Add the ginger and garlic and let it lightly brown for 10 seconds.
5. Shallow-fry the steak until lightly browned, about 1 minute. Remove from the wok and set aside.
6. Remove and discard all but 2 tablespoons of the oil.
7. Add the onion to the wok and stir-fry for 1 minute.
8. Add the chile and stir-fry for 1 minute.
9. Add the soy sauce mixture and stir until a glaze is formed.
10. Return the beef to the wok and stir to coat.
11. Garnish with the sesame seeds and scallions. Serve over rice.

Gingered Kimchi with Korean Beef Bowl

Prep time: 15 minutes | Cook time: 6 minutes | Serves 4

- 2 tablespoons cooking oil
- 1 tablespoon crushed, chopped ginger
- 2 garlic cloves, crushed and chopped
- 1 pound (454 g) ground beef
- 2 tablespoons soy sauce
- 1 medium onion, diced
- 2 tablespoons gochujang
- 1 cup kimchi
- 1 teaspoon hot sesame oil
- 1 tablespoon sesame seeds
- 4 scallions, cut into ½-inch pieces

1. In a wok over high heat, heat the cooking oil until it shimmers.
2. Add the ginger, garlic, beef, soy sauce, and onion and stir-fry for 1 minute.
3. Stir in the gochujang, kimchi, and sesame oil and stir-fry for 1 minute.
4. Garnish with the sesame seeds and scallions. Serve over steamed rice.

Paprika with Garlicky Lamb Curry

Prep time: 15 minutes | Cook time: 5 minutes | Serves 4

- 2 tablespoons cooking oil
- 2 tablespoons crushed, chopped ginger
- 4 garlic cloves, crushed and chopped
- 1 medium onion, cut into ¼-inch pieces
- 1 tablespoon paprika
- 1 pound (454 g) boneless leg of lamb or rump, sliced into ¼-inch strips against the grain
- 1 chile, cut into ¼-inch rounds
- 1 tablespoon soy sauce
- 1 tablespoon rice vinegar
- 1 tablespoon brown sugar
- 1 teaspoon hot sesame oil
- 4 scallions, cut into 1-inch pieces

1. In a wok over high heat, heat the cooking oil until it shimmers.
2. Add the ginger, garlic, onion, paprika, and lamb and stir-fry for 1 minute.
3. Add the chile, soy sauce, rice vinegar, and brown sugar and stir-fry for 1 minute.
4. Add the sesame oil and scallions and toss lightly.
5. Serve over steamed rice.

Sugared Ginger with Curry Lamb

Prep time: 15 minutes | Cook time: 10 minutes | Serves 4

- 1 tablespoon red Thai curry paste
- ¼ cup canned coconut milk

- 1 tablespoon fish sauce
- 1 tablespoon brown sugar
- 1 tablespoon cornstarch
- 2 tablespoons coconut oil
- 1 tablespoon crushed, chopped ginger
- 2 garlic cloves, crushed and chopped
- 1 pound (454 g) boneless lamb leg or shoulder, cut into 1-inch pieces
- 1 medium onion, cut into 1-inch pieces
- 4 ounces (113 g) mushrooms, sliced
- 1 bird's eye chile, thinly sliced
- 2 cups chopped bok choy

In a small bowl, whisk together the curry paste, coconut milk, fish sauce, brown sugar, and cornstarch. Set aside.

In a wok over high heat, heat the coconut oil until it shimmers.

Add the ginger, garlic, and lamb and stir-fry for 1 minute.

Add the onion, mushrooms, and bird's eye chile and stir-fry for 1 minute.

Add the bok choy and stir-fry for 30 seconds.

Add the curry paste mixture and stir until a glaze forms.

Serve over coconut rice.

Cilantro with Spicy Cumin Lamb

Prep time: 15 minutes | Cook time: 5 minutes | Serves 4

- 2 tablespoons cooking oil
- 1 tablespoon crushed, chopped ginger
- 2 garlic cloves, crushed and chopped
- 1 pound (454 g) boneless leg of lamb or shoulder, cut into 1-inch pieces
- 1 medium onion, diced
- 1 tablespoon ground cumin or cumin seeds
- ½ teaspoon ground black pepper
- ¼ teaspoon kosher salt
- 1 red bell pepper, cut into ½-inch pieces
- 1 tablespoon rice wine
- 1 tablespoon rice vinegar
- 2 tablespoons soy sauce
- 1 tablespoon cornstarch

- ½ cup coarsely chopped cilantro

1. In a wok over high heat, heat the cooking oil until it shimmers.
2. Add the ginger, garlic, and lamb and stir-fry for 1 minute.
3. Add the onion, cumin, black pepper, and salt and stir-fry for 1 minute.
4. Add the bell pepper and stir-fry for 1 minute.
5. Add the rice wine, rice vinegar, soy sauce, and cornstarch and stir until a glaze forms.
6. Garnish with the cilantro and serve over steamed rice.

Garlicky Scallions with Tortillas

Prep time: 10 minutes | Cook time: 8 minutes | Serves 4

- 2 tablespoons peanut or vegetable oil, divided
- 2 teaspoons toasted sesame oil
- 1 pound (454 g) pork tenderloin, cut into thin strips
- 3 garlic cloves, minced
- 6 scallions, thinly sliced
- 1 (8-ounce / 227-g) bag shredded carrots
- 1 (10-ounce / 283-g) bag premade coleslaw mix
- 4 tablespoons hoisin sauce, plus additional for serving
- 2 tablespoons soy sauce
- 10 flour tortillas

1. Heat your wok on high heat until a drop of water sizzles on contact. Add 1 tablespoon of peanut oil and the sesame oil to the wok, and swirl to coat the wok. Add the pork and garlic, and stir-fry for 2 to 3 minutes. Transfer the pork to a plate and set aside.
2. Wipe out the wok if necessary. Heat the wok on high heat. Add the remaining 1 tablespoon of peanut oil. Then add the scallions, carrots, and coleslaw, and stir-fry for 4 to 6 minutes, or until they are crisp-tender. Add the hoisin sauce and soy sauce to the vegetables and mix to combine. Reduce the heat to medium, and return the pork to the wok. Mix everything together and stir-fry for about 2 minutes.
3. Serve the pork and vegetables with additional hoisin sauce and tortillas on the side for taco-style

wrapping.

Tamari with Beef and Pea Pods

Prep time: 10 minutes | Cook time: 6 minutes | Serves 4

- 2 tablespoons cooking oil
- 1 tablespoon crushed, chopped ginger
- 2 garlic cloves, crushed and chopped
- 1 pound (454 g) sirloin tips, cut into ¼-inch strips
- 2 tablespoons tamari
- 2 cups sugar snap or snow pea pods
- 2 tablespoons mirin
- 2 tablespoons brown sugar
- 1 tablespoon cornstarch

1. In a wok over high heat, heat the cooking oil until it shimmers.
2. Add the ginger and garlic and stir-fry for 30 seconds.
3. Add the steak and tamari and stir-fry for 1 minute.
4. Add the pea pods and stir-fry for 1 minute.
5. Add the mirin, sugar, and cornstarch and stir until a light glaze forms.
6. Serve over steamed sushi rice.

Syrupy Fried Ribs with Sesame

Prep time: 15 minutes | Cook time: 7 minutes | Serves 6

- 2 pounds (907 g) pork ribs, cut into 1-inch nuggets
- 1 large piece red fermented bean curd
- ½ teaspoon ground white pepper
- 1 teaspoon sesame oil
- 1 teaspoon five spice powder
- 2 tablespoons Shaoxing wine
- 1 tablespoon soy sauce
- 1 tablespoon maple syrup
- ½ teaspoon garlic powder
- ½ teaspoon onion powder
- ½ teaspoon baking soda
- ¼ cup cornstarch
- 3 cups canola oil

1. Mix bean curd, white pepper, sesame oil, spice powder, wine, soy sauce, maple syrup, garlic powder, onion powder, baking soda, and cornstarch in a bowl.
2. Stir in pork ribs and mix well to coat.
3. Cover the pork and marinate for 1 hour in the refrigerator.
4. Add 3 cups canola oil in a deep wok and heat up to 350ºF (180ºC).
5. Deep fry the pork chunks for 7 minutes until golden-brown.
6. Serve warm.

Pork Stir-Fry with Snow Peas

Prep time: 10 minutes | Cook time: 10 minutes | Serves 4

- 2 teaspoons Shaoxing rice wine
- 2 teaspoons light soy sauce
- ½ teaspoon chili paste
- ¾ pound boneless pork loin, thinly sliced into julienne strips
- 2 tablespoons vegetable oil
- 4 peeled fresh ginger slices, each about the size of a quarter
- Kosher salt to taste
- 4 ounces (113 g) snow peas, thinly sliced on the diagonal
- 2 tablespoons hoisin sauce
- 1 tablespoon water

1. In a bowl, stir together the rice wine, light soy, and chili paste. Add the pork and toss to coat. Set aside to marinate for 10 minutes.
2. Heat a wok over medium-high heat until a drop of water sizzles and evaporates on contact. Pour in the oil and swirl to coat the base of the wok. Season the oil by adding the ginger and a pinch of salt to taste. Allow the ginger to sizzle in the oil for about 30 seconds, swirling gently.
3. Add the pork and marinade and stir-fry for 2 to 3 minutes, until no longer pink. Add the snow peas and stir-fry for about 1 minute, until tender and translucent. Stir in the hoisin sauce and water to loosen the sauce. Continue to toss and flip for 30 seconds, or until the sauce is heated through and the pork and snow peas are coated.
4. Transfer to a platter and serve hot.

Gingered Coriander Meatballs

Prep time: 20 minutes | Cook time: 17 minutes | Serves 8

- 1 pound (454 g) beef, minced
- ½ cup cold water
- ½ teaspoon baking soda
- ½ teaspoon ginger, minced
- 1 teaspoon scallion whites, minced
- 1 teaspoon sugar
- 1 ⅛ teaspoon salt
- 1 tablespoon cornstarch
- 1 tablespoon vegetable oil
- ¼ teaspoon sesame oil
- 2 teaspoons Shaoxing wine
- ¼ teaspoon white pepper
- 1 ¼ teaspoon dried tangerine peel
- ¼ teaspoon coriander powder
- 1 egg white
- 2 bunches fresh watercress, boiled and chopped
- ¼ cup cilantro, chopped

Mix beef with watercress, cilantro, and rest of the ingredients in a food processor for 15 seconds.

Make golf ball-sized meatballs out of this mixture.

Fill a cooking pot with water, place it over medium heat and set a steamer basket in it.

Add the meatballs to the steamer and cover the lid.

Cook the meatballs in the steam for 12 minutes.

Sear the meatballs with some cooking oil in a Mandarin wok for 5 minutes.

Serve warm.

Beef with Lo Mein Noodles

Prep time: 25 minutes | Cook time: 13 minutes | Serves 4

For the Beef and Marinade:

- 12 ounces / 340 g flank steak, sliced
- 1 teaspoon cornstarch
- 1 teaspoon soy sauce
- 1 teaspoon vegetable oil
- ¼ teaspoon baking soda

For the Sauce:

- 1 tablespoon light soy sauce
- 1 tablespoon oyster sauce
- 2 teaspoons dark soy sauce
- ½ teaspoon sesame oil
- ½ teaspoon salt
- ¼ teaspoon sugar
- ¼ teaspoon white pepper

For the Noodles:

- 1 pound (454 g) fresh lo Mein noodles, boiled
- 1 garlic clove, minced
- 1 carrot, julienned
- ½ red bell pepper, julienned
- ½ cup mushrooms, sliced
- ½ cup bamboo shoots, sliced
- 2 cups Napa cabbage, shredded
- ⅔ cup snow peas
- 2 cups mung bean sprouts
- 2 tablespoons vegetable oil
- 1 tablespoon Shaoxing wine
- 2 scallions, julienned

1. Mix soy sauce and all the ingredients for the sauce in a bowl.
2. Coat the beef cubes with cornstarch, soy sauce, and baking soda.
3. Sear the beef with vegetable oil in a skillet until golden-brown.
4. Sauté ginger, carrot, cabbage, bell pepper, mushrooms, snow peas, bean sprouts, wine, scallion, and garlic with oil in a Cantonese wok for 7 minutes.
5. Add beef cubes and sauce into the wok, then mix well.
6. Stir and cook the mixture for 5 minutes until beef is done.
7. Serve warm.

Honeyed Orange Beef

Prep time: 15 minutes | Cook time: 10 minutes | Serves 4

- 1 teaspoon sea salt
- 1 tablespoon plus
- 1 teaspoon cornstarch, divided
- 1 teaspoon minced garlic
- 1 teaspoon red pepper flakes
- 1 pound (454 g) sirloin steak, cut into strips
- 1 teaspoon grated orange rind
- ¼ cup orange juice
- 2 teaspoons honey
- 1 teaspoon sesame oil

- 3 tablespoons soy sauce
- 1 tablespoon peanut oil
- 3 scallions, cut into 1-inch strips

1. In a large bowl, mix the sea salt, 1 teaspoon of the cornstarch, garlic, and crushed red pepper. Add the beef, tossing it to coat all sides. Let the beef sit for 10 minutes.

2. In a small bowl, make the sauce by combining the orange rind, orange juice, the remaining 1 tablespoon of cornstarch, honey, sesame oil, and soy sauce. Set aside.

3. Heat your wok over high heat until a drop of water sizzles on contact. Add the oil and swirl to coat the wok. Add the beef and scallions, and stir-fry for 1 to 2 minutes, or until the beef is cooked. Add the sauce to the wok, stir to combine, and cook about 2 minutes, or until the sauce thickens.

4. Serve with rice.

Spicy Cashew with Gingered Steak

Prep time: 15 minutes | Cook time: 10 minutes | Serves 4

- ¼ cup soy sauce
- 2 tablespoons sugar
- 2 tablespoons cornstarch
- ½ teaspoon ground ginger
- 1 pound (454 g) sirloin steak
- 2 tablespoons peanut or vegetable oil, divided, plus additional, if needed
- 1 large sweet onion, cut into 1-inch squares
- 1 red bell pepper, cut into 1-inch squares
- 1 yellow bell pepper, cut into 1-inch squares
- 1 zucchini, halved and cut into rounds
- 3 scallions, cut into 1-inch strips
- ½ cup cashews

1. In a large bowl, mix the soy sauce, sugar, cornstarch, and ground ginger, stirring until the sugar has dissolved.

2. Slice the steak across the grain into ¾-inch-thick slices. Add the slices to the cornstarch marinade, and coat them well on all sides. Let the beef sit for 10 minutes.

3. Heat your wok until a drop of water sizzles on contact. Add 1 tablespoon of peanut oil, and

swirl to coat the wok. Add the beef and stir-fry it until it has browned, about 3 minutes. Add the remaining 1 tablespoon of peanut oil and the onion, and stir-fry about 2 minutes. If more oil is needed, add it to the wok. Add the bell peppers, zucchini, and scallions and stir-fry for another 3 minutes. Finally, add the cashews, stir everything to combine, and remove the wok from the heat.

4. Serve with rice.

Cilantro with Brothy Mongolian Beef

Prep time: 15 minutes | Cook time: 10 minutes | Serves 4

- 2 tablespoons Shaoxing rice wine
- 1 tablespoon dark soy sauce
- 1 tablespoon cornstarch, divided
- ¾ pound flank steak, cut against the grain into ¼-inch-thick slices
- ¼ cup low-sodium chicken broth
- 1 tablespoon light brown sugar
- 1 cup vegetable oil
- 4 or 5 whole dried re Chinese chilies
- 4 garlic cloves, coarsely chopped
- 1 teaspoon peeled finely minced fresh ginger
- ½ yellow onion, thin sliced
- 2 tablespoons coarse chopped fresh cilant

1. In a mixing bowl, stir together the rice wine, dar soy, and 1 tablespoon of cornstarch. Add the slic flank steak and toss to coat. Set aside and marin for 10 minutes.

2. Pour the oil into a wok and bring it to 375°F (190°C) over medium-high heat. You can tell the oil is at the right temperature when you dip the end of a wooden spoon into the oil. If the oil bubbles and sizzles around it, the oil is ready.

3. Lift the beef from the marinade, reserving the marinade. Add the beef to the oil and fry for 2 to minutes, until it develops a golden crust. Using a wok skimmer, transfer the beef to a clean bowl a set aside. Add the chicken broth and brown suga to the marinade bowl and stir to combine.

4. Pour out all but 1 tablespoon of oil from the wo and set it over medium-high heat. Add the chili

peppers, garlic, and ginger. Allow the aromatics to sizzle in the oil for about 10 seconds, swirling gently.

. Add the onion and stir-fry for 1 to 2 minutes, or until the onion is soft and translucent. Add the chicken broth mixture and toss to combine. Simmer for about 2 minutes, then add the beef and toss everything together for another 30 seconds.

. Transfer to a platter, garnish with the cilantro, and serve hot.

Soy Sauce with Lamb and Leeks

Prep time: 15 minutes | Cook time: 15 minutes | Serves 4

- ¾ pound (340 g) (boneless leg of lamb, cut into 3 chunks, then thinly sliced across the grain
- Kosher salt to taste
- 2 tablespoons Shaoxing rice wine
- 1 tablespoon dark soy sauce
- 1 tablespoon light soy sauce
- 1 teaspoon oyster sauce
- 1 teaspoon honey
- 1-2 teaspoons sesame oil
- ½ teaspoon ground Sichuan pepper corns
- 2 teaspoons cornstarch
- 2 tablespoons vegetable oil
- 1 tablespoon peeled and finely minced fresh ginger
- 2 leeks, trimmed and thinly sliced
- 4 garlic cloves, finely minced

In a mixing bowl, season the lamb lightly with 1 to 2 pinches of salt. Toss to coat and set aside for 10 minutes. In a small bowl, stir together the rice wine, dark soy, light soy, oyster sauce, honey, sesame oil, Sichuan pepper, and cornstarch. Set aside.

Heat a wok over medium-high heat until a drop of water sizzles and evaporates on contact. Pour in the vegetable oil and swirl to coat the base of the wok. Season the oil by adding the ginger and a pinch of salt to taste. Allow the ginger to sizzle in the oil for about 10 seconds, swirling gently.

Add the lamb and sear for 1 to 2 minutes, then begin to stir-fry, tossing and flipping for 2 minutes

more, or until no longer pink. Transfer to a clean bowl and set aside.

4. Add the leeks and garlic and stir-fry for 1 to 2 minutes, or until the leeks are bright green and soft. Transfer to the lamb bowl.

5. Pour in the sauce mixture and simmer for 3 to 4 minutes, until the sauce reduces by half and turns glossy. Return the lamb and vegetables to the wok and toss to combine with the sauce.

6. Transfer to a platter and serve hot.

Cucumber with Cumin Lamb Burgers

Prep time: 15 minutes | Cook time: 10 minutes | Serves 4

- 1 tablespoon cumin seeds
- 1 teaspoon Sichuan peppercorns
- ½ teaspoon red chili flakes
- 1 pound (454 g) ground lamb
- 1 teaspoon salt
- 1 medium red onion, sliced
- 1 jalapeno, thinly
- sliced
- 1 small red bell pepper, thinly sliced
- 1 tablespoon vegetable oil
- 1 cup plain Greek Yogurt
- 2 garlic cloves, minced
- 4 brioche or potato buns
- 1 cucumber, diced

1. Toast peppercorns, cumin seeds, and red chili flakes in a skillet.

2. Transfer the mixture to a pestle and grind with a mortar.

3. Mix the lamb with half of the toasted spice mixture and salt and make 4 patties out of it.

4. Set a wok with oil on medium heat and sear the patties for 2 minutes per side.

5. Transfer the patties to a plat and keep them covered aside.

6. Add peppers, and onion to the skillet until caramelize.

7. Mix yogurt with salt, garlic, and remaining spice mixture in a bowl.

8. Place one patty in each bun then divide caramelized onion, cucumber, and yogurt sauce in

the burgers.

9. Serve.

Cumin Lamb with Cilantro Dish

Prep time: 15 minutes | Cook time: 15 minutes | Serves 4

- **Marinate the Lamb:**
- 1 pound (454 g) lamb shoulder, cut into 2-inch pieces
- 1 tablespoon cumin
- 1 ½ teaspoon cornstarch
- 1 tablespoon oil
- 1 tablespoon light soy sauce
- 1 tablespoon Shaoxing rice wine
- 2 tablespoons cumin seeds
- 2 tablespoons oil
- 2 red chili peppers, chopped
- ½ teaspoon Sichuan red pepper flakes
- ¼ teaspoon sugar
- 2 scallions, chopped
- Large handful of chopped cilantros
- Salt, to taste

For the Dish:

1. Mix soy sauce, cornstarch, wine, and cumin in a bowl, and toss in lamb pieces.
2. Cover and marinate for 1 hour in the refrigerator.
3. Add oil and marinated lamb to a skillet then sear for minutes per side.
4. Mix chili peppers, Sichuan red pepper flakes, sugar, scallions, cilantro, salt, cumin seeds, and oil in a Cantonese wok.
5. Sauté for 1 minute, then add the seared lamb to the wok.
6. Continue cooking the lamb for 5 minutes.
7. Serve warm.

Chili Cumin and Lamb Skewers

Prep time: 10 minutes | Cook time: 12 minutes | Serves 4

- 1 pound (454 g) lamb shoulder, diced
- 2 teaspoons cumin seeds
- 1 tablespoon dried chili flakes
- Salt, to taste
- 1 tablespoon oil
- Bamboo skewers

1. Grind cumin seeds with chili flakes, oil, and salt to taste in a mortar with pestle.
2. Rub this mixture over the lamb cubes and cover to a marinate for 30 minutes.
3. Thread the lamb cubes on the skewers.
4. Sear the lamb skewers for 6 minutes in a preheated and greased wok.
5. Enjoy.

Kimchi with Korean Beef Stir-fry

Prep time: 15 minutes | Cook time: 5 minutes | Serves 4

- 8 ounces / 227 g ground beef
- 2 garlic cloves, crushed and chopped
- 1 tablespoon crushed and chopped peeled ginger
- 1 large onion, cut into ½-inch dice
- 2 tablespoons gochujang
- 2 cups white kimchi
- 1 tablespoon cornstarch
- 1 tablespoon sesame seeds
- 4 scallions, green and white parts, cut diagonally into ¼-inc pieces
- 1 cup bean sprouts
- Cooked rice or noodles, for serving

1. Heat a wok until it begins to smoke.
2. Put the beef, garlic, and ginger in the wok. Stir-fry for 1 minute, or until the garlic and ginger are fragrant.
3. Add the onion and stir-fry for 1 minute, or until it is tender crisp.
4. Add the gochujang, kimchi, and cornstarch. Stir-fry for 1 minute, or until all of the ingredients are well combined.
5. Add the sesame seeds, scallions, and bean sprout. Toss. Serve over rice or noodles.

Chapter 8: Soups, Rice, and Noodles

Peppered Beef with Soy Sauce

Prep time: 15 minutes | Cook time: 17 minutes | Serves 4

¼ cup Shaoxing rice wine

¼ cup light soy sauce

2 tablespoons cornstarch

1½ tablespoons dark soy sauce

1½ tablespoons dark soy sauce

½ teaspoon sugar

Ground white pepper

¾ pound (340.5 g) flank steak or sirloin tips, cut across the grain into ⅛-inch-thick slices

1½ pounds (680

g) fresh wide rice noodles or ¾ pound dried

· 2 tablespoons sesame oil, divided

· 3 tablespoons vegetable oil, divided

· 4 peeled fresh ginger slices, each about the size of a quarter

· Kosher salt

· 8 scallions, halved lengthwise and cut into 3-inch pieces

· 2 cups fresh mung bean sprouts

In a mixing bowl, stir together the rice wine, light soy, cornstarch, dark soy, sugar, and a pinch of white pepper. Add the beef and toss to coat. Set aside to marinate for at least 10 minutes.

Bring a large pot of water to a boil and cook the rice noodles according to package instructions. Reserve 1 cup of the cooking water and drain the rest. Rinse with cold water and drizzle with 1 tablespoon of sesame oil. Set aside.

Heat a wok over medium-high heat until a drop of water sizzles and evaporates on contact. Pour in 2 tablespoons of vegetable oil and swirl to coat the base of the wok. Season the oil by adding the ginger and a pinch of salt. Allow the ginger to sizzle in the oil for about 30 seconds, swirling gently.

Using tongs, add the beef to the wok and reserve the marinating liquid. Sear the beef against the wok for 2 to 3 minutes, or until a seared, browned crust develops. Toss and flip the beef around the wok for 1 more minute. Transfer to a clean bowl and set aside.

5. Add 1 more tablespoon of vegetable oil and stir-fry the scallions for 30 seconds, or until soft. Add the noodles and lift in a scooping upward motion to help separate the noodles if they have stuck together. Add the cooking water, 1 tablespoon at a time, if the noodles have really glued themselves together.

6. Return the beef to the wok and toss to combine with the noodles. Pour in the reserved marinade and toss for 30 seconds to 1 minute, or until the sauce thickens and coats the noodles and they turn a deep, rich brown color. If you need to, add 1 tablespoon of the reserved cooking water to thin out the sauce. Add the bean sprouts and toss until just heated through, about 1 minute. Remove the ginger and discard.

7. Transfer to a platter and drizzle with the remaining 1 tablespoon of sesame oil. Serve hot.

Carrot and Sesame Lo Mein

Prep time: 15 minutes | Cook time: 7 minutes | Serves 4

· 2 tablespoons soy sauce

· 2 teaspoons sugar

· 1 teaspoon sesame oil

· 1 teaspoon chili sauce (optional)

· 1 tablespoon peanut oil

· 2 garlic cloves, minced

· 1½ cups cremini or button mushrooms, sliced

· 1 red bell pepper, julienned

· ¼ cup shredded carrots

· ½ cup snow peas

· 2 scallions, cut into 1-inch pieces

· ½ pound lo mein, cooked according to package directions and drained well

1. In a small bowl, make the sauce by mixing the soy sauce, sugar, sesame oil, and chili sauce (if using). Set aside.

2. Heat your wok on high heat until a drop of water sizzles on contact. Add the peanut oil and swirl to coat the wok. Add the garlic, cremini mushrooms, red bell pepper, and carrots to the wok, and stir-fry for 3 to 4 minutes, tossing often. Add the snow peas and scallions, and stir-fry for another 2 to 3 minutes.

3. Add the lo mein and the sauce mixture to the wok.

Toss everything together to combine, and turn off the heat. Serve immediately.

Garlicky Pork Congee

Prep time: 15 minutes | Cook time: 92 minutes | Serves 4

- 10 cups water
- ¾ cup jasmine rice, rinsed and drained
- 1 teaspoon kosher salt
- 2 teaspoons peeled minced fresh ginger
- 2 garlic cloves, minced
- 1 tablespoon light soy sauce, plus more for serving
- 2 teaspoons Shaoxing rice wine
- 2 teaspoons cornstarch
- 6 ounces (170 g) ground pork
- 2 tablespoons vegetable oil
- Pickled Chinese vegetables, thinly sliced, for serving (optional)
- Scallion-Ginger Oil, for serving (optional)
- Fried Chili Oil, for serving (optional)
- Sesame oil, for serving (optional)

1. In a heavy-bottomed pot, bring the water to a boil. Stir in the rice and salt and reduce the heat to a simmer. Cover and cook, stirring occasionally, for about 1½ hours, until the rice has turned to a soft porridge-like consistency.

2. While the congee is cooking, in a medium bowl, stir together the ginger, garlic, light soy, rice wine, and cornstarch. Add the pork and allow it to marinate for 15 minutes.

3. Heat a wok over medium-high heat until a drop of water sizzles and evaporates on contact. Pour in the vegetable oil and swirl to coat the base of the wok. Add the pork and stir-fry, tossing and breaking up the meat, about 2 minutes. Cook for another 1 to 2 minutes without stirring to get some caramelization.

4. Serve the congee in soup bowls topped with the stir-fried pork. Garnish with your toppings of choice.

Vinegary Hakka Noodles

Prep time: 15 minutes | Cook time: 9½ minutes | Serves 4

- ¾ pound (340.5 g) fresh flour-based noodles
- 3 tablespoons sesame oil, divided
- 2 tablespoons light soy sauce
- 1 tablespoon rice vinegar
- 2 teaspoons light brown sugar
- 1 teaspoon sriracha
- 1 teaspoon Fried Chili Oil
- Kosher salt
- Ground white pepper
- 2 tablespoons vegetable oil
- 1 tablespoon peeled finely minced fresh ginger
- ½ head green cabbage, shredded
- ½ red bell pepper, sliced into thin strips
- ½ red onion, sliced into thin vertical strips
- 1 large carrot, peeled and julienned
- 2 garlic cloves, finely minced
- 4 scallions, thinly sliced

1. Bring a pot of water to a boil and cook the noodles according to package instructions. Drain, rinse, and toss with 2 tablespoons of sesame oil. Set aside.

2. In a small bowl, stir together the light soy, rice vinegar, brown sugar, sriracha, chili oil, and a pinch each of salt and white pepper. Set aside.

3. Heat a wok over medium-high heat until a drop of water sizzles and evaporates on contact. Pour in the vegetable oil and swirl to coat the base of the wok. Season the oil by adding the ginger and small pinch of salt. Allow the ginger to sizzle in the oil for about 10 seconds, swirling gently.

4. Add the cabbage, bell pepper, onion, and carrot and stir-fry for 4 to 5 minutes, or until the vegetables are tender and the onion begins to caramelize slightly. Add the garlic and stir-fry until fragrant, about 30 seconds more. Stir in the sauce mixture and bring to a boil. Turn the heat down to medium and simmer the sauce for 1 to 2 minutes. Add the scallions and toss to combine.

5. Add the noodles and toss to combine. Increase the heat to medium-high and stir-fry for 1 to 2 minutes to heat the noodles. Transfer to a platter, drizzle with the remaining 1 tablespoon of sesame oil, and serve hot.

Sesame with Soy Sauce Noodles

Prep time: 5 minutes | Cook time: 10 minutes | Serves 4

- ½ pound (227 g) egg noodles, dried or fresh
- 2 tablespoons peanut or vegetable oil
- 1 cup bean sprouts, rinsed and dried
- 2 scallions, cut into 1-inch pieces
- 2½ tablespoons soy sauce
- ½ teaspoon sesame oil

If using dried noodles, parboil them for 3 minutes. Drain very well before they are added to the wok.

Heat your wok on high heat until a drop of water sizzles on contact.

Add the peanut oil and swirl to coat the wok.

Add the noodles and cook for about 4 minutes while continuously tossing and stir-frying.

Add the bean sprouts, scallions, soy sauce, and sesame oil to the wok, and stir-fry for another 3 to 4 minutes, or until the noodles are browned and serve.

Garlicky Shrimp Mei Fun

Prep time: 15 minutes | Cook time: 4 minutes | Serves 4

- 1 tablespoon Shaoxing wine
- 1 teaspoon sugar
- 1 tablespoon soy sauce
- 1 tablespoon oyster sauce
- 1 teaspoon sesame oil
- 2 tablespoons peanut or vegetable oil
- 1 onion, thinly sliced
- 1 garlic clove, minced
- 1 red bell pepper, sliced into strips
- 1 cup shrimp, pork, chicken, beef, or tofu, thinly sliced
- 2 eggs, beaten
- 10 ounces (283 g) rice noodles, soaked, drained well
- 1 scallion, cut into slivers

In a small bowl, make the sauce by combining the rice wine, sugar, soy sauce, oyster sauce, and sesame oil. Set aside.

Heat your wok on high until a drop of water sizzles on contact. Add the peanut oil and swirl to coat the wok. Add the onion, garlic, and red bell pepper, and stir-fry for about 20 seconds. Add the shrimp and stir-fry for 1 to 2 minutes. Slowly stream in the eggs to create egg threads, and stir-fry for about 1 minute more. Add the rice noodles and stir-fry for about 2 minutes, tossing everything together.

3. Add the sauce mixture to the wok. Stir-fry for 1 to 2 minutes, making sure everything is combined. Add the slivered scallion, give it a quick toss, and turn off the heat.

4. Serve with rice and chili sauce or sambal oelek on the side.

Mushroom and Chicken Noodle Soup

Prep time: 10 minutes | Cook time: 11 minutes | Serve 4

- 2 teaspoons vegetable oil
- 2 tablespoons minced garlic
- ⅓ cup fresh ginger, finely chopped, peeled
- 5 ounces (142 g) fresh shiitake mushrooms, stemmed and thinly sliced
- ½ cup Shaoxing wine or good dry sherry
- 6 cups low-sodium chicken broth
- 1½ pounds (680 g) boneless chicken thighs, fat trimmed,
- cut into bite-size pieces
- 5 scallions, green part only, cut into 1-inch pieces
- 3 carrots, cut into matchsticks
- 2 tablespoons soy sauce
- Sea salt
- Freshly ground black pepper
- ½ pound (227 g) rice stick noodles, soaked in boiling water for 10 minutes and then drained

1. Heat your wok to medium-high heat, and then add the oil. Add the garlic, ginger, and shiitake mushrooms to the wok, and stir-fry for about 1 minute. Stir in the rice wine, reduce the heat to medium, and cook for 2 to 3 minutes. Add the chicken broth to the wok, and bring it to a hard simmer.

2. Add the chicken, scallions, and carrots to the soup, stir, and let it simmer for about 3 minutes. Then reduce the heat to low, and simmer for another 5 to 6 minutes. Add the soy sauce to the soup, stir

3. Divide the noodles among 4 soup bowls. Ladle the soup over the noodles and serve.

Egg Noodles Chow Mein

Prep time: 15 minutes | Cook time: 20 minutes | Serve 4

- 1 teaspoon ground ginger
- 2 garlic cloves, minced
- 3 tablespoons ketchup
- 1 tablespoon oyster sauce
- 2 tablespoons soy sauce
- 3 tablespoons water
- 3 nests egg noodles
- 1 tablespoon peanut oil
- 2 small chicken breasts, cut into strips
- 1 large green bell pepper, cut into strips
- 1 celery stalk (not from the outside), cut into strips
- 4 scallions, trimmed and cut into 1-inch strips

1. In a small bowl, make the sauce by combining the ginger, garlic, ketchup, oyster sauce, soy sauce, and water. Set aside.

2. Boil the noodles for 4 minutes or according to the package directions. Drain the noodles well and set aside.

3. Heat your wok over high heat until a drop of water sizzles on contact. Add the oil and swirl to coat the wok. Add the chicken and stir-fry it for about 1 minute. Add the green bell pepper and celery, and stir-fry for another 1 to 2 minutes.

4. Add the sauce to the wok. Cook and stir until the sauce starts to simmer. Add the noodles and scallions to the wok, and stir to combine the ingredients and coat the noodles with the sauce. Turn off the heat and serve.

Brothy Rice Noodles

Prep time: 10 minutes | Cook time: 31 minutes | Serve 4

- ½ cup chicken broth
- ¼ cup soy sauce
- 2 tablespoons Shaoxing wine
- 2 teaspoons minced garlic
- ½ teaspoon ground ginger

- 1 teaspoon sambal oelek
- 1 tablespoon peanut oil
- 1 red bell pepper and 1 green bell pepper
- 2 shallots, thinly sliced
- 1½ cups bean sprouts
- 1 teaspoon curry powder
- 1 cup sliced mushrooms
- 6 ounces (170 g) thin rice noodles, soaked, drained well
- 1 scallion, sliced (optional)

1. In a medium bowl, make the sauce by combining the chicken broth, soy sauce, rice wine, garlic, ginger, and sambal oelek. Set aside.

2. Heat your wok over high heat until a drop of water sizzles on contact. Add the oil and swirl to coat the wok. Add the bell peppers, shallots, bean sprouts, and curry powder, and stir-fry for 2 to 3 minutes. Add the mushrooms and stir-fry for another 2 minutes, or until the peppers are crisp-tender.

3. Reduce the heat to medium, and add the noodles to the wok with 3 tablespoons the sauce. Stir-fry and toss so that the noodles and sauce are combined with the other ingredients, about 2 minutes.

4. Turn off the heat and slowly pour in the remaining sauce, mixing everything to combine. Don't use all the sauce if you like it with less.

5. Serve the noodles garnished with the sliced scallion (if using).

Vinegary Chinese Noodles

Prep time: 5 minutes | Cook time: 1 minute | Serves 4

- 1 pound (454 g) Chinese egg noodles
- Sesame oil, divided
- 6 tablespoons soy sauce
- 2 tablespoons balsamic vinegar
- 4 tablespoons sugar
- 1 tablespoon sea salt
- 2 teaspoons chili oil
- 12 scallions, trimmed and cut into 1-inch pieces

1. Cook the noodles according to the package directions until they are al dente. Rinse quickly with cold water to cool.

2. Drain the noodles well, moving them around the colander so all the water is removed.

Line a wide flat plate with paper towels and spread out the noodles on it to make sure they are completely dry.

In an extra-large bowl, whisk together ⅓ cup plus 1 tablespoon cup sesame oil, the soy sauce, vinegar, sugar, sea salt, and chili oil. Add the scallions.

Heat up your wok on medium-high heat and add the remaining 1 tablespoon sesame oil.

Using a slotted spoon, transfer the scallions to the wok and stir-fry for 1 to 2 minutes. Toss to avoid burning. Return the scallions to the sauce in the bowl.

Add the noodles to the bowl and toss with the sauce and scallions to combine. Cover with plastic wrap and chill in the refrigerator for at least 1 hour. Toss the noodles again with the sauce before serving.

ggy Fried Rice with Rice

ep time: 10 minutes | Cook time: 7 minutes | rves 4

- 4 tablespoons peanut oil, divided
- 2 tablespoons garlic, minced
- 2 tablespoons fresh ginger, grated
- 1 small sweet onion, diced
- 4 cups cooked long-

- grain or jasmine rice (day-old rice is best)
- 4 large eggs, beaten
- 2 teaspoons sesame oil
- 4 teaspoons soy sauce
- Sea salt
- Freshly ground pepper

Heat your wok over medium-high heat. Add 3 tablespoons peanut oil, and swirl to coat the wok. Add the garlic and ginger, and stir-fry for about 1 minute. Add the onion and stir-fry for about 3 minutes, or until the onion is tender.

Reduce the heat to medium. Add the rice to the wok, and stir everything together. Continue stir-frying for about 2 minutes.

Move the rice to the edges of the wok. Pour the eggs into the center of the wok, first adding the remaining 1 tablespoon peanut oil, if necessary. Scramble the eggs, about 1 minute.

When the eggs are scrambled, turn the heat off. Mix the eggs into the rice. Add the sesame oil and

soy sauce to the rice, and mix everything together. Season with the sea salt and pepper.

Brothy Chicken Congee

Prep time: 10 minutes | Cook time: 5 minutes | Serve 4

- 5 cups chicken broth
- 4 cups water
- 1 cup short-grain rice, rinsed well
- 2 cups cooked chicken, cut into small pieces
- Sea salt
- Soy sauce, for garnish (optional)
- Toasted sesame oil, for garnish (optional)

- Scallions, thinly sliced, for garnish (optional)
- Cilantro, chopped, for garnish (optional)
- Roasted unsalted peanuts, chopped, for garnish (optional)
- Chili oil, for garnish (optional)

1. In your wok, bring the chicken broth and water to a boil.

2. Add the rice, cover the wok, and reduce the heat to a gentle simmer. Let the rice simmer, stirring once in a while, for about 1 hour. The rice will have a porridge-like consistency.

3. Stir in the chicken and season with the sea salt. Let the congee simmer for about 5 more minutes.

4. Ladle it into bowls. Serve with the soy sauce, sesame oil, scallions, cilantro, peanuts, and chili oil on the side for individual garnishing (if using).

Honeyed Chow Mein

Prep time: 10 minutes | Cook time: 5 minutes | Serves 4

- ¼ cup cooking oil
- 1 pound (454 g) cooked noodles
- 1 tablespoon crushed, chopped ginger
- 2 garlic cloves, crushed and chopped
- 1 medium onion, cut into 1-inch pieces
- 1 red bell pepper, cut into 1-inch pieces

- 2 cups sugar snap or snow pea pods
- ¼ cup hoisin sauce
- 2 tablespoons honey
- 2 tablespoons soy sauce
- 2 tablespoons Shaoxing rice wine
- 4 scallions, cut into 1-inch pieces

1. In a wok over high heat, heat the cooking oil until it shimmers.

2. Add the noodles and stir-fry for 2 minutes until lightly browned.

3. Remove the noodles and drain off all but 2 tablespoons oil.

4. Add the ginger, garlic, and onion to the wok and stir-fry for 1 minute.

5. Add the bell pepper and pea pods and stir-fry for 1 minute.

6. Add the noodles, hoisin sauce, honey, soy sauce, and rice wine and stir-fry for 1 minute.

7. Garnish with the scallions and serve.

Spicey Seafood Lo Mein

Prep time: 15 minutes | Cook time: 3 minutes | Serves 4

- 2 tablespoons cooking oil
- 1 tablespoon crushed, chopped ginger
- 2 garlic cloves, crushed and chopped
- ¼ pound (113 g) ground pork
- 1 medium onion, cut into 1-inch pieces
- 1 red bell pepper, cut into 1-inch pieces
- ¼ pound (113 g)

- medium shrimp, peeled, deveined, and cut in half lengthwise
- ¼ pound (113 g) sea scallops, cut in half widthwise
- 2 tablespoons soy sauce
- 2 tablespoons rice wine
- ¼ cup oyster sauce
- 1 pound (454 g) cooked noodles

1. In a wok over high heat, heat the cooking oil until it shimmers.

2. Add the ginger, garlic, pork, and onion and stir-fry for 1 minute.

3. Add the bell pepper and shrimp and stir-fry for 1 minute.

4. Add the scallops and stir-fry for 30 seconds.

5. In a small bowl, whisk together the soy sauce, rice wine, and oyster sauce, then add the mixture to the wok.

6. Add the noodles and stir-fry for 30 seconds.

7. Serve immediately.

Spicy Mirin Yaki Udon

Prep time: 15 minutes | Cook time: 15½ minutes | Serves 6

- 1 pound (454 g) frozen udon noodles
- 2 tablespoons butter
- 1 garlic clove, minced
- 2 teaspoons dashi powder
- 1 tablespoon oil
- 4 ounces (113 g) pork shoulder
- 4 ounces (113 g) oyster mushrooms, sliced

- 2 tablespoons mirin
- 2 cups cabbage, shredded
- 1 medium carrot, julienned
- ⅛ teaspoon black pepper
- 2 tablespoons soy sauce
- 1 tablespoon water
- 2 scallions, julienned

1. Boil the dry noodles in hot water as per package' instructions then drain.

2. Sauté garlic with butter in a Mandarin wok for 3(seconds.

3. Stir in pork shoulder, then sauté for 5 minutes.

4. Add mushrooms along with remaining except th noodles.

5. Cover and cook for 10 minutes until pork is tend

6. Stir in noodles and mix well.

7. Serve warm.

Garlicky Asian Noodles

Prep time: 10 minutes | Cook time: 1 minutes | Serves 6

- 12 ounces (340 g) thin spaghetti
- 4 tablespoons unsalted butter
- 8 garlic cloves, peeled and sliced
- ⅛ teaspoon turmeric
- 1 tablespoon oyster sauce

- 1 tablespoon soy sau
- 1 to 2 teaspoons bro sugar
- 1 teaspoon sesame o
- 1 to 2 whole scallion chopped
- ¼ cup Parmesan cheese

1. Boil the spaghetti in hot water as per package's instructions then drain.

2. Sauté garlic with butter in a Cantonese wok ove for 30 seconds.

1. Mix turmeric, soy sauce, oyster sauce, brown sugar, sesame oil, scallions, and Parmesan cheese in a bowl.

2. Pour this mixture into the wok and cook for 30 seconds.

3. Toss in boiled spaghetti and mix well with the sauce.

4. Serve warm.

Chili Singapore Noodles with Stock

Prep time: 15 minutes | Cook time: 7½ minutes | Serves 6

- 5 ounces (142 g) dried vermicelli rice noodles
- 12 large frozen shrimp; peeled, deveined, and butterflied
- 2½ tablespoons vegetable oil
- 2 eggs, beaten
- 2 garlic cloves, chopped
- 4 ounces (113 g) char Siu, Chinese Roast Pork
- 3 dried red chili peppers
- 9 ounces (255 g) Napa cabbage, shredded
- 1 medium carrot
- 1 tablespoon Shaoxing wine
- 2 tablespoons curry powder
- 2 teaspoons salt
- ¼ teaspoon sugar
- ⅛ teaspoon white pepper
- 2 to 4 tablespoons chicken stock
- 1 tablespoon vegetable oil
- ½ teaspoon sesame oil
- 1½ teaspoons soy sauce
- 1 scallion, julienned
- ½ cored onion, thinly sliced

Boil the dry noodles in hot water as per package's instructions then drain.

Sauté garlic with oil in a Cantonese wok for 30 seconds.

Stir in cabbage, carrot, and onion, then sauté for 5 minutes.

Add shrimp and rest of the (except the noodles).

Cover and cook for 2 minutes until shrimp turn white.

Stir in noodles and mix well.

7. Serve warm.

Honeyed Pork Fried Rice

Prep time: 15 minutes | Cook time: 12 minutes | Serves 6

- 1 tablespoon hot water
- 1 teaspoon honey
- 1 teaspoon sesame oil
- 1 teaspoon Shaoxing wine
- 1 tablespoon soy sauce
- 1 teaspoon dark soy sauce
- ¼ teaspoon white pepper
- 5 cups cooked Jasmine rice
- 1 tablespoon oil
- 1 medium onion, diced
- 1 pound (454 g) Chinese BBQ pork, cut into ½-inch chunks
- 1 teaspoon salt
- ½ cup bean sprouts
- 2 eggs, scrambled
- 2 scallions, chopped

1. Sauté onion, bean sprouts, and pork with oil in a Mandarin wok for 7 minutes.

2. Stir in rest of the along with eggs (except rice).

3. Mix well and cook for 5 minutes.

4. Stir in rice and mix gently.

5. Serve warm.

Egg with Fried Brown Rice

Prep time: 15 minutes | Cook time: 15 minutes | Serves 8

- 4 cups cooked brown rice
- 8 ounces (227 g) beef, chicken, or pork, cut into ½-inch pieces
- 1 tablespoon water
- 1½ teaspoon dark mushroom soy sauce
- 1 teaspoon vegetable oil
- 1 teaspoon cornstarch
- ¼ teaspoon granulated sugar
- ⅛ teaspoon ground white pepper
- ½ teaspoon sesame oil
- 1 teaspoon dark soy sauce
- 1 tablespoon light soy sauce
- 3 tablespoons vegetable oil
- 2 eggs, beaten
- 1 medium onion, chopped
- ¾ cup carrots, chopped
- 1 tablespoon Shaoxing wine
- 1 cup frozen peas

- 1 scallion, chopped

1. Beat eggs with salt and wine in a bowl.
2. Pour this mixture into a greased wok and stir cook for 1 minute. Transfer it to a plate.
3. Mix cornstarch with water, soy sauce, white pepper, and sesame oil in a bowl.
4. Sauté onion, carrot, and peas with oil in a cooking pot for 5 minutes.
5. Stir in meat then sauté for 7 minutes.
6. Pour in prepared sauce and mix well.
7. Add cooked eggs, rice, wine, and scallions, then mix well to cook for 2 minutes.
8. Serve warm.

Classic Vietnamese Pho

Prep time: 15 minutes | Cook time: 5 hours | Serves 6

- 2 (3-inch) pieces ginger, cut in half lengthwise
- 2 onions, peeled
- 5 pounds (2.3 kg) beef marrow
- 2 pounds (907 g) beef chuck, cut into 2 pieces
- 2 scallions, cut into 4-inch lengths
- ⅓ cup fish sauce
- 2½ ounces rock sugar
- 8-star anise
- 6 cloves
- 1 cinnamon stick
- 1 black cardamom pod
- 2 teaspoons fennel seeds
- 2 teaspoons coriander seeds
- 1 tablespoon salt
- 1 pound (454 g) dried pho noodles, boiled
- ⅓ pound (151 g) beef sirloin, sliced

1. Sauté onions and ginger with oil in a large wok for 5 minutes.
2. Stir in meat and beef marrow then cover to cook for 40 minutes.
3. Toast all the whole spices in a dry skillet for 3 minutes then seal the spices in a spice infuser.
4. Place the spice infuser to the broth and cover to cook for 4 hours.
5. Stir in sugar, salt, and fish sauce, then mix well.
6. Remove the spice infuser from the soup.
7. Add remaining including noodles then cook for 5

minutes.

8. Serve warm.

Vinegary Glass Noodle Soup

Prep time: 10 minutes | Cook time: 3 minutes | Serves 4

- 2 tablespoons cooking oil
- 1 tablespoon crushed, chopped ginger
- 2 garlic cloves, crushed and chopped
- ½ pound (227 g) ground pork
- 1 medium carrot, julienned
- 12 cups meat or vegetable broth
- 8 ounces (227 g)
- dry vermicelli glass noodles
- ¼ cup rice vinegar
- 1 teaspoon hot sesame oil
- 4 eggs, cracked into a bowl with yolks unbroken
- 1 cup chopped bok choy
- 1 scallion, cut into ½-inch pieces

1. In a wok over high heat, heat the cooking oil until it shimmers.
2. Add the ginger, garlic, pork, and carrot and stir-fry for 1 minute.
3. Add the broth, noodles, rice vinegar, and sesame oil and bring to a boil.
4. Distribute the eggs into the boiling broth without breaking the yolks and poach for 1 minute.
5. Sprinkle the bok choy into the soup and let it cook for 1 minute.
6. Garnish with the scallion and serve with one poached egg in each bowl.

Brothy Wonton Soup

Prep time: 5 minutes | Cook time: 0 minutes | Serves 4

- 6 cups chicken broth, homemade or store-bought
- 1 scallion, finely chopped
- 12 to 15 wontons

1. In your wok, bring the chicken broth to a boil. Carefully add the wontons, one at a time; lower the heat to a simmer. The wontons are ready when they float to the top of the broth.

Spoon the soup into individual bowls, and garnish with the chopped scallion.

Eggy Pork Drop Soup

Prep time: 10 minutes | Cook time: 1½ minutes | Serves 4

- 13¼ cups vegetable or meat broth, divided
- ¼ cup cornstarch
- 1 pound (454 g) ground pork
- 1 tablespoon crushed, chopped ginger
- 2 garlic cloves, crushed and chopped
- 1 ounce dried, sliced shiitake or tree ear mushrooms
- 4 eggs, beaten
- 1 cup chopped bok choy
- 4 scallions, cut into ½-inch pieces

Combine 1 cup the broth with the cornstarch and stir to form a slurry. Set aside.

In a wok over high heat, boil ¼ cup the broth.

Add the pork, ginger, and garlic and cook for 1 minute.

Add the remaining 3 quarts broth and the mushrooms to the wok. Bring to a boil.

Stir the cornstarch slurry into the boiling broth until the broth thickens.

Stir the broth in one direction while drizzling the beaten eggs into the wok.

Stir the bok choy into the broth and let cook for 30 seconds.

Garnish with the scallions, squeezing them to bruise while dropping them into the broth. Serve immediately.

Spicy Hot Seafood Soup

Prep time: 15 minutes | Cook time: 5 minutes | Serve 4

- 3½ L vegetable, fish, or meat broth
- 1 tablespoon hot sesame oil
- ¼ cup rice vinegar
- 2 tablespoons cornstarch
- 1 tablespoon cooking oil
- 2 garlic cloves, crushed and chopped
- 1 tablespoon crushed, chopped ginger
- ¼ pound (113 g) ground pork
- ½ cup julienned carrots
- 1 cup chopped bok choy
- ¼ pound (113 g) medium shrimp, shelled and deveined
- ¼ pound (113 g) white fish (like cod or haddock), cut into 1-inch pieces
- ¼ pound (113 g) sea scallops, cut in half widthwise
- 4 scallions, cut into ½-inch pieces

1. In a large bowl, whisk together the broth, sesame oil, rice vinegar, and cornstarch. Set aside.
2. In a wok over high heat, heat the cooking oil until it shimmers.
3. Add the garlic, ginger, and pork and stir-fry for 1 minute.
4. Add the carrots and stir-fry for 1 minute.
5. Add the broth mixture to the wok and stir until the cornstarch dissolves and the broth comes to a boil.
6. Add the bok choy and let cook for 1 minute.
7. Add the shrimp, followed by the fish and scallops. Cook for 2 minutes.
8. Garnish with the scallions and serve immediately.

Brothy Chicken Stir-Fry Soup

Prep time: 10 minutes | Cook time: 1½ minutes | Serves 4

- 2 tablespoons cooking oil
- 1 tablespoon crushed, chopped ginger
- 2 garlic cloves, crushed and chopped
- 1 pound (454 g) ground or finely chopped chicken
- 1 medium onion, diced
- 1 bell pepper (any color), cut into ½-inch pieces
- 1 cup bok choy, chopped
- 12 cups meat or vegetable broth
- 4 scallions, cut into ¼-inch pieces

1. Fresh chopped herbs such as cilantro, mint, parsley, or basil, for garnish
2. In a wok over high heat, heat the cooking oil until it shimmers.
3. Add the ginger, garlic, chicken, onion, and bell pepper and stir-fry for 1 minute.

4. Add the bok choy and stir-fry for 30 seconds.

5. Add the broth and bring to a gentle boil.

6. Add the scallions, squeezing them to bruise while sprinkling them into the soup.

7. Serve the soup topped with chopped herbs.

Eggy Seaweed Drop Soup

Prep time: 10 minutes | Cook time: 2 minutes | Serves 6

- 2 tablespoons dried seaweed
- 4 cups chicken stock
- 1 cup water
- 5 g dried shrimp flakes
- ¼ to ½ teaspoon
- sesame oil
- ¼ teaspoon white pepper
- 2 eggs, beaten
- 1 scallion, sliced

1. Sauté seaweed in a Cantonese wok for 2 minutes, then add water and chicken stock.

2. Boil the stock then add shrimp flakes, sesame oil, seaweed, and white pepper.

3. Cook the mixture to a boil, then stir in eggs and scallions.

4. Serve warm.

Cornstarch with Sesame Noodle Soup

Prep time: 10 minutes | Cook time: 20 minutes | Serves 8

For the Pork:

- 4- to 6-ounce (113- to 170-g) pork shoulder, cut into thin strips
- 1 teaspoon cornstarch
- 1 teaspoon vegetable oil
- 1 teaspoon Shaoxing wine
- 1 teaspoon oyster sauce
- ⅛ teaspoon salt

For the Soup:

- 8 ounces (227 g) fresh white noodles, cooked
- 4 cups chicken stock
- 1 tablespoon vegetable oil
- 7 ounces (198 g) pickled mustard stems
- ¼ teaspoon sugar
- ½ teaspoon sesame oil
- 1 scallion, chopped

1. Mix cornstarch with wine, oyster sauce, and salt in a bowl.

2. Stir in pork slices and mix well. Cover to marinate for 10 minutes.

3. Add oil and marinated pork to a wok then sear them until golden-brown.

4. Transfer this brown pork to a plate and set it aside.

5. Sauté mustard stems and scallions with sesame and vegetable oil in a Mandarin wok for 1 minute.

6. Stir in stock, sugar, pork, and noodles.

7. Cook the pork soup for 10 minutes.

8. Serve warm.

Spiced Egg Drop Soup

Prep time: 10 minutes | Cook time: 11 minutes | Serves 4

- 2 tablespoons oil
- 10 ounces (283 g) tomatoes; cut into chunks
- 1 cup chicken stock
- 2 cups water
- 2 teaspoons light soy sauce
- ½ teaspoon sesame oil
- ¼ teaspoon white
- pepper
- Salt, to taste
- 1 egg, beaten
- 1½ teaspoons cornstarch mixed with 2 tablespoons water
- 1 scallion, chopped
- 2 tablespoons cilantro, chopped

1. Sauté tomatoes with oil in a deep wok for 5 minutes.

2. Stir in stock, water, soy sauce, sesame oil, white pepper, and salt, then cook for 5 minutes.

3. Pour in cornstarch slurry then cook until the soup thickens.

4. Stir in egg and cook for 1 minute.

5. Garnish with scallion and cilantro.

6. Enjoy.

Eggy Meatballs with Melon Soup

Prep time: 15 minutes | Cook time: 2 minutes | Serves 6

For the Meatballs:

- 1 pound (454 g) ground pork
- 2 tablespoons water
- 2½ tablespoons light soy sauce

2 tablespoons Shaoxing wine

1 teaspoon sesame oil

½ teaspoon ground white pepper

½ teaspoon sugar

1 egg white

1 tablespoon ginger, minced

1 scallion, chopped

¼ teaspoon salt

or the Soup:

1 package glass noodles, boiled

- 1 pound (454 g) winter melon, peeled and diced
- 1 tablespoon oil
- 2 scallions, chopped
- 4 cups chicken stock
- 2 cups water
- ½ teaspoon ground white pepper
- ½ teaspoon sesame oil
- Salt, to taste
- 1 handful of cilantros, chopped

Mix pork with water, soy sauce, wine, sesame oil, white pepper, sugar, egg white, ginger, scallions, and salt in a bowl.

Make small meatballs out of this pork mixture.

Sauté meatballs with 1 tablespoon oil in a deep wok until golden-brown.

Stir in scallions and melon then sauté for 2 minutes.

Add the remaining soup along with boiled noodles.

Cook the soup for 10 minutes on medium heat until meatballs are done.

Serve warm.

Gingered Carrots with Pork Soup

Prep time: 10 minutes | Cook time: 3 hours | Serves 14

4 dried shiitake mushrooms, soaked and drained

1⅓ pounds (605 g) lean pork shoulder,

1 pound (454 g) large carrots, cut into chunks

2 tablespoons dried red dates, pitted and

halved

- 2 tablespoons dried goji berries
- 1 large chunk ginger, smashed
- 14 cups water
- 1 pound (454 g) Chinese yams, peeled and cut into chunks
- Salt, to taste

1. Add pork, mushrooms, carrots, red dates, goji berries, ginger, water, and salt to a wok.

2. Cover and cook for 2 hours on a simmer, then add Chinese yam.

3. Cook for another 1 hour on a simmer.

4. Serve warm.

Goji Berries with Pork Ribs Soup

Prep time: 10 minutes | Cook time: 4 hours | Serves 6 to 8

- 1 pound (454 g) pork ribs, cut into 1-inch pieces
- 1 pound (454 g) lotus root, peeled and cut into ¼-inch-thick rounds
- ½ teaspoon peppercorns
- 12 cups water
- 2 tablespoons soy sauce
- 1 teaspoon salt
- ¼ cup dried goji berries
- ½ cup dried red dates (optional)

1. Place the pork ribs, lotus root, peppercorns, red dates (if using), and water in a wok.

2. Simmer over low heat for at least 4 hours, and up to 6 hours.

3. Turn off the heat and add the soy sauce, salt, and goji berries.

4. Allow the soup to sit for about 15 minutes for the goji berries to reconstitute, then serve.

Milky Laksa Noodle Soup

Prep time: 15 minutes | Cook time: 11 minutes | Serves 6

- 4 bone-in chicken thighs
- 4 tablespoons vegetable oil
- 1 garlic clove, minced
- 1½ tablespoons ginger, minced
- 1 stalk lemongrass, minced
- 2 Thai chilies, minced
- ½ cup laksa paste
- 1 tablespoon brown sugar
- 4 cups chicken stock
- 1 can coconut milk
- 1 tablespoon fish sauce
- 1 package soy puffs, halved
- 4 portions noodles

- 1 to 3 limes, juices
- 3 large shallots, thinly sliced
- ¼ cup all-purpose flour
- 12 large shrimp
- 2 cups mung bean sprouts
- ½ cup fresh cilantro leaves

1. Season the chicken thighs with black pepper and salt.
2. Place them in a baking tray and bake for 40 minutes at 400ºF (205ºC).
3. Meanwhile, sauté ginger and garlic with 2 tablespoons oil for 1 minute in a deep wok.
4. Stir in chilies and lemongrass then sauté for 3 minutes.
5. Add brown sugar and laksa paste, then cook for 3 minutes.
6. Stir in fish sauce, coconut milk, and chicken stock, then cook this mixture to a boil.
7. Add soy puffs, cover the soup, and cook for 10 minutes on a simmer.
8. Cook the noodles in boiling water according to the package's instructions.
9. Add noodles along with remaining to the soup.
10. Cook for 5 minutes, then serve warm.

Scallion with Chicken Feet Soup

Prep time: 10 minutes | Cook time: 2⅓ hours | Serves 12

- 2 tablespoons dried seaweed, soaked
- 1 cup raw shelled peanuts
- 1½ pounds (680 g) chicken feet
- 2 tablespoons
- Shaoxing wine
- 4 ginger slices
- 12 cups water
- Salt, to taste
- 1 scallion, chopped

1. Add water, ginger, wine, chicken feet, seaweed, peanuts, and salt in a large wok.
2. Cook the chicken feet soup for 20 minutes, then reduce the heat to low.
3. Continue cooking for 2 hours, then garnish with scallions.
4. Serve warm.

Eggy Matzo Ball Soup

Prep time: 10 minutes | Cook time: 1⅓ hours | Serves 8

- 1 cup matzo meal
- ¼ cup vegetable oil
- ¼ cup chicken stock
- 4 large eggs
- ¼ teaspoon nutmeg
- ½ teaspoon baking powder
- Salt and black pepper to taste
- 6 cups chicken stock
- 4 ribs celery, diced
- 3 medium carrots, diced
- 1 small onion, diced

For the Soup:

1. Mix matzo meal with eggs, salt, black pepper, nutmeg, vegetable oil, baking powder and stock in a bowl.
2. Cover and refrigerate this mixture for 3 hours.
3. Add chicken stock, onion, carrots, and celery to a deep wok.
4. Cook the soup for 40 minutes on low heat until veggies are soft.
5. Meanwhile, set pot filled with salted water. Make small balls out of the matzo mixture.
6. Add the matzo balls to the water and cook for 35 minutes.
7. Transfer the matzo balls to the soup and cook for minutes. Serve warm.

Egg with Spicy Tofu Soup

Prep time: 10 minutes | Cook time: 20 minutes | Serves 6

- 8 ounces (227 g) frozen Shepherd's purse
- ½ block silken tofu
- 4 cups homemade chicken stock
- 1½ teaspoons salt
- 1 teaspoon sesame oil
- ¼ teaspoon ground white pepper
- ¼ cup cornstarch, mixed with ¼ cup water
- 3 egg whites

1. Sauté tofu and shepherd's purse with sesame oil a wok for 5 minutes.
2. Stir in stock, salt, and white pepper, then cook th mixture on a simmer for 10 minutes.
3. Mix cornstarch with water and pour into the sou

Cook the soup until it thickens.

Beat egg whites and pour into the soup.

Cook for 5 minutes, then serve warm.

Cilantro with Scallions Noodles

Prep time: 10 minutes | Cook time: 3½ minutes | Serves 4

- ¾ pound (340 g) egg noodles
- 3 tablespoons sesame oil, divided
- 2 tablespoons vegetable oil
- 6 to 8 fresh shiitake mushrooms, stems removed and caps thinly sliced
- ½ pound (227 g) medium shrimp (U41/50), peeled and deveined
- 1 shallot, thinly sliced
- Kosher salt
- 4 ounces char shiu (Chinese barbecue pork), sliced into thin strips
- ½ cup frozen edamame beans, shelled and thawed
- 1 tablespoon light soy sauce
- 2 teaspoons Shaoxing rice wine
- 4 scallions, trimmed, white and green parts thinly sliced
- 3 tablespoons coarsely chopped fresh cilantro

Bring a pot of water to a boil and cook the noodles according to package instructions. Drain and rinse the noodles under cold water. Drizzle the noodles with 1 tablespoon sesame oil and set aside.

Heat a wok over medium-high heat until a drop of water sizzles and evaporates on contact. Pour in the vegetable oil and swirl to coat the base of the wok. Add the mushrooms and toss to coat with the oil. Let the mushrooms sit against the wok and sear for 1 to 2 minutes. Toss and flip the mushrooms around for another 30 seconds, or until golden brown.

Add the shrimp and shallot and toss with the mushrooms. Stir-fry for 2 to 3 minutes, until the shrimp turns opaque and pink. Season with a pinch of salt. Add the char shiui and edamame, tossing and flipping until heated through, about another minute. Drizzle in the light soy and rice wine and toss to coat.

Add the scallions and cilantro, reserving a small bit of each for garnish, and toss until the cilantro wilts slightly. Add the noodles and another pinch of salt. Toss and scoop, lifting upward to separate the noodle strands and combine with the shrimp and vegetables.

5. Transfer to a platter and drizzle with the remaining 2 tablespoons sesame oil. Garnish with the reserved scallions and cilantro. Serve immediately. Happy Birthday!

Steamed Rice with Bok Choy

Prep time: 10 minutes | Cook time: 20 minutes | Serves 4

- 1½ cups jasmine rice
- 4 lap cheung (Chinese sausage) links or Spanish chorizo
- 4 baby bok choy heads, each sliced into 6 wedges
- ¼ cup vegetable oil
- 1 small shallot, thinly sliced
- 1-inch fresh ginger piece, peeled and
- finely minced
- 1 garlic clove, peeled and finely minced
- 2 teaspoons light soy sauce
- 1 tablespoon dark soy sauce
- 2 teaspoons Shaoxing rice wine
- 1 teaspoon sesame oil
- Sugar

1. In a mixing bowl, rinse and swish the rice 3 or 4 times under cold water, swishing the rice around in the water to rinse off any starches. Cover the rice with cold water and soak for 2 hours. Drain the rice through a fine-mesh sieve.

2. Rinse two bamboo steamer baskets and their lids under cold water and place one basket in the wok. Pour in 2 inches of water, or enough to make the water level come above the bottom rim of the steamer by ¼- to ½-inch but not so high that the water touches the bottom of the steamer.

3. Line a plate with a piece of cheesecloth and add half the soaked rice to the plate. Arrange 2 sausages and half the bok choy on top, and loosely tie up the cheesecloth so there is enough space around the rice so that it can expand. Place the plate in the steamer basket. Repeat the process with another plate, more cheesecloth, and the remaining sausage and bok choy in the second steamer basket, then stack it on top of the first and cover.

4. Turn the heat to medium-high and bring the water to a boil. Steam the rice for 20 minutes, checking the water level often and adding more as needed.

5. While the rice is steaming, in a small saucepan, heat the vegetable oil over medium heat until it just begins to smoke. Turn off the heat and add the shallot, ginger, and garlic. Stir together and add the light soy, dark soy, rice wine, sesame oil, and a pinch of sugar. Set aside to cool.

6. When the rice is ready, carefully untie the cheesecloth and transfer the rice and bok choy to a platter. Slice the sausages diagonally and arrange on top of the rice. Serve with the ginger soy oil on the side.

Brothy Bok Choy with Rice

Prep time: 10 minutes | Cook time: 25 minutes | Serve 4

- 1 tablespoon butter
- 1 head of chopped bok choy
- 2 cups chicken broth
- 1 cup uncooked jasmine rice
- 1 tablespoon olive oil
- 1 tablespoon chopped fresh chives, or to taste
- 1 pinch ground black pepper

1. Melt the butter in a deep wok or large saucepan over medium heat. Add the bok choy and stir-fry for about 5 minutes until soft.

2. Add the chicken stock and turn up the heat on high. Bring to a boil. Add rice, olive oil and chives and stir well.

3. Cover with a tightly fitting lid, reduce the heat to a boiling point and cook for 20 minutes. After 10 minutes, check the rice to make sure it is pacing well; overcooking will make the rice dry, overcooking will result in hard rice.

4. Season with pepper and serve.

Garlicky Mushroom with Apple Rice

Prep time: 15 minutes | Cook time: 22 minutes | Serves 4

- 170 g prawns, peeled, veined and cut into pieces
- 1 pinch salt and ground black pepper, to taste
- 1 teaspoon corn starch
- 1 tablespoon vegetable oil, or more as needed
- 1 teaspoon minced garlic
- 1 egg, beaten
- 1 cup diced mushrooms
- ¾ cup frozen mixed vegetables
- 1 apple, peeled, cored and diced
- 2 tablespoons raisins
- 1 tablespoon curry powder
- 1 tablespoon light soy sauce
- 2 cups white rice steamed overnight
- 1 green onion, diced

1. Mix salt, pepper and prawns in a bowl then mix with cornstarch. Heat a wok with oil over medium heat and add the shrimp mixture. Cook the shrimp mixture, about 5 minutes, until it turns light brown.

2. Put the cooked shrimp mixture on a plate. Fry the garlic in the same wok for about 1 minute until fragrant.

3. Add the egg and cook for 3 minutes or until you have scrambled eggs. Place the mixed vegetables in the wok and cook for 3 to 5 minutes, stirring until soft.

4. Put the mixed vegetables in the wok and cook for 3 to 5 minutes, stirring until soft. Add the raisins, apple and curry powder. Put the rice in the wok and season with salt, pepper and soy sauce.

5. Boil for 3 minutes and stir until fragrant. Cook and stir everything for 3 to 5 minutes or until the rice is heated through.

6. Put the rice in the wok and season with salt, pepper and soy sauce. Add the spring onions and prawns and let everything cook for 2 to 4 minutes and stir everything for 2 to 4 minutes until the rice is heated through.

Turmeric with Fried Rice and Prawns

Prep time: 10 minutes | Cook time: 4 minutes | Serves 4

- 2 kg pineapple
- ½ cup paprika
- 3 thinly sliced spring onions
- 2 teaspoons chopped fresh jalapeño pepper
- ½ tablespoon soy sauce

½ teaspoon sugar

1 teaspoon anchovy paste

½ teaspoon turmeric

2 tablespoons vegetable oil

- 1 pound (454 g) small shrimp, peeled and chopped
- 2 garlic cloves, chopped
- 5 cups cooked rice

Cut the pineapple in half lengthways, cut out the pulp, leaving 1.2 cm thick

pods and reserve the peel. Discard the core and cut enough of the pineapple into pieces to measure 1½ peels and reserve the remaining pineapple for other use.

Mix the pineapple pieces, paprika, spring onions and jalapeño pepper in a bowl. In a small bowl, stir together the soy sauce, sugar, anchovy paste, turmeric and 1 tablespoon water. Heat 1 tablespoon oil in a wok or heavy pan over moderate heat until hot but not smoked, fry the prawns in it for 1½ minutes or until just firm, stirring, and transfer to a bowl.

Heat the remaining 1 tablespoon oil over moderate heat until it is hot but not smoking, and fry the garlic in the oil for 5 seconds while stirring or until it is golden brown. Add the rice and saute the mixture for 30 seconds or until the rice is hot. Add the soy mixture and sauté the mixture for 1 minute while stirring.

Add the pineapple mixture and prawns, sauté the mixture for 1 minute or until hot, then stir in the coriander. Serve the fried rice in the reserved pineapple bowls as desired. (Fried rice is served separately.)

Brothy Grapes with Rice Stir Fry

Prep time: 5 minutes | Cook time: 3 minutes | Serves 4

1 tablespoon vegetable oil

1 cup sliced red grapes

1 cup diced cooked

chicken

- 2 cups cooked rice
- ¼ cup chicken broth

Heat the vegetable oil in a large pan or wok over medium to high heat. Add the chicken and grapes. Cook for about 3 minutes until the grapes are

tender and the chicken is well heated.

3. Pour in the chicken broth and rice. Keep cooking

Easy Steamed White Rice

Prep time: 5 minutes | Cook time: 17 minutes | Serves 4 to 6

- 2 cups jasmine rice
- 3 cups water, plus

water for rinsing the rice

1. First wash the rice. Pour the rice into a medium pot. Rinse the rice by filling the pot halfway with cold tap water, running your fingers through the rice to loosen the starch, then pouring out the murky water. Repeat three or four times, draining as much water as possible. Alternatively, put the rice in a mesh strainer and rinse it under running tap water.

2. To cook the rice, pour 3 cups of water over the rice in the pot.

3. Bring to a boil over high heat, uncovered.

4. When most of the water has been absorbed and you can see the surface of the rice, reduce the heat to low and cover the pot with a lid. (If you use a pot with a heavy base that retains heat well, you can turn off the heat completely at this point, leaving it covered. The rice will continue to steam and won't burn.)

5. Simmer the rice for an additional 12 minutes. No peeking!

6. Turn off the heat. Allow the rice to sit, covered, for 5 minutes.

7. Uncover. Just before serving, fluff the rice using a spatula or chopsticks.

Classic Steamed Brown Rice

Prep time: 5 minutes | Cook time: 35 minutes | Serves 4 to 6

- 2 cups medium- or long-grain brown rice
- 4 cups water, plus

more for rinsing the rice

- 1 teaspoon salt

1. First wash the rice. Pour the rice into a medium pot. Rinse the rice by filling the pot halfway with cold tap water, running your fingers through the rice to loosen the starch, then pouring out the murky water. Repeat three or four times, draining

as much water as possible. Alternatively, put the rice in a mesh strainer and rinse it under running tap water.

2. To cook the rice, pour 4 cups of water into the pot with the rice, then add the salt. Bring to a boil over high heat, uncovered.

3. When most of the water has been absorbed and the top of the rice is visible, reduce the heat to low and cover the pot.

4. Simmer the rice for 20 minutes. No peeking!

5. Turn off the heat. Let the rice sit, partially uncovered, for 15 minutes.

6. Fluff with a spatula or chopsticks before serving.

Basic Cornstarch with Egg Drop Soup

Prep time: 10 minutes | Cook time: 1 minutes | Serves 4

- 1½ tablespoons cornstarch
- 3 tablespoons water
- 4 cups basic Chinese chicken stock, or store bought
- 1 teaspoon salt
- 2 eggs, lightly beaten
- 1 medium tomato, diced
- Pinch ground white pepper
- 1 scallion, chopped

1. In a small bowl, combine the cornstarch and water.

2. In a wok over medium-high heat, bring the chicken stock to a boil. Add the salt.

3. Stir in the cornstarch-water mixture. Return to a boil.

4. Using a pair of chopsticks, swirl the soup, and at the same time slowly pour the beaten eggs into the soup. Swirl faster for a thinner, silky consistency; or slower for a thicker, chunky egg consistency.

5. Add the tomato and pepper, stir, and simmer for 1 minute.

6. Garnish with the scallion, and serve.

Shrimp with Pork Meatball Soup

Prep time: 10 minutes | Cook time: 33 minutes |

Serves 8 to 10

For the Pork Meatballs:
- ½ pound (227 g) ground pork
- ¼ pound (227 g) minced shrimp
- ¼ cup water chestnuts, finely diced
- 1 teaspoon soy sauce
- ½ teaspoon sugar
- ½ teaspoon salt
- Pinch ground white pepper

- 1½ tablespoons cornstarch

For the Soup:
- 10 cups Basic Chinese chicken stock, or store bought
- ½ head napa cabbage, cut into 1-inch pieces
- 1 carrot, sliced
- 2 teaspoons salt
- 2 teaspoons sesame oi
- 2 teaspoons soy sauce

To Make the Meatballs

1. In a bowl, mix the ground pork, shrimp, water chestnuts, soy sauce, sugar, salt, pepper, and cornstarch. Set aside to marinate for about 15 minutes.

To Make the Soup

2. In a wok over high heat, bring the chicken stock to a boil.

3. Add the cabbage and carrot, and simmer for abou 30 minutes.

4. Roll about 1 heaping tablespoon of pork mixture into a ball and continue until all the pork mixture is used. Carefully drop the meatballs into the boiling soup one at a time. Avoid stirring. As the meatballs cook, they will rise to the top. They wil take about 3 minutes to cook through.

5. Add the salt, sesame oil, and soy sauce just before turning off the heat.

Spicy Berry Pork Soup

Prep time: 10 minutes | Cook time: 3⅔ hours | Serves 6 to 8

- 12 cups water, divided
- ½ pound (227 g) pork ribs or pork shoulder, cut into 1-inch pieces
- 6 to 10 dried red dates
- ¼ cup dried goji

- berries
- 1 pound (454 g) watercress
- 1 tablespoon salt
- 3 pinches ground white pepper

1. In a wok, bring 2 cups of water to a boil. Blanch th

pork for about 5 minutes. Rinse the pork and the wok, and set the pork aside.

In the wok, bring the remaining 10 cups of water to a boil.

Return the pork to the wok. Reduce the heat to low and simmer, partially covered, for 3½ hours.

Add the red dates, goji berries, watercress, salt, and pepper. Simmer for 10 more minutes, and serve.

Classic Peanut Soup

Prep time: 5 minutes | Cook time: 2 hours | Serves 4 to 6

- ½ pound (227 g) raw peanuts, shelled and skinned
- 1 tablespoon baking soda
- 8 cups water, plus more for soaking
- 4 tablespoons sugar

Soak the peanuts in a bowl of water overnight.

Rinse the peanuts, sprinkle them with the baking soda, then cover in fresh water to soak for 1 to 2 more hours.

Thoroughly rinse the peanuts.

In a wok over high heat, bring the 8 cups of water to a boil.

Add the peanuts to the boiling water, reduce the heat to low, and simmer, partially covered, for 2 hours.

Add the sugar in increments until the soup reaches your desired sweetness.

Serve the soup at room temperature, hot, or cold, with an almond or butter cookie, if desired.

Carrot and Mushroom with Rice Soup

Prep time: 10 minutes | Cook time: 22 minutes | Serves 4

- 1 cup cooked rice
- 4 cups low-sodium chicken broth
- 4 fresh shiitake mushrooms, stems removed and caps
- thinly sliced
- 1 large carrot, peeled and cut into ¼-inch-thick slices
- 2 teaspoons light soy sauce

- 2 teaspoons sesame oil
- 1 teaspoon Shaoxing rice wine
- 2 baby bok choy heads, chopped into
- bite-size pieces
- 10 to 12 medium shrimp (U41/50), peeled and deveined
- 3 cups vegetable oil

1. Preheat the oven to 300°F (150°C). Line a baking sheet with parchment paper or aluminum foil. Spread the rice in an even layer and bake for 15 to 20 minutes, until it feels dry. Set aside to cool.

2. In a soup pot, bring the chicken broth to a boil over high heat. Lower the heat to medium-high and add the mushrooms and carrot. Add the light soy, sesame oil, and rice wine to the soup and simmer for 5 minutes.

3. Add the bok choy and bring to a boil over high heat. Turn the heat down to simmer and add the shrimp. Stir to distribute the vegetables and shrimp and simmer over low heat while you fry the rice.

4. Pour the oil into the wok; the oil should be about 1 to 1½ inches deep. Bring the oil to 375°F (190°C) over medium-high heat. You can tell the oil is at the right temperature by dipping the end of a wooden spoon into the oil. If the oil bubbles and sizzles around it, the oil is ready.

5. Fry the rice a scoopful at a time, until golden brown and crispy, 2 to 3 minutes. Use a wire skimmer to lift the rice in clumps out of the oil and transfer to a paper towel–lined plate.

6. When ready to serve, divide the soup and vegetables among 4 soup bowls. Top each bowl with the crispy rice and serve while still sizzling.

Oyster Sauce with Chicken Chow Mein

Prep time: 15 minutes | Cook time: 1⅓ minutes | Serves 4 to 6

For the Chicken Marinade:

- 2 teaspoons soy sauce
- 1 teaspoon oyster sauce
- 2 teaspoons cornstarch

- 1 (5-ounce / 142-g) chicken breast, cut into bite-size pieces

For the Sauce:

- 2 tablespoons soy sauce
- 1 tablespoon oyster sauce

- 2 teaspoons Shaoxing wine
- 1 teaspoon brown sugar
- 1 teaspoon sesame oil
- ½ teaspoon salt
- 2 pinches ground white pepper

For the Stir-Fry:

- 2 tablespoons peanut oil, plus more if needed
- 2 garlic cloves, minced
- 2 cups shredded cabbage
- 1 small carrot, julienned
- 1 pound (454 g) fresh chow mein noodles or fresh egg noodles, cooked according to package directions
- 2 scallions, cut into 1-inch pieces

1. Pour the soy sauce, oyster sauce, and cornstarch over the chicken in a medium bowl and marinate at room temperature for 20 minutes.

2. In a small bowl, prepare the sauce by combining the soy sauce, oyster sauce, Shaoxing wine, brown sugar, sesame oil, salt, and pepper.

3. In a wok over medium-high heat, heat the peanut oil. As soon as the wok starts to smoke, add the chicken and stir-fry until fully cooked. Remove the chicken and set it aside.

4. Add a little more oil to the wok if needed, add the garlic, and stir-fry for about 20 seconds, until aromatic.

5. Add the shredded cabbage and carrot, and stir-fry until the cabbage wilts slightly.

6. Add the noodles, stir in the sauce, and return the chicken to the wok.

7. Stir-fry for about 1 minute, combining all the ingredients.

8. Turn off the heat, add the scallions, and stir to combine. Transfer to a serving dish.

Gravy with Shrimp and Rice Noodles

Prep time: 15 minutes | Cook time: 3 minutes | Serves 4 to 6

For the Gravy:

- 2 cups basic Chinese chicken stock, or store bought
- ½ cup water
- 3 tablespoons cornstarch
- 2 tablespoons soy sauce
- 2 teaspoons oyster sauce
- 1 teaspoon Shaoxing wine
- ½ teaspoon sugar
- 2 pinches ground white pepper

For the Stir-Fry:

- 2 tablespoons peanut oil, plus 2 teaspoons
- 1 pound (454 g) fresh flat rice noodles
- 1½ tablespoons soy sauce, divided
- ¾ teaspoon dark soy sauce, divided
- ½ pound (227 g) rice vermicelli noodles, soaked in warm water for 30 minutes
- 2 garlic cloves, minced
- 10 to 12 large shrimp, peeled and deveined
- 1 stalk choy sum or 2 baby bok choy, cut into 1-inch pieces
- 1 small carrot, sliced

1. In a large bowl, prepare the gravy by mixing the chicken stock, water, cornstarch, soy sauce, oyster sauce, Shaoxing wine, sugar, and pepper. Set it aside.

2. In a wok over high heat, heat 2 tablespoons of peanut oil.

3. Add the flat rice noodles and stir in 1 tablespoon of soy sauce and ½ teaspoon of dark soy sauce. Stir-fry slowly for about 1 minute, being careful not to over-stir so as to allow some parts of the noodles to get slightly charred. Remove the flat noodles from the wok and set them aside.

4. Add the vermicelli noodles, the remaining ½ tablespoon of soy sauce, and the remaining ¼ teaspoon of dark soy sauce. Stir-fry for about 1 minute.

5. Return the flat rice noodles to the wok, stirring just to combine with the vermicelli noodles. Remove from the wok and set aside.

6. Reduce the heat to medium-high and add the remaining 2 teaspoons of oil to the wok.

7. Add the garlic and stir-fry for about 20 seconds, until aromatic.

8. Pour the gravy into the wok. Add the shrimp, choy sum, and carrot. Gently stir and allow the gravy boil for about 1 minute. Transfer to a large bowl.

9. When ready to serve, pour the gravy, shrimp, and vegetable mixture over the fried noodles.

Goji Berries with Mushroom Soup

Prep time: 10 minutes | Cook time: 21 minutes | Serves 6 to 8

- 1 tablespoon olive oil
- ½ onion, sliced
- 2 garlic cloves, minced
- 1 carrot, cut into thin slices
- 4 or 5 large shiitake mushrooms, cut into thin slices
- 5 or 6 white or brown button mushrooms, cut into thin slices
- 1 small bunch enoki mushrooms, roots removed
- 8 cups vegetable stock
- ¼ cup dried goji berries
- 2 teaspoons sesame oil
- 1 tablespoon soy sauce
- 1 teaspoon salt

In a wok over medium heat, heat the olive oil.

Sauté the onion and garlic until the onion turns slightly translucent.

Add the carrot, shiitake mushrooms, button mushrooms, and enoki mushrooms. Sauté for about 1 minute.

Pour in the vegetable stock and bring to a boil.

Add the goji berries, sesame oil, soy sauce, and salt.

Simmer over low heat for about 20 minutes before serving.

Egg with Chicken and Scallion Soup

Prep time: 10 minutes | Cook time: 10 minutes | Serves 6 to 8

- 2 (14.75-ounce / 418-g) cans cream-style sweet corn
- 8 cups Basic Chinese Chicken Stock or store bought
- 2 cups cooked shredded chicken
- 1 teaspoon salt
- 1 teaspoon sesame oil
- 3 teaspoons cornstarch mixed with 2 tablespoons water (optional)
- 2 eggs, lightly beaten
- 1 scallion, chopped

In a wok over high heat, add the corn to the chicken stock and bring to a boil.

2. Add the shredded chicken, salt to taste, and sesame oil. Return to a boil.

3. Stir in the cornstarch mixture (if using) to thicken the soup. Return to a boil.

4. Use chopsticks to stir the soup and while stirring, pour the beaten eggs into the soup. The faster you swirl and the faster you pour, the silkier the egg. Swirl and pour slowly for a chunkier egg texture.

5. Garnish with the chopped scallion just before serving.

Garlicky Egg Drop Soup

Prep time: 10 minutes | Cook time: 10 minutes | Serves 4

- 4 cups low-sodium chicken broth
- 2 peeled fresh ginger slices, each about the size of a quarter
- 2 garlic cloves, peeled
- 2 teaspoons light soy sauce
- 2 tablespoons cornstarch
- 3 tablespoons water
- 2 large eggs, lightly beaten
- 1 teaspoon sesame oil
- 2 scallions, thinly sliced, for garnish

1. In a wok or soup pot, combine the broth, ginger, garlic, and light soy and bring to a boil. Reduce to a simmer and cook for 5 minutes. Remove and discard the ginger and garlic.

2. In a small bowl, mix the cornstarch and water and stir the mixture into the wok. Return the heat to medium-high and stir for about 30 seconds, until the soup thickens.

3. Reduce the heat to a simmer. Dip a fork into the beaten eggs and then drag it through the soup, gently stirring as you go. Continue to dip the fork into the egg and drag it through the soup to create the egg threads. When all the egg has been added, simmer the soup undisturbed for a few moments to set the eggs. Stir in the sesame oil and ladle the soup into serving bowls. Garnish with the scallions.

Meat with Rice Cake Soup

Prep time: 15 minutes | Cook time: 15 minutes | Serves 8

For the Meat:

- ½ pound (680 g) lean

- pork, cut into strips
- 2 teaspoons Shaoxing wine
- 1 tablespoon light soy sauce
- ½ teaspoon sesame oil
- ¼ teaspoon white pepper
- 2 teaspoons cornstarch
- 1 teaspoon water

For the Soup:

- 4 tablespoons vegetable oil
- 4 ginger slices, julienned
- 3 scallions, sliced
- 1 small carrot, sliced
- 1 ¼ pounds (567g) Napa cabbage, cut into 1-inch pieces
- 4 cups chicken stock
- 4 cups water
- ½ teaspoon white pepper
- 1 teaspoon sesame oil
- 1 tablespoon light soy sauce
- 1 pound (454 g) rice cakes, oval-shaped slices

1. Mix pork with soy sauce, sesame oil, water, cornstarch, white pepper, and wine in a bowl.
2. Cover the pork and marinate for 20 minutes.
3. Sauté pork with remaining oil in a Mandarin wok until brown.
4. Stir in ginger and rest of the ingredients, then sauté for 4 minutes.
5. Pour in water, stock, white pepper, soy sauce, and cook the soup for 10 minutes.
6. Add the rice cakes and cook for 1 minutes on medium heat.
7. Serve warm.

Peppered Sesame Noodle Soup

Prep time: 20 minutes | Cook time: 20 minutes | Serves 6

- 3 tablespoons roasted soybeans
- 3 ½ ounces (99g) dried sweet potato noodles
- 2 ½ cups stock
- 1 ginger slice, minced
- 2 garlic cloves, minced
- 1 teaspoon toasted sesame seeds
- 1 teaspoon Sichuan chili flakes
- 2 tablespoons vegetable oil
- 2 tablespoons Chinese black vinegar
- 2 tablespoons light soy sauce
- ½ teaspoon dark soy sauce
- ½ teaspoon sugar
- ½ teaspoon Sichuan peppercorn powder
- ¼ teaspoon white pepper
- ½ teaspoon sesame oil
- 1 tablespoon chili oil
- ¼ cup pickled mustard stems
- 1 scallion, finely chopped
- 1 tablespoon cilantro, chopped

1. Sauté soybeans, scallion, ginger, garlic, and mustard stem with oil in a deep wok for 5 minutes
2. Stir in stock and all other ingredients and cover to cook for 15 minutes.
3. Serve warm.

Parsley and Noodle Wonton Soup

Prep time: 15 minutes | Cook time: 17 minutes | Serves 6

For the Wontons:

- 1 pound (454 g) ground chicken
- ½ cup parsley, finely chopped
- 1 garlic clove
- ¼ cup water
- 2 tablespoons dry sherry
- Juice of ½ a lemon
- 1 tablespoon oil
- 1 teaspoon salt
- 1 teaspoon sugar
- ½ teaspoon dried thyme
- ½ teaspoon black pepper
- 2 tablespoons butter, melted
- 1 package wonton wrappers

For the Soup:

- 1 tablespoon oil
- ½ white onion, diced
- 3 medium carrots, diced
- 3 stalks celery, diced
- 5 cups chicken broth
- Salt and black pepper to taste

1. Mix chicken, oil, salt, sugar, thyme, garlic, ginger, black pepper, parsley, lemon juice, and sherry in bowl.
2. Spread the wonton wrappers on the working surface.
3. Divide the filling on top of the wrappers and wet the edges.
4. Fold the wrappers in half and seal the two edges the wontons.

Sauté onion, carrot, and celery with oil in a Mandarin wok for 5 minutes.

Pour in stock, black pepper, salt to taste, and prepared wontons.

Cover and cook the soup for 12 minutes on medium heat.

Serve warm.

Vinegary Tofu with Mushroom Soup

Prep time: 20 minutes | Cook time: 11 minutes | Serves 9

- ½ cup lily flowers
- ⅓ ounce (9.6 g) dried wood ear mushrooms, soaked
- ⅔ ounce (19 g) dried shiitake mushrooms, soaked
- 3 ounces (85 g) spiced dry tofu, soaked
- 4 ounces (113 g) fresh firm tofu
- 7 cups vegetable stock
- ½ teaspoon salt
- ¼ teaspoon sugar
- 2 dried red chili peppers, chopped
- 1-2 teaspoons ground white pepper
- 1 ½ teaspoon mushroom dark soy sauce
- 1 tablespoon light soy sauce
- 1 teaspoon sesame oil
- ⅓ cup white vinegar
- 5 ounces (142 g) bamboo shoots
- ¼ cup cornstarch, whisked with ¼ cup water
- 1 large egg, beaten
- 1 scallion, chopped

Sauté all the veggies and tofu with cooking oil in a deep wok until golden.

Pour in spices, sauces, vinegar, sugar, stock, and lily flowers.

Cook the soup for 10 minutes on a simmer.

Stir in cornstarch slurry then cook until it thickens.

Slowly pour in the egg and cook for 1 minute with a stir.

Serve warm.

Mushroom with Beef and Sesame Soup

Prep time: 15 minutes | Cook time: 8 minutes |

Serves 4

- 2 tablespoons cooking oil
- 1 tablespoon crushed chopped ginger
- 2 garlic cloves, crushed and chopped
- 1 medium carrot, julienned
- 1 medium onion, cut into 1-inch pieces
- 1 pound (454 g)
- mushrooms, sliced
- 3 quarts vegetable or meat broth
- 1 teaspoon hot sesame oil
- ¼ cup rice vinegar
- 1 cup chopped bok choy
- 1 pound (454 g) shaved steak

1. In a wok over high heat, heat the cooking oil until it shimmers.
2. Add the ginger, garlic, and carrot and stir-fry for 30 seconds.
3. Add the onion and mushrooms and stir-fry for 30 seconds.
4. Add the broth, sesame oil, and rice vinegar and bring to a boil.
5. Add the bok choy and steak and stir for 30 seconds.
6. Serve immediately.

Egg with Peppered Tofu Soup

Prep time: 10 minutes | Cook time: 15 minutes | Serves 6

- 8 ounces / 227 g frozen Shepherd's purse
- ½ block silken tofu
- 4 cups homemade chicken stock
- 1 ½ teaspoon salt
- 1 teaspoon sesame oil
- ¼ teaspoon ground white pepper
- ¼ cup cornstarch, mixed with ¼ cup water
- 3 egg whites

1. Sauté tofu and shepherd's purse with sesame oil to a wok for 5 minutes.
2. Stir in stock, salt, and white pepper to taste, then cook this mixture on a simmer for 10 minutes.
3. Mix cornstarch with water and pour into the soup.
4. Cook the soup until it thickens.

5. Beat egg whites and pour into the soup.

6. Cook for 5 minutes, then serve warm.

Gingered Broth and Tofu Soup

Prep time: 10 minutes | Cook time: 8 minutes | Serves 4

- 2 tablespoons cooking oil
- 2 garlic cloves, crushed and chopped
- 1 tablespoon crushed, chopped ginger
- 1 pound (454 g) tofu, well drained, patted dry, and cut into 1-inch pieces
- 1 red bell pepper, cut into ¼-inch pieces
- 4 ounces (113 g) mushrooms, cut into slices
- 1 cup chopped bok choy
- 1 teaspoon hot sesame oil
- 2 quarts vegetable or meat broth
- 4 eggs, beaten

1. In a wok over high heat, heat the cooking oil until it shimmers.

2. Add the garlic, ginger, and tofu and stir-fry until the tofu begins to brown.

3. Add the bell pepper and stir-fry for 1 minute.

4. Add the mushrooms and stir-fry for 30 seconds.

5. Add the bok choy and stir-fry for 30 seconds.

6. Add the sesame oil, then add the broth and bring to a boil.

7. Drizzle the beaten eggs over the broth and let the eggs float to the top. Serve the soup hot as an appetizer or main dish.

Garlicky Quinoa with Fried Rice

Prep time: 10 minutes | Cook time: 5 minutes | Serves 4

- 2 tablespoons peanut oil
- 2 eggs, lightly beaten
- 3 garlic cloves, minced
- 3 or 4 string beans, cut into ¼-inch pieces
- 1 cup frozen peas and carrots (no need to thaw)
- 6 cups Steamed Quinoa
- 2 tablespoons soy sauce
- 1 scallion, chopped

1. In a wok over medium-high heat, heat the peanut oil.

2. In the wok, scramble the eggs until cooked, then transfer them to a small bowl.

3. Add the garlic to the wok and stir-fry for about 20 seconds. Add the string beans and stir-fry for 20 30 seconds.

4. Add more peanut oil if necessary, then add the peas and carrots, and stir-fry for 30 seconds.

5. Add the quinoa and return the scrambled egg to the wok, stirring to combine.

6. Add the soy sauce. Stir-fry gently to combine, using a wok spatula.

7. Transfer to a serving dish and garnish with the chopped scallion.

Indonesian Nasi Goreng

Prep time: 15 minutes | Cook time: 8 minutes | Serves 4

- 3 tablespoons cooking oil, divided
- ½ pound (227g) ground meat of your choice
- 1 tablespoon crushed, chopped ginger
- 2 garlic cloves, crushed and chopped
- 1 medium onion, diced
- 2 cups cold, cooked rice
- ¼ cup kecap manis
- 1 teaspoon hot sesame oil
- 4 scallions, cut into ½-inch pieces
- 4 eggs
- 2 tomatoes, sliced
- 1 cucumber, sliced

1. In a wok over high heat, heat 2 tablespoons of the cooking oil until it shimmers.

2. Add the meat, ginger, garlic, and onion and stir-fry for 1 minute.

3. Add the rice, kecap manis, sesame oil, and scallions and stir-fry for 1 minute. Remove from the wok and place in a serving bowl.

4. Add the remaining 1 tablespoon of cooking oil to the wok and, when the oil is shimmering, fry the eggs sunny-side up.

5. Serve each portion of rice with a fried egg on top and sliced tomatoes and cucumbers on the side.

Gingered Bacon with Kimchi Fried Rice

Prep time: 15 minutes | Cook time: 8 minutes | Serves 4

- ½ pound (227g) thick-sliced bacon, cut into 1-inch pieces
- 1 tablespoon crushed, chopped ginger
- 2 garlic cloves, crushed and chopped
- 4 ounces (113 g) sliced mushrooms
- 1 cup kimchi, cut into ½-inch pieces
- 2 cups cold, cooked rice
- 1 teaspoon sesame oil
- 4 scallions, cut into ½-inch pieces
- 1 tablespoon soy sauce
- ¼ cup kimchi juice
- 4 large eggs

Place the bacon, ginger, and garlic in a wok over high heat and stir-fry for 2 minutes, or until the bacon is lightly browned.

Drain off all but 2 tablespoons of the bacon fat from the wok and set aside.

Add the mushrooms to the wok and stir-fry for 1 minute.

Add the kimchi and stir-fry for 30 seconds.

Add the rice, sesame oil, scallions, soy sauce, and kimchi juice. Stir-fry for 30 seconds, then remove from the wok and place on a serving dish.

Return 2 tablespoons of the reserved bacon fat to the wok and fry the eggs sunny-side up.

Serve the rice with the fried eggs on top.

Oniony Scallions with Fried Rice

Prep time: 15 minutes | Cook time: 5 minutes | Serves 4

- 2 tablespoons cooking oil
- 1 tablespoon crushed, chopped ginger
- 2 garlic cloves, crushed and chopped
- ½ teaspoon kosher salt
- 2 large eggs, beaten
- 1 medium onion, diced
- ½ pound (227g) medium shrimp, peeled, deveined, and halved lengthwise
- 1 cup frozen peas, thawed
- 2 cups cold, cooked rice
- 1 teaspoon sesame oil
- 1 tablespoon soy sauce
- 4 scallions, cut into ½-inch pieces

1. In a wok over high heat, heat the cooking oil until it shimmers.
2. Add the ginger, garlic, salt, and eggs and stir-fry for 1 minute, or until the eggs are firm.
3. Add the onion and shrimp and stir-fry for 1 minute.
4. Add the peas, rice, sesame oil, and soy sauce and stir-fry for 1 minute.
5. Garnish with the scallions and serve immediately.

Simple Japanese Yakimeshi

Prep time: 10 minutes | Cook time: 8 minutes | Serves 4

- ½ pound (227g) thick-sliced bacon, cut into 1-inch pieces
- 1 tablespoon crushed, chopped ginger
- 2 garlic cloves, crushed and chopped
- 3 eggs, beaten
- 2 cups cold, cooked rice
- 1 teaspoon sesame oil
- 4 scallions, cut into ½-inch pieces
- 2 tablespoons sesame seeds
- Kosher salt to taste
- Ground black pepper to taste

1. In a wok over high heat, stir-fry the bacon, ginger, and garlic for 2 minutes, or until the bacon is lightly browned.
2. Remove the bacon and set aside.
3. Add the eggs and stir-fry until they are firm and dry.
4. Add the cooked bacon, rice, and sesame oil and stir-fry for 1 minute.
5. Add the scallions and sesame seeds and toss for 30 seconds.
6. Serve with salt and pepper to taste.

Classic Indian Fodni Bhaat

Prep time: 15 minutes | Cook time: 8 minutes | Serves 4

- 2 tablespoons cooking oil
- 1 tablespoon crushed, chopped ginger

- 1 medium onion, diced
- 1 teaspoon mustard seeds
- 2 garlic cloves, crushed and chopped
- 2 bird's eye chiles, sliced into ¼-inch circles
- 1 teaspoon hot sesame oil
- ½ teaspoon turmeric
- ½ teaspoon ground coriander
- ¼ teaspoon kosher salt
- 2 cups cold, cooked basmati rice
- ¼ cup coarsely chopped mint leaves

1. In a wok over high heat, heat the cooking oil until it shimmers.
2. Add the ginger, onion, mustard seeds, and garlic to the wok and stir-fry for 1 minute.
3. Add the bird's eye chiles, sesame oil, turmeric, coriander, salt, and rice and stir-fry for 1 minute.
4. Garnish with the mint and serve immediately.

Eggy Pineapple with Peppered Fried Rice

Prep time: 10 minutes | Cook time: 11 minutes | Serves 9

- 1 cup pineapple, diced
- 1 scallion, chopped
- 2 eggs, beaten
- ¼ teaspoon salt
- ½ teaspoon Shaoxing wine
- 4 tablespoons vegetable oil
- 1 tablespoon fish sauce
- 1 tablespoon light soy sauce
- ½ teaspoon ground white pepper
- 1 ½ teaspoons sesame oil

1. Beat eggs with salt and wine in a bowl.
2. Pour this mixture into a greased wok and stir cook for 1 minute.
3. Sauté onion, carrot, peas, ham, and pineapple with oil in a cooking pot for 7 minutes.
4. Stir in rest of the ingredients along with eggs, and rice.
5. Mix well and cook for 3 minutes.
6. Serve warm.

Spicy Fried Rice with Egg

Prep time: 10 minutes | Cook time: 5 minutes |

Serves 4

- 2 tablespoons cooking oil
- 2 garlic cloves, crushed and chopped
- 1 tablespoon crushed and chopped peeled ginger
- 4 large eggs, beaten
- 4 scallions, green and white parts, cut diagonally into ¼-inch
- pieces
- 2 cups day-old cooked rice
- ½ teaspoon salt
- ½ teaspoon black or white pepper
- 1 tablespoon soy sauce
- 1 teaspoon toasted sesame oil

1. In a wok, heat the cooking oil over high heat until it begins to smoke.
2. Add the garlic, ginger, and eggs. Stir-fry for 2 minutes, or until the eggs are cooked.
3. Add the scallions, rice, salt, pepper, soy sauce, and sesame oil. Stir-fry for 1 minute, or until all of the ingredients are well combined. Serve immediately.

Chicken with Grapes Stir-fry

Prep time: 5 minutes | Cook time: 10 minutes | Serves 4

- 1 tablespoon vegetable oil
- 1 cup of sliced red grapes
- 1 cup of diced cooked
- chicken
- 2 cups of cooked rice
- ¼ cup chicken broth

1. Heat the vegetable oil in a large pan or wok over medium to high heat. Add the chicken and grapes
2. Cook for about 3 minutes until the grapes are tender and the chicken is well heated.
3. Pour in the chicken broth and rice. Keep cooking

Mushroom Rice with Gingered Pork

Prep time: 10 minutes | Cook time: 10 minutes | Serves 8

- 1 cup shiitake mushrooms, diced
- 8 ounces / 227 g pork
- belly, cut into ¼-inch thick pieces
- 2 tablespoons oil

3 ginger slices, minced

1 ½ tablespoons Shaoxing wine

3 tablespoons light soy sauce

¾ tablespoon dark soy sauce

- 1 tablespoon sugar
- ½ to ¾ cup water
- 4 cups cooked rice
- 1 scallion, chopped

Sauté ginger with oil in a Mandarin wok for 30 seconds.

Stir in pork, mushrooms, all the sauces, sugar, and water.

Mix well and cook for 7 minutes with occasional stirring.

Stir in rice and scallions then mix well.

Serve warm.

Eggy Sausage with Fried Rice

Prep time: 20 minutes | Cook time: 7 minutes | Serves 8

3 Chinese sausages, diced

1 medium onion, chopped

5 cups cooked white rice

¾ teaspoon salt

¼ teaspoon sugar

2 teaspoons hot water

¼ teaspoon sesame oil

1 teaspoon soy sauce

½ teaspoon dark soy sauce

- ⅛ teaspoon white pepper
- 3 tablespoons vegetable oil
- 2 eggs, beaten
- ⅔ cup frozen green peas
- 1 cup mung bean sprouts, boiled
- 2 scallions, chopped
- 1 teaspoon Shaoxing wine

Sauté onion, with oil in a Mandarin wok for 2 minutes.

Stir in sausages, bean sprouts, eggs, all the sauces, sugar, spices, and peas.

Mix well and cook for 5 minutes with occasional stirring.

Stir in rice and scallions then mix well.

Serve warm.

Lettuce with Trout and Fried Rice

Prep time: 15 minutes | Cook time: 10 minutes | Serves 4

- 2 large eggs
- 1 teaspoon sesame oil
- Kosher salt to taste
- Ground white pepper to taste
- 1 tablespoon light soy sauce
- ½ teaspoon sugar
- 3 tablespoons ghee or vegetable oil, divided
- 1 teaspoon peeled finely minced fresh ginger
- 2 garlic cloves, finely minced
- 3 cups cold cooked rice
- 4 ounces (113 g) smoked trout, broken into bite-size pieces
- ½ cup thinly sliced hearts of romaine lettuce
- 2 scallions, thinly sliced
- ½ teaspoon white sesame seeds

1. In a large bowl, whisk the eggs with the sesame oil and a pinch each of salt and white pepper to taste until just combined. In a small bowl, stir the light soy and sugar together to dissolve the sugar. Set aside.

2. Heat a wok over medium-high heat until a drop of water sizzles and evaporates on contact. Pour in 1 tablespoon of ghee and swirl to coat the base of the wok. Add the egg mixture and, using a heatproof spatula, swirl and shake the eggs to cook. Transfer the eggs to a plate when just cooked but not dry.

3. Add the remaining 2 tablespoons of ghee to the wok, along with the ginger and garlic. Stir-fry quickly until the garlic and ginger just become aromatic, but take care not to let them burn. Add the rice and soy mixture and stir to combine. Continue stir-frying, about 3 minutes. Add the trout and cooked egg and stir-fry to break them up, about 20 seconds. Add the lettuce and scallions and stir-fry until they are both bright green.

4. Transfer to a serving platter and sprinkle with the sesame seeds.

Classic Japanese Gyudon

Prep time: 15 minutes | Cook time: 5 minutes |

Serves 4

- 2 tablespoons cooking oil
- 1 tablespoon crushed, chopped ginger
- 2 garlic cloves, crushed and chopped
- 1 medium onion, halved and cut into ¼-inch strips
- ½ cup dashi broth
- 1 tablespoon mirin
- 1 tablespoon sake
- 1 tablespoon tamari
- 1 tablespoon sugar
- 1 pound (454 g) shaved steak
- 3 scallions, cut into ½-inch pieces

1. In a wok over high heat, heat the cooking oil until it shimmers.
2. Add the ginger, garlic, and onion and stir-fry for 1 minute.
3. Add the dashi, mirin, sake, tamari, and sugar and bring to a boil.
4. Stir in the steak. Add the scallions and stir for 1 minute.
5. Serve over steamed sushi rice.

Cilantro with Eggy Pad Thai Chicken

Prep time: 15 minutes | Cook time: 6 minutes | Serves 4

- 2 tablespoons tamarind paste
- 1 tablespoon fish sauce
- 1 tablespoon soy sauce
- 2 tablespoons brown sugar
- 1 tablespoon cornstarch
- 2 tablespoons cooking oil
- 1 tablespoon crushed, chopped ginger
- 2 garlic cloves, crushed and chopped
- 2 eggs, beaten
- 1 pound (454 g) boneless chicken thighs, cut into 1-inch pieces
- 2 bird's eye chiles, sliced into ¼-inch circles
- 1 pound (454 g) cooked rice noodles
- ½ cup chopped peanuts
- 1 cup bean sprouts
- Coarsely chopped cilantro
- Lime wedges

1. In a small bowl, whisk together the tamarind paste, fish sauce, soy sauce, brown sugar, and cornstarch. Set aside.
2. In a wok over high heat, heat the cooking oil until it shimmers.
3. Add the ginger, garlic, and eggs and stir-fry for 1 minute.
4. Add the chicken and bird's eye chiles and stir-fry for 1 minute.
5. Add the tamarind paste mixture and stir until a glaze forms.
6. Serve over the noodles and garnish with the peanuts, bean sprouts, cilantro, and lime wedges.

Garlicky Mushroom with Pancit Canton

Prep time: 20 minutes | Cook time: 8 minutes | Serves 4

- 2 tablespoons cooking oil
- 1 tablespoon crushed, chopped ginger
- 2 garlic cloves, crushed and chopped
- ¼ pound (114 g) boneless chicken thighs, cut into 1-inch pieces
- 1 medium carrot, julienned
- ¼ pound (114 g) thinly sliced sirloin steak, cut into 1-inch pieces
- 1 medium onion, cut into 1-inch pieces
- 4 ounces (113 g) shiitake mushrooms, sliced
- ¼ pound (114 g) medium shrimp, peeled, deveined, and cut in half lengthwise
- 1 tablespoon fish sauce
- 2 tablespoons soy sauce
- ¼ cup oyster sauce
- ¼ cup meat or vegetable broth
- 1 pound (454 g) cooked Hong Kong–style noodles
- 4 scallions, cut into 1-inch pieces
- Lemon wedges

1. In a wok over high heat, heat the oil until it shimmers.
2. Add the ginger, garlic, chicken, and carrot and stir-fry for 1 minute.
3. Add the steak, onion, and mushrooms and stir-fry for 1 minute.
4. Add the shrimp, fish sauce, soy sauce, oyster sauce

and broth and stir-fry for 1 minute.

. Add the noodles and stir-fry for 1 minute.

. Garnish with the scallions and serve with the lemon wedges

Buttered Peanut Noodles

Prep time: 15 minutes | Cook time: 6 minutes | Serves 4

- ¼ cup peanut butter
- ¼ cup peanut oil
- 1 tablespoon hot sesame oil
- 2 tablespoons powdered sugar
- 2 tablespoons soy sauce
- 2 tablespoons cooking oil

- 1 tablespoon crushed, chopped ginger
- 2 garlic cloves, crushed and chopped
- 1 pound (454 g) cooked noodles
- 4 scallions, cut into ½-inch pieces
- 1 tablespoon sesame seeds

In a medium bowl, whisk together the peanut butter, peanut oil, sesame oil, powdered sugar, and soy sauce until smooth. Set aside.

In a wok over high heat, heat the cooking oil until it shimmers.

Add the ginger, garlic, and noodles and stir-fry for 1 minute.

Add the peanut butter mixture and toss for 30 seconds.

Garnish with the scallions and sesame seeds and serve.

Butter and Ham with Brown Rice

Prep time: 10 minutes | Cook time: 10 minutes | Serves 8

- 3 tablespoons of peanut oil, divided, or more as needed
- ½ onion (chopped)
- 2 large eggs
- 1 cup diced fully cooked ham
- 2 tablespoons of

- butter
- 3 cups of cooked brown rice
- Kosher salt and freshly ground black pepper to taste
- ½ cup of grated cheddar cheese

1. Preheat a wok or pan on a high flame for 1 minute. Thoroughly add 2 tablespoons of peanut oil to the wok and reduce the flame to medium temperature. Boil the onion and stir until it starts to soften, about 3 minutes.

2. Beat the eggs directly into the wok. Stir ham into the wok and only cook until the eggs start to set but are still runny, stir ham into the wok for about 1 ½ minutes, 1 minute and only cook until it is warmed through.

3. Stir butter and the remaining 1 tablespoon of peanut oil into the wok for 1 minute; Let heat for 10 seconds. Add rice and stir for 3 to 4 minutes, stirring constantly, when the rice starts to stick; season fried rice with salt and pepper to taste; top with cheddar cheese.

Coriander with Pork Noodles

Prep time: 15 minutes | Cook time: 6 minutes | Serves 4

- 2 tablespoons cooking oil
- 1 tablespoon crushed, chopped ginger
- 2 garlic cloves, crushed and chopped
- 1 pound (454 g) ground pork
- 1 medium carrot, julienned
- 1 medium onion, diced
- 1 cup shredded cabbage

- 1 pound (454 g) cooked noodles
- 1 tablespoon fish sauce
- 1 tablespoon soy sauce
- 1 tablespoon hoisin sauce
- 1 teaspoon ground coriander
- 1 teaspoon hot sesame oil
- 1 scallion, cut into ½-inch pieces

1. In a wok over high heat, heat the oil until it shimmers.

2. Add the ginger, garlic, and pork and stir-fry for 1 minute.

3. Add the carrot, onion, and cabbage and stir-fry for 1 minute.

4. Add the noodles and stir-fry for 1 minute.

5. Add the fish sauce, soy sauce, hoisin, coriander, and sesame oil and stir-fry for 1 minute.

6. Garnish with the scallion and serve.

Garlicky Sinangag

Prep time: 5 minutes | Cook time: 6 minutes | Serves 4

- 2 tablespoons cooking oil
- 8 cloves garlic, crushed and chopped
- 2 cups cold, cooked rice
- ¼ teaspoon kosher salt
- 4 scallions, cut into ¼-inch pieces

1. In a wok over medium-high heat, heat the cooking oil and garlic. Stir-fry for 2 minutes until the garlic turns golden brown but does not burn.
2. Remove half the garlic and reserve it for garnishing.
3. Gently sprinkle the rice and salt into the wok and stir-fry for 1 minute.
4. Garnish with the chopped scallions and caramelized garlic before serving.

Mirin with Udon Noodles

Prep time: 15 minutes | Cook time: 16 minutes | Serves 6

- 1 pound (454 g) frozen Udon noodles
- 2 tablespoons butter
- 1 garlic clove, minced
- 2 teaspoons dashi powder
- 1 tablespoon oil
- 4 ounces (113 g) pork shoulder
- 4 ounces (113 g) oyster mushrooms, sliced
- 2 tablespoons mirin
- 2 cups cabbage, shredded
- 1 medium carrot, julienned
- ⅛ teaspoon black pepper
- 2 tablespoons soy sauce
- 1 tablespoon water
- 2 scallions, julienned

1. Boil the dry noodles in hot water as per package's instructions then drain.
2. Sauté garlic with butter in a Mandarin wok for 30 seconds.
3. Stir in pork shoulder, then sauté for 5 minutes.
4. Add mushrooms along with remaining ingredients except the noodles.
5. Cover and cook for 10 minutes until pork is tender.
6. Stir in noodles and mix well.

7. Serve warm.

Cornstarch with Sesame and Soy Sauce

Prep time: 15 minutes | Cook time: 10 minutes | Serves 4

- ¼ cup Shaoxing rice wine
- ¼ cup light soy sauce
- 2 tablespoons cornstarch
- 1½ tablespoons dark soy sauce
- 1½ tablespoons dark soy sauce
- ½ teaspoon sugar
- Ground white pepper to taste
- ¾ pound (340g) flank steak or sirloin tips, cut across the grain into ⅛-inch-thick slices
- 1½ pounds (680 g) fresh wide rice noodles or ¾ pound dried
- 2 tablespoons sesame oil, divided
- 3 tablespoons vegetable oil, divided
- 4 peeled fresh ginger slices, each about the size of a quarter
- Kosher salt to taste
- 8 scallions, halved lengthwise and cut into 3-inch pieces
- 2 cups fresh mung bean sprouts

1. In a mixing bowl, stir together the rice wine, light soy, cornstarch, dark soy, sugar, and a pinch of white pepper. Add the beef and toss to coat. Set aside to marinate for at least 10 minutes.
2. Bring a large pot of water to a boil and cook the rice noodles according to package instructions. Reserve 1 cup of the cooking water and drain the rest. Rinse with cold water and drizzle with 1 tablespoon of sesame oil. Set aside.
3. Heat a wok over medium-high heat until a drop of water sizzles and evaporates on contact. Pour in 2 tablespoons of vegetable oil and swirl to coat the base of the wok. Season the oil by adding the ginger and a pinch of salt to taste. Allow the ginger to sizzle in the oil for about 30 seconds, swirling gently.
4. Using tongs, add the beef to the wok and reserve the marinating liquid. Sear the beef against the wok for 2 to 3 minutes, or until a seared, browned crust develops. Toss and flip the beef around the wok for 1 more minute. Transfer to a clean bowl and set aside.

Soups, Rice, and Nood

Add 1 more tablespoon of vegetable oil and stir-fry the scallions for 30 seconds, or until soft. Add the noodles and lift in a scooping upward motion to help separate the noodles if they have stuck together. Add the cooking water, 1 tablespoon at a time, if the noodles have really glued themselves together.

Return the beef to the wok and toss to combine with the noodles. Pour in the reserved marinade and toss for 30 seconds to 1 minute, or until the sauce thickens and coats the noodles and they turn a deep, rich brown color. If you need to, add 1 tablespoon of the reserved cooking water to thin out the sauce. Add the bean sprouts and toss until just heated through, about 1 minute. Remove the ginger and discard.

Transfer to a platter and drizzle with the remaining 1 tablespoon of sesame oil. Serve hot.

piced Chicken with Rice Noodles

ep time: 20 minutes | Cook time: 10 minutes | rves 6

r the Rice Noodles:

- 7 ounces (198 g) dried rice vermicelli noodles
- 1 teaspoon vegetable oil
- ½ teaspoon dark soy sauce

r the Chicken:

- 7 ounces (198 g) chicken breast, cut into strips
- 1 teaspoon cornstarch
- 1 tablespoon water
- 1 ½ teaspoon oyster sauce
- 2 teaspoons Shaoxing wine
- ¼ teaspoon white pepper
- 1 pinch five spice powder

- 1 teaspoon vegetable oil

For the Dish:

- 2 ginger slices, julienned
- 4-5 small shallots, sliced
- 1 medium carrot, julienned
- 5 ounces (142 g) cabbage, shredded
- 3 scallions, cut into 2-inch pieces
- 3 tablespoons vegetable oil
- 1 ½ tablespoon light soy sauce
- ½ teaspoon sesame oil
- ¼ teaspoon white pepper
- Salt, to taste

- 2 tablespoons water

1. Boil the dry noodles in hot water as per package's instructions then drain.
2. Sauté noodles with oil and soy sauce in a skillet and keep it aside.
3. Mix chicken with cornstarch, water, oyster sauce, wine, spice powder, and white pepper in a bowl.
4. Heat oil in a Cantonese wok and sear the chicken over medium heat until golden-brown.
5. Stir in shallots, carrots, and cabbage, then sauté for 3 minutes.
6. Toss in rest of the ingredients along with the noodles then mix well.
7. Serve warm.

Shredded Carrots with Garlic

Prep time: 10 minutes | Cook time: 10 minutes | Serves 4

- 2 tablespoons soy sauce
- 2 teaspoons sugar
- 1 teaspoon sesame oil
- 1 teaspoon chili sauce (optional)
- 1 tablespoon peanut oil
- 2 garlic cloves, minced
- 1½ cups cremini or button mushrooms, sliced

- 1 red bell pepper, julienned
- ¼ cup shredded carrots
- ½ cup snow peas
- 2 scallions, cut into 1-inch pieces
- ½ pound (227g) lo mein, cooked according to package directions and drained well

1. In a small bowl, make the sauce by mixing the soy sauce, sugar, sesame oil, and chili sauce (if using). Set aside.
2. Heat your wok on high heat until a drop of water sizzles on contact. Add the peanut oil and swirl to coat the wok. Add the garlic, cremini mushrooms, red bell pepper, and carrots to the wok, and stir-fry for 3 to 4 minutes, tossing often. Add the snow peas and scallions, and stir-fry for another 2 to 3 minutes.
3. Add the lo mein and the sauce mixture to the wok. Toss everything together to combine, and turn off

the heat. Serve immediately.

Vinegary Dan Dan Noodles

Prep time: 15 minutes | Cook time: 15 minutes | Serves 4

- 2 tablespoons peanut or vegetable oil
- 12 ounces / 340 g ground pork
- Sea salt to taste
- Freshly ground black pepper to taste
- 2 tablespoons fresh chopped, peeled ginger
- ¾ cup chicken broth
- 2 tablespoons chili oil
- 1 tablespoon rice vinegar
- 2 tablespoons soy sauce
- ½ teaspoon sesame oil
- 2 tablespoons peanut butter
- 1 teaspoon Sichuan peppercorns
- ½ pound (227g) dried egg noodles, cooked according to package directions, well drained
- 2 tablespoons chopped, roasted peanuts
- 3 scallions, thinly sliced

1. Heat your wok over medium heat. Add the peanut oil and swirl to coat the wok. Add the pork, season it with the sea salt and pepper to taste, and stir-fry it for about 2 minutes. Add the ginger and stir-fry it with the pork for about 2 minutes.

2. Add the chicken broth, chili oil, rice vinegar, soy sauce, sesame oil, peanut butter, and Sichuan peppercorns. Mix everything well to combine, and simmer 6 to 8 minutes, until the sauce thickens.

3. Turn off the heat and remove the wok from the heat. Add the noodles, peanuts, and scallions to the wok, and toss everything together to combine. Serve immediately.

Spicy Cold Skin Noodles (Liangpi)

Prep time: 10 minutes | Cook time: 12 minutes | Serves 4

- For the Sauce:
- ¼ cup chili oil
- 2 teaspoons Chinese black vinegar
- 1 tablespoon light soy sauce
- 1 teaspoon sesame oil
- 1 tablespoon toasted sesame seeds
- 1 teaspoon Sichuan peppercorn powder
- ½ teaspoon sugar
- ¼ teaspoon salt
- 2 garlic cloves, minced
- For the Dish:
- 8 ounces / 227 g fresh Liangpi noodles
- 1 ½ cups bean sprout
- 4 ounces (113 g) whea gluten
- ¼ cup cilantro leaves
- 1 small cucumber, julienned

1. Boil the dry noodles in hot water as per package's instructions then drain.
1. Mix all the ingredients for the liquid sauce in a small bowl.
1. Pour this sauce into a wok and cook for 30 seconds.
1. Stir in bean sprouts, wheat gluten, cucumber, an cilantro leaves.
1. Mix well then add the noodles and cook for 1 minute.
1. Serve warm.

Limey Butter Noodles

Prep time: 10 minutes | Cook time: 12 minutes | Serves 6

- 7 ounces (198 g) fresh white noodles
- 2 garlic cloves, minced
- 1 ½ teaspoon ginger, minced
- ⅓ cup peanut butter
- 2-3 tablespoons hot water
- 1 tablespoon Thai
- black soy sauce
- 2 teaspoons light soy sauce
- 2 teaspoons fish sau
- ½ teaspoon sesame o
- 1 tablespoon lime juice
- 2 teaspoons chili oil

1. Boil the dry noodles in hot water as per package instructions then drain.
2. Sauté garlic and ginger with peanut butter in a Cantonese wok for 30 seconds.
3. Stir in all the sauces, water, lime juice, and chili oil.
4. Mix well and cook it for 1 minutes then toss in noodles.
5. Mix well and serve warm.

Soups, Rice, and Noo

Oniony Carrot and Fennel

Prep time: 15 minutes | Cook time: 5 minutes | Serves 8

- 2 tablespoons cooking oil
- 2 garlic cloves, crushed and chopped
- 1 tablespoon crushed and chopped peeled ginger
- 1 medium carrot, julienned
- 1 medium onion, julienned
- 1 fennel bulb, julienned
- ¼ cup soy sauce
- 2 tablespoons brown sugar
- 1 tablespoon mirin
- 1 pound (454 g) cooked al dente soba, well drained and tossed with 2 tablespoons toasted sesame oil
- 1 tablespoon sesame seeds
- ¼ cup coarsely chopped fennel fronds
- 1 cup bean sprouts

In a wok, heat the cooking oil over high heat until it begins to smoke.

Add the garlic, ginger, and carrot. Stir-fry for 1 minute, or until the garlic and ginger are fragrant.

Add the onion and fennel. Stir-fry for 1 minute, or until they are lightly coated with oil.

Add the soy sauce, sugar, mirin, and soba. Stir-fry for 1 minute, or until all of the ingredients are well combined.

Add the sesame seeds, fennel fronds, and bean sprouts. Toss. Serve immediately.

Gingered Sesame with Fried Rice

Prep time: 10 minutes | Cook time: 10 minutes | Serves 4

- 2 tablespoons peanut or vegetable oil
- 3 garlic cloves, minced
- 2 teaspoons grated fresh ginger
- 1 cup of beef, chicken, or shrimp, thinly sliced (if desired)
- 2 tablespoons soy
- sauce
- 1 tablespoon kecap manis
- 1 teaspoon sesame oil
- 4 cups cooked long-grain or jasmine rice (day-old rice is best)
- 4 eggs, fried sunny-side up

- Sambal oelek, for garnish

1. Heat your wok over high heat until a drop of water sizzles on contact. Add the peanut oil and swirl to coat the wok. Add the garlic and ginger, and stir-fry for about 20 seconds. Add the beef (if using) and stir-fry for 2 minutes.

2. Turn the heat down to medium-low, and add the soy sauce, kecap manis, sesame oil, and rice. Mix and stir to combine the ingredients. Stir-fry for another 2 to 3 minutes.

3. Serve in four portions, with a fried egg on top and sambal oelek on the side.

Broccoli with Shirataki Stir-Fry

Prep time: 15 minutes | Cook time: 15 minutes | Serves 4

- 1 pound (454 g) shirataki noodles
- ¼ cup soy sauce
- 2 teaspoons hoisin sauce
- 1 tablespoon cornstarch
- ½ cup warm or room temperature water
- 1 tablespoon peanut oil
- 2 cups broccoli florets
- ½ pound (227g)
- boneless, skinless chicken breast, cut into thin strips
- 1 cup bean sprouts, washed and dried well
- ½ cup chopped cremini mushrooms
- ½ cup thinly sliced zucchini
- ¼ cup shredded carrots
- 2 scallions, chopped

1. Rinse the shirataki noodles very well under cool running water. After draining them well, use cooking shears to cut them into smaller pieces twice. Set aside.

2. In a small bowl, make a sauce by combining the soy sauce, hoisin sauce, cornstarch, and water. Set aside.

3. Heat your wok over medium-high heat. Add the oil and swirl to coat the wok. Add the broccoli and chicken, and stir-fry for 5 to 6 minutes, or until the chicken is cooked. Add the bean sprouts, mushrooms, zucchini, carrots, and scallions, and stir-fry for 2 to 3 minutes.

4. Pour the sauce into the wok, stir to combine it with

the chicken and broccoli, and cook until the sauce has thickened, about 2 minutes. Add the noodles to the wok, mix them with the other ingredients, and cook, stirring occasionally, for 2 to 3 minutes, until the flavors are combined.

Cream and Buttered Uni Roe Pasta

Prep time: 15 minutes | Cook time: 10 minutes | Serves 2

- 2½ teaspoons kosher salt, divided
- ¼ pound (114 g) linguine, or pasta of your choice
- 1 tablespoon olive oil
- 1 tablespoon unsalted butter
- 1 garlic clove, finely minced
- ¼ teaspoon red chili flakes
- ¼ cup heavy cream
- 5 ounces (142 g) fresh uni
- ½ teaspoon white pepper
- 1 tablespoon fresh chives, finely diced
- 1 teaspoon toasted sesame seeds
- ¼ cup seasoned nori (seaweed), chiffonade

1. Bring a large pot of water to boil and add 2 teaspoons salt. Add the linguine and cook the pasta for 8-10 minutes or until al dente.

2. In a wok over medium heat, melt the olive oil and butter together. Add garlic and sauté for 1-2 minutes.

3. Add the chili flakes and heavy cream. Bring to a slight slimmer and add all but 4 pieces of the uni.

4. Remove from heat and whisk items together until the uni has broken down into the sauce. Toss in the cooked pasta until the noodles have been evenly coated. Season with remaining salt and white pepper to taste.

5. Transfer pasta to a plate and place the remaining whole uni segments on top. Sprinkle the tops with chives, sesame seeds, and nori. Serve immediately.

Chili Peanut and Sesame Noodles

Prep time: 10 minutes | Cook time: 5 minutes | Serves 4

- 2½ tablespoons creamy peanut butter
- 2½ tablespoons tahini paste
- 3 tablespoons soy sauce
- 1 tablespoon honey
- 2 teaspoons Chinese black vinegar, rice vinegar, or balsamic vinegar
- 1½ tablespoons
- sesame oil
- 2 tablespoons chili oil
- 1 tablespoon peanut oil
- 12 ounces / 340 g fettuccine noodles or spaghetti, cooked according to package directions, drained well
- 3 scallions, chopped, for garnish

1. In a small bowl, mix the peanut butter, tahini paste, soy sauce, honey, black vinegar, sesame oil, and chili oil. If the peanut butter is too stiff, microwave everything for 30 seconds at 50 percent power, and stir well to combine the ingredients.

2. Heat your wok on medium-high heat. Add the peanut oil and swirl to coat the wok. Add the noodles and stir-fry for about 1 minute. Add the peanut butter sauce to the wok, and stir-fry for 1 to 2 minutes.

3. The noodles can be served at room temperature or cold. If serving cold, chill them in the refrigerator. Garnish with the scallions before serving.

Quick and Easy Vegetable Congee

Prep time: 10 minutes | Cook time: 20 minutes | Serves 8

- ¾ cup white rice
- 4 ounces (113 g) pork shoulder, julienned
- ½ teaspoon corn-starch
- 1 teaspoon oyster sauce
- 1 teaspoon vegetable oil
- 7 cups water
- 2 eggs; boiled, peeled and diced
- 3 ginger slices
- ¼ teaspoon ground white pepper
- Salt, to taste
- Chopped scallion and cilantro

1. Mix pork with oyster sauce, cornstarch, and vegetable oil in a bowl.

2. Cover and marinate the pork for 20 minutes.

3. Sear the pork in 1 teaspoon vegetable oil in a dee

wok until golden-brown. Set the pork aside.

Add 7 cups water, rice, ginger, white pepper, and salt to a soup pot.

Cover and cook the congee for 15 minutes on a simmer.

Add eggs and pork to the congee and cook for 5 minutes on a simmer.

Garnish with cilantro and scallions.

Serve warm.

Chapter 9: Appetizers and Dessert

Cornstarch with Berries and Pork Balls

Prep time: 10 minutes | Cook time: 35 minutes | Serves 4

- ½ cup sticky rice
- 1 egg
- 1 (1 inch) piece ginger root, minced
- 2 teaspoons soy sauce
- Salt, to taste
- 4 ounces (113 g) ground pork
- 2 tablespoons cornstarch
- 1 tablespoon pork stock
- ¼ cup water
- 1 teaspoon dried goji berries

Soak the rice in water for 2 hours in a bowl.

Mix pork stock, pork, water, salt, soy sauce, ginger, cornstarch, and goji berries in a bowl.

Divide the mixture into meatballs.

Fill a cooking pot with water and set a steamer basket inside.

Boil the water and spread the balls in the basket.

Cover and steam these balls for 30 minutes.

Coat these steamed balls with rice.

Sear the steamed balls in a Mandarin wok greased with oil for 5 minutes.

Serve warm.

Peppered Sesame with Edamame

Prep time: 5 minutes | Cook time: 5 minutes | Serves 4

- 1 (16 ounces / 454 g) package frozen edamame
- 2 teaspoons sesame seeds
- 3 tablespoons white sugar
- 2 tablespoons soy sauce
- 2 teaspoons olive oil
- 1 teaspoon red pepper flakes

1. Fill a cooking pot with boiling water and soak the edamame in the water for 6 minutes.
2. Transfer the edamame to a salad bowl.
3. Sauté edamame with olive oil in a Mandarin wok for 5 minutes.
4. Stir in sugar, sesame seeds, soy sauce, and red pepper flakes.
5. Mix well and serve.

Salt and Sugar Fried Shrimp Balls

Prep time: 10 minutes | Cook time: 0 minutes | Serves 16

- 1 pound (454 g) shelled and deveined shrimp
- 1 egg white, lightly beaten
- 1 teaspoon salt
- 1 teaspoon sugar
- 1 tablespoon cornstarch
- ½ teaspoon sesame oil
- 3 dashes white pepper powder
- 8 pieces spring roll wrapper

1. Blend shrimp with egg white, salt, sugar, cornstarch, sesame oil, and white pepper in a bowl.
2. Cut the roll wrappers into strips and keep them in a bowl.
3. Make small meatballs out of the shrimp mixture and wrap them with the roll wrapper strips.
4. Heat oil in a Cantonese wok and deep fry the shrimp ball until golden-brown.
5. Serve warm.

Cucumber with Koya Dofu

Prep time: 10 minutes | Cook time: 7 minutes | Serve 6

- 1 Koya dofu, sliced
- 1 katakuriko
- 2 tablespoons vegetable oil
- 3 tablespoons ketchup
- 1 tablespoon soy sauce
- 2 teaspoons sugar
- 1 cucumber, peeled and sliced

1. Squeeze the dofu and slice it.
2. Coat the dofu slices with Katakuriko.
3. Mix ketchup, soy sauce, and sugar in a bowl.
4. Add oil to a wok and sear the dofu for 4 to 5 minutes per side.
5. Stir in the prepared sauce and cook it for 3 minutes on a simmer.
6. Garnish with cucumber.
7. Serve warm.

Chili Cilantro and Seaweed Salad

Prep time: 15 minutes | Cook time: 16 minutes | Serves 12

- 12 ounces (340 g) fresh kelp
- 4 garlic cloves, minced
- 3 thin ginger slices, minced
- 3 Thai chilies, sliced
- 2 scallions, chopped
- 3 tablespoons vegetable oil
- 1 tablespoon Sichuan peppercorns
- 1½ teaspoons sugar
- 2 teaspoons Chinese black vinegar
- 2½ tablespoons light soy sauce
- 1 teaspoon oyster sauce
- ½ to 1 teaspoon sesame oil, to taste
- ¼ teaspoon salt
- ¼ teaspoon five-spice powder
- 1 tablespoon cilantro, chopped

1. Boil kelp in a pot filled with water for 5 minutes in a cooking pot.
2. Drain the kelp and rinse it under cold water.
3. Mix ginger, garlic, Thai chilies, and scallion in a bowl.

4. Sauté garlic mixture, and peppercorns with 3 tablespoons oil in a Mandarin wok for 10 minutes
5. Stir in vinegar, sugar, soy sauce, salt, sesame oil, five-spice powder, and oyster oil.
6. Add cilantro and scallions then sauté for 1 minut
7. Pour this sauce over the boiled kelp leaves.
8. Serve warm.

Oniony Coconut Shrimp

Prep time: 10 minutes | Cook time: 0 minutes | Serves 4

- 1 pound (454 g) shrimp
- ¼ cup all-purpose flour
- 1 teaspoon cornstarch
- ¼ teaspoon baking powder
- ¼ teaspoon baking soda
- ¼ teaspoon salt
- ¼ teaspoon garlic powder
- ¼ teaspoon onion powder
- ¼ cup ice water
- ½ cup coconut flakes
- Peanut oil, for frying

1. Whisk flour, cornstarch, baking powder, baking soda, salt, garlic powder, and onion powder in a bowl.
2. Dredge the shrimp through the flour mixture the dip in the water.
3. Coat the shrimp with coconut flakes.
4. Deep the fry the shrimp in a Cantonese wok fille with oil at 350ºF (180ºC), until golden-brown.
5. Transfer these shrimps to a plate lined with a paper towel.
6. Serve warm.

Fried Sesame with Sugar Balls

Prep time: 10 minutes | Cook time: 0 minutes | Serves 8

- 1½ cups glutinous rice flour
- ⅓ cup granulated sugar
- ¼ cup boiling water
- ¼ cup water
- 7 ounces (198 g) lotu paste or red bean paste
- ¼ cup sesame seeds
- 4 cups peanut oil, fo frying

1. Mix sugar, ¼ cup rice flour, and ¼ cup warm water in a bowl and leave for 5 minutes.

2. Stir in remaining water, and remaining rice flour.

3. Mix well, cover the dough, and leave it for 30 minutes.

4. Meanwhile, make 8 small balls out of the lotus paste.

5. Divide the prepared dough into 8 pieces and spread each piece of dough into a round.

6. Place one lotus paste ball at the center of each dough round and wrap it around the ball.

7. Roll to smooth out the balls then coat them with sesame seeds.

8. Add 4 cups oil in a deep wok and heat it to 320ºF (160ºC).

9. Deep fry the sesame balls until golden-brown.

10. Serve.

Gingered Vegetable Dumplings

Prep time: 15 minutes | Cook time: 8 minutes | Makes 15 to 20 portions

For the Dumplings:

- 2 teaspoons olive oil
- 4 cups shredded cabbage
- 1 carrot, shredded
- 2 scallions, chopped
- 5 to 8 garlic chives, cut into 1-inch pieces
- 1-inch piece of ginger, peeled and minced
- 1 tablespoon water
- 2 teaspoons sesame oil, plus 2 teaspoons for brushing
- Salt and pepper
- 15 to 20 round wonton wrappers

For The Dipping Sauce:

- 2 tablespoons soy sauce
- 2 teaspoons sesame oil
- 2 teaspoons rice vinegar
- 1 teaspoon chili oil
- 1-inch piece of ginger, peeled and finely minced

In a wok over medium heat, heat the olive oil.

Add the cabbage, carrot, scallions, garlic chives, and ginger to the wok. Stir-fry for about 1 minute.

Add the water to help steam the vegetables. Stir-fry until most of the water has evaporated. Drizzle 2 teaspoons sesame oil over the vegetables.

Season with salt and pepper, and toss. Remove from the heat and set it aside to cool.

4. Place about 1 teaspoon of vegetable mixture in the middle of a wonton wrapper.

5. Dampen the edges of the wonton wrapper with a little water, fold the wrapper in half so that it forms a triangle, and gently press down to seal the edges.

6. Brush the dumplings with a light coating of sesame oil.

7. Line a bamboo steamer with parchment paper liners or napa cabbage leaves. Arrange the dumplings on top and steam for 8 minutes, or until the wonton wrappers look slightly translucent.

8. While the dumplings are steaming, make the dipping sauce. Combine the soy sauce, sesame oil, rice vinegar, chili oil, and ginger in a small bowl.

9. Serve the dumplings with the dipping sauce.

Milky Coconut and Peanut Mochi

Prep time: 10 minutes | Cook time: 18 minutes | Serve 14

For the Dough:

- 1½ cups sweet rice flour
- ¼ cup cornstarch
- ¼ cup caster sugar
- 1 ½ cups coconut milk
- 2 tablespoons coconut oil

For the Filling:

- ½ cup peanuts
- ½ cup coconut flakes, chopped
- 3 tablespoons sugar
- 1 tablespoon melted coconut oil

For the Coconut Peanut Mochi:

- A large piece of wax paper
- 1 cup coconut flakes, chopped
- 16 small paper cupcake cups

1. Add peanuts to a Mandarin wok and roast them for 3 to 5 minutes until golden-brown.

2. Allow the peanuts to cool, then chop them finely.

3. Layer a 11-inch by 11-inch cake pan with wax paper and brush with vegetable oil.

4. Whisk rice flour, sugar, cornstarch, coconut oil,

and coconut milk in a bowl.

5. Boil water in a suitable cooking pot, place the steam rack inside and add the dough in the steamer.

6. Cover and cook for 15 minutes in the steamer then allow the dough to cool.

7. Meanwhile, mix peanuts with 1 tablespoon coconut oil, sugar, and coconut flakes in a bowl.

8. Spread the prepared dough in the prepared pan and cut it into 14 squares.

9. Add a tablespoon the filling at the center of each square.

10. Pinch the edges of each square and roll it into a ball.

11. Coat all the balls with coconut flakes and place them in the cupcake cup.

12. Leave them for 20 minutes.

13. Serve.

Cabbage with Spicy Potstickers

Prep time: 15 minutes | Cook time: 3 minutes | Serves 6

- ½ pound (227g) ground pork
- 1 cup finely shredded cabbage
- 2 scallions, sliced
- 2 teaspoons minced ginger
- 2 tablespoons soy sauce
- 1 teaspoon sesame oil
- ½ teaspoon pepper
- 24 dumpling skins
- 2 tablespoons vegetable oil
- ¼ cup water
- ¼ cup chopped scallions

1. In a large bowl, combine the pork, cabbage, scallions, ginger, soy sauce, sesame oil, and pepper. Refrigerate for 30 minutes.

2. Take 1 dumpling skin and use your finger to brush water along the edge of the circle. Place about 1 tablespoon of the mixture in the center of the skin. Fold the dumpling skin over and firmly press the sides to seal completely. While you are forming the potstickers, create a flattened bottom. You can also pleat the edges if you like.

3. Heat the oil in a wok over medium heat. Place the

potstickers, flattened side down, in one layer and fry for 1 to 2 minutes.

4. Carefully pour the water into the wok and cover. Allow the pot stickers to steam for an additional 2 to 3 minutes. Remove the lid and continue cooking until the water has evaporated.

5. Place the potstickers on a plate and sprinkle the tops with scallions. Serve hot.

Limey Parsley Calamari

Prep time: 10 minutes | Cook time: 2 minutes | Serves 4

- ½ cup Tequila Lime Marinade
- 1 pound (454 g) calamari tubes, cut into 1" pieces
- 2 tablespoons vegetable oil
- 1 tablespoon lime
- juice
- 2 tablespoons extra-virgin olive oil
- 2 tablespoons chopped Italian parsley
- ½ teaspoon kosher sa

1. Combine the marinade with the calamari in a large bowl. Refrigerate for 5 minutes.

2. Heat a wok to medium-high heat and add the vegetable oil. Swirl the oil around the wok and add the calamari. Toss and stir-fry the calamari for 2 3 minutes.

3. Remove the calamari to a plate and drizzle with lime juice, olive oil, and parsley. Season with salt to taste and serve immediately.

Carrots and Scallion Egg Rolls

Prep time: 15 minutes | Cook time: 5 minutes | Makes 12

- 1 pound (454 g) lean ground pork
- 1 tablespoon dark soy sauce
- 2 tablespoons oyster sauce
- 1 teaspoon minced garlic, divided
- 1 teaspoon minced
- ginger, divided
- 1 cup shredded carro
- 2 scallions, finely chopped
- 1 teaspoon sesame oi
- 1 teaspoon black pepper
- 25 (6 × 6) egg roll wrappers

2 eggs, beaten

vegetable oil

2 cups peanut or

In a large bowl, mix together the ground pork, soy sauce, oyster sauce, garlic, ginger, carrots, scallions, and sesame oil. Add the black pepper.

One at a time, place an eggroll wrapper on a flat surface with one of the points facing toward you. Spoon about 2 tablespoons of the filling in a line toward the bottom half of the wrapper. Brush the top corner and sides with the beaten egg. Fold in the sides of the wrapper and tightly roll the egg roll up until it is closed. Press to seal, set aside, and continue with the remaining ingredients.

Heat the oil in a wok over high heat to 375ºF (190ºC). In batches, fry the egg rolls until golden brown, about 5 to 6 minutes. Remove the fried egg rolls to plates lined with paper towels to drain. Serve hot.

ettuce Spring Rolls

ep time: 15 minutes | Cook time: 2 minutes | rves 4

- ½ pound (227g) shrimp, peeled and deveined
- 2 garlic cloves, minced
- 2 tablespoons fish sauce
- ¼ teaspoon black pepper
- 2 tablespoons vegetable oil
- 8 rice paper spring roll wrappers

- 8 lettuce leaves
- 2 cups cooked vermicelli noodles
- 1 cup cucumbers, thinly sliced
- 1 cup shredded carrots
- 1 cup fresh mint leaves
- 1 cup cilantro leaves
- 1½ cups Nuoc Cham Sauce

In a medium bowl, mix the shrimp, garlic, fish sauce, and black pepper together. Refrigerate for 10 minutes.

Heat a wok with the oil over medium-high heat. Add the shrimp and stir-fry for 2 to 3 minutes, until they turn pink. Remove to a plate.

Take 1 piece of rice paper and dip into a shallow dish of water to soften. Lay the softened rice paper on a plate. Place 1 piece of lettuce in the center and top with ¼ cup of the noodles in a line. Top with a few cooked shrimp, slices of cucumber,

carrots, mint leaves, and cilantro. Fold in the sides and tightly roll up until it is closed. Repeat with the remaining ingredients.

4. Serve with Nuoc Cham Sauce.

Cilantro and Mushroom Garbanzo

Prep time: 10 minutes | Cook time: 25 minutes | Serves 2

- 2 tablespoons oil
- 1 tablespoon. oregano
- 1 tablespoon. chopped basil
- 1 clove garlic, crushed
- ground black pepper to taste
- 2 cups cooked

- garbanzo beans
- 1 large zucchini, halved and sliced
- ½ cup sliced mushrooms
- 1 tablespoon. chopped cilantro
- 1 tomato, chopped

1. Heat oil in a skillet over medium heat. Stir in oregano, basil, garlic and pepper. Add the garbanzo beans and zucchini, stirring well to coat with oil and herbs. Cook for 10 minutes, stirring occasionally.

2. Stir in mushrooms and cilantro; cook 10 minutes, stirring occasionally. Place the chopped tomato on top of the mixture to steam. Cover and cook 5 minutes more.

Vinegar and Honeyed Chicken Salad Cups

Prep time: 15 minutes | Cook time: 8 minutes | Makes 15 to 20

FOR THE CHICKEN CUPS:

- 4 ounces (113 g) skinless, boneless chicken tenderloins
- Salt and Pepper to taste
- 3 tablespoons olive oil, divided
- 15 to 20 wonton wrappers
- 1 small head romaine

- lettuce, shredded
- 1 carrot, julienned
- 2 scallions, chopped
- ¼ cup sliced almonds
- ¼ cup chopped fresh cilantro

FOR THE SALAD DRESSING:

- 4 tablespoons apple cider vinegar
- 2 tablespoons sesame

oil   • 2 tablespoons honey

1. Season the chicken tenderloins with salt and pepper to taste. In a wok over medium heat, heat 1 tablespoon of olive oil. Add the chicken and sear on both sides until cooked through, about 1 minute per side. Remove the chicken from the wok and chop it finely.

2. Preheat the oven to 375ºF (190ºC).

3. Brush each wonton wrapper on both sides with a thin layer of olive oil. Arrange the wonton wrappers in a regular-size muffin pan to form little cups.

4. Bake the wrappers for 6 minutes. Allow them to cool completely.

5. While the wrappers are baking, make the salad dressing. Combine the apple cider vinegar, sesame oil, and honey in a small bowl, and mix well.

6. In a large bowl, combine the chicken, lettuce, carrot, scallions, almonds, and cilantro with the salad dressing and toss well.

7. Fill each wonton cup with the salad and serve.

Gingered Shrimp Shumai

Prep time: 15 minutes | Cook time: 10 minutes | Makes 20 to 25

- ½ pound (227g) shrimp, peeled and deveined
- ½ pound (227g) ground pork
- 3 tablespoons sesame oil
- 1 tablespoon cornstarch
- 1 tablespoon soy sauce
- 1 teaspoon grated

- ginger
- ½ teaspoon salt
- 2 pinches ground white pepper
- 2 teaspoons Shaoxing wine
- 20 to 25 round wonton wrappers
- ½ carrot, finely minced

1. Mince the shrimp by flattening each piece with the side of a knife, then roughly chopping each one.

2. Mix together the shrimp and the ground pork.

3. Add the sesame oil, cornstarch, soy sauce, ginger, salt, pepper, and Shaoxing wine to the shrimp and pork. Combine thoroughly.

4. Make an "O" with your thumb and index finger. Place one wonton wrapper on the "O" and gently

press it down to create a small cup.

5. Using a teaspoon, fill the wonton cup to the top with some of the pork and shrimp mixture. Use th back of the teaspoon to press the filling into the cup.

6. Line a bamboo steamer with parchment paper liners or napa cabbage leaves. Arrange the shuma on top of the liners or leaves. Top each shumai with a bit of minced carrot.

7. Steam for 10 minutes or until the meat is cooked through.

Eggy Crab Lettuce Warps

Prep time: 10 minutes | Cook time: 10 minutes | Serves 4 to 6

- 1 head lettuce
- 4 eggs, lightly beaten
- Pinch salt to taste
- Pinch ground white pepper to taste
- ½ teaspoon soy sauce
- 2 scallions, chopped
- 3 tablespoons peanut

- oil
- ½ cup diced water chestnuts
- 1 small onion, thinly sliced
- ¾ cup crabmeat
- ¼ cup Basic Sambal (here) (optional)

1. Wash and separate the lettuce leaves. Chill the lettuce leaves in the refrigerator until just before serving.

2. Put the beaten eggs into a medium bowl. Add the salt, pepper, soy sauce, and scallions to the eggs. Stir gently just to combine.

3. In a wok over medium-high heat, heat the peanu oil.

4. Stir-fry the water chestnuts and onion until the onion is slightly translucent.

5. Add the crabmeat to the wok, then the egg mixture, and let it sit for a moment. When the bottom of the egg is cooked through, flip, and co on the other side.

6. Using a wok spatula, break up and scramble the egg.

7. Serve with the chilled lettuce leaves and samba using).

Oniony Chicken Phyllo Rolls

Prep time: 10 minutes | Cook time: 15 minutes | Serves 12

- 2 tablespoons olive oil
- 1 small onion, sliced
- 2 scallions, chopped
- 3 garlic cloves, minced
- 2 teaspoons curry powder
- 2 cups cooked chicken, shredded
- 1 tablespoon cilantro, chopped
- 1 lime, zested
- 2 tablespoons lime juice
- Salt, to taste
- Black pepper, to taste
- 4 tablespoons butter, melted
- 8 sheets phyllo dough
- ¼ cup panko breadcrumbs

Sauté onion, scallions, and garlic with oil in a Mandarin wok until soft. Stir in chicken and rest of the ingredients (except the phyllo dough). Sauté for about 1 minute then remove the filling from the heat.

Spread a sheet of dough phyllo in a baking pan and brush it with butter. Drizzle breadcrumbs on top, repeat the layers with three more phyllo sheets.

Top the four phyllo sheets with ½ of the chicken filling. Roll the sheets to make a phyllo roll.

Repeat the same steps with remaining phyllo and filling.

Place the rolls in a baking tray and brush them with butter. Bake the phyllo rolls for 12 minutes in the oven at 375ºF (190ºC).

Slice and serve warm.

Cheesy Cream Wontons

Prep time: 10 minutes | Cook time: 20 minutes | Serves 6

- 8 ounces (227 g) cream cheese
- 2 teaspoons sugar
- ½ teaspoon salt
- 4 scallions, chopped
- 1 pack wonton wrappers
- Vegetable oil, for frying

Mix cream cheese with sugar, salt, and scallions in a bowl. Spread the egg roll wrappers on the working surface.

2. Divide the cream cheese filling at the center of each wrapper.

3. Wet the edges of the wrapper, fold the two sides, then roll the wrappers into an egg roll.

4. Add oil to a deep wok to 325ºF (163ºC) then deep fry the egg rolls until golden-brown.

5. Transfer the golden egg rolls to a plate lined with a paper towel.

6. Serve warm.

San Xian Wontons

Prep time: 10 minutes | Cook time: 20 minutes | Serves 12

- 8 ounces shrimp; peeled, deveined, and chopped
- 8 ounces ground pork
- 8 ounces ground chicken
- 1 tablespoon ginger, minced
- ¼ cup scallion, chopped
- 2 tablespoons vegetable oil
- 2 tablespoons light soy sauce
- 1 tablespoon oyster sauce
- ½ tablespoon sesame oil
- ½ teaspoon ground white pepper
- ½ cup water
- 2 packages wonton wrappers

1. Sauté scallions and ginger with oil in a Mandarin wok until soft.

2. Stir in pork, chicken, shrimp, and rest of the ingredients (except the wrappers).

3. Sauté for about 8 minutes, then remove the filling from the heat.

4. Allow the filling to cool and spread the egg roll wrappers on the working surface.

5. Divide the pork-shrimp filling at the center of each wrapper.

6. Wet the edges of the wrapper, fold the two sides then roll the wrappers into an egg roll.

7. Add oil to a deep wok to 325ºF then deep fry the egg rolls until golden-brown.

8. Transfer the golden egg rolls to a plate lined with a paper towel.

9. Serve warm.

Scallion and Cabbage Salad

Prep time: 20 minutes | Cook time: 0 minutes | Serves 4 as a side

- 1 tablespoon toasted sesame oil
- 1 tablespoon soy sauce
- 3 tablespoons rice vinegar or white vinegar
- 1 tablespoon sugar
- 3 cups finely shredded napa cabbage
- 1 cup shredded carrots
- 1 scallion, finely slivered

1. In a large bowl, whisk together the sesame oil, soy sauce, rice vinegar, and sugar. Add the cabbage, carrots, and slivered scallion. Toss to combine.

Vinegary Tofu with Avocado Salad

Prep time: 10 minutes | Cook time: 5 minutes | Serves 4

- 7 ounces (198 g) silken tofu, sliced
- 1 ripe avocado, peeled and sliced
- 2 garlic cloves, grated
- 1 teaspoon ginger, grated
- 2 tablespoons light soy sauce
- 1 teaspoon sesame oil
- ½ teaspoon sugar
- ½ teaspoon Chinese black vinegar
- ¼ teaspoon white pepper
- 2 teaspoons water
- Salt, to taste
- 1 scallion, finely chopped

1. Sauté tofu with sesame oil in a Mandarin wok for 5 minutes.
2. Toss tofu with rest of the salad ingredients in a salad bowl.
3. Mix well and serve.
4. Enjoy.

Sugar and Vinegar with Cucumber Salad

Prep time: 10 minutes | Cook time: 2 minutes | Serves 4

- 6 garlic cloves, minced
- 3 tablespoons oil
- 2 English cucumbers, sliced
- 1 ½ teaspoon salt
- 1 teaspoon sugar
- ⅛ teaspoon MSG
- ¼ teaspoon sesame oil
- 1 tablespoon rice vinegar

1. Sauté garlic with oil in a Cantonese wok for 30 seconds.
2. Stir in sugar, MSG, sesame oil, rice vinegar, and salt.
3. Cook for 1 minute, then toss in cucumber.
4. Mix well and serve.

Eggy Scallion Dumplings

Prep time: 10 minutes | Cook time: 15 minutes | Serves 4

- 2 tablespoons vegetable or peanut oil
- ½ teaspoon toasted sesame oil
- 1 teaspoon minced garlic
- 4 large eggs, beaten
- Sea salt to taste
- Freshly ground black pepper to taste
- 2 scallions, trimmed and chopped
- 24 to 30 dumpling, gyoza, or pot sticker wrappers

1. To a hot wok, add the vegetable oil and sesame oil. Add the garlic and cook for about 30 seconds.
2. Add the eggs to the wok, and season with the sea salt and pepper to taste. Scramble the eggs with a heat-proof spatula for about 30 seconds, or until done. Add the scallions and mix with the scrambled eggs. Transfer the eggs to a plate, and set aside to cool until they can be handled.
3. Spoon a heaping teaspoon of the egg and scallion filling into the center of a dumpling wrapper. Wet the edges of the wrapper with water, fold the wrapper to enclose the filling, and seal the dumpling by pinching the wrapper at its edges. Repeat with the remaining wrappers and filling. Make sure the uncooked dumplings don't touch each other. They will stick together until they're cooked.
4. Steam, pan-fry, boil, or deep-fry the dumplings, or use them in soup.

Pepper and Ginger Shrimp Dumplings

Prep time: 10 minutes | Cook time: 8 minutes | Serves 4

- ½ pound (227g) raw shrimp, peeled, deveined
- 1 teaspoon oyster sauce
- 1 tablespoon vegetable oil
- ¼ teaspoon white pepper
- 1 teaspoon sesame oil
- ¼ teaspoon salt
- 1 teaspoon sugar
- ½ teaspoon ginger, minced
- ¼ cup bamboo shoots, chopped
- 12 dumpling wrappers

Blend shrimp with all the filling ingredients (except bamboo shoots) in a blender. Add bamboo shoots to the blended filling and mix well. Cover and refrigerate this filling for 1 hour.

Meanwhile, spread the dumpling wrappers on the working surface. Divide the shrimp filling at the center of each dumpling wrapper. Wet the edges of the dumplings and bring all the edges of each dumpling together. Pinch and seal the edges of the dumplings to seal the filling inside.

Boil water in a suitable pot with a steamer basket placed inside.

Add the dumplings to the steamer, cover and steam for 6 minutes.

Meanwhile, heat about 2 tablespoons oil in a Mandarin wok.

Sear the dumpling for 2 minutes until golden.

Serve warm.

Sesame Steamed Egg Custard

Prep time: 10 minutes | Cook time: 10 minutes | Serves 4

- 4 large eggs, at room temperature
- 1¾ cups low-sodium chicken broth or filtered water
- 2 teaspoons Shaoxing rice wine
- ½ teaspoon kosher salt
- 2 scallions, green part only, thinly sliced
- 4 teaspoons sesame oil

1. In a large bowl, whisk the eggs. Add the broth and rice wine and whisk to combine. Strain the egg mixture through a fine-mesh sieve set over a liquid measuring cup to remove air bubbles. Pour the egg mixture into 4 (6-ounce / 170-g) ramekins. With a paring knife, pop any bubbles on the surface of the egg mixture. Cover the ramekins with aluminum foil.

2. Rinse a bamboo steamer basket and its lid under cold water and place it in the wok. Pour in 2 inches of water, or until it comes above the bottom rim of the steamer by ¼ to ½ inch, but not so much that it touches the bottom of the basket. Place the ramekins in the steamer basket. Cover with the lid.

3. Bring the water to a boil, then reduce the heat to a low simmer. Steam over low heat for about 10 minutes or until the eggs are just set.

4. Carefully remove the ramekins from the steamer and garnish each custard with some scallions and a few drops of sesame oil. Serve immediately.

Turmeric and Spiced Popcorn

Prep time: 15 minutes | Cook time: 10 minutes | Serves 4

For the Spice Blend:

- 1 whole star anise, seeds removed and husks discarded
- 6 green cardamom pods, seeds removed and husks discarded
- 4 whole cloves
- 4 black peppercorns
- 1 teaspoon coriander seeds
- 1 teaspoon fennel seeds
- 1 teaspoon ground cinnamon
- 1 teaspoon ground ginger
- ½ teaspoon ground turmeric
- ⅛ teaspoon ground cayenne pepper

For the Popcorn:

- 2 tablespoons vegetable oil
- ½ cup popcorn kernels
- Kosher salt to taste

TO MAKE THE SPICE BLEND

1. In a small sauté pan or skillet, combine the star anise seeds, cardamom seeds, cloves, peppercorns, coriander seeds, and fennel seeds. Heat the skillet over medium heat and gently shake and swirl the spices around the pan. Toast the spices for 5 to 6

minutes, or until you can smell the spices and they start to pop.

2. Remove the pan from the heat and transfer the spices to a mortar and pestle or spice grinder. Cool the spices for 2 minutes before grinding. Grind the spices to a fine powder and transfer to a small bowl.

3. Add the ground cinnamon, ginger, turmeric, and cayenne pepper and stir to combine. Set aside.

TO MAKE THE POPCORN

4. Heat a wok over medium-high heat until it just begins to smoke. Pour in the vegetable oil and ghee and swirl to coat the wok. Add 2 popcorn kernels to the wok and cover. Once they pop, add the rest of the kernels and cover. Shake constantly until the popping stops and remove from the heat.

5. Transfer the popcorn to a large paper bag. Add 2 generous pinches of kosher salt and 1½ tablespoons of the spice blend. Fold the bag closed and shake! Pour into a large bowl and enjoy immediately.

Gravy with Simple Egg Foo Young

Prep time: 10 minutes | Cook time: 10 minutes | Serves 4

For the Gravy:

- ¾ cup chicken broth
- 1½ tablespoons hoisin sauce
- 1 tablespoon cornstarch dissolved in 2 tablespoons cold water

For the Egg Foo Young:

- 3 to 3½ tablespoons peanut or vegetable oil, divided
- 3 or 4 shiitake or cremini mushrooms, thinly sliced
- 4 scallions, thinly sliced
- 1½ cups fresh bean sprouts
- ¼ cup chopped ham or Canadian bacon
- 1½ teaspoons soy sauce
- 1 teaspoon sesame oil
- 6 large eggs

1. Heat a wok over medium-high heat until a drop of water sizzles on contact. Add 1 tablespoon of peanut oil, and swirl to coat the bottom of the wok.

2. Add the shiitake mushrooms, scallions, and bean sprouts to the wok, and stir-fry them for about 3

minutes. Add the ham, soy sauce, and sesame oil to the wok, and stir-fry them for another 1 to 2 minutes. Remove the filling mixture from the wok and set it aside.

3. In a medium bowl, beat the eggs. Add the filling mixture to the eggs and mix to combine.

4. Heat the wok to medium-high, and add 1 tablespoon of peanut oil. Pour in one quarter of the egg mixture to make an omelet. Cook the egg mixture until it is golden brown, 1 to 2 minutes per side. Transfer the omelet to a plate. Repeat this step with the rest of the egg mixture to make total of 4 omelets. For each subsequent omelet, u only 1½ teaspoons or less of the remaining peanu oil.

5. To serve, pour some gravy over each omelet.

Creamy Almond Sponge Cake

Prep time: 10 minutes | Cook time: 20 minutes | Makes 8

- Nonstick cooking spray
- 1 cup cake flour, sifted
- 1 teaspoon baking powder
- ¼ teaspoon kosher salt
- 5 large eggs, separate
- ¾ cup sugar, divided
- 1 teaspoon almond extract
- ½ teaspoon cream of tartar

1. Line an 8-inch cake pan with parchment paper. Lightly spray the parchment with nonstick cooking spray and set aside.

2. Into a bowl, sift the cake flour, baking powder, a salt together.

3. In a stand mixer or hand mixer on medium, beat the egg yolks with ½ cup of sugar and the almond extract for about 3 minutes, until pale and thick. Add the flour mixture and mix until ju combined. Set aside.

4. Clean the whisk and in another clean bowl, whip the egg whites with the cream of tartar until frothy. While the mixer is running, continue to whisk the whites while gradually adding the remaining ¼ cup of sugar. Beat for 4 to 5 minute until the whites turn shiny and develop stiff pea

5. Fold the egg whites into the cake batter and gen combine until the egg whites are incorporated.

Transfer the batter to the prepared cake pan.

3. Rinse a bamboo steamer basket and its lid under cold water and place it in the wok. Pour in 2 inches of water, or until it comes above the bottom rim of the steamer by ¼ to ½ inch, but not so much that it touches the bottom of the basket. Set the center pan in the steamer basket.

4. Bring the water to a boil over high heat. Place the cover on the steamer basket and turn the heat down to medium. Steam the cake for 25 minutes, or until a toothpick inserted into the center comes out clean.

5. Transfer the cake to a wire cooling rack and cool for 10 minutes. Turn the cake out onto the rack and remove the parchment paper. Invert the cake back onto a serving plate so that it is right side up. Slice into 8 wedges and serve warm.

Buttered Egg Puffs

Prep time: 10 minutes | Cook time: 20 minutes | Makes 8

- ½ cup water
- 2 teaspoons unsalted butter
- ¼ cup sugar, divided
- Kosher salt to taste
- ½ cup all-purpose unbleached flour
- 3 cups vegetable oil
- 2 large eggs, beaten

In a small saucepan, heat the water, butter, 2 teaspoons of sugar, and a pinch of salt to taste over medium-high heat. Bring to a boil and stir in the flour. Continue stirring the flour with a wooden spoon until the mixture looks like mashed potatoes and a thin film of dough has developed on the bottom of the pan. Turn off the heat and transfer the dough to a large mixing bowl. Cool the dough for about 5 minutes, stirring occasionally.

While the dough cools, pour the oil into the wok; the oil should be about 1 to 1½ inches deep. Bring the oil to 375ºF (190ºC) over medium-high heat. You can tell the oil is ready when you dip the end of a wooden spoon in and the oil bubbles and sizzles around the spoon.

Pour the beaten eggs into the dough in two batches, vigorously stirring the eggs into the dough before adding the next batch. When all the eggs have been incorporated, the batter should look satiny and shiny.

4. Using 2 tablespoons, scoop the batter with one and use the other to gently nudge the batter off the spoon into the hot oil. Let the puffs fry for 8 to 10 minutes, flipping often, until the puffs swell to 3 times their original size and turn golden brown and crispy.

5. Using a wok skimmer, transfer the puffs to a paper towel–lined plate and cool for 2 to 3 minutes. Place the remaining sugar in a bowl and toss the puffs in it. Serve warm.

Cinnamon with Caramel Granola

Prep time: 10 minutes | Cook time: 5 minutes | Serves 8

- 2 cups of quick-boiling oats
- 1 cup of brown sugar
- 2 tablespoons of ground cinnamon
- ½ cup melted butter
- 5 tablespoons of caramel sauce
- 2 tablespoons of white sugar

1. Mix the oats, brown sugar and cinnamon in a wok or a large pan over high heat, cook for 5 to 10 minutes; remove from heat and add butter and caramel sauce; stir evenly.

2. Spread the mixture in a thin layer on a flat plate or baking sheet. Sprinkle the white sugar over the muesli. Let cool completely before serving.

Ginger with Sugared Dessert Soup

Prep time: 10 minutes | Cook time: 10 minutes | Serves 4

- 3 cups water
- ¾ cup granulated sugar
- ¼ cup light brown sugar
- 2-inch fresh ginger piece, peeled and
- smashed
- 1 tablespoon dried chrysanthemum buds
- 2 large yellow peaches, peeled, pitted, and sliced into 8 wedges each

1. In a wok over high heat, bring the water to a boil, then lower the heat to medium-low and add the granulated sugar, brown sugar, ginger, and chrysanthemum buds. Stir gently to dissolve the sugars. Add the peaches.

2. Simmer gently for 10 to 15 minutes, or until the peaches are tender. They may impart a beautiful rosy color to the soup. Discard the ginger and divide the soup and peaches into bowls and serve.

Milky Mango Pudding

Prep time: 5 minutes | Cook time: 0 minutes | Serves 4

- ½ pound frozen mango chunks
- ¼ cup sugar
- ½ cup hot water
- 1 packet unflavored gelatin
- ½ cup evaporated milk
- Raspberries or kiwi slices, for garnish (optional)

1. In a blender, purée the mango and sugar until smooth.

2. In a large bowl, mix the hot water and gelatin. Let it stand for a few minutes.

3. Add the evaporated milk to the gelatin, and stir until they are combined. Add the mango purée and mix until well combined.

4. Pour the pudding into individual small cups or ramekins. Cover each one with plastic wrap, and chill in the refrigerator for at least 2 hours.

5. Before serving, garnish each pudding with the raspberries or kiwi (if using).

Chapter 10: Sauces

Lime and Honeyed Parsley Sauce

Prep time: 15 minutes | Cook time: 0 minutes | Makes 1 cup

- 1 cup roughly chopped fresh cilantro
- 1 cup roughly chopped Italian parsley
- 4 sprigs fresh oregano
- 2 teaspoons minced garlic
- 1 serrano chili pepper, seeded and diced
- ½ tablespoon grated lime zest
- 2 tablespoons lime juice
- ¼ teaspoon red pepper flakes
- 1 tablespoon honey
- ½ cup olive oil
- ½ tablespoon kosher salt

- ¼ tablespoon black pepper

1. In a food processor or blender, add the cilantro, parsley, oregano, garlic, serrano chili, lime zest and juice, red pepper flakes, and honey. Pulse several times to break down the herbs.

2. Stream in the olive oil and blend until the items have fully incorporated. Season with salt and pepper to taste. Sauce can be stored in a sealed container in the refrigerator for up to 1 week.

Hot and Spicy Sriracha

Prep time: 10 minutes | Cook time: 10 minutes | Makes 1 cup

- 1½ pounds (680 g) spicy red chile peppers, such as red jalapeño (hotter peppers make hotter sriracha)
- ½ cup apple cider vinegar
- 10 garlic cloves, finely minced
- ¼ cup tomato paste
- 1 tablespoon tamari or coconut aminos
- ½ teaspoon stevia
- 1 teaspoon sea salt

1. Stem, seed, and chop the chile peppers.

2. In a food processor or blender, combine all of the ingredients and purée until smooth.

3. In a small saucepan, bring the purée to a simmer over medium-high heat, and cook, stirring frequently, for about 10 minutes, until it's thick.

4. Store in a sterile container in the refrigerator for up to 1 month.

Sugar and Vinegar Stir-Fry Sauce

Prep time: 10 minutes | Cook time: 0 minutes | Makes ½ cup

- 3 tablespoons soy sauce
- 3 tablespoons water
- 1 tablespoon oyster sauce
- 2 teaspoons red wine vinegar
- 2 teaspoons granulated sugar
- 1 teaspoon garlic salt
- ¼ teaspoon black pepper

1. Combine all the ingredients in a small bowl. Add this simple sauce in the final stages of stir-frying. If you like, thicken the sauce by adding 1 teaspoon of cornstarch dissolved in 4 teaspoons of water.

Add the cornstarch and water mixture directly into the sauce in the wok or skillet, stirring quickly to thicken.

Tip: store in a sealed container in the refrigerator until ready to use. (Use the sauce within 3 or 4 days.)

Shallot with Garlicky Black Bean Sauce

Prep time: 10 minutes | Cook time: 10 minutes | Makes 2 cups

- ½ cup fermented black beans
- 1 cup vegetable oil, divided
- 1 large shallot, finely minced
- 3 tablespoons peeled and minced fresh ginger
- 4 scallions, thinly sliced
- 6 garlic cloves, finely minced
- ½ cup Shaoxing rice wine

put the black beans in a small bowl, cover with hot water, and let soak for 10 minutes to soften. Drain and coarsely chop the beans.

Heat a wok over medium-high heat. Pour in ¼ cup of oil and swirl to coat the pan. Add the shallot, ginger, scallions, and garlic and stir-fry for 1 minute, or until the mixture has softened.

Add the black beans and rice wine. Lower the heat to medium and cook for 3 to 4 minutes, until the mixture is reduced by half.

Transfer the mixture to an airtight container and cool to room temperature. Pour the remaining ¾ cup of oil over the top and cover tightly. Keep in the refrigerator until ready to use.

This fresh bean sauce will keep in the refrigerator in an airtight container for up to a month. If you wish to keep it for longer, freeze it in smaller portions.

Vinegary Orange Sauce

Prep time: 10 minutes | Cook time: 0 minutes | Makes ⅔ cup

- 6 tablespoons orange juice
- 1 tablespoon fresh orange zest
- 2 tablespoons water
- 1 tablespoon rice vinegar

- 1 tablespoon dark soy sauce
- 2 teaspoons light soy sauce
- 2 teaspoons brown sugar
- ¼ teaspoon red pepper flakes

1. Combine the orange juice, zest, water, rice vinegar, dark soy sauce, light soy sauce, brown sugar, and red pepper flakes in a bowl. Either use immediately in a stir-fry recipe or store in a sealed container in the refrigerator until ready to use. (Use the sauce within 3 or 4 days.)

Chili Cornstarch and Sesame Sauce

Prep time: 10 minutes | Cook time: 0 minutes | Makes ½ cup

- 4 tablespoons chicken broth
- 2 tablespoons red wine vinegar or Chinese red rice vinegar
- 2 tablespoons soy sauce
- 2 tablespoons sesame oil
- ½ tablespoon granulated sugar
- ¼ teaspoon chili paste
- 2 garlic cloves, finely minced
- 2 teaspoons cornstarch

1. Combine the chicken broth, vinegar, soy sauce, sesame oil, sugar, chili paste, and garlic in a bowl.

2. Whisk in the cornstarch. Either use the sauce immediately or store in a sealed container in the refrigerator until needed. (Use the sauce within 3 or 4 days.) Stir the sauce before adding to the stir-fry to bring up any cornstarch that has settled on the bottom.

Tips: Sesame sauce makes a great dipping sauce for spring rolls, or it can be added to a stir-fry dish at the end of cooking. If chili paste is already included in the recipe, do not add it to the sauce.

Brothy Kung Pao Sauce

Prep time: 10 minutes | Cook time: 0 minutes | Makes 1 ¼ cups

- ¾ cup low-sodium chicken broth
- 3 tablespoons soy sauce
- 2½ tablespoons Shaoxing rice wine
- 1½ tablespoons Chinese black vinegar

- 1 teaspoon toasted sesame oil
- 2 teaspoons cornstarch

1. Whisk the ingredients together in a small bowl. Use immediately or store in a glass jar in your refrigerator.

Tips: If you make this sauce and keep it in your fridge, making Kung Pao Chicken (or kung pao pork or beef) will be a snap.

Garlicky Mirin Teriyaki Sauce

Prep time: 10 minutes | Cook time: 8 minutes | Makes ¾ cup

- ¾ cup low-sodium soy sauce
- ½ cup water
- 1 tablespoon mirin
- 1 tablespoon sake
- 3 tablespoons light
- brown sugar
- ½ tablespoon minced garlic
- 1 tablespoon minced ginger

1. In a small saucepan over medium heat, whisk together all the ingredients and let the liquids come a low boil.
2. Reduce the heat to low and simmer the sauce until thickened, about 8 to 10 minutes. Use immediately or store covered in the refrigerator for 1 week.

Tips: This quick sauce can be thickened with the addition of ½ teaspoon cornstarch dissolved in 2 tablespoons of water.

Sugar and Vinegar Ketchup Sauce

Prep time: 5 minutes | Cook time: 0 minutes | Makes 1 cup

- ¼ cup granulated sugar
- ¼ cup vinegar
- 2 tablespoons ketchup
- ¾ cup water
- 1 tablespoon cornstarch

1. Combine the sugar, vinegar, ketchup, and water in a medium bowl.
2. Whisk in the cornstarch. Use as called for in the stir-fry recipe. Stir the sauce before adding to the stir-fry to bring up any cornstarch that has settled

on the bottom. If not using immediately, store the sauce in a sealed container in the refrigerator. (Use the sauce within 3 or 4 days.)

Tips: To turn this into a dipping sauce, simply bring the ingredients to a boil in a medium saucepan over low heat, stirring constantly. Use the dipping sauce immediately or store in a sealed container in the refrigerator until ready to serve.

Buttered Peanut and Vinega Sauce

Prep time: 10 minutes | Cook time: 0 minutes | Makes 1 ½ cup

- 1 cup creamy peanut butter
- 1 tablespoon grated ginger
- 2 teaspoons sesame oil
- 1 tablespoon soy sauce
- 2 garlic cloves, minced
- 1 teaspoon red peppe flakes
- 2 tablespoons rice vinegar
- ¼ teaspoon kosher s
- ¼ cup peanut oil

1. In a blender, add the peanut butter, ginger, sesame oil, soy sauce, garlic, red pepper flakes, ri vinegar, and salt. Blend until combined.
2. On the lowest setting, stream in the peanut oil until completely emulsified, approximately 2 to 3 minutes. Sauce should be used within the sam day.

Soy Sauce with Chili Dip

Prep time: 5 minutes | Cook time: 0 minutes | Makes ¼ cup

- 4 tablespoons soy sauce
- 1 to 2 teaspoons
- Chinese chili sauce
- ½ teaspoon sesame

1. Whisk the ingredients together in a small bowl.

Tips: This is a quick dipping sauce for dumplings, fried wontons, or egg rolls.

Classic Sesame and Stir-Fr Sauce

Prep time: 10 minutes | Cook time: 0 minutes | Makes 1 cup

¼ cup low-sodium soy sauce

¼ cup oyster sauce

2 tablespoons Shaoxing wine

2 tablespoons honey or brown sugar

- 2 tablespoons water
- 1½ tablespoons sesame oil
- 1 tablespoon cornstarch
- 1 teaspoon chicken stock granules

- Pinch ground white pepper.
- Pour all the ingredients into a small jar or sealable container.
- Shake until well combined.
- Store in the refrigerator for up to 2 weeks.

Stocky Brown Sauce

Prep time: 5 minutes | Cook time: 0 minutes | Makes 1 cup

1 cup basic Chinese chicken stock, or store bought

2 tablespoons oyster sauce

1 tablespoon soy sauce

- 2 teaspoons cornstarch
- 1 teaspoon brown sugar
- ½ teaspoon sesame oil

Put all the ingredients in a small bowl and stir to combine. Stir well before using.

Alternatively, put all the ingredients in a small jar, seal, and gently shake to combine. Shake well before using.

Garlic with Honey Dipping Sauce

Prep time: 10 minutes | Cook time: 0 minutes | Makes ½ cup

4 tablespoons soy sauce

3 tablespoons rice wine vinegar

1 clove garlic, minced

- 1 tablespoon honey
- 1 teaspoon sesame oil
- 1 teaspoon sesame seeds

Whisk all the ingredients together in a small bowl.

Sesame and Vinegar Dipping Sauce

Prep time: 5 minutes | Cook time: 0 minutes | Makes ⅓ cup

- 3 tablespoons soy sauce
- 2 tablespoons Chinese

- black vinegar
- 1 teaspoon sesame oil

1. Whisk all the ingredients together in a small bowl.

Chinese Broccoli with Oyster Sauce

Prep time: 10 minutes | Cook time: 0 minutes | Serves 6 to 8

- 2 tablespoons peanut oil
- 4 garlic cloves, peeled and halved
- ½ (2-inch) piece ginger, peeled and julienned
- 1 pound (454 g)

- Chinese broccoli (kai lan), rinsed and cut into bite-size pieces
- 2 tablespoons oyster sauce
- 1 teaspoon sugar
- Pinch ground white pepper

1. In a wok over medium heat, heat the peanut oil.

2. Add the garlic. As soon as it starts to turn golden brown, add the ginger and give it all a quick stir.

3. Increase the heat to high and immediately add the kai lan, oyster sauce, sugar, and pepper.

4. Stir the kai lan well. Add a tablespoon or two of water to help steam it, if desired.

5. When the kai lan turns bright green and softens a little, remove it from the heat and serve immediately.

Vinegary Sauce with Gingered Mussels

Prep time: 10 minutes | Cook time: 5⅓ minutes | Serves 4 to 6

For the Sauce:

- 1 cup water
- 1 tablespoon black bean sauce

- 1 teaspoon rice vinegar
- 1 teaspoon sugar
- 1 teaspoon soy sauce

- ½ teaspoon dark soy sauce

For the Stir-Fry:

- 1 tablespoon peanut oil
- 2-inch piece ginger, peeled and julienned
- 2 garlic cloves, minced
- 2 pounds (907 g) fresh mussels, scrubbed and debearded
- 1 teaspoon sesame oil
- 1 scallion, chopped into 1-inch pieces

1. In a small bowl, prepare the sauce by combining the water, black bean sauce, rice vinegar, sugar, soy sauce, and dark soy sauce. Set it aside.

2. In a wok over medium-high heat, heat the peanut oil.

3. Add the ginger and garlic and stir-fry for about 20 seconds or until aromatic.

4. Add the mussels and sauce. Stir and reduce the heat to low.

5. Cover the wok for about 5 minutes, uncovering to stir the contents every minute or so.

6. When most of the shells have opened, turn off the heat and stir in the sesame oil and scallions. Discard any unopened mussels.

7. Transfer to a serving dish and serve immediately.

Limey Red Chili Sauce

Prep time: 5 minutes | Cook time: 0 minutes | Makes ¾ cup

- 6 fresh red chiles
- 2 garlic cloves, chopped
- 1 small shallot, thinly
- sliced
- 1 teaspoon freshly squeezed lime juice
- Pinch salt

1. Remove the seeds from the chiles, then cut the chiles into thin slices.

2. Put the sliced chiles, garlic, and shallot into a small blender or food processor. Blend for a few seconds or until it forms a paste. Alternatively, use a mortar and pestle to mash the ingredients.

3. Once the mixture is a paste, add the lime juice and salt. Stir to combine.

Plum Sauce

Prep time: 10 minutes | Cook time: 50 minutes | Makes 2 cup

- 4 cups coarsely chopped plums (about 1½ pounds)
- ½ small yellow onion, chopped
- ½-inch fresh ginger slice, peeled
- 1 garlic clove, peeled and smashed
- ½ cup water
- ⅓ cup light brown sugar
- ¼ cup apple cider vinegar
- ½ teaspoon Chinese five spice powder
- Kosher salt

1. In a wok, bring the plums, onion, ginger, garlic, and water to a boil over medium-high heat. Cover, reduce the heat to medium, and simmer, stirring occasionally, until the plums and onion are tender, about 20 minutes.

2. Transfer the mixture to a blender or food processor and blend until smooth. Return to the wok and stir in the sugar, vinegar, five spice powder, and a pinch of salt.

3. Turn the heat back to medium-high and bring to a boil, stirring frequently. Reduce the heat to low and simmer until the mixture reaches the consistency of applesauce, about 30 minutes.

4. Transfer to a clean jar and cool to room temperature. Refrigerate for up to a week or freeze for up to a month.

Appendix 1 Measurement Conversion Chart

MEASUREMENT CONVERSION CHART

VOLUME EQUIVALENTS(DRY)

US STANDARD	METRIC (APPROXIMATE)
1/8 teaspoon	0.5 mL
1/4 teaspoon	1 mL
1/2 teaspoon	2 mL
3/4 teaspoon	4 mL
1 teaspoon	5 mL
1 tablespoon	15 mL
1/4 cup	59 mL
1/2 cup	118 mL
3/4 cup	177 mL
1 cup	235 mL
2 cups	475 mL
3 cups	700 mL
4 cups	1 L

VOLUME EQUIVALENTS(LIQUID)

US STANDARD	US STANDARD (OUNCES)	METRIC (APPROXIMATE)
2 tablespoons	1 fl.oz.	30 mL
1/4 cup	2 fl.oz.	60 mL
1/2 cup	4 fl.oz.	120 mL
1 cup	8 fl.oz.	240 mL
1 1/2 cup	12 fl.oz.	355 mL
2 cups or 1 pint	16 fl.oz.	475 mL
4 cups or 1 quart	32 fl.oz.	1 L
1 gallon	128 fl.oz.	4 L

TEMPERATURES EQUIVALENTS

FAHRENHEIT(F)	CELSIUS(C) (APPROXIMATE)
225 °F	107 °C
250 °F	120 °C
275 °F	135 °C
300 °F	150 °C
325 °F	160 °C
350 °F	180 °C
375 °F	190 °C
400 °F	205 °C
425 °F	220 °C
450 °F	235 °C
475 °F	245 °C
500 °F	260 °C

WEIGHT EQUIVALENTS

US STANDARD	METRIC (APPROXIMATE)
1 ounce	28 g
2 ounces	57 g
5 ounces	142 g
10 ounces	284 g
15 ounces	425 g
16 ounces (1 pound)	455 g
1.5 pounds	680 g
2 pounds	907 g

Appendix 2 Index

[193]

Complete Wok Cookbook

In

The Complete Wok Cookbook

V

W-Z

Printed in Great Britain
by Amazon

40648424R00117